The Mammoth Dictionary of Symbols

Also available

The Mammoth Book of Classic Science Fiction
The Mammoth Book of Golden Age Science Fiction
The Mammoth Book of Vintage Science Fiction
The Mammoth Book of New Age Science Fiction
The Mammoth Book of Fantastic Science Fiction
The Mammoth Book of Modern Science Fiction
The Mammoth Book of Private Eye Stories
The Mammoth Book of Great Detective Stories
The Mammoth Book of Spy Thrillers
The Mammoth Book of True Murder
The Mammoth Book of True Crime
The Mammoth Book of True Crime 2
The Mammoth Book of Short Horror Novels
The Mammoth Book of True War Stories
The Mammoth Book of Modern War Stories
The Mammoth Book of the Western
The Mammoth Book of Ghost Stories
The Mammoth Book of Ghost Stories 2
The Mammoth Book of the Supernatural
The Mammoth Book of Astounding Puzzles
The Mammoth Book of Terror
The Mammoth Book of Vampires
The Mammoth Book of Killer Women
The Mammoth Book of Zombies
The Mammoth Book of Historical Whodunnits
The Mammoth Book of Werewolves
The Mammoth Book of Frankenstein
The Mammoth Book of Golden Age Detective Stories
The Mammoth Book of Contemporary SF Masters
The Mammoth Book of Astounding Word Games
The Mammoth Book of Mindbending Puzzles
The Mammoth Book of Historical Detectives
The Mammoth Book of Battles
The Mammoth Book of Victorian & Edwardian Ghost Stories

The Mammoth Dictionary of SYMBOLS

NADIA JULIEN

Translated by Elfreda Powell

Carroll & Graf Publishers, Inc.
NEW YORK

Carroll & Graf Publishers, Inc.
260 Fifth Avenue
New York
NY 10001

First Carroll & Graf edition 1996

A copy of the Cataloguing in Publication Data for this title is available from the Library of Congress

ISBN 0–7867–0301–6

Printed and bound in the UK

10 9 8 7 6 5 4 3 2 1

Introduction

A symbol is a material object used to denote a difficult abstract concept or an idea that has hidden truths.

Man has always employed symbols to describe thoughts and feelings, or to protect secret truths from common knowledge. This is how the mysteries evolved, with their imagery that only the initiated can understand.

Symbols have been used to express profound truths, such as explanations of cosmic phenomena, or the dynamic structure of the universe, or how the mind works, and these have been passed down from generation to generation, through folklore, fairy tales, myths and legends. You only have to reread these, and delve deeper into their meanings, to discover a mass of symbols that have a common origin, and to see how many human motivations would be difficult to understand without them.

These images and allegories belong to everyone. In fact, they have an identical value in civilizations far removed from one another. This is because, originally, primitive peoples found it quite natural to think by way of analogy. Today this seems irrational to us, because we tend to compare it with our own way of thinking, without taking into account the thousands of years of slow evolution that have shaped our minds and given us a materialistic vision, in which we see things in a matter-of-fact way that makes the symbol seem outmoded.

And yet symbols have survived, not only in folklore but in everyday life and religion. Take, for example, the Union Jack, the Cross, the Lamb of God. These are symbols that have as much meaning as the written word or gestures. Then there are customs like wearing black at funerals, crowns, wedding-rings, that are symbolic props. Legends and fairy tales use a symbolic language, just like dreams. For symbolism is the only language that can be understood by the unconscious, that part of our mind affecting our behaviour and emotions, and expressed through what Jung called archetypes – primitive mental images inherited from our earliest ancestors – which hold the key to its interpretation.

And so the symbol, like Ariadne's thread, can lead us into undreamed-of worlds; it can act as a guide to our ego and its complex mechanisms, our mutinous feelings, frustrations and desires buried deep in the unconscious, and it can carry coded messages from the unconscious that cannot be understood through normal reasoning.

Discovering the world of symbols will give you almost unlimited scope for reflection and meditation, and enable you to go right back, through thousands of years of culture and evolution, to the very origins of the human race: every symbol is like a translucent egg, containing an almost inexhaustible source of knowledge and research. You will be able to delve deeper into these images, transcending time and matter and conventional meanings. You will pass from the tangible to the intangible, rise to a world of the spirit, and profit from the experience of countless earlier generations.

Far from being just an intellectual amusement, the interpretation of symbols is an individual way of approaching the problems of life, mankind and the universe. Macrocosm and microcosm are united in these images, these eternal, universal signs.

You must use your intuition when studying symbols. Their language might seem abstract at first, so it is a good idea to ignore familiar meanings, set aside your academic knowledge and forget modern ideas about things.

Symbols generally contain more than one meaning,

which can be psychological, religious or moral. Avoid digressing into a maze of detail when you interpret them, and approach them in their context. Above all, be receptive; keep an open mind to any associations they suggest.

The sources for this book have been many and various, and its scope is worldwide. I have drawn particularly on the Cabbalah (medieval Jewish mysticism), the tarot, astrology, alchemy, Freemasonry, Zorastrianism, Hinduism, Buddhism and Islam, but ancient Egyptian, American Indian, Celtic, ancient Greek, Roman, Persian and Assyrian and Japanese cultures are also very well represented, and it is surprising how images, particularly in creation myths, recur.

(Numbers in brackets in the text refer to the Bibliography on pp. 519–24.)

ABYSS

source of wisdom buried deep in the mind or the unconscious, accessible through intuition

In all the theories of the origin of the universe, the abyss symbolizes both the genesis and end of universal evolution. It is often conceived as mythological monsters who swallow humans, then regurgitate them renewed and transformed.

• In Greek and Latin, it denotes indefinite depths or heights and, universally, symbolizes the informal states of existence in which transformation can take place: evolution as opposed to a solid, fixed state. Man has to confront his personal abyss at least four times in a lifetime, that is, he has to reconsider his convictions and question his motives in order to achieve maturity (the four ages of man).

• The depths of the abyss relate to the land of the dead and the chthonian mother (earth goddess), from whom Jung took his interpretation, which associates the symbolism of the abyss with the maternal archetypal image of a mother who is simultaneously loving and cruel.

• The bottomless depths of the abyss are a symbol of the uncertainty of childhood, as well as the absence of distinction when life ends. However, dreaming of an abyss is positive: it is an invitation to plumb one's inner depths, to explore the most intimate parts of one's personality, that is, the unconscious, which contains an immense source of life and vitality.

ACACIA
initiation, and knowledge of unseen things

Acacia is similar to the thorn and hawthorn in its symbolism.

• In ancient Egypt acacia symbolized spiritual regeneration; on some Egyptian monuments there are coffins with acacia growing from them and the motto 'Osiris thrusts forth', meaning 'Out of death comes life' or rebirth. Acacia is a symbol of this in Freemasonry.

• Acacia wood was used to make the *arani*, a fire-making device used by Vedic priests, and therefore has sacred associations with the sun god. The acacia tree was a symbol of immortality in Nature, and later came to denote vitality.

Its connection with sun worship has given it a religious value: in India, the sacrificial ladle, an attribute of the supreme god Brahma, was carved from acacia wood. The Ark of the Convenant was also made of acacia and plated in gold.

ACROBAT
critical situation

This is an image that appears frequently in dreams. The acrobat who can defy the laws of gravity symbolizes the overturning of established order, emancipation from everyday routine and social conventions, and reveals a critical situation, which can be resolved through movement and action.

• Acrobatics symbolize physical ecstasy, the soaring flight towards a superhuman situation. They depict the search for an identification with divinity, as in the sacred dances of India, Java and Bali. Acrobatics are linked to the Hanged Man (the twelfth arcana of the tarot).

ADAM

origins of human life, the comprehensiveness of traditional wisdom

Adam, as the first man and the image of God, symbolizes the appearance of the spirit in material form endowed with consciousness, reason, autonomy and intelligence. Every tradition mentions a first man, a mythical ancestor. In ancient Persia there was a prototype man, Gayomart, who emitted rays of light. On his death, all the metals sprang from his body, and his soul was transformed into gold. From his sperm scattered on the ground the first couple was born. In ancient China, the first man was Pan-Ku, who is shown covered in leaves, while the Irish acknowledge a racial ancestor who came into their country from a foreign land.

• Each great historical period has a primordial man, an Adam. The Gnostics were quick to identify this first man with an inner psychic image, and for the Hindus an immortal part of each human being was the Purusha, which appears in the symbolic myths of ancient India as simultaneously living deep in man's heart and filling the universe.

• In the tradition of the Cabbalah (Jewish mystical teachings based on medieval texts), Adam represents the synthesis of humanity, and encapsulates the soul of all future mankind, beyond individual life. To create Adam,

God put together red, black, white and yellow earth (*adamah*) which had been taken from the four corners of the earth (the cardinal points). And so his soul was made up of an infinite number of strands, like a lamp wick.

• In Christian doctrine, the first Adam committed original sin through his wish to equal God, and is therefore a symbol of the perversion of the mind and a refusal to submit, which earned him a devastating punishment, that is, death. A second Adam then appeared in the form of Jesus Christ, who, out of sheer grace and perfection, was the first man, the incarnation of the Word, he man-God who is no longer an image but a reality, and capable of conferring on humanity the grace and eternal life that his predecessor took away.

According to Jung, this new Adam symbolizes the advent of a new humanity amidst the ashes of the old. He represents the certainty of the Resurrection.

• From a psychological viewpoint, this cosmic man is a source of psychic energies associated with 'old men' and produced from painful experiences. In dreams, he appears in the guise of a monk, a patriarch, a philosopher or a pope, signifying a wise old man, associated with the archetype of the father or the ancestor.

The appearance of this sage reveals a need to progress, and realize one's personality through synthesizing one's potential into an integrated and dynamic whole.

AEROPLANE

The symbolism of the aeroplane is a combination of the car, ascension, the bird and air. It also symbolizes the idea of detachment from material things, and flight.

AGES or PERIODS
the division of time

People once thought the world was divided into four periods: (1) the *Golden Age* under the rule of Saturn, which was an age of happiness, innocence and abundance, where work was unnecessary; (2) the *Silver Age* ruled by Jupiter; (3) the *Bronze Age* dominated by injustice, looting and wars; and (4) the *Iron Age*, associated with human misfortune, greed and drought.

These periods correspond to the four stages in the process of regeneration in alchemy: the black of the unconscious, the white of air (when the anima appears in the unconscious), the red of the energy of fire, and the gold of the transformation.

• In the Etruscan world, the seers or *aruspices* divided the duration of the world, society and man into periods. Human life consisted of twelve periods of seven years (a number reached by dividing the lunar month by 4), the seventh year being a critical period in each case. During the first ten periods, expiatory rites could delay the onset of death; but in old age, fate could no longer be deflected through the intervention of the gods, for 'the sum of predestined events was immutable for the whole of the twelve periods.'[98]

These periods corresponded to the modifications undergone by the human body and mind, and marked the growth, static state and decline of vitality: childhood (which lasted until about seven); adolescence (until about eighteen); adulthood (until forty – the age of maturity); the change of life (until sixty), and old age. Transition between these ages required adaptation.

• The duration of city and state life was divided into periods of an age, the length of which was based on human life (for the druids an age was equal to thirty years, the average length of human life).

AIR
spiritualization

Air is one of the four elements, the intermediary between heaven and earth, fire and water. Air is where divine inspiration, a symbol of spiritualization, is manifested.

• In Hindu mythology, it is represented as a spiritual vehicle, by Vayu, god of the region of subtlety, and of the wind that rides a gazelle, the god whose standard floats in the eight cosmic winds connected to the eight directions of space.

Associated with Prâna, a dynamic energy underlying the vital, nervous activities that underpin man's mental energies, Vayu rules over the vital levels that connect the physical being to the purely mental one, and is identified with the Word, which is itself 'inspiration', or an intake of air.

• In the Book of Genesis, air was an 'emanation of the breath of the Spirit of God which moved upon the face of the waters to divide them and create the firmament.'[30]

ALCHEMY
the road to perfection

In its secular sense, alchemy involved a series of chemical processes, which were meant to lead to the transformation of base metal into gold. It was also a scientific, philosophical system, directed at discovering the hidden laws ruling the universe.

In its spiritual sense, it is the art of men's intellectual and moral self-improvement.

• The gold alchemists strived to produce was, symbolically, human perfection.[18]

This spiritual alchemy used symbolic media, such as the male element of sulphur, an expansive energy coming from the heart of an individual, and the female element of mercury, as energy emanating from the exterior, which can penetrate everything. These antagonistic forces are balanced in salt, a crystallizing substance which symbolized the stable part of a human being.

• The alchemist went through six consecutive operations: first there was calcination, a stage corresponding to the colour black and the extinction of desires; then putrefaction, which separated the charred elements; solution, corresponding to the colour white and symbolizing the wise man resisting temptations; fermentation and congelation, corresponding to the colour red and the union of opposites; and sublimation, corresponding to gold, symbol of perfection.

• The alchemist is the sage who, 'having noted its symbolic dimension, enters into a kind of "laboratory" that becomes an oratory for his thoughts. He stands in the centre of the world, or more exactly in the centre of a world in the process of being formed, that he must make coherent. Then he discovers the cosmos, a harmony of heavenly voices . . . the universe, the divine word in its infinity of worlds and universes.'[80]

• For Jung, 'the processes of alchemy' symbolize the process of individuation, the search for self, the essence of personality, identical to the *athanor*, the alchemist's crucible. This quest begins in the total blackness of the unconscious, continues in the analysis of the psyche and its division into separate components, until the true values of existence are assimilated into the conscious and used in the here and now.

• The Taoists' art of long life and immortality was based on an internal alchemy, directed at 'dissolving the form, remaking the body, refining it through the process of alchemy.' It involved breathing, gymnastic and dietary techniques. To obtain the elixir of gold and transmuted cinnabar[63] this base cinnabar was modelled on the yin–yang (the Chinese concept of two opposite and complementary forces in Nature) and conformed to systems of numbers. Using a symbolic language, a logical system was organized, that relied on the 'fundamental idea of dynamic, transcendent connections between man, heaven and earth, and on the balance of yin and yang in the human organism; man was thought to be an exact replica of the macrocosm'.[65]

The aim was to act on the primordial elements of 'essence, inspiration and vital spirit', through concentration and inner contemplation and through the practice of embryonic breathing, a kind of regression to the 'state of the infant in the womb'.

Inspiration was sought 'in the Sea of Inspiration, near the lower region of cinnabar . . . from where it would be brought up to the brain, then circulated throughout the whole body, ensuring that normal breathing continued, although reduced as much as possible.'[64]

ALCOHOL

release of the unconscious, creative inspiration

Alcohol is a synthesis of two opposing elements, water and fire, and symbolizes vital energy, 'the fire of life'; and, for Sufis, fire and love.

On an individual level, it has the effect of lifting prohibitions and taboos, releasing vital forces and the imagination.

ALMOND – ALMOND TREE

reality behind appearance

This nut, concealed in an outer skin, symbolizes the essence hidden within things of little importance: Christ whose divine nature was hidden by his human form, the secret in the shadows, waiting to be discovered so that it can be eaten.

• In the esoteric language of the Middle Ages, the mystic almond symbolized Mary's virginity (and from this came the elliptical halo that can be seen surrounding her in pictures). Bodies of saints are also enveloped in an almond shape, divided by three lines representing the Trinity, to which they are united through a beatific vision.

• In India, the almond is the vulva, the *yoni*, and eating it signifies the sexual act.

• In the *Upanishads* it is used as a 'symbol of the cosmic waters and the turbulent agitation of infinite possibilities of existence.'

• A dream featuring almonds can mean a difficult problem about something essentially precious, very often connected with sex.

• As the Tree of Wisdom in the Book of Genesis, the spring-flowering almond tree signifies renewal, and also fragility, as the flowers are sensitive to wintry weather.

• In mythology it is an attribute to Atys, who was conceived by a virgin from an almond.

• For Jews, it symbolizes a new life, and, according to a Jewish myth, the base of an almond tree forms the entrance to the underworld city of Luz, home of the immortals. Luz was also the name of the city where Jacob had a vision of the House of God (Bethel).

ALPHA AND OMEGA
wholeness

These two letters are the first and last of the Greek alphabet and are supposed to contain the key to the universe; they symbolize the beginning and end of everything that exists. Juxtaposed, they represent the cycle of time, where the end once more joins the beginning. (See *Snake*, *Ouroboros*.)

ALPHABET

see *Letters*

AMBER
spiritual bond

Yellow amber (in Greek: *electron*, hence electricity), which possesses the property of generating electricity through rubbing, is used to make rosaries and amulets, which can be turned into real condensers of electric current, discharging it when fingered or touched.

• It can be likened to a psychic thread, linking individual energy to cosmic energy, and it is a symbol of solar, spiritual and divine attraction.

• In Christian imagery the saints sometimes have amber faces, reflecting their inner heavenly light.

• Symbolically, these invisible powers correspond to the ladder of human values based on everyday behaviour, with the highest spirituality attained by mystics at the top, and at the bottom, the total degradation of those who have yielded to their basest instincts.

Inconographically they are shown with wings, testifying to their immaterial essence, and with a white habit, symbol of purity.

In Jung's view, demons represent inferior functions stirring in the dark areas of the human unconscious.

AMETHYST

the inner centre, resignation

The Amethyst (in Greek: *amethustos*, not inebriated), symbol of temperance, is worn by bishops who must be on their guard against all intoxication, even spiritual. Its symbolism has similarities to that of precious stones and the colour purple.

ANGELS

positive and negative energies of the unconscious

In every tradition, in both the Old and New Testament, and in religious theory in ancient Egypt, Persia, India and China, there is a belief in spiritual creatures superior to man. Creation was thought of as a ladder, with its top rung occupied by angels, immaterial beings made of pure spirit, whereas man consisted of both matter and spirit, a body and a soul.

• According to the teachings of the Church, angels were created in a state of grace and happiness and with freedom to choose between good and evil. Some of them sinned through pride and were condemned to eternal torture; these are the demons who drive men along the path of evil.

Each individual is helped along the road to goodness by a guardian angel, a symbol of conscience.

The legions of angels who make up the armies of heaven are divided into three hierarchies, which in turn are divided into three choirs: (1) seraphim, cherubim and thrones; (2) dominations, virtues, powers; and (3) principalities, archangels and angels.

ANDROGYNE

mystery of creation, primordial unity

The oldest image of androgyny is the menhir, an almost round block of rough stone, standing alongside a similarly shaped stone lying on the ground, simultaneously representing the moment of birth of the new sum or winter solstice, man and woman, and by extension strength, the active male element on the one hand, and matter, the passive, life-giving female element on the other. These symbols have survived in the Hindu *lingam* and *yoni*.[136]

Later, as can be seen in ancient sculptures, a great number of figures were devised that possessed organs of both sexes: gods and goddesses of the solstice with two heads looking in opposite directions, or bearded women. Even 'priests came to be dressed in women's clothes.'[136] All these images symbolize 'organized matter from primeval times, from the very moment when it had emerged from chaos, and had not as yet been permeated by the Creator's ethereal essence,' and was therefore still undifferentiated.[83]

• The androgyne symbolizes the mystery of creation; it is an anthropomorphic depiction of the cosmic egg, the origin of life in the universe which began the cosmologic cycle. The androgyne is the Sumerians' *An* (heaven) and *Enlil* (earth); the Japanese Izanagi and Izanami merging in the cosmic egg; in Egypt it is Ptah; in China Fu-hi and Niu-ka joined by their snake's tails; in India Shiva, tightly embracing Shakti, his own energy conceived as a woman, to form a single being – this is an example of the androgyne's informal manifestation; Cupid, god of love; the Word made flesh, described in the Cabbalah and the eleventh-century Christian Gnostic scriptures as an androgynous being;[66] and Adam created in the image of God, therefore bisexual, who becomes Adam and Eve. 'The way the female element changes into a different shape symbolizes the beginning of the fall from a state of perfection into duality.'[66]

It follows from this primeval androgyny that woman is man's complement (according to Plato, marriage is an attempt to restore this androgynous unity that was lost for eternity). Woman is also man's future, because she makes certain that his line is continued.

• Androgyny illustrates the fundamental duality that exists throughout the natural world, expressed in T'ai-chi; in Chinese philosophy.

Androgyny is dualism and totality; like alpha and omega it symbolizes the beginning and end of time, birth and death. Death recreates the unity that originally existed, as man regains the completeness inherent in the absence and separation of the sexes.

These ancient beliefs, which echo biological discoveries on man's bipolarity help explain the rites of circumcision and excision, which attempt to establish gender definitively (the woman's clitoris is considered to be a remnant of the penis, and the man's prepuce, a remnant of the female labia).

The dogma of androgyny has a wide application beyond the world of the gods: bronze, composed of copper (a female element) and tin (a male element) was regarded as androgynous and used in the magic ritual of purification: in ancient Rome, the chief priest at the temple of Jupiter could only have his hair cut with bronze razors, and the Etruscans used a bronze plough to mark the boundaries of their brand new city.[136]

ANIMAL

instincts, conscious and unconscious, often primitive and dangerous

In ancient times, it was thought that all men, animals and plant life had been impregnated with some of the divine essence spread throughout the universe. 'Animal and plant characteristics were regarded not only as manifestations of divine power, but also as permanent, true emanations of its essence.[83]

And so sacred animals – such as the deer, snake, bull, cow, etc. – were held to be images of divine power.

• The ancient hunting, fishing and pastoral cultures that preceded agrarian, astral or astronomical religions were characterized by representations of animals, some of which survived in the Chaldaean, Chinese and Mexican zodiacs and in Egyptian religion.

Later, Christianity used animal symbols extensively: to illustrate physical appearance: – the gospel writers are shown as an ox (Saint Luke), a lion (Saint Mark), an eagle (Saint John) – or an animal was linked to their spiritual characteristics – Christ with a lamb (symbol of the sacrifice on the Cross) or a fish (symbol of the secrecy of the early Christians) and the Holy Spirit with a dove.

One can often see animals hidden among creeping plants on the capitals of pillars in churches. These symbolize the interlacing of plant and human life where one can so easily get lost, and the need for self-knowledge in order to find one's way.

• The animal is a vessel for cosmic energy, and in the Middle Ages, at New Year, men and women dressed up in the skins of horse, wolf or ox so that they could be infiltrated by this vital force. 'This copied an ancient Egyptian idea of "transformation" in which the initiate acquired the particular virtue of each of the creatures into which he was transformed.'[80]

• Chinese and medieval art offer a wide range of mythical beasts: dragons or two-headed eagles (the duality of human nature), foxes with nine tails (the nine regions of Middle Earth), wild beasts with eight human heads (the number 8 symbolizing cosmic balance), phoenixes, gargoyles, chimaeras, unicorns.

In medieval bestiaries, these same symbols from Eastern, Etruscan and Tyrrhenian civilizations, served as symbolic aids in teaching doctrines and moral precepts: they illustrated the fundamental Christian virtues and helped explain the mysteries of religion. These archaic concepts are testimonies of the survival of the collective unconscious, and have survived so well long after these civilizations have become extinct that today they are found in the contemporary art world, in complex visual fantasies, particularly of the surrealist school.

• Writers of fables (Aesop, Hesiod, Florian, La Fontaine) have also exploited animal symbolism and used it to express improving morals.

In this symbolism the animal generally depicts negative qualities in human nature, or the sublimation of instincts (using the addition of wings to reverse the symbol; for example, a winged horse, snake or dragon). Killing the snake signifies overcoming or taming an instinct.

• These symbols are seen in psychological tests and dreams as archetypes that illustrate human characteristics, and throw light on hidden or unknown aspects of the personality: passions, and often repressed instincts whose unsuspected influence is endangering the dreamer's balance of mind; or alternatively they reveal the 'beast' lurking in the depths of each of us.

In fact, according to Jung, being attracted or repelled by animals and their appearance in our dreams reveals unconscious aspects of the psyche, repressed desires, the shadow, the anima, the animus, the inferior functions in their ancient form.

Whether they are life companions or wild beasts, animals reflect the rudimentary instincts that motivate human behaviour: self-preservation, reproduction, the gregarious instinct, aggression . . . And so, people's taste for leather clothes or fur is an expression of an unsatisfied need for pleasure or luxury, and beards or long hair expresses a need for simplicity or naturalness repressed by the exigencies of civilized life or everyday routine.

If we can recognize and understand the animal within us, we can tame it, that is, we can use the repressed energy in the unconscious that it symbolizes. For it is a negative force that can dominate our conscious existence and poison relationships, because we project these animal elements and the delusive images they suggest on to others.

ANKH
eternity

The Egyptian looped cross is held in the hand by their gods and features on important people's tombs. (See *Knot*, *Cross*.)

Ankh: the looped cross

ANNIVERSARY

memory

Anniversaries, celebrated in every country and every religion and every family, are in some way symbols of past events. The Jewish Passover recalls the exodus from Egypt, Pentecost evokes the promulgation of law on Mount Sinai. The Christian world celebrates Christmas, Epiphany, Ascension as the very days when the mysteries took place. New Year's Day for the Romans marked the day when their city was founded. For Moslems it evoked the day when Mohammed fled from Mecca.

In China, they celebrate the anniversary of Buddha, and of the goddess of the sea, Tin Hau, during the third lunar month; Taoists have their festival on the fifteenth day of the seventh lunar month.

• As far as the individual is concerned, anniversaries symbolize the important phases in our life cycle, and mark the length of a marriage: one year of marriage = paper wedding; five years = wood; ten years = tin; twenty-five years = silver; fifty years = gold; sixty years = diamond.

ANTIMONY
the little king

Antimony is a metal that combines easily with ordinary gold which it then purifies. It was once known as *regulo* (little king).

• Practitioners of the Hermetic art (an early form of alchemy) used it as everlasting water or heavenly water to cleanse the philosopher's gold/stone of all impurity, an operation which corresponded to the penultimate stage of the alchemist's process of changing base metal into gold.

• In Jungian terms, it symbolizes a state close to the final stage of evolution, the state of individuation. The most difficult remains to be done, the transformation of lead into gold, releasing opacity from matter. Antimony therefore came to express the possibility of a final boost or a final obstacle. It is linked to the symbolism of grey.

APOCALYPSE
the fate of the world

The Apocalypses are the Jewish/Christian scriptures that contain revelations about mankind's fate, the end of the world and the arrival of the day of Judgement. These works are based on symbolic data: numbers, colours, precious stones. personalities (Michael, angels, woman, the new-born, the prostitute), animals (dragon, lion, ox, eagle, beast), objects, etc. The Apocalypse has come to symbolize the end of the world, with catastrophes of every kind: floods, earthquakes, etc.

APPLE, APPLE TREE
the guarantee of immortality

In Irish tradition, the apple is a fruit that guarantees immortality: cut in half, crossways, it reveals a five-pointed star, the pentagram, a symbol of the 'five stations from birth to death and rebirth.'

• Apples were part of the Orphic cult and also symbolized the goddess Venus (to whom they were sacred), who, according to Robert Graves, 'was worshipped as the evening star, Hesper, on one half of the apple, and as Lucifer, son of morning, on the other.'[107]

• Jung interpreted the apple eaten by Adam and Eve as a symbol of life.

In dreams, a red and green apple is the expression of a harmonious organic life. A maggoty apple reveals an apparently healthy relationship which has been eaten away on the inside.

APRON
work

Worn in the Middle Ages by masons, cathedral builders, the apron is the essential item of apparel for Freemasons, 'builders of the symbolic temple of future mankind.' Originally it had a magnetic belt that was meant to contain a disk of etheric matter, separating the lower part of the body from the upper part so that the formidable energies that the Masonic ceremony was intended to bring into play would not escape to the lower regions of the anatomy.[108]

• Made of sheepskin, a symbol of purity, the Apprentice's apron is a symbol of work and (in French Freemasonry) has a raised bib forming a five-pointed figure, a symbol of quintuple man. The Companion wears the bib pulled down, and the Master Mason has a double bib in red.

• In England, the Master Mason of the Grand Lodge has an apron which is double and edged with blue. It has two lines of influence or spiritual energy, each ending in seven silver lines, which indicate the colours of a prism and symbolize the seven temperaments.[108]

Aquarius
20 January–18 February

Aquarius is the eleventh sign of the zodiac, a fixed airy sign, ruled by Saturn (and Uranus) which is its house. The sun is in exile, and Neptune falling.
Characteristics: freedom, frankness, waves, explosion, invention.
Correspondences: wetness, winter, day, positiveness, maleness, sterility, violence. Metal: lead. Stones: sapphire, black pearl.
In the body: vessels, calves and heels, cerebral electricity, cardiac rhythms.[14, 122]
Principle qualities: sense of brotherhood, of peace and discovery.
Negative qualities: intolerance of legitimate, established social norms, revolutionary spirit lacking creative power.

ARA
solar fire

An ara is a parrot with a powerful beak, long red tail and distinct, brilliantly coloured plumage. It was used in Mayan culture as a symbol of fire and solar energy. The people of Central America use its feathers for decoration and ritual.

ARABESQUE
Islamic mandala

The arabesque is a basic element of Islamic art. As a religious art it uses only a combination of lines and colours, since the Koran forbids the representation of living things and man.

• As an infinite repetition of the same theme, with a regular rhythm, the arabesque serves as an aid to meditation and contemplation; it helps one escape from temporal conditioning, and is reminiscent of a maze, access to its centre being achieved only by a complicated route. It is an image of individuation directed at reaching the centre of the personality.

ARCH

see *Bow*

ARCHETYPE
collective ancestral heritage

Archetypes, a term developed by Carl Jung, are special mental constructs that belong to each individual and also to everyone in general. In some ways they are the mental equivalent of biological instincts which combine to form our models of behaviour; unconscious motivations on the one hand; conscious on the other.

The notions of God, mother, father, anima and animus, horse, snake, and others are 'primordial images, innate in the human mind' according to Jung. They have been present since the human race began, and have persisted across thousands of years, forming a sediment in the mind of every human being.

Aries
21 March–20 April

A masculine, cardinal fiery sign. Aries is in the house of Mars. The sun and Pluto are exalted in Aries, Venus is in exile, Saturn falls.

Characteristics: intrepidity, courage, love of action and of conception, speed, ardour, vitality.

Correspondences: red, ruby, spicy plants. Loyalty, swords, sabres, daggers, iron, industry, factories, metals, sheep, buck, lancets, burins, anything that cuts.

In the body: head, brain, nose, face.[122]

Negative aspects: instinct for destruction, unruly impatience, impulsiveness, egocentricity, egotism.[14]

ARK
the house of God

Egyptian temples contained God's holy ark wrapped in precious veils, which was solemnly carried by priests in processions.

It is found again as an object of veneration by Jewish nomads in the Ark of the Covenant. Jews thought of it as God's earthly home.

The rectangular wooden chest plated in gold (a symbol of the divine character of the glorified Church) had a lid of pure gold called a propitiatory, on which were placed two cherubim in beaten gold (cherubim symbolizing divine love, divine power). This *kapporet* (Hebrew for propitiatory) symbolized justice, Jehovah's immutable principle.[19]

As a materialization of Jehovah's design he had conceived before the beginning of creation, the ark symbolized God's eternal design, the hidden mystery, the Christ.[20]

This Holy of Holies was the very heart of the Temple. itself in the heart of Jerusalem, in the heart of the land of Israel, at the heart of the world.[19]

ARM
power

Arms symbolize physical vigour, authority, power and projection.

- In the Middle Ages, the power of lay judges was referred to as the secular arm; they had the responsibility of carrying out the orders of the ecclesiastical judges (in, for example, the case of Joan of Arc).
- In India, the goddess Kali, who symbolizes 'cosmic

power, the totality of the universe, harmony of all opposite couples'[66] is herself symbolized by her four arms, representing her universal power.

• In Christian liturgy, arms are raised to signify a prayer for grace to descend on the supplicant, and for his soul to receive God's blessing.[1] Raising the arms is also an act of submission and surrender, of giving up the fight.

ARROW

the father-protector

The arrow is the most widespread popular symbol of the Heavenly Father and of human fathers in general, and is linked to the symbolism of the sun's rays, a fertilizing element of Nature, the origin of the obelisk. This explains the words of the psalm: 'As arrows are in the hand of a mighty man; so are children of the youth. Happy is the man that hath his quiver full of them.'

• The arrow embodies an intrinsic idea of elevation. Sagittarius symbolizes overtaking and excess.

• A bow and quiver, Diana's attributes, symbolize female power, which can be both creative and destructive.

Solar rosace of a female archer (drawing on an Assyrian obelisk)[121]

AURA
colours of the soul

Buddhists think that the aura, the magnetic field surrounding the human body, reveals the colours of the soul and reflects an individual's state of health and feelings.

This halo is the vital force itself, formed by coloured radiations emanating from various parts of the body.

AXE
separation, penetration

All ancient traditions associated the axe with lightening, water and fertility, and attributed the power of making or stopping rain to it.

In antiquity it appears as a sign of divinity and royalty in almost every religion. There were cults of the axe in Egypt, Assyria, Greece and among the Parthians. In Egyptians hieroglyphics, 'the sign of the axe meant separation because oaths or sacred matters were separate from other things'.[9]

• It is a symbol of spiritual penetration '(to the very heart of the mystery), as well as an instrument of deliverance. It opens up the ground and enters it; that is, it symbolizes union with heaven, fertilization.'[1]

• It is an instrument of separation, of differentiation; it cuts, separates, grades. With the blow of an axe to Zeus' skull, Hephaistos brought Athens, goddess of wisdom and intelligence, into the world, armed and helmeted. (This act also illustrates lightning intuition, enlightenment.)

• In the hands of warrior gods, it is a symbol of destruction and anger.

Axe

• In China, the axe (*fu*) is one of twelve insignia of imperial power; it is the symbol of the patron of carpenters and of a mediator.

• The axe was used symbolically in wedding ceremonies to cut branches (the betrothed) from two tree trunks (the respective families), which were then bound up into faggots.

BAG
riches

In ancient Egypt a sack of wheat was a symbol of intelligence, prudence and proprietorship of lands. Mercury, god of material and intellectual riches, was represented with a purse in his hand.

• In ancient China, where wine was stored in bags (*bu-dai*), there was a god of bags, said to be identical to primal man (faceless but with six feet and four wings), who lived on the mountain of heaven. That is why in popular language a bag is called 'chaos' (*hun-dun*) like *wun tun* (the Cantonese pronunciation for tiny balls of meat contained in tiny bags of pastry and cooked in boiling water, served in Chinese restaurants).

• In dreams, the soldier's haversack is loaded with useless things, all of which are a superfluous burden we carry along the road of life, while a woman's handbag is associated with femininity.

BANQUET
satisfaction of desire

The banquet is a symbol of participation in a ritual, project or festival, a place of exchange where class or racial distinctions are of less importance, and where participants share the same dishes, 'prepared by the subtle art of cooking.'[80]

• In Christianity, the ritual of the Eucharist is reminiscent of a banquet and symbolizes the communion of the saints who share the same grace and the same life.

• Ritual banquets are common to all religions: in Hindu ritual, whoever celebrates the Vedic sacrifice absorbs *soma*, the mystic wine which 'reveals the divine essence.' Sharing a meal with a god symbolizes the height of wisdom or happiness.

BEAR
unfinished

The Egyptians imagined that a child was unformed at birth and was subsequently shaped by the maternal caresses of a she-bear in cub, because 'she gives birth to condensed blood and transforms it by heating it on her breast and finishes shaping it by licking it.'

This process is similar to creation (the world began, unshaped, by Chaos, and was finished through the love of God), and this legend, which symbolized the malleability of matter used in formal creation, was taken up in the bestiaries

Bear. Painting on the façade of a North American Indian House[142]

• The bear is a solitary, cunning creature, of terrifying strength but fond of fruit and honey, a creature of contrasts. For the Celts it was a symbol of the warrior class, unlike the wild boar which was a symbol of spiritual authority. The Gauls associated the bear with Artio, goddess of earthly prosperity.[95]

The bear's association with the state of being unfinished makes it a symbol of the first step in the alchemical process, the base substance, the blackening or *nigredo*, the chaos from which primal matter will emerge, the stone, the goal of the work.

• In China, the bear (*xiong*) is a symbol of valiance and man, with the snake symbolizing woman; but the bear also symbolizes violence: 'in the ideological debate between the Republic of China and the Soviet Union, the Russian bear features as the aggressor.'[7]

• According to Jung, the bear represents danger caused by the uncontrollable contents of the unconscious. In dreams it can mean a period of regression.

BEARD
wisdom

The philosophers of ancient India, Assyria and Chaldaea and Jewish elders allowed their beards to grow as a sign of their wisdom and often as an adornment. They took the greatest care of it, even sprinkling it with scent. People kissed it as a sign of respect.

• In Perrault's fairy tale of Bluebeard (who killed women and locked their corpses in a secret room), the beard is a symbol of bestiality and the possessive instinct (blue symbolizing fear). The character of Bluebeard symbolizes 'violent, destructive feelings . . . sombre aspects of sexuality which could be well hidden behind a permanently bolted and closely guarded door.'[67]

On a cosmic scale, this tale has similarities with the death of dawn, killed by the sun.

BEE
activity, vigilance, organization

In all traditional cultures the bee is an attribute of the gods: sometimes it symbolizes priestesses; sometimes it is associated with Rê, the sun-god of ancient Egypt, whose hieroglyph is a bee. With its six feet, it also alludes to the solar wheel.

• Most frequently it symbolizes the soul where, in Indian legend, the vital principle resided. In Siberia and South America, the bee is the incarnation of the soul after it has left the body. On tombs, it signifies resurrection.

• Because it produces honey, a pure, scented food and the source of nectar, the drink of the gods, the bee symbolizes the sacred task of refining and distillation. This, in turn, suggests the initiation process, and the bee's reappearance in the hive after hibernation reinforces this analogy (the initiatory resurrection).[30]

• In Egyptian art and tradition, it denotes sacred inspiration.

• In Christian tradition, it is the emblem of Christ, of his forgiveness (through analogy with the sweetness of its honey), with his justice (through its sting), Christian virtues (because of the exemplary way worker bees behave towards their queen).

• As a symbol of organization, activity and vigilance, it has served, as the emblem of Chaldaean and Egyptian monarchs, of king and emperor (for example, Napoleon), representing the master of order and prosperity, the civilizing hero who assures harmony and prosperity through his wisdom and two-edged sword.

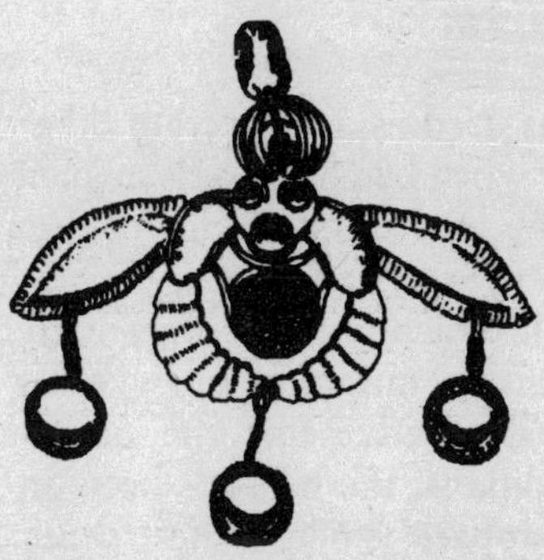

The bee, emblem of kings. The illustration shows a pendant found in a necropolis on Crete c.1700 BC

• In the fables of the Sudanese living at the mouth of the Niger, the bee symbolizes man and his social organizations.

• In Greece, the bee was 'A drop of light fallen from the sun at dawn'[30] and denoted eloquence, poetry and intelligence (bees settled on Pindar's and Plato's lips). In ancient Ireland, it symbolized perfection.

• In China, the bee (*mi-feng*) illustrates zeal and economy.

• The hive symbolizes the family or an organized group, or a town, etc.

• Honey, used in the preparation of nectar, drink of the immortals, symbolizes initiation, wisdom, immortality of the soul.

• In dreams, the diligent bee is a positive symbol, a dynamic figure of courage, prosperity, but also violent restlessness.

BELT
union and liaison

Whether it was used as a protection, like the chastity belt or virgin's belt worn by young girls in ancient Greece, or to please, like the *cestus* or girdle of Venus which held magical powers of seduction, or to cure, like the miraculous belt which until the thirteenth century had the power to perform miracles, or whether it was purely utilitarian or decorative like the precious *zona* of the Greeks and Romans, the belt has been an item of civilian and religious apparel since earliest times. In the Bible it symbolized close union with God.

• It was worn as a symbol of servitude by the high priest of the Jews, for he was a servant of justice (this was a forerunner of liturgical sashes). A widow who gave away her chattels to the community in order to avoid paying her late husband's debts 'would throw her belt to the ground.'

• It was also a symbol of deprivation, of restrictions and frustration, as can be seen in the monk's knotted rope, symbolizing his vows of chastity and continence . . . and in the popular expression of tightening one's belt.

• Its different colours denote grades or degrees, as in the army or in judo.

BIRD
freedom, spiritual quest

Because a bird can soar beyond the limits of the earthly plane, flying freely in the air, perhaps reaching heaven, it was thought to be a messenger of the gods. And so, in Mithraic sacrifice, the divine angel-messenger is a crow, a representation of Hermes, chosen by the Egyptians to express the immateriality of the soul.

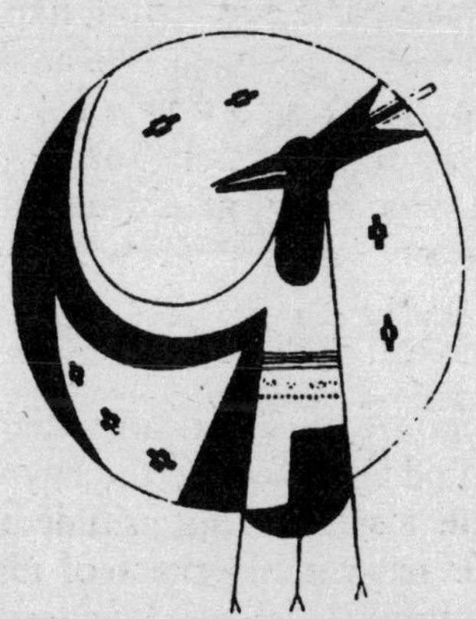

A bird design on prehistoric pottery of the Hopi North American Indians[144]

Bird

• In numerous myths, a bird is associated with the sun: Garuda, the fantastic Hindu bird was a symbol of immortality; the Egyptian phoenix and giant Vedic eagle are sun-gods. Often, it is a bird which brings fire from heaven to man. In folk tales, men metamorphose into birds. The bird is an attribute of Minerva, and symbolizes knowledge of the unconscious, the basis of wisdom.

• Wings symbolize the idea of spiritual ascension connected to superior states of consciousness. The wings of a bird have been used many times to depict the divine spirit, and, by analogy, the human soul (in India, Egypt, Assyria, Scandinavia, Brazil, Mexico).

Wings attached to certain animals (such as snakes and dragons) symbolize the capacity to rise above material obstacles and commune with the heavenly world, home of the spirit. Wings attached to claws or to Hermes–Mercury's helmet, symbolize lightness and speed. A bird's lightness also symbolizes intelligence, imagination, speed of comprehension, fantasy and caprice.[104]

Quetzecoatl, the Aztec sun-god[48]

• Feathers symbolize an American Indian chief's spiritual authority. The goddess Maat, in the Egyptian *Book of the Dead*, wears them on her head as a symbol of truth and justice.[10] In the same book, the soul of the deceased is symbolized in a falcon.

• In the Koran, supreme knowledge is depicted in the

language of birds, and this language is understood by the hero who conquers the dragon who has acquired this wisdom and gained virtual immortality. Similarly, Chinese tales tell of sages who have found salvation and spiritual riches through the medium of bird language.

• Dreams of birds, the archetypal image of the soul, announce the beginning of psychic transformation.

A bird's flight represents freedom of the soul from materialism. It can equally signal the danger manifest in obsessive ideas or preoccupations, when it flies unceasingly within a limited space.[24]

BLIND MAN
introversion

Blindness symbolizes a refusal to see reality, or it can refer to inner vision. Hindus consider a blind man to be a foreigner who can 'see other things, another world.'

• In dreams, it can mean that one's behaviour is too introverted, and one's life is becoming impoverished by this.

BLINDFOLD
retreat/retirement

The blindfold covering Thetis' eyes symbolizes her impartiality as the Greek goddess of justice. Over Eros' eyes it symbolizes chance.

• On an esoteric level, the blindfold symbolizes retreat into oneself, contemplation: the white canvas headband worn by nuns represents self-denial, abandonment of worldly things.

BLOOD
vehicle of life

Blood shares the colour red's symbolism and that of fire and the sun: it signifies life, strength and vigour. In the Greek myth of Adonis, blood symbolizes the resurrection of Nature in springtime (the god's blood is turned into an anemone, the first spring flower, and the flower of Aphrodite, his lover; blood also colours white roses red).

• Blood is the vehicle of life and contains the principle of vital heat, which is the basis of Moses' taboo to the Jews regarding eating the blood of animals.

In ancient times blood was thought to be the seat of the passions and familiar demons, or 'divine emanations.'[83]

• Australian Aborigines and many so-called primitive tribes anticipate an increase in vigour from blood, which for them is the principle of life and energy, and is also endowed with the virtue of purification. They cover their bodies in blood because they think that it will 'increase the element of life and fortify their all too volatile soul.'

These tribes use blood in all their rituals and sacred ceremonies: bloodletting accompanies offerings of food at initiation rites, and blood is sprinkled on the sacred stone inhabited by the spirit of a mythical person. 'Blood is drunk at some meetings as a sign of reconciliation.' In fertility rites, which take place when the new harvest is sown, the field is sprinkled with the blood of a buffalo, pig or chicken.

• The same idea is also found at the sacrifices (originally human, then animal) that accompanied Aztec and Mayan agrarian rituals, with the symbol of fire being added to that of blood. (The new fire was lit by a priest on the chest of the sacrificial victim stretched out on an altar.)

They attributed healing powers to blood, and sprinkled it over the bodies of the sick, or used red ochre, which to them seemed a 'real' visual equivalent of the vital fluid.

When blood was taken from the penis, it acquired a magical virtue and communicated invulnerability.

Blood is also the vehicle of the soul, and so it was also sprinkled on the ground during ritual sacrifices.[39]

• For the Chinese, fresh, red blood (*hsue*) is the symbol of life, home of the soul, and endowed with a magic force that it communicates to everything it touches. Idols are given life by painting their eyes with blood. But contact with 'unclean' blood, such as menstrual blood, leads to bad luck and sickness.[7]

• If blood appears in a dream it is a symbol of the soul's secret wounds manifested in a state of incomprehensible anguish, the deep cause of which can be found in too disciplined and inhibited a lifestyle.[24]

BLUEBIRD

peace, tranquillity, blind happiness

This fabled bird was dedicated to Thetis, one of the Nereids, and is associated with water and air. It symbolizes spiritual and material fecundity, no matter how threatened by the elements or how jealous the gods. It avoids the danger of self-satisfaction, knowing happiness can only come from heaven.

BOAT
journey

Symbol of a crossing. Charon, ferryman of the underworld, rowed the souls of the newly departed to the other side. The ancient Egyptian *Book of the Dead* described a solar barque in which the dead crossed the twelve regions of the underworld encountering dangers, demons and snakes on the way.

This boat, which bore the sun's disk (symbolizing the solar principle) inscribed on a crescent moon, was the symbol of supreme salvation. The disk amalgamated two opposing elements which had once been united and formed part of the earth before separating from it and splitting up, and so heralding the beginning of the biblical Fall. The joint rule of sun and moon symbolizes the defeat of 'sex and death, the two harmful consequences of the Fall.' The boat was the means of assuring progress towards evolution.

• Yoga compares the human body to a boat, conveying man to the other shore of the ocean of existence.

• The boar also symbolizes security in the perilous journey of life, and is affiliated to the symbolism of the mother.

BOOK
gnosis

The book symbolizes gnosis, knowledge. In Revelation, the Book of Life is at the centre of paradise 'where the Tree of Life is.'

• In holy scriptures such as the Koran and the Vedas, it contains the word[85], the divine message.

• The Sibyl's oracles were written down on linen canvas in the Sibylline Books, which contained the fate of Rome.

• Books have accompanied man into the life beyond, and people attaching great importance to death have left a Book of the Dead. The Egyptian one is made up of a series of advisory pictures intended to help the deceased lead his posthumous existence. The Book of the Dead of the Maya, who believed in metempsychosis, describes the complete ritual that accompanied the deceased from the time of his agony to his reincarnation in the entrails of a pregnant woman, passing through various metamorphoses of the soul.[30]

• In China the book (*shu*) is a symbol of erudition; learned and erudite systems of thought always rely on books: five classic books, four books of Confucianism.

• In dreams, an open book reproduces an action or an event that recalls the psychic situation in which the dreamer finds himself. Its title evokes an important moment, 'an extract from psychic life . . . The titles of these books encountered in dreams should be read because they tell us what is going on inside us.'

BOW/ARCH
desire

As the oldest projectile in hunting and war, the bow and its string and arrows have sexual implications, because of the tension, relaxation and release involved when it is used. The stretched bow consequently means desire, and physical and mental tension.

• As a weapon used in chivalry, if stretched upwards, the bow symbolizes sublimation of desire.

• Both bow and arch, like an upright loop, are similar to the rope in their symbolism, and are regarded as protective agents against demons. In numerous traditions, people walk under an arch formed by tree branches in order to rid themselves of illness, invisible enemies and ghosts. These are the narrow entrances associated with the arched doorways, arcades and vaults giving access to holy places.

• Triumphal arches, replicas of natural arches erected on an army's route, symbolize a psychological gate isolating survivors from the souls of soldiers killed in combat.

• In certain dances (such as the French Provençal farandole), arches formed by raised arms have a similar meaning to the bow and arch.

BOX
secret

A box symbolizes the mother's body and the unconscious.

• When closed, it symbolizes a secret, fragile, precious or fearsome thing.

• In Greek myth, Pandora's box symbolized taboos, for it enclosed every kind of evil which then affected mankind, spreading throughout the world, through the curiosity of a woman (just like Eve and the apple?). Its contents were the hidden forces of the unconscious, which can destroy evolution, but also serve it, for at the bottom of the box there is hope.

BOXWOOD

permanence

Boxwood is sacred to Hades, lord of the underworld, and to Cybele, goddess of fertility, who holds the key to earthly riches. And so boxwood has an ambivalent interpretation: it is a symbol of eternity for the Gauls, and also immortality (death–resurrection), which explains why it was so often planted in cemeteries and can also be seen on Egyptian tombs. It also signifies firmness and perseverance, because of the wood's hardness and the fact that its foliage is evergreen.

• In addition, it is an attribute of Satan, because of its strong smell and its association with the lord of the underworld.

BRANCH

strength

A green branch symbolizes regeneration and immortality. Mistletoe is known as golden branch because its leaves are gold in spring and the druids would only cut it with a gold sickle. It is a symbol of light, knowledge and spiritual strength.

BREAD

psychic nourishment

Because the process of making bread is long and labouring, bread is a symbol of cultural and psychic development. Each stage in breadmaking represents a stage in creation: sowing the grain, its growth, harvesting, milling, sifting, kneading, baking in the oven, sharing it at the family table . . .

At the Eucharist or Holy Communion, Christ becomes the bread of life, a symbol of material and spiritual nourishment. The Old Testament's twelve loaves of the bread of the presence were symbolic of the special food reserved for those who were in outer darkness, as opposed to 'the new beings engendered by God through the word of truth.'[20] This bread later symbolized the Christian Church's role in feeding the faithful and communicating strength and knowledge to them, and also, according to Josephus, symbolized the year and cycle of the zodiac.

• Yeast, the active agent in leavening bread, was a symbol of spiritual transformation: unleavened bread from which the host is made symbolized deprivation and sacrifice.

• Dreams about bread are never negative. They evoke vital elementary values, spiritual and mental psychic nourishment and often mark the end of psychological difficulties.

Bread in dreams can be a metaphor for the body of a loved one,[24] or refer to everyday married life or the sacrament of marriage.[135]

BREAST
tenderness

The breast is linked to fertility and milk, and is a symbol of abundance which has been assimilated into the cup which quenches thirst.

• It is inseparable from mother's milk and evokes protection, love and tenderness.

• In ancient China, secretions from the breast or the 'elixir of the breast' were one of the elements in the theory of the medicine of the three peaks, along with woman's saliva and vaginal secretions.

• In the iconography, goddesses' breasts symbolize nutritive power.

• In dreams breasts represent the archetype of the mother, and may appear in the form of a monster, dragons, or whale, and remind the person of the need to separate himself definitively from the cosy world of childhood and confront his responsibilities as an adult.[25]

BREATHING
achievement of immortality

In numerous traditions, the rhythm of breathing symbolizes the production and reabsorption of the universe, known in India as *kalpa* and *pralaya*, centripetal and centrifugal movements coming from the heart of the vital centre.

• Controlled breathing is one of the disciplines of Taoism, used in the art of feeding the vital principle (along with gymnastics, diet and the art of making love). It allows that which is in harmony to assimilate the power of the air and escape from the ascendancy of illness, old age and death, and to free the Taoist of all fear and the domination of time and space. 'True man breathes through his heels,' according to Chuang-tu, and according to Lao-tse, the ideal method consists in concentrating your breathing until you become soft, like a baby who expends no energy and preserves his power of life intact.

This embryonic breathing (breathing like a foetus in the womb) circulates breath in the body, eases communication between the five viscera and six receptacles, eliminating obstructions in the channels, stretches and contracts knots, and sustains the vital spirits.[65]

Breathing within an enclosed circuit enables you to return to the primal state in an attempt to achieve immortality.

• Yogis, as Buddhists, practise rhythmic breathing in order to improve mental concentration.

BRIDGE
crossing

A bridge symbolizes communication with heaven and relations with the gods: many myths refer to a tree trunk stretching from the summit of the cosmic mountain, the centre of the world, up into heaven.[92]

• A rainbow is a link between heaven and earth, a bridge of light easing the passage from the sensory world to the supernatural one; there was the rainbow which Buddha borrowed to descend to earth, and in ancient Greek myth, Iris's scarf.

• Since a bridge is a way of crossing from one bank to another, it has become a symbol of travel or crossing. Initiatory journeys in secret Chinese societies included crossing bridges (*quiao*): the golden bridge was symbolized by a white scarf; iron or copper bridges, reminiscent of the *nigredo* stage in alchemy (of turning to black or red), was symbolized by a sword.

• In dreams, a bridge symbolizes the passage from one state to another, higher one, like an ascension; it lies between two situations, or at the end of one cycle and the beginning of another.

BULL
divine strength

The bull is a symbol of divine power and divine creative strength. The wild bull breaking the egg of chaos with its horns once symbolized the creator releasing the fertile sperm from the restraints of inert matter. In the iconography, the reproductive organs were attached to the animal's head, indicating that the creator used his power to create sentient beings.[83]

• In India the bull and cow are male and female symbols, and also symbols of reproduction, nutrition, power and divinity.[83] Shiva has the bull Nandi as a mount, a symbol of justice, strength and law (*dharma*). Vrishabha, the powerful, male Vedaic bull, is assimilated into Soma as 'the Father of abundance, the supreme bull, dappled with the great variety of its manifestations'.[44] Each of the bull's hooves symbolizes an age (*yuga*) in the total cycle (*maha-yana*), and at each age it loses a foot.

• In Sioux mythology, this bull-dharma has become a bison (symbol of the universe comprising the totality of manifested forms), an animal incarnation of the earth principle manifested in the visible earth.

Each of its parts corresponds to a category of creation, and its feet correspond to the four ages of the cosmos. At the beginning of the cycle it is in the west, holding back the waters that threaten the earth.

Each year it loses a hair, and in each cyclic age it loses a foot. When it has lost all its hair and its four feet, the waters will flood the earth and that will be the end of the cycle.[131]

• In ancient civilizations, the bull was a symbol of fertility, and was associated with the gods of the atmosphere. Its bellowing was part of storms and thunder, its horns the crescent moon.

• As a virility symbol of natural reproductive forces, it symbolized the Nile, the great fertile force of Egypt. The bull Onuphis was sacred to Amon the Begetter, and was taken to be the incarnation of Osiris, god of death and resurrection,[124] while the cow Masre, begetter of the sun, was the attribute of Neith, mother of the god Phré (the sun). The bull Apis, bearing Uraeus and the sun disk between its horns, was a fertility symbol, protector of flocks, and associated with Osiris.

• In dreams, the bull has a symbolism similar to red and blood, and is the incarnation of powerful natural forces (in particular the sexual drive); they are ready for action, but must be controlled, for the dreamer risks becoming a victim of them. The bull 'contains a blind, indomitable impulsiveness.'[24]

BULL-ROARER
false thunder

The bull-roarer is used in Aborigine initiation ceremonies in south-east Australia.

It consists of a wooden board with a piece of string through one end. When whizzed around in the air, it gives off a humming, throbbing sound, similar to a bull's roar. This sound is known only to initiates. If it is heard in the night by the uninitiated, it is terrifying as it sounds like the voice of spirits or ancestors, 'from which they divine the approach of a god.'[21]

BUTTERFLY
lightness

In ancient tradition, the butterfly symbolized the etheric principle.

Its metamorphosis is reminiscent of the state of man in his earthly form 'in which the vigour and activity of the heavenly soul is hampered and confused with the material being.'

• The torpor and lack of feeling in the motionless, dormant chrysalis is reminiscent of death, 'the transitory state between the living functioning of the body and the final deliverance of the soul which takes place through fire.'

• The butterfly fluttering through the air is 'the image of the heavenly soul breaking the bonds of the material world in order to melt again into the ether from which it emanated.'[83]

• In China, the butterfly (*hu-die*) is, as it was in ancient Greece, a symbol of the soul, of renewal and immortality. The Chinese also thought of it as a symbol of man in love who had just drunk from the flower's chalice (i.e., woman). The expression, 'the butterfly mad with love and the wild bee' symbolized sexual union.

• In the iconography, a butterfly and a plum tree signify a long life and virgin beauty; a butterfly and a cat express the wish that someone should live until he or she is eighty.[7]

• In the West, a butterfly symbolizes lightness and fickleness.

• In dreams, it is a symbol of rebirth, linked to the process of psychic transformation, liberation from the fetters of the ego.[25]

CABBALAH
the secret of creation

The Cabbalah, the rabbinical basis of esoteric knowledge, is a Jewish mystical doctrine that, some say, goes back to Moses. It is transmitted by initiates, who take their text from four books: the *Heikhalot* books, the *Sefer Yetzira* (book of creation which also contains the 'thirty-two paths of wisdom'), the *Sefer ha-Zohar*, referred to as *Zohar* (book of splendour) and the *Bahir* (book of brilliance).

According to this doctrine, God established degrees of subordination between himself and the angels, between the angels and the stars, and between the stars and the world. These fundamental connections are contained in letters, numbers and symbols. From this basic belief the Cabbalists developed their theories of the influence of stars and spirits, and the symbolic properties of beings and things.[114]

Esoteric teaching begins with the study of the twenty-two letters of the Hebrew alphabet and their numerical values, and the first ten numbers, the *sephiroth*.

To make esoteric interpretations, several different procedures are used: *gematria* which consists of replacing a word by another whose letters add up to the same total; *notariqon*, which uses the initial letters of words in a sentence to compose a secret world; the *temura*, or anagram, and the *tsiruphim* or metagram, which consists of changing the alphabetical order by substituting the first letter with the last, etc.[19]

CADUCEUS

conveyance

The caduceus consists of two snakes entwined around a stick, crowned by two small wings. Made of gold, it was the attribute of Bacchus, Ceres, and especially Mercury/Hermes, who received it from Apollo.

Caduceus is a Latin word derived from the Greek *kerukeion*, meaning a herald's staff. It possesses the virtue of ridding someone of anger, and is regarded as an emblem of mediation and peace. (Tradition has it that the snakes represent Jupiter and Rhea, reconciled by Mercury after a quarrel.)

• The stick, which here has the same symbolic meaning as the sceptre, depicts the power man needs to run his life; he must master his conscious and unconscious impulses in order to develop his spirituality (according to Jung). Note too a parallel with the symbolism of the tree, which is the axis of the world, the Hindu *kundalini* symbolizing a transmutation of instinctive sexual drives in order to attain the superhuman level (symbolized by wings).

• The symmetrically placed snakes are reminiscent of the double spiral, and symbolize evolution, progressive development, the infinite repetition of the cycles of life.[8] The journey can be made in two directions (upwards, towards superior states, and downwards, towards inferior states), and so the snakes symbolize the duality of opposing and balancing forces.

Also inherent in this symbol is the harmony of cosmic forces created by Mercury from primordial chaos.

This idea is present on a human level too: the caduceus is

the attribute of Aesculapius, and symbolizes psychosomatic balance (psycho = mind; soma = body), the harmony of vital, psychic forces and their growth and balance, which is one of medicine's goals. The double spiral has remained the doctor's symbol, and a single snake the chemist's.

Lion bearing the caduceus[47]

• Wings signify spiritual ascension, divinity and infinity, and symbolize both the freeing of man's instinctive drives and his identification with the cosmos.

• An equivalent of the caduceus can be seen in the Brahman baton. And also in the American Indian peace pipe decorated with two eagle feathers, surrounded by intertwined locks of female hair (the equivalent of the wings on the caduceus). Also similar to the caduceus is the representation of two *nadi* in hatha-yoga. Here, currents of physical and psychic energy are entwined around the axis of the vertebral column (*sushumma*) where activity relating to the senses, mind and emotions circulates; by an act of will this must be made to flow upwards, towards the supreme beatitude of the *sahaja*, the One who is immanent in us.[11]

• The caduceus is also sometimes used as a symbol of commerce, which is the domain of Mercury, as a god of many values.

• The caduceus is therefore a dynamic symbol of movement, of conveyance and spiritual development.

CAIN
guilt

Cain, meaning 'vanquished' in Hebrew, was the first son of man, the first farmer, the first man to make sacrifices, the first murderer, the first nomad. He opened up the era of human responsibility, of willpower, and posed the problem of owning property, and the warring feelings that ensue as a result: jealousy, envy, the desire for vengeance, feelings of injustice (God preferred his brother's offering to his) and guilt.

This episode in the Bible also symbolizes the struggle between the ego and the shadow (the dark side of our personality), between opposing tendencies that constantly clash in the mind of man.

CANCER
feminity, dream

Cancer is the legendary crab, sent by Hera to help Hydra of Lerna. Heracles killed the crab after she had nipped his foot, and Hera bore her off to heaven.

Cancer
21 June–20 July

Fourth sign of the zodiac, Cancer is a female, watery, cardinal sign. House of the moon, Jupiter is exalted, Saturn is in exile, and Mars falls.

Cancer governs all the pockets in the body: such as the stomach and womb.

Characteristics: sensitivity, fertility, maternity, the past, tradition, memory.

Negative aspects: prolonged adherence to the maternal element, difficulty in ridding oneself of protective frameworks. Predominant emotionalism. Its association with the aquatic universe makes Cancer a symbol of the primeval waters and the mystery of deep water (a taste for secrecy and intimacy).[14]

Correspondences: metals: silver, platinum. Minerals: selenite, soft white stones, emerald. Colour: dull white.

CANDLESTICK
God's word

The Book of Exodus describes the menorah, a beaten gold candlestick placed in the Tabernacle by Moses, with seven branches bearing a bowl on each branch, and representing the entire Church, whose seven stages of development were exemplified in the seven congregatioins of Asia Minor.

These bowls were almond-shaped because fruit forms on the almond tree before the leaves appear, just as the priesthood bears fruit before the leaves of manifestation appear.[20]

The candlestick is a symbol of God's word and its light,

the holy illumination of the spirit of truth. It enlightens the Church on profound, divine matters that are entirely hidden from man. Only those who are truly holy are authorized to see this light deeply hidden in the holy of holies.

CAPRICORN

self-control, pessimism

This monster of Greek myth, half-goat, half-fish, was sacred to Pan, and was carried up to heaven by Zeus to become the southern constellation of Capricorn, whose appearance preludes winter.

Capricorn
21 December–19 January

The tenth sign of the zodiac. A female, cardinal, earth sign. House of Saturn, Mars is exalted, the moon is in exile, and Jupiter falls.
Characteristics: solidity, learning, rigidity, mistrust, silence, yoke.
Negative aspects: slave or slave driver, harshness, intransigence.
Correspondences: cold, dry, night, sterility, violence, weakness of material means. Metal: lead. Minerals: onyx. Governs bones and knees.

CAR
ego

The car is the modern equivalent of the horse and carriage, and frequently appears in dreams. The engine (horses) symbolizes man; the driver (coachman) symbolizes intelligence.

A car in motion symbolizes development and the experiences that accompany it, as well as the subject's adaptations to this development, which is linked to the state of the vehicle.

The bodywork reflects the persona, that is, the impression one is trying to give other people.

As an integral part of modern man's life, the car is also an image of the ego. Driven by someone else, it betrays difficulty in leading one's life as one understands it, or the existence of a complex.

A bad driver who puts the lives of the car's occupants at risk reveals lack of self-control, irresponsibility, a need to keep his or her impulses under control

If there is no fuel, one has overestimated one's strength, or at base one has none.

Large vehicles, such as lorries or trailers, blocking the road can be the incarnation of someone close to the dreamer whose presence or attitude is blocking his or her advance.

Buses symbolize social life. If they appear too often in dreams, it is time to look again at one's behaviour and think of one's personal development, which has been neglected in favour of gregariousness.

CARDINAL POINTS
cosmic order

Through the number 4, considered to be the root of everything, man has been able to orientate himself in space by determining the cardinal points: North, South, East and West, to which can be added the centre and the zenith.

• These points are emblems of cosmic order, and in every civilization they are the focus of significant symbolism; they can be found in artefacts as early as the stone circles around Iron Age tombs which are marked by bigger stones which indicate the position of the solstices and equinoxes. The symbolism of cardinal points is always related to the idea of guardianship, be it animal or divine:

– the four sentinels in ancient Persia (Tascher, guardian of the East, Satevis of the West, Venant of the South and Haftorang of the North) who keep watch over the celestial armies (stars seen as legions of soldiers) divided into twelve battalions which relate to the zodiacal constellation;[3]

– the four rivers flowing out from the Hindu Mount Meru, containing the hidden power of the gods;

– the four rivers of Christian paradise compared by St Ambrose to the cardinal virtues;

– the four sons of Horus in ancient Egypt, guarding the heart and entrails of Osiris.

• The Maya turned the cardinal points into gods whom they saw as pillars upholding the earth, and associated each with a different colour and animal.

• Chaldaean cosmogonical theories established relationships between the cardinal points and the elements: North – winter, water; South – summer, fire; East – autumn, earth; West – spring, air.[21]

• The Lydians associated the cardinal points with the seasons, the ages of man, and parts of the tree of life. North – winter solstice, Atlas, root; East – vernal equinox, Hel, the child, the stem; South – summer equinox, Hanom, adult man, the fruit; West – autumn equinox, Ahan Dor, the old man, the seed.

• Navajo Indians honoured the cardinal points with precious stones. North – black stone; South – turquoise; East – white pearl and rock crystal; West – conch shell.[126]

• The Annamese depicted them as symbolic animals: North – snake, tortoise; South – red sparrow; East – white dragon; West – white tiger.

In Indo-European sun worship, they were shown as the lion, eagle, bull and female angel.[3]

• The American Indians showed the cardinal points special homage: all their rites included offerings and ritual greetings to the four directions, beginning with the South (source of life, from which man emerged to walk towards the setting sun of his life).[13]

• The Navajo showed the cardinal points through symbolic colours which played a significant role in their iconography and worship: white symbolized the East; blue the South; yellow the West; and black the North.[66]

• According to the Aztecs, all the ills afflicting humanity came from the North, home of Tezcatlipoca, god of the nocturnal heaven and winds. From the North came rain, violent winds which destroyed the maize crops, bad habits, and the evil air which caused sickness. In the North lay the Milky Way, the moon and *Mictlampa ehecatl*, the Mayan hell. It was to there that the dead journeyed. Its colour was black, red for the Maya; its emblem obsidian, *tectpatl*.

The South was the source of light and was symbolized by the rabbit, *tochtli*. It belonged to Uitzilopochti, god of the midday sun. It was the land of fire.

The East, where Venus and the sun were born, symbolized by the reed, was the home of Tlaloc, god of rain, the house of green feathers. Its colour was red.

The West, symbolized by the house, was the residence of mother-goddesses and the god of maize, Centeotl, and of women who had died in childbirth who accompanied the sun from its zenith to the western horizon (while the men lived in the east). It was the region of decline, the gate of mystery. Its colour was yellow, the colour of maize.

• For the Sioux Indians, the 'four quarters of the universe' represents the four essential divine manifestations and consequently their prototypes in man. The North is associated with the great white wind that purifies and gives strength. The South, linked with the yellow wind, which brings in the summer, is the source of life and growth. In the West, associated with the black wind, live the creatures of thunder who send rain, that is to say, revelation and grace. The East, from which light and knowledge spring and where the morning star lives which gives man knowledge, corresponds to the red wind. These four spirits personify complementary aspects of the universal spirit, which unites them all within itself, 'just as all colours are united in light.'

• Among the Arapaho, the four principles are personified in four old men emanating from the sun; they watch over the inhabitants of the earth, and to them are attributed daytime in the south-east, summer in the south-west, night in the north-west and winter in the north-east. The north–south axis symbolizes the 'good red road'. the 'way of happiness and felecity', the good, straight path similar to the Christian 'strait and narrow way'. It is the vertical line of the cross, the axis of possibility. The east–west axis is the 'blue or black path', the way of error and destruction. 'Anyone who travels along this path . . . is distracted, dominated by the senses, living for himself rather than society.'[13]

• An identical orientation existed in ancient Rome: the *Cardo* ran from south to north; the *Decumanus* from west to east; the *tribus* were in four divided sections which made up the four *curies*.

• The Jews divided their twelve tribes into four groups of three tribes, each of which had a chief tribe: Judah in the East; Reuben in the South; Ephraim in the West, and Dan in the North.[4]

• This kind of distribution is also found in India, where there was a correspondence between cardinal points, castes, mountains, and sacred animals made of different metals and colours: the North was a region of darkness and death; it was the traditional point of departure and was associated with brown or black, iron, and the Shudras (serfs). The South was associated with red, copper and the Kshatriyas (the warrior class). The West was a place of spiritual darkness and corresponded to yellow, gold and the Vaishyas (the merchant class). The East corresponded to white, silver and the Brahmin (the highest class). The centre was Mount Meru, centre of the world.[4]

• In Chinese cosmology, North is associated with water, South with fire, West with clouds, and East with lightning. And there is a sort of similarity with the Hindu regions, in the orientation of the celestial palaces: East, symbolized by a full moon in the autumn equinox, is green; West is white; the central palace, associated with Saturn, the planet of the north, is yellow, the colour of the earth.

• The orientation of medieval cathedrals was related to the cardinal directions. The façade faced East, the place where light is generated and from which 'creative impulses arise' while the West is the place of the Last Judgement. The South is the place of shining light, and the North of cold and darkness, 'where uncreated light is generated' on the path of initiation. ('The alchemists gathered at the little north door to discuss beginning the Great Work.') 'In the north are sculpted scenes from the Old Testament, the foundations of Christianity and the foundations of Man whose edification begins.'[80]

CASTLE
individuation

The castle, difficult of access, surrounded by fortifications, high walls, towers and bastions, is a symbol of protection.

• While it acts as a refuge in times of danger, it also illustrates solitude, the often necessary isolation involved in the process of individuation, or psychic maturity (according to Jung): the heroines of fairy tales sleep in it as they wait for Prince Charming to awaken them (a symbol of the awakening of the conscious mind).

• It can reflect ostentation, luxury or the abandonment of hope (a black castle).

• In darkness or with windows closed, it symbolizes the unconscious, a confused mind and indecision; lit up, it reflects lucid consciousness, a realization of one's wishes.

The revolving castle of the Holy Grail[47]

• At a higher level, the almost inaccessible castle is a symbol of the difficulty of achieving self-realization, of finding the Self, while the need to attack the fortress's defences reflects the need to fight unconscious forces and the irrational tendencies of the super-ego.

CAT
femininity

In Egypt, the cat (*aelurus*) was a symbol of the moon. It was worshipped in the form of the great cat, Mau, who, in the *Book of the Dead*, struck down the mythological snake Apophis who had tried to capsize the solar barque.

It was also the goddess Bast, a personification of the sun's power of fertility. Bast protected the sun against snakes while it slept.

The Thebans called the female cat lady of heaven.

• Muslims thought the cat a lucky animal with seven lives, but a black cat had magical powers.

• In China, the cat (*mao*) is a symbol of clairvoyance, linked to the moon and to everything that characterizes it. In some regions, it is thought to have demonic powers, and be able to see spirits at night.

White cats were thought to transform themselves by night into harmful spirits because they had stolen the moon's rays.[7]

• Traditionally, the cat was thought to have a feminine nature, and the Pawnee Indians of North America use the wild cat as a symbol of shrewdness and ingenuity. Just as in fairy tales it personifies *savoir-faire* with a penchant for lies and hypocrisy.

In other traditions, it is malevolent because it possesses the subtlety and evasiveness of the devil, and is thought of as a symbol of death.

• In dreams a cat signifies an agonizing situation; and is often resented as hostile, aggressive and formidable.[23] According to Aeppli, who retains the Pawnee's symbolic interpretation, this animal with 'shiny fur that crackles when stroked, and offers a velvet paw at one moment and strikes with all claws out the next, appears particularly in women's dreams, just when they are becoming aware of feline characteristics within their own natures.'[24]

CAVE, CAVERN
rebirth

The dark cave which served early man as both house and temple is seen as the door to the underworld, the cave of mysteries. In former times initiation rites were practised there: the postulant entered as into a tomb, to be reborn to a new life, after leaving his rudimentary passions and instincts behind in the cave.

A cave is associated with the idea of a test, or of the difficulties encountered at the stage in self-discovery that precedes the integration of the personality's different elements. And so, in myths, the cave is haunted by monsters, symbolizing the dangerous (because as yet unknown) contents of the unconscious.

• The caves of initiation rites were sacred to Isis in Egypt, to Hera, Pallas or Demeter in Greece, and to the Virgin Mary for the early Christians. They were a symbol of regression, of the return to the maternal womb to be reborn . . . and given new life. The burial of the dead in crypts and tombs comes from this ancient belief: return to the earth, to the universal matrix from which life was born. The enthusiasm of cavers for descent to the bottom of chasms and caverns is related to a desire to return to one's origins, to plunge into the unconscious.

• In dreams, the cave is the maternal archetype, the process of psychic transformation.[25] This semi-obscure place is the place of inner rebirth.[24]

CENTRE

the origin of movement

The centre of the world is the omphalos, the earth's navel, symbolized by the fat prehistoric figures of Venus.

Later, with the advent of a patriarchal society, this centre was symbolized by a mound on which a stone in the shape of a phallus was erected, a central pillar on which the continuation of the human race depended. Each tribe had its own centre/axis of the world: it may have been a sacred mountain like the Hindu Mount Meru, a temple or a royal palace. These were their sources of reality.

• The cosmic centre/axis, like the tree of life, which served as the central pivot of space and time, has its equivalent in the body: this is the vertebral column, on which different levels of consciousness (the Indian *chakras*) are set out in tiers; the highest represents fraternization with the gods, and freedom, the lowest is devoted to instinct.

• The centre also symbolizes order, in the administrative law (central power, centralization) of the state, and, on a higher level, of the world, and of thought, and spiritual ascensions.

• It is also the heart of the new Jerusalem – a symbol of accomplished man. To reach the centre of his personality implies integrating the three levels of consciousness (in Freudian terms): the id (instinctive impulses), the ego (consciousness) and the super-ego (the subconscious, superior mental processes), This integration leads to psychological maturity.

• The symbolism of the centre is linked to the point, the pivot on which everything depends.

CHARIOT
movement

In the seventh arcana of the tarot, the young charioteer, reminiscent of the Lover (the emotions) and the Magician (thinking element) and bearing a sceptre like the Emperor (will), is the incarnation of superior elements in the human personality, and represents the intellectual soul – the alchemist's antimony.

His chariot, a visible support to the invisible, symbolizes a dynamic realization of the body (the wheel being a symbol of vital ardour, kept alive by movement).

This young prince represents the enlightened conscious, which can reconcile opposing tendencies within the personality, symbolized by the two sphinxes in contrasting colours, which he controls superbly.

The arcana symbolizes unification through movement.

Divinatory meaning: victory, self-control, talent, success due to personal merit, ambition, advancement.

Reverse meaning: incapability, lack of talent and of tact; shocking behaviour.[17, 19, 114]

CHILD
naturalness

In every tradition, including Christian mysticism, a child is symbolic of freshness, spontaneity, simplicity and naturalness.

• In dreams, this image can symbolize the beginning of psychological development: 'a new possibility of life is rising out of unconscious into the conscious that is overburdened with conflict . . . The child comes to the rescue bringing harmony.'[24]

The presence of a child can also signal the existence of a complex that causes childish behaviour; this must be overcome if we are to begin the process of development.

CHIMAERA
divine powers

The chimaera, a monster described by Homer, part goat, part lion and part snake, expelling fire from its mouth, symbolized God's powers of creation (the goat), destruction (the lion) and conservation (the snake), 'united and given life through fire, the divine essence of the three.'[83]

CIRCLE
the continual development of creation

Early man used a circle to denote the cycle of the seasons that make up the year. He named them by making a circle with his lips and emitting sounds: *on*, *aen*, *ain*, which the Greeks turned into *ennos* (year), the Romans, *annulus* (a ring), and the Assyrians, *Anou* (god of the heavens).[121]

The symbolism of the circle expressed the triple notion of continually evolving life, time, and divinity.

• If the centre is the point from which movement and, by extension, life emanates, the circle is a development of the central point, 'in every direction'[17]; it shows the constant return of time, the seasons, life, death, day and night.

Circle

• It implies an idea of movement, and symbolizes the cycle of time, the perpetual motion of everything that moves, the planets' journey around the sun (the circle of the zodiac) which can be seen in circular temples, arenas, circuses, the round dances of the whirling dervishes, the circumambulation of Arab pilgrims around the Ka'aba, of Buddhists around stupas (a domed edifice containing a relic), of the priest around the altar with the censer, symbols of their participation in the great rhythm of the universe.

• In Islam the circle symbolizes perfection, in ancient Egypt, divinity (the solar disk) and light. As an image of that which has no beginning and no end, the circle symbolizes eternity. This aspect is illustrated by the snake (an emblem of life) biting its tail (known as the ouroboros) and symbolizing eternity. The ouroboros has a motto: 'One for all' – raw matter, rarefied until it is imperceptible, forms the inanimate essence of things, the immaterial foundation of all matter.

• In astrology, it is a symbol of the sun and an image of the sun's generative power (the Egyptian *kneph* or winged disk). The idea of the circle can be seen in circular walks and marches, ritual worship and assistance for the sun god, who needs to be sustained in the difficult moments of his annual cycle, such as the solstices, equinoxes and eclipses.[136]

• The circle is also zero in our system of numbering, and symbolizes potential, or the embryo. If it has a central point, it illustrates the 'manifest being', evoking the concept of order in the universe, and harmony.[22] It also looks like a wheel.

• It has a magical value as a protective agent, and symbolizes an impenetrable barrier, warding off demons and keeping them at bay. In China, a chalk circle around a bonfire on which a bowl containing demons is burnt symbolizes a fortress with no exit, from which it is impossible to escape; or, around tombs, a barrier to fend off *pretas* who steal the offerings intended for the dead.[6]

• The Chinese wear a rigid gold collar as an amulet, with a large clasp called a long-life clasp, signifying that the spirit of long life and good luck is safe, locked away, and will continue to dispense its blessings to the wearer. These good-luck charms in gold or silver are given to new-born babies on the nineteenth day of the second lunar month, the anniversary of Buddha's birth.[75]

• Associated with the magic circle are chains of defence, drawn by sorcerers around persons or plants to ward off noxious influences and procure supernatural virtues for them: there are circles containing magic names to conjure up spirits and genies, circles drawn on the ground which the magician stands inside and will not cross until certain compacts have been made.

• In Japan, the *shimenawa* (sacred rope made of rice straw which, according to myth, prevents the sun from disappearing for ever) fulfils an identical function. It is wrapped around objects as a protection, for example, around sacred trees and rocks, and buildings or building sites which can be built on only after purification. Putting the ropes in place involves an impressive ceremonial ritual. They are hung above the entrances of private houses or temples at New Year.[77]

• Note also that the magic ring worn by a sorcerer or magician to protect his fingers from dangerous influences, was the forerunner of modern rings, bracelets, and diadems, formerly intended to secure the cohesion between body and soul, which is indispensable for man's survival (they were taken off at death to allow the soul to escape).

• The *kyilkhov* (meditation circle) used by Tibetan lamas is simultaneously a magic tool that circumscribes spiritual impulses, and a mandala. Drawn on fabric, paper, metal or on the ground using coloured powders, this diagram has a god at its centre symbolized by a *torma* or small paste pyramid.

• In dreams, the circle is a symbol of the Self and indicates the end of the process of individuation, of striving towards a psychic wholeness and self-realization.[24]

• The sphere is a three-dimensional circle. According to the Hermetica (a body of Hellenistic mystical philosophy), God was conceived as a sphere whose centre was not only in heaven, but everywhere, on earth and in the underworld. This is reminiscent of the ancient Egyptians' three divisions of heave, earth and duat.

• The sphere also symbolizes psychic dynamism.

CIRCUMCISION
entry into adult life

A rite that boys still undergo to free the penis from its protective prepuce, through a kind of aggression on the part of the circumciser. Circumcision symbolizes and marks a definitive break from babyhood and the maternal world.

This rite is still practised by (Jewish and Islamic) societies who have purged their mythology of every female element. See also *Androgyne*.

CLOTHES
the persons

Clothing is the external symbol of spiritual activity and is meant to reflect the function and dignity of the wearer. The ancient Egyptians were already depicting Isis with clothes that varied in colour and had complicated pleats to indicate 'that passive physical power takes multiple forms and diverse paths in order to adapt more readily to the influence of active or ethereal power.' Osiris' clothes, on the other hand, were 'simple and of a luminous colour in order to show his essential unity and the inimitable universality of his power.'[83]

• In the Middle Ages, the king, who synthesized society, had to wear the best clothes. The pope's clothes made him a living representation of the universe. 'Earth is symbolized in his knee breeches woven from fine linen, the sea that surrounds the continents by shoulder belts, air by his hyacinth tunic, fire by his mitre.'[83]

• The high priest of the Jews wore glorious, beautiful clothes: his tunic of white linen symbolized purity which was essential in his sacrificial role; his embroidery symbolized the development of his pure character in works of grace. His tiara, a fine band of white linen tied with a blue cord, showed that the crown of justice belonged to him. His linen mitre proclaimed the perfect justice of the leader of officiating priests during sacrifice. His belt (a symbol of slavery) of linen (justice) indicated a just servant. His blue robe symbolized fidelity. His ephod of purple, blue and scarlet fabric, interwoven with gold thread and in two parts, represented the two great alliances: the alliance of Abraham and the new alliance.[20]

• Clothing was impregnated with the prestige and power of the wearer: during processions people touched the pope's clothes, as they had once done the king's clothes, gloves, and shoes.

Clothes

• The cloak worn by the king at his coronation was a symbol of heaven.

• Headwear, such as a peaked cap or helmet, is sometimes a symbol of social distinction. Like Buddha's golden umbrella, it is also a symbol of power.

• Clothes can sometimes by a symbol of belonging, like a monk's cassock or uniforms. Casting them off is a symbol of abandoning the community, or of breaking ties.

• In ancient China, imperial dress was a synthesis of the universe. It was made from the essence of the world, square below, a symbol of earth, the circular dais of his square chariot being the equivalent of heaven, 'the most powerful constellations being present in the symbols of the flags and choice of insignia (sun, moon, the constellations, lightning, etc.) which are shown on his clothes, the emperor found himself in direct contact with the most efficacious of beneficent forces.'[34]

Chinese imperial costume had to form a harmonious ensemble in which all the details were adapted to the law of correspondences. 'An officer's tunic had to be one of five basic colours, his under garment in the corresponding intermediary colours'. The bonnet, the noblest part of his clothing, had to suit the occasion: whether mourning, abstinence, disgrace, business meetings, or presence of a superior, etc.

To be received at court, the nobility had to wear clothes befitting their rank, the season and the emperor's circumstances and, of course, the emperor's dignity.

'Dress must be made of twelve bands as the year is made of twelve months . . . with round sleeves imitating a circle with a neck cut square, the back stitching as straight as a die, as a symbol of rectitude and correctness, with the bottom edge as level as the beam on a pair of balanced scales.'[134]

• Clothes symbolize the persona: the image of ourselves that others see, our social function, profession and social life.

In dreams new clothes symbolize a new attitude, a different sense of how we want to behave in our lives and towards others. A torn garment (or one that is inappropriate for the occasion) betrays wounded vanity or a feeling of inferiority. Wearing a uniform reveals a lack of originality or an automized way of life.

CLOUD
confusion

Clouds are intermediaries between heaven and earth, spirit and matter, dream and reality, and as such they symbolize nebulousness, an obscured vision of things, and also melancholy and sadness.

• In stories disappearing in a cloud means being transformed into pure energy.[68]

• In China clouds (*yun*) are produced by the union of yin and yang. In the iconography, clouds of five colours are a symbol of happiness and peace: the cloud-mountains or very distant mountains symbolize separation and nostalgia. A mist of clouds is a ravishing brassière.

• In dreams clouds reveal the collective unconscious and express floating, changing feelings of insecurity.

COCK
vigilance, pugnaciousness

The king of the farmyard is renowned for his virility and fertility (while a castrated cock or capon is a picture of cowardice).

• It was as a symbol of vigilance (in Greek *alektruor*, meaning he who does not sleep), the guardian of souls, that early Christianity showed a cock in the company of Jesus and Peter, and placed him high up on church towers, 'where he could survey the horizon and frighten away demons.'

In his double role of vigilant protector and courageous defender of his children, the cock symbolizes Christ who, from on high, watches over the church militant here on earth, and defends it against squalls and tempests from whatever direction they come.[31]

The cock's vigilance was apparent when he called Saint Peter to order with his three crows.

His call, which ends the medieval *danse macabre* (dance of death), symbolizes life victorious in death, and a trace of this lingers in the popular tradition which says that the cock-crow that heralds the dawn also heralds God's divine powers and chases away nocturnal ghosts.

• By signalling the sun's daily arrival, the cock symbolizes the sun itself, and for this reason it was sacred to Apollo. It was also a symbol of vitality and as such an attribute of Aesculapius, god of medicine, and because of the cock's penchant for fighting and his courage, an attribute of Bellone, companion of Mars, god of war.

• The cock also symbolizes victory because he would rather die than ever abandon a fight.

On French republican coinage, he features as a symbol of union and the armed forces.

• In heraldry, the cock rampant indicates pride and vigilance 'with his beak open to crow his alarm and awakening call'.

• The *coq gaulois* takes its name from the Latin *gallus* meaning both cock and Gaul.[31]

• In Egypt the cock, together with the eagle and fire, form a trinity of initiation symbols. The white cock was sacred to Jupiter and the sun and moon, and Pythagoras forbade his followers to eat it on any occasion other than at a ceremonial Pythagorean supper.

• For the Incas, who were sun worshippers, the cock was a sacred animal because he announced the coming of divine light.

• In India, he personified solar energy, and in the Tibetan wheel of fate he features as lust, desire and voluptuousness (along with the snake and pig); these were considered negative impulses that a wise man should rid himself of, as a first stage in spiritual development.

• The cock (*ji*) is the tenth sign in the Chinese zodiac. It confers an attractive personality, pride and vanity, precision, a developed critical sense, and a taste for polemics.

The Year of the Cock is marked by discussions and disputes, displays of egoism at every level. During this period, prudence in every kind of enterprise and initiative is recommended.

COLOURS
life

Three of the six colours are primary: blue, yellow and red. The other three are a mixture of two primary ones: green (blue and yellow), orange (red and yellow) and purple (blue and red). Neither white nor black are in the spectrum, although white was once thought to be a synthesis of all colours.

Colours have had exceptional importance in traditional symbolism ever since mankind began, and it appears that in earliest times, colours had the same significance for every people.

The language of colour, which is intimately linked to

religion, spread through India, China, Egypt and Greece to Rome, and reappeared in the Middle Ages. Explanations for the stained glass windows in Gothic cathedrals can be found in Zen texts, in Vedic scriptures, and in paintings in Egyptian temples.[32]

• Colours have had a cosmic significance and have symbolized gods in a range of cosmologies. In Amerindian (Mayan, Aztec, Incan) cultures, red was associated with the east, the land of the sun; blue or white with the north (a cold land); black, with the west (land of shadow); yellow or white with the south (the Incan Valhalla) and was connected with the ages of creation.[126]

• The Japanese recognized particularly subtle significances in colours that were outside man's normal descriptive powers. The Shinto school taught their initiates the following correspondences:
black (*kuro*) and purple (*murasaki*) – north – *ara-mitama* – primitive, origin, paradise;
blue or green (*ao*) – east – *kushi-mitama* – life, creation;
red (*aka*) – south – *sachi-itama* – harmony and expansion;
white (*shiro*) – west – *nigi-mitama* – integration and impulses;
yellow (*ki*) – centre – *nao-hi* (sun rays) – creator, unity.

This series of five colours dominated the ritual when the emperor made a gift of fabric to a kami (god). It was essential at the very least to have a piece in each colour; banners were made up in bands of five colours, and ribbons in the five colours hung from the little bells worn by the dancers during special sacred dances.[77]

The way we like or dislike certain colours can reveal our hidden emotions, forgotten feelings, confused states of mind imprinted deep in our memories, and, through colour preference, we can attempt to penetrate the conscious.

White

Once thought to be the synthesis of all colours, white is light, and ancient civilization deemed it the colour of divinity: the Egyptians wrapped their dead in a white shroud to show that death delivers the pure soul from its perishable envelope of flesh

• For the Jews, the tunic of white linen represented the purity of the priest officiating at a sacrifice, and divine justice.

• White was the colour of the vestal virgins (priestesses who were burnt alive if they broke their vow of chastity) and of the druids and initiates.

• Other white symbols indicating purity, virtue and chastity are the white first communion or confirmation dress, the bridal gown, the bouquet of orange blossom, lilies, doves, linen, ivory, swans, diamonds, snow . . .

• In its malevolent aspect, moon whiteness has the lividness of a corpse and shroud.

Red

In Egypt, red symbolized divine love. It was the colour of fresh or tainted blood, and fire which, according to ancient belief, created the world and would ultimately destroy it. It symbolizes life, warmth and reproduction, but also destruction.

• In the sacred language of Christians, Egyptians, Jews and Arabs, this colour has always been associated with fire and divine love, and has symbolized divinity and religion.

Red has been a colour worn by generals, the nobility, patricians and emperors in Rome; and Roman Catholic cardinals have inherited this symbol of sovereignty. In Peru, red was associated with war and symbolized the army.

Colours

• In coats-of-arms, red or *gules* expresses valiance, fury, cruelty, anger, murder and carnage.

• Bright or light red is the 'vital force of the triumphant hero, wealth and love.' But red's negative side corresponds to egoism, hatred and infernal love (red is the devil's colour).

• On a psychological level, red represents the joy of living, optimism, vigour, the fighting instinct and its aggressive tendencies, sexual drive, sexual desire, passion and the need to conquer.

Here we can recognize the animus and its physical strength, its power of creation and procreation. Red is also the colour of the psychological function of feeling. 'The soul is ready for action, feeling is presented in the form of conquest or suffering, total sacrifice, and distress.'[24]

Yellow

Yellow is the colour of light, gold, and honey. It is the colour of heavenly light revealed to man, the religious doctrine taught in the temples.[32]

• But lunar yellow, colour of tarnished gold and sulphur, symbolizes inconstancy, jealousy, depraved passions, adultery, guilt, treason (in many countries Jews were forced to wear yellow garments because they were said to have betrayed Christ; in France, traitors' door were daubed in yellow. Judas is shown in paintings as wearing yellow garments).

• From a psychological viewpoint and in dreams, yellow is the colour of intuition and symbolizes a capacity for renewal, liveliness, youth and audacity, but also instability and vanity.[33]

It shows a need to be superior and, at the extreme, a blind will to power manifested in exaggerated pretensions to a false superiority (often compensation for unconscious or residual feelings of inferiority).

Orange

Orange, which is a mixture of yellow and red, symbolizes the revelation of divine love to the human soul and was the symbol of indissoluble marriage, but also, reversing the symbol, of adultery and lust, and, in heraldic symbolism, dissimulation and hypocrisy.

• In dreams, this hot, brilliant colour, emblematic of lust, expresses an intense need for sexual pleasure and expansion, and reflects a fragile balance, and the dreamer's need to control his or her impulses.[33]

Orange is an attribute of Typhon (the monster who, by attacking the gods on Olympus, began the fight between light and the forces of the underworld). In everyday mythology, tawny (*tenne* in heraldry) symbolizes man's animal tendencies, extravagant fertility, perversion, concupiscence, and their consequences: intemperance, debauchery, violence, egoism.

• It is the colour of the psychological function of sensation, the instinct for propagation and all that that entails.

Green

Green, the colour of Nature and lustral (purifying) water, is endowed with the power of regeneration; it captures solar energy and transforms it into vital energy, thus becoming a symbol of spiritual regeneration.

• As the colour of springtime buds that announce the end of winter, it symbolizes hope.

• In heraldry, *sinoper* testifies to the knight's courtesy, honour, joy and vigour.

Colours

• In Egypt green is an attribute of the god Ptah, creator and stabilizer, and of water, because in the Egyptian cosmology water was the primordial agent of creation. It signifies the foundation of time, the creation of the world, and physical and spiritual birth – in other words, the mysteries of initiation.[9]

• Being a mixture of yellow and blue, green has a dual character: it is the colour of Venus, a symbol of renewal, but also of vengeance; of the Aztec serpent-god, inventor of the arts and identified with the Egyptian god Thoth and Roman Mercury, and also with Lug of the Gauls, a doctor, magician, satirist and artisan. Green is also identified with the Islamic Kisr whose task was to reconcile extremes (this function of creating a synthesis can also be seen in the caduceus).

• In China, green designated the east, springtime, woods and charity, and in Christianity, regeneration and charity, but also, paradoxically, moral degradation and folly, despair.

• Flecked with yellow (the colour of dragons' and snakes' eyes), green is the colour of stagnant water, putrefaction and harmful influences.

• On a psychological level and in dreams, green is the colour of sexual vigour and reflects a need to open up, a need for self-esteem, self-actualization, culture and knowledge.[33]

Blue

In all the mythologies blue is associated with divinity: with Amon-Rê, god of the rising sun in ancient Egypt; in Greece, with Jupiter, father of gods and man, and with Juno, the incarnation of female blossoming fertility; in India, with Vishnu, dispenser of justice.

• In China, it symbolizes the Tao, the sacred path, the unfathomable principle of human life.

• For the Egyptians, Jupiter's blue, the cold colour of the void, is the colour of truth; in Christian tradition, it represents eternal truth, immortality, faithfulness, chastity, loyalty and justice.

• Blue is identified with air and wind, and symbolizes spirituality, contemplation, passivity; it helps in meditation and rest.

• On a psychological level and in dreams, blue is the colour of tolerance and stands for balance, self-control, tendencies towards generosity and kindness, a reflective demeanour and a need for serenity.

Light blue reflects the inaccessible, the miraculous, the evasive.[33]

Purple

Red and blue are used in equal portions to make purple, which signifies a love of truth, and the truth of love. It was the symbol of the mystic marriage of Our Lord and the Church, of his Passion and the martyrs, and signifies the total identification of Father and Son.

• It is also a colour used by widows, bishops and martyrs, and is a symbol of death for the Chinese.

• In psychology, purple, the colour of loving fusion and submission expresses the need for union, for the approbation of and identification with a loved one.[33]

But this red turned cold has a faded quality about it; it expresses a melancholy state of mind, accompanying a need for tenderness and gentleness.

Pink

A mixture of red and white, the colour of flesh and regenerative dew and seduction, pink symbolizes love, purity, fidelity (like the rose praised in song by minstrels and poets down through the ages).

Black

Black, negative of light, is a symbol of nothingness, of error, and of what does not exist, and is associated with night, ignorance, evil and everything false. It signifies ignorance born of evil and of all the selfish, hateful passions.[9]

It is the colour of coal, reminding us of combustion, the prelude to regeneration in alchemy; it encompasses the idea of resurrection.

Ancient initiation rites included tests that took place in the dark: the postulant had to step over a symbolic corpse in a dark place in order to become a new man, reborn into a spiritual life.

• In heraldry, it is known as sable and signifies prudence, wisdom and constancy in times of sadness and adversity.

• Black also contains a hint of the fear of abandonment complex, inseparable from melancholy and often accompanied by a fear of life, and despair, tendencies reflected in dreams, as well as a need for independence.

Grey

Grey combines the white of innocence with the black of guilt. For Christians it was the emblem of earthly death and spiritual immortality, of calumnied, blackened innocence, condemned by opinion or by law.[33]

• It is also the colour of sadness, of anxiety, of vague dreaming.[33]

• In the Bible, it is the colour of ashes, a symbol of persistence (on Ash Wednesday, an occasion for public penitence, the priest makes a mark of ashes on the forehead of penitents; in former times the bishop would spread ashes over sinners' heads). Ashes were also a sign of mourning (the Jews covered themselves with ashes at funerals as an expression of their grief).

• Grey is an equivocal colour, a refusal a lack of vigour, asthenia (debility), depression, egoism, a refusal to participate, narcissistic inwardness, and in dreams, excessive indifference, boredom, coldness, a need for tranquility.[33]

Brown

Brown, colour of earth and autumn leaves, contains ideas of degradation and death.[33]

• In Christian symbolism, reddish-black, a mixture of fire, smoke, ash and soot is the symbol of infernal love and treachery.[32]

• As the colour of things material, brown corresponds to the sado-anal stage, with latent or open aggression, wickedness, obstinacy, avarice, egoism.

In dreams, it signifies a need for physical comfort and security.[33]

COLUMN

axis

The idea of the column representing the axis of the world derives from the tree or post, just as the tower, pillar and obelisk do.

The columns on the Jewish Tabernacle were made of wood, a corruptible material, and represented vindicated but not perfect believers. The Jews were guided across the Sinai desert by a pillar of fire (probably a solar column, a luminous pillar that occasionally appeared at sunset and shone intensely) that led them to the Promised Land. It symbolizes the torch which lights man and leads him towards the centre of his personality (self-realization).

COMB
magic arch

The comb (*kushi*) has an important role in Japanese myth. It acts as an intermediary between heaven and earth and is a sacred sign used when a human being enters into contact with the kami (gods). And so the comb belonging to Izanagi, the kami-creator of the world, is endowed with the supernatural power of metamorphosis. It protects him from the 'female horrors' who pursue him and the redoubtable dragon intent on devouring him. He can turn himself into a stand of bamboo. He can use one of the comb's teeth as a torch to look at his wife, whom he wants to lead back from the kingdom of the dead.

Putting a comb in a woman's hair makes her a daughter of the kami, which is explained in a tale which tells of the emperor Sujin who placed a farewell comb in his daughter's hair when he gave her the divine mirror in which Amaterasu-Omikami (the sun goddess) resided.

- Like the pillar, axis, and hub of a wheel, the comb has a central role. 'It holds together all the component parts of what symbolizes man's strength, nobility, and relationship with the gods: in short, what he considers the most precious and most specific elements of his personality.'

- Its teeth have a protective role. They guard the different components of an individual's personality that are held together by the whole comb.[77]

COW
mother

The cow (*go*, *gau*, *dhemu*, *usrah*) is a sacred animal in India, a symbol of food and generosity, likened to Aditi, the great mother, to the earth, and sometimes even to the universe.[50] A cow in calf is the female symbol of the earth's generative and nutritive powers. A cow and bull together make up the male and female procreative and nutritive symbols of divinity.[83]

• In the Vedas, cows are associated with dawn and the sun, and are 'imperishable'; they are mothers said to possess the triple nature of the supreme world. They are the hidden rays of Surya, the sun god, the sun's flock, and they symbolize (mental) light, enlightening thoughts, emanating from the super-conscious and coming from the sun, light and truth.[44]

Meh-urt, the Egyptian cow of heaven[124]

• In ancient Greece, a cow symbolized divinity, and 'was frequently shown licking a calf which was bunting her, or licking herself to symbolize the increase of her divine strength through the exercise of her nutritive power over herself.'[83]

• In ancient Egypt, in Memphis, the cow was a symbol of

passive creative power, incarnated in Venus.[83]

• The cow fulfilled a cosmic role: the cow of heaven, Meh-urt, gave birth to the sky, and incarnated the heavenly ocean (Methyer for the Greeks). The sky was upheld by the four feet of the great mother, Hathor, Egyptian goddess of the cosmos and cow-goddess, whose belly was the firmament. Every evening Horus the sun entered her mouth in the form of an eagle, and every morning was reborn.[124]

• In dreams, a cow is the incarnation of the maternal and vegetative side of life. For women, it counsels patience, kindness, humility and submission.[124]

CRAB
withdrawal

In Egypt the crab was used on medallions of ancient cities as a symbol of water's productive power because the crab has the ability to separate mutilated limbs from its body and generate new ones.[83]

• The eighteenth card of the tarot confuses it with a crayfish, and shows it eating rotting vegetation in a lake. Here it symbolizes renewal, the need to rid oneself of useless thoughts which clutter the mind and should be discarded in the same way that the crab does its shell once it has become too heavy.

• On certain English coats-of-arms, the crab is a symbol of inconstancy because of the way it continually advances and retreats.

CRANE
regeneration

If, nowadays, the crane is regarded as a symbol of stupidity and clumsiness, in heraldry it represents prudence and vigilance.

• As a bird sacred to Athena and Artemis in Greece, it was considered to have inspired Hermes' invention of letters; it was associated with poets and initiation. The dance of the cranes, performed around an altar adorned with horns, reproduced the circles which wound and unwound in the initiatory labyrinth.[107]

• In China, the crane (*he*) is often pictured with a pine tree and a rock, as the triple symbol of long life.

It is the symbol of wisdom, for wounding or useless words are blocked by its long sinuous neck, which allows time to prepare more constructive speech. Consequently the crane is the bird of the Taoist immortals. They believed that it lived for a thousand years and could breathe with its neck bent, a technique the Taoists imitated to make breathing more supple.

The immaculate whiteness of its feathers was naturally a symbol of purity, but its cinnamon-coloured head shows that it has within it the power of life and that inside it is purely yang and deprived of yin, the death principle. The crane is also able to mount the skies like the immortals flying towards the heavens.[64]

Along with the phoenix, heron, duck and wagtail, which evoke five types of relations between man, the crane features the relationship between father and son.

CROSS
the union of opposites

The cross is one of the oldest of cosmic symbols, and signifies the harmony between God and earth.[15] It is the basis of all the symbols of orientation, since it demonstrates the four cardinal points: on earth, in heaven, in space and time. A vertical line links the poles to the equator; a horizontal line the equinoxes and solstices. The point where they meet is the centre.

• The Latin cross is a Christian version of the tree of life, of the axis linking heaven and earth; it was once called God's seal, and it symbolizes the crucified Christ.

In the same way, making the sign of the cross is an admission of faith, it is the sign of the whole, of redemption. On the cross, Jesus saved the whole of mankind: by this, he sanctifies the whole of mankind to the very depths of their being.

• As a symbol of faith, a red cross on a white background served as a rallying signal for crusaders when they fought to capture the Holy Sepulchre in Jerusalem.

• The *tau* or T-shaped, headless cross was the emblem of creation and generation long before it was adopted by the Christian religion as a sign of salvation: it was erected at crossroads and in churchyards. According to Holy Scripture, an angel of the Apocalypse marked the foreheads of the prophets with a T-shaped cross (Saint Augustine's seal).

• When the cross is inscribed within a circle, it signifies the process of creation; once it symbolized the sun.[15]

• The cross makes the union of opposites a tangible

The Assyrian solar cross

Solar cross on the tympanum at Little Paxton Church, England[121]

reality. According to the alchemists, the crossing of an 'upright active' vertical line 'representing the activity of male energy that penetrates and fertilizes' with the 'recumbent, passive, female' horizontal line 'is essentially a sign of life, of a fertile joining together, of creative power.'[17] This is an echo of the *lingam–yoni* couple.

• The Egyptians' looped cross (a T-shaped cross surmounted by a loop) is also called the key of the Nile, and symbolizes the specific intention of giving life. This cross provided the origin for the layout of cathedrals.[3] See also *Ankh*.

In fact, the cross is one of the essential forms of the medieval church, 'a meeting place between time and space, heaven and earth. Man found the centre of his being in the crucified body of the cathedral. All wandering ceased at the centre of the cross, which was not an instrument of torture, but an enduring symbol.'[80] For on Calvary, this place of death, the cross, the tree of life had been planted. 'Its roots went down to hell where Christ had descended to save the souls of the damned; its branches rose into the heavens, from where he now reigns.'[30]

• The swastika which is also known in the West as the gamma cross because its branches are similar to the Greek

Solar cross engraved on a shell found in a tumulus in Mississippi

The solar wheel and the swastika on either side of the tree of life on an ancient Indian coin[121]

letter gamma, was a symbol of life. Like the cross within a circle, it has a rotating movement around a fixed centre, the sun: 'the activity of the principle in relation to the world.' A relationship has been established between this symbol and the double spiral, which is in turn linked to the T'ai-chi of the Far East.

In the Christian world, the inside part of the swastika represented Christ, and the four gammas pointing in different directions, the four evangelists.[35] Subsequently it became horribly degraded as a symbol through its association with Nazism, which turned it into an atrocious symbol of intolerance and death

CROSSROADS
choice

In every tradition, there are monuments, statues, altars and stones that have been built or placed at crossroads with the aim of conciliating the gods who haunt them, such as the formidable Hecate, who stands at crossroads holding a torch, followed by a horde of demons and ghosts.

• In China, crossroads are places to get rid of demons: in the ceremony of the devil hunt, the magician, under the influence of a supernatural power, imprisons the demons in an incense holder placed in a bowl, and covers the bowl with five differently coloured sheets of paper held solidly together. Once he has arrived at a crossroads, he sets fire to the bowl and the devils are burnt alive.[6]

• As a crossing of paths, a crossroads symbolizes a moment of solitude, of coming face to face with fate. It invites the traveller to stop and pause before taking a decision, and so it implies choice and action.

• The crossroads evokes the cross of the transept of a church, between the small and great mysteries, where the pilgrim must make a decisive choice in his quest for motivation. The centre of the crossroads corresponds to the centre of the cross.

• Since it is a point of transition from one place to another, a crossroads also symbolizes the journey from one world to another, from one state to another, from life to death. Different travellers meet there so it is a symbol of social life. But as no one lingers, it also symbolizes an invitation to continue on one's way.

In dreams a crossroads is a dangerous place, open to ambush, and prudence and vigilance are recommended.

CROWN/WREATH

full consciousness

The crown is similar to the circle and head in its symbolism and often signifies accomplishment and perfection.

Crown/Wreath

• Originally crowns and wreaths were made of plaited foliage or flowers and had a religious purpose. In Egypt only gods and pharaohs had a right to wear them. In Greece, every god had his or her own, loaded with symbolism: an oak wreath for Zeus, laurels for Apollo, myrtle for Aphrodite, vine for Dionysos, and in ceremonies, the effigy of the god, priests, worshippers and followers, and the victims offered for sacrifice were crowned with these wreaths. From this originated the custom of putting wreaths on graves.

• A crown signifies reward: Christians hope to receive in heaven the everlasting crown, shown on monuments as being held in the hand of God the Father; the bride's coronet was a sign of her virginity.

• The halo/nimbus is a crown of the Trinity, which, like the mandorla (the oval halo that surrounds images of saints in paintings) symbolizes immortal praise and union with God.

• In Tantric yoga the crown is known as the *sahasrara*, and is shown as a lotus flower with a thousand petals on top of the head; it is a symbol of the highest degree of spiritual development possible, and is totally androgynous, beyond time and space.[12]

• In the secular world, the crown has come to mean success (crowns are given to winners of games or contests); it is a symbol of dignity and sovereignty.

CYCLOPS
instinct for cruelty

These fabled giants with only one eye in the centre of their forehead devoured humans, but also forged the thunderbolts and lightning that enabled Zeus to conquer the throne of heaven.

They symbolize brutality, cruelty and blindness caused through the domination of instincts and passions. In Irish legend, they symbolize the dark side of creation comparable to the powers of hell.

DANCE

ecstasy, identification with the One

In ancient times the movement of the planets was thought to be like a dance. In fact, in Sophocles' *Ajax*, Pan is mentioned as creator and choreographer of the dances of the gods, 'the cause and effect of the regular movement of the universe, depicted in these dances which he has created.'

• The dance therefore played a role in the cosmos by establishing a relationship between heaven and earth; it symbolized universal harmony. The most complete illustration of the symbol is the Hindu god Shiva, the cosmic dancer whose movements awakened dormant energies that gave the world form.

Shiva is the incarnation and manifestation of eternal energy, of cosmic power that is both procreative and destructive; he dances to the music of time. He is the principle of creation through the beating of the drum that he holds in his right hand.

His role of creator is shown by his right foot resting on a dwarf's back, a symbol of the passage of souls from the divine world into matter; his role as divine guide is shown through his second left hand which points to his left foot raised in the position of the elephant, 'opening up a path through the jungle of the world.'

The god's creative energy is shown in the bracelets and rings (living snakes) on his arms and ankles, and in his Brahmanic sash (the sash worn over the left shoulder to the right hip by high castes, symbolizing the threshold).

His destructive role is illustrated in the tongue of flame which he holds in his first left hand, a symbol of the fire that will destroy the created world, while his second right hand gestures reassuringly.

His raised left foot (which points to his left hand) signifies the deliverance of the soul.

His powers of regeneration are shown in the skull (a symbol of death) that adorns his hair, shaped like a crescent moon (symbol of birth and growth), and in the effigy of the goddess of the Ganges placed above his head (the Ganges, descending from heaven, pours out the living waters of salvation that the god distributes to humanity, thus regenerating mankind physically and spiritually).

The balance, or harmony of opposites is represented by a man's earring which hangs from his right ear and a woman's which hangs from his left, dominating the thrust of his arms (creation) and the rhythmic beating of his right heel (destruction).

The calm centre, the passing beyond the joy and pain of this world, is shown in his impassive face.[66]

• Divine activities are symbolized in Hindu ritual dances that reproduce the battles of the Titans and relate to secret occult powers, through gestures of the hands (the famous *mudras*) and the spreading of the arms, each movement having a deep, very secret meaning.[38]

• Japanese traditional dances, which also have a link with cosmology (the *otome-mai* or dance of a young girl, the *gosechi-no-mai* or dance in five movements executed for the first time by a female angel who came down from heaven, the *shishi-mai*, a lion or dragon dance which chases away evils, the dance of red skirts . . .), retraced a whole episode of Japanese cosmology and were intended to pacify, console and delight the kami (gods).[77]

• In the Middle Ages, a similar idea lay behind the French dance of the twelve canons (symbolizing the signs of the zodiac) on Easter Day, around the maze at Auxerre cathedral, 'a manifestation of the movement of the heavenly spheres around the holy city.'[80] At this period, even popular dances were choreographed to mimic the movement of the planets, such as the round dance, the *carol*, the 'continuous chain formed by the dancers.'

• In ancient China, the dance was linked to the symbolism of numbers and had a role in the organization of the world: the chief dancer 'danced on one foot to fertilize the natural world because his dancing induced the sap to rise'.

Dancing conjures up images of ecstatic inebriation: during feasts offered to the ancestors people would dance without a break, like whirlwinds, as a prelude to ecstasy.

These occurrences were part of Taoist practice, where 'even holy men who had access to the most rarefied secrets could not stop slapping their thighs and leaping about like sparrows.'[8]

Prayer and appeal, sacred or priestly dance could be a cry of joy (like David's before the Ark), but above all else there was a search for freedom in ecstasy, an attempt to identify with the One God. The bacchic orgies or bacchanalia celebrating the cult of Dionysos (Bacchus) were linked with water and sap, the primordial source of all vegetation; they were also a hymn to life.

• The prayer-dance formed a part of agrarian and solar religions: in certain rituals it was like an endurance test, for example, the Sioux's 'dance-which-looks-at-the-sun', danced around the murmuring-tree/the axis of the world, which was a 'way of sending their wishes to the Great Spirit,'[13] or the Aztec dance around a pole, where the dancers personified the cardinal points, representing the religious cycle of fifty-two years in the ritual calendar.[36] The dancers stood in a circle, similar to the circumambulation of the whirling dervishes or the magic propitiatory dances of the Aborigines of Australia, South Africa or Papua.[39]

All these dances are a ritual repetition of the cycle of time and of the earth's movement around its axis.

• In dreams, a dancer can reveal that the dreamer's behaviour is too introvert and indicate the need to 'participate in the vertiginous, invisible cycle of life.' A dance partner is an 'aspect of the other sex within ourselves.'[24]

DAWN
birth

Sunrise is a symbol of birth or rebirth, and of awakening.

• In dreams, the coming of dawn indicates that an element of the unconscious has become accessible, and is ready to be used.

DEATH
rebirth

Death symbolizes the perishable, impermanent side of existence, but also revelation. Chronos is an allegorical representation of it. He is seen carrying a scythe, a tool used for harvesting, both a symbol of death and of 'the new hope the harvest brings.'[36]

• Death and annihilation have always been linked with a new beginning, with evolution. This explains the similarity between the symbolism of death and the mother, and the foetal position of skeletons in prehistoric tombs – awaiting rebirth, a new beginning of life.

• The death of the sun followed by its resurrection, as the

death and annual resurrection of wheat, and, by extension, agrarian divinities, have become symbols of the death and resurrection of man: Quetzalcoatl, the Mexican maize god, and the planet Venus which periodically disappears and reappears; and Osiris, the Egyptian sun god into whom the deceased was assimilated and by whom he was led into the sky, all became proof of the immortality of the human soul.[98]

• These images of disappearance and dissolution represent initiatic death, which consists of passing from one state of imperfection into a superior state. This is the death exacted from the Freemason, symbolized by the period he has to remain in the darkness of a tomb, or in a place of study and reflexion, the death of the old personality after work on the Self.

• Alchemy translates this transition into the appearance of the colour black, symbolized by Saturn's crow, itself a symbol of constructive energy, the 'basis of individual egoism', in the early stages of the Great Work: it is the death of the world and its frivolities.[17, 18]

• Initiatic death is the subject of the thirteenth arcana of the tarot, which shows a skeletal reaper holding a scythe with a red handle, symbol of the fire of passion which burns up vital reserves and causes their extinction, but which devours the dried-up forces, the straw which no longer draws up the sap. Death therefore revivifies.

This arcana, which is ruled by the number 13 (meaning renewal, a new beginning), reveals the need for a radical change in life, of a fundamental rethink: an aspect of one's personality must disappear in order to leave room for new feelings or concepts.

Divinatory meaning: disillusion, clear judgement, detachment, asceticism. Fatality, necessary ending, radical transformation. Heritage. Sadness, mourning, corruption.[17]

• Dreams of death are generally about the dreamer's persona: it could concern the disappearance of attitudes and outworn concepts, ideas and feelings.

The death of a known person, according to Jung, indicates mystical detachment from him or her, the end of a relationship or love, dramatized in this psychic event.

DECANATE
a portion of eternity

Decanates are actually the thirty-six divisions of the zodiac (each being 10 degrees), which in ancient Egypt represented 'the state of heaven at a particular moment in the horoscope of eternity, that is to say, on one's way towards the eternal residence.' They were represented by genies, each of whom reigned for ten days of the year.

Decanates played an important part in establishing the horoscope.

Here are the symbols of the decanates according to G. Muchery:

Aries

• *1st decanate* Mars is its lord (in a desert landscape, a leaping ram in front of a sturdy castle): symbolizes pride, impetuosity, imprudence, or lack of reflection, jealousy and inconstancy in love, excessive appetites and desires.[41]

• *2nd decanate* Sun (Andromeda on her rock at the mercy of a sea monster, with a winged horse flying to her rescue): symbolizes will and courage.

• *3rd decanate* Venus (an amorphous but very agile and dangerous (because unpredictable) sea mammal): symbolizes chance, insecurity, imprudence, egoism and a taste for pleasure.

Taurus

• *1st decanate* Mercury is its lord (a bull, with flicking tail and damp muzzle, arrested in mid-leap by a heifer): symbolizes concentration, timidity and fear, materialism and patience.

• *2nd decanate* Moon (the hideous mask of one of the three gorgons, Medusa, whose hair consists of live snakes): symbolizes jealousy and excess; reveals bad luck and envy.

• *3rd decanate* Saturn (the seven sons of Atlas, in despair over their father's death, flying towards the star-encrusted heavens): symbolizes a brimming imagination, instability; favours travel.

Gemini

• *1st decanate* Jupiter is its lord (two joined cherubim, smiling, chatting, holding the arrow of sardonic irony, the lyre of the arts and the wand of sacred knowledge): symbolizes a penetrating ironic, trenchant mind, good taste, *savoir-faire*.

• *2nd decanate* Mars (Amathea, Jupiter's nurse, holding a horn of plenty full of delicious fruit in her hand): symbolizes anxiety, physical or moral impotence preventing one from profiting from a good opportunity, fear of failure, fear of anything.

• *3rd decanate* Sun (Sirus and Orion: a dog lying at the feet of a magnificent hunter): symbolizes physical dexterity, intellectual cleverness that creates winners, a lively optimism, diplomacy, good sense and ability to bluff, a desire to please.

Decanate

Cancer

• *1st decanate* Venus is its lord (a woman with an oval face, abundant hair, and pale grey eyes, holding a gently waving veil on which there is the sign of a crayfish): symbolizes infidelity, love of change, slowness, the absence of moral and physical courage, capriciousness and day-dreaming; brings mystery into the way life is led.

• *2nd decanate* Mercury (a ship with all its sails hoisted, clouds scudding before a storm, choppy waves, and, on a rock, a young man who is fainting, thunderstruck): symbolizes false security, discord, the threat of an incident that will disturb one's peace of mind or health.

• *3rd decanate* Moon (a figure descending from the clouds, clutching a torch, dissipating the darkness of night): symbolizes friendship, reliance, the possibility of conquering difficulties with a minimum of risks.

Leo

• *1st decanate* Saturn (the fabled lion which Heracles overcame in the valley of Nemea, the sun shining on the horizon): symbolizes power, control, violent ambition, impatience, love of every kind of pleasure.

• *2nd decanate* Jupiter (the great heavenly dog, on the alert, inquisitive, salacious, tenacious and violent): symbolizes strength and kindness under a boorish exterior, faithfulness, long-held grudges, unhealthy curiosity, gossip.

• *3rd decanate* Mars (the slimy, constantly reborn, many-headed Hydra in a foul sewer): symbolizes innumerable difficulties and upsets; advises making a 'clean sweep' by attacking as soon as an obstacle presents itself.

Virgo

• *1st decanate* Sun (a sad, solitary young woman holding an olive branch in one hand and in the other a hexagon, the magic symbol of balance): symbolizes uprightness, balance, fear of self-deception, and shows prejudice against others; there is a factor of elevation and perfection.

• *2nd decanate* Venus (a ship in a storm, with ripped hold, broken masts, yet surviving and reaching port): symbolizes difficult enterprises, contretemps, disillusionment and wounded vanity which will heal with time, and the necessity of never abandoning the fight.

• *3rd decanate* Mercury (the face of a beautiful woman, framed by blond hair sprinkled with stars): favours love affairs, pure chance; brings natural physical and intellectual gifts, but engenders bad feelings with children and in-laws.

Libra

• *1st decanate* Moon (a pair of scales held in a strong hand, representing justice, equity and law): symbolizes balance, a sense of correctness, spiritual equality, optimism, good humour, indulgence without cowardliness.

• *2nd decanate* Saturn (an old sage with tousled hair and an active mind, pouring over an ancient manuscript, hoping to extract its essence): symbolizes knowledge which frees the spirit from matter; a factor of intelligence, comprehension of everything, of success in his chosen field.

• *3rd decanate* Jupiter (a sturdy tree bearing golden fruit, symbol of man's well-regulated work, a ripe ear of wheat heavy with golden grain): symbolizes the abundance of good things that hard work and *savoir-faire* can bring, the pleasures of life and the satisfaction of duty well done; a factor of concern about lineage.

Decanate

Scorpio

• *1st decanate* Mars (a scorpion near brackish eater prudently and slyly advancing in search of a victim): symbolizes slyness, dissimulation, a tendency to distrust, to mock, to presume; obstinacy in often fatally erroneous ways; facilitates satisfaction of appetites.

• *2nd decanate* Sun (a coiled snake wrapped round a ringed planet) symbolizes perfection in work, perseverance; factors of health, vitality, courage, prudence and eloquence, dissimulation, astuteness, provoking alternatives of rising and falling.

• *3rd decanate* Venus (a wolf howling at death under a full moon): symbolizes physical strength, vitality, cowardice and amorality.

Sagittarius

• *1st decanate* Mercury (a centaur, half-man, half-horse, armed with bow and arrow): symbolizes spiritual and social elevation, self-control, optimism, sensuality; sometimes incites to excess.

• *2nd decanate* Moon (a colossus opening a lion's jaws); symbolizes power, domination, courage, willpower in the service of desire; brings consideration and power, but causes enemies and powerful jealousies.

• *3rd decanate* Saturn (a winged dragon, with fiery tongue, and steely claws): symbolizes vigilance, clairvoyance, indicating that one should not allow oneself to be lulled into a false sense of security.

Capricorn

• *1st decanate* Jupiter (a fabulous animal with a billy goat's head and a body that is half-goat, half-fish) symbolizes lewdness, sadness, envy; incites pessimism, bitterness or idealism; factors of discord, disturbance, long life and continuity.

• *2nd decanate* Mars (a winged bird of prey watching from the top of an inaccessible crag, observing its unsuspecting prey): symbolizes distrust, perspicacity, the gift of observation, jealousy, solitude, pessimism, sadness.

• *3rd decanate* Sun (a solitary eagle hovering in the inaccessible heights suddenly swooping down on someone): symbolizes pride, awareness of one's own strength, distrust of lower regions, faithfulness, brutal and capricious fate; factors of health and long life.

Aquarius

• *1st decanate* Venus (a sea shell pouring out limpid, life-giving water): symbolizes reason, an accurate and elevated view of things; factors of kindness, understanding, indulgence, generosity; exposed to ingratitude and deceit; incites, with age, solitude, bitterness and distrust.

• *2nd decanate* Mercury (an aquatic mammal sliding graciously and silently through the water): symbolizes duplicity, hypocrisy, blackmail, scandalmongering, vested interests; tendencies to allow oneself to be duped by appearances.

• *3rd decanate* Moon (Pegasus, winged racehorse, snorting and bucking, ready to fly to the home of the immortals): symbolizes the creative imagination, grants protection; saves one from a brutal fall.

Pisces

• *1st decanate* Saturn (two fleeing fish which seem to be confiding in one another on a sombre glaucous field of water): symbolizes deceit, scandalmongering, bad faith; a predisposition to unconscious cruelty, egoism, nonchalance.

• *2nd decanate* Jupiter (a majestic swan, with a deceptive appearance, advances nonchalantly on the object of its amorous, short-lived desire): symbolizes unstable feelings, duplicity, adultery, deceitful venal love, love of pleasure; factors of vitality and long life.

• *3rd decanate* Mars (a river slowly rising from its bed, upturning everything in its path): symbolizes good or bad luck, abuse of every kind, followed by long periods of abstinence and wisdom; a predisposition to continuing effort, and resignation in suffering. Time works in the native's favour.[41]

DEGREES
image symbols

Each of the 360 degrees of the zodiac has a special attribute and significance. There are male and female degrees, light and dark, informal, ceremonial, empty, veiled, etc., that the symbolic key images represent.

DEVIL, DEMON
materiality, uncontrolled energy

Theologians interpret devils as fallen angels, and name Satan (the enemy, the evil one) or Lucifer (the light-bearer, the shining one) as their chief. He is also known as Azazel or Beelzebub. His names allude to the brilliance he enjoyed before his downfall.

• The devil is depicted as hairy, with horns, a long tail, and cloven hooves, and symbolizes the spirit of wrongdoing and lying, and the unconscious forces that influence the conscious and cause the individual to regress into moral and physical evil, leading to the breakdown of his personality. Satan is the enemy of spirituality, of spiritual elevation; he is symbolized in the black half of Amphisbaena (see *Snake*), a symbol of spiritual death.

• In Jewish tradition, demons were divided into ten hierarchies, revealing the ten shadowy *sephiroth*, each personifying a passion or a vice. Their supreme leader was Samael, the angel of poison and death, Shatan of the Scriptures who, according to the *Zohar* (see *Cabbalah*), seduced the first woman.

His wife Lilith was the mistress of evil and debauchery, a nocturnal power in the Cabbalah, which regards these demons as blind forces of creation, beings inferior to man.[19]

• In ancient theology, these familiar demons were divine emanations who lived in blood which contains the principle of vital heat; 'as a consequence Moses forbade the consumption of animal blood.'[83]

• Astrology interprets the devil as the harmful influence of the planets: 'gods, demons, saints and devils are different faces of the same planetary forces, and the devil is the shadow or the dark side of God . . . inseparable from God as the evil side of a planet is inseparable from its good side.'

• Cabbalists say that Satan's real name is Jehovah spelt backwards.[4]

• According to Jung, demons are neuroses and complexes, 'that is to say, hidden affective themes, liable to provoke permanent disturbances in our psychic life.'[42] They are what makes us 'mistake the shadow for the substance: they symbolize the inevitable imperfections of the kingdom of shadows.'[66]

• In the fifteenth arcana of the tarot, the Devil represents man's primary instincts and personifies deep-rooted egoism. 'He is the cause of strife, the enemy of unity, he sets one man against another . . . The devil possesses us when we come into the world . . . but we are destined gradually to free ourselves from the tyranny of our innate instincts': pride, laziness, anger, greed, envy, meanness and lust.

Happily the devil (our animal body, our elementary instincts) 'is not so black as he is painted: he is our inescapable associate in life.' But if we act upon these base instincts, we lose our 'beneficent magic power . . . The divine spark within us must conquer gross instinct,'[77] and tame the beast in order to maintain the harmony between body–matter–instincts and spirit.

Divinatory meaning: Over-excitement, lack of balance, madness, desire, excesses of every kind. This links up with the Confucian belief that the devil is the epitome of evil, self-centredness, obstinacy, the need to monopolize, the desire to set one man against another, who, unsatisfied, turns to violence.[8]

DIAMOND
indomitable strength

The generic meaning of a diamond is uncreated light or universal matter, or, in Hebrew terminology, *yesod*.

• It is the talisman of the Alexandrian Hermetic philosophers.[114]

• Its unrivalled hardness makes this stone, along with its

'particularly spectacular optical effects'[43] a symbol of solidity, firmness and imperishability.

• In the Middle Ages, the diamond was thought to contain a dangerous unconquerable power.

• In Christianity it is God the Father's raiment of light, a symbol of divine wisdom; in Tantric Buddhism, it is *vajra*, the magic sword, a symbol of unchangeableness, of invincible spiritual power.

• Its purity symbolized perfection and achievement; in popular tradition, it was an emblem of purity, constancy and fame, the stone of reconciliation which sustained love between husband and wife.

• Ancient philosophers attributed it with magical and prophylactic properties: it warded off fear, rewarded chastity, subjugated ghosts and nocturnal terrors. As a cut stone it was used to make splendid artefacts, 'to honour the sacred.'[80]

DISK
the sun

Linked to the symbolism of the circle, the disk and its derivatives (the rosace, halo, shield, ball and tonsure) are sun emblems which, with the stick and eye, are related to the four aspects of solar divinity (simultaneously *one* and *three* different entities). It symbolizes a judgemental god or a boundary-spirit endowed with the power to separate light from shadow, good from evil.[3]

Egyptian sun-disk[121]

DISTAFF
flow of time

The distaff is a symbol of time, of the inexorable flow of days. It is an attribute of the Fates, the spinners who spin the web of man's life and cut the thread.

• The distaff is also a phallic symbol, like the spindle, belonging in tales and legends to bad fairies, dangerous characters: a prick from a spindle plunges Sleeping Beauty into a hundred-year sleep.

DOG
guardian of the threshold

In most mythologies, the dog is associated with earth, water and the moon, and therefore with vegetative, female, divinatory and sexual functions of the unconscious.

• In the Bible a dog is a symbol of cowardice and servility.

• For Muslims, it is a repellent animal. It is the devil's companion (Mephistopheles' yellow dog), used in certain black magic rituals and thought of as an enemy of god.

• As a guardian of the flock, a pontiff's emblem, it is also a symbol of obedience, vigilance and fidelity.

• In ancient Mexico and Egypt, it fulfilled the role of psychopomp (conducting souls to the place of the dead: dog-faced baboon spirits, servants of Thoth, masters of wisdom, were 'seated at the prow of Rê's barque announcing the lord of the world's orders.'[10]

• In myths, the dog symbolizes dangerous, primitive instincts, the unconscious animus acting without reserve: the ferocious dogs of Artemis, the howling pack of the redoubtable, evil Hecate, messenger of demons, and symbol of the authoritarian or possessive mother.

• The dog also symbolizes motherliness (certain vanished tribes used to let their dead be devoured by dogs, whose belly symbolized the maternal womb where the dead would await their resurrection, and maternity that both nurtures and devours.[25]

As Cerberus, guardian of the entrance to the underworld, the dog symbolizes 'the defensive potential of the unconscious ego.'[114]

• The Dog (*gou*), the eleventh sign in the Chinese zodiac, confers honesty, loyalty and a sense of justice.

The Year of the Dog brings stability and harmony to a household, but is marked by important confrontations on the world stage.[118]

• On a psychological level, the dog is an archetype of individuation and represents the first step in psychic evolution: Cerberus, the dog with three heads and poisonous teeth guards the door to the underworld, a symbol of the threshold separating the conscious from the unconscious, the first step in evolution.

In dreams, the dog becomes an animal-brother, a symbol of reconciled friendship. But if it appears abandoned or hurt, it means that our instinctive drives have been neglected or maltreated.[24]

DONKEY

poverty, patience, resignation

The donkey plays a beneficial role in numerous religious texts found in Asia, the Near East and the West, where it is associated with holy men: for example, the white ass of the immortals in China, the female donkey bearing Christ into Jerusalem.

• In Egypt, it is the incarnation of Seth, god of evil, but also god of vital power.

• In the Nativity story, the donkey in the stable illustrates the humble, deprived conditions in which Christ was born.

• In fairy tales, it is renowned for its patience, calmness and sobriety.

• Bestiaries in the Middle Ages linked it to the passage of time and knowledge, for the 'wild ass (onager) on the twenty-fifth day of March brays twelve times in the night and the same number of times during the day . . . for wild asses can indicate the time of day by braying.' Apuleus' humble golden ass was able to transmute back into human form, after acquiring the knowledge transmitted through a crown of roses offered by a priest of Isis.

• Nietzshe made the donkey into a symbol of wisdom when he compared it with kings who no longer valued outward appearance.

• However, by night, the donkey is associated with infidelity: formerly, women who were guilty of adultery were paraded on an ass.

• In numerous sacred Hebrew writings, a red donkey symbolizes the devil, evil and harmful fire. In Egypt, a red donkey is one of the greatest dangers encountered by the dead on their final journey. In India, it is ridden by gods of death: Nairrita, guardian of the land of the dead, and Kalaratri, Devi's negative side. The *asura* (demon) Dhenuka is shown as a donkey.

• In the Greek myth of Midas, a donkey symbolizes a lack of reflection and stupidity in someone who places too much emphasis on material pleasures and wordly riches,

Midas was given ass's ears (symbols of stupidity) by Apollo, for having preferred Marsyas' flute to the great god's lyre.

In shame, Midas hid his ears under a Phrygian cap (a symbol of debauchery, since the Prygians were renowned for their self-indulgence) until the day when his barber, who could no longer contain his secret made a hole in the ground and cried into it: 'King Midas has ass's ears.' On that very spot, reeds grew (revelation), and as they rustled they repeated his secret.

The donkey here symbolizes the importance of instinctive life and sexual pleasure at the expense of spirituality. This is the conflict it reveals when it appears in dreams.

DOOR

transition, metamorphosis

A door is an important element of a house, a symbol of passage from one place to another, one state to another, from light to darkness.

• Entrances to holy places (temples, cathedrals) are no invitation to participate in the mysteries contained inside. The act of passing over the threshold means that the faithful must set aside their personality and materialism, as they are forced to confront the inner silence and meditation that it symbolizes.

This is why at temple entrances giant or frightening animals (dragons, lions, winged bulls, etc.) keep vigilant guard. Even Japanese temples, which are preceded by several *torii* (gateways), often monumental in size, have their guardian gods (*zui-jin*) put there to symbolize this passage from the profane to the sacred and to stop any malevolent influences.

The door of an Egyptian temple was seen as giving access to the 'Amenta, where the soul was united with the immortal spirit and where, from then on, it remained.'[108]

• The door has a role in initiation rites. When you cross the threshold, you abandon old, emotional ideas, concepts and plans which are no longer appropriate; the familiar horizon is enlarged.

This process is symbolized in the Sumerian goddess Inanna's descent into the underworld, passing through seven doors to arrive before the seven judges of the lower world;[66] the twelve doors passed through by the solar barque in the beyond (twelve stages of initiation); and the three doorways preceding the Masonic lodge (simultaneously a symbol of the universe and of the superior world that the Mason enters on leaving the physical world), which represent the qualities acquired successively through the stages crossed – these are discrimination, absence of desires, self-control.[108]

• As an access to a refuge or the warmth of a hearth, a door also symbolizes communication, contact with others and with the outside world. An open door attracts because it signifies welcome, invites discovery, but a door can also signify imprisonment, isolation. A closed door signifies rejection, exclusion, secrecy, but also protection against dangers and the unknown.

DRAGON

vital energy, Diana complex

The dragon is a symbol of the spirit of evil in Christian legend and stories of chivalry (and defeated by St Michael, St George, St Martha in order to illustrate the battle between good and evil). It is depicted as a winged saurian (lizard), of terrifying aspect, and combines air, fire and earth.

• For alchemists, the dragon's six positions symbolize the stages in the Great Work: *hidden*, putrefaction; *in the fields*, fermentation; *visible*, coagulation; *leaping*, the solution; and *gliding*, sublimation.

• In China, the dragon (*Long*), which symbolized the emperor, is the active principle, with the six sides of the *Khien* hexagram featuring its stages of manifestation, as opposed to the tiger which rules the west and death.

Cosmology makes a distinction between heavenly dragons, symbols of celestial regenerative forces; spirit-dragons who make rain; earth-dragons who rule the waves and springs; and dragon guardians of treasure. They are tended by four kings who rule the four seas surrounding the earth.

'Upper-class ceremonial dress is distinguished by the number of claws the dragons display on garments; the emperor's robe would have dragons with five claws, princes had the right to four; other functionaries only had three.'[7]

The dragon yang (masculine force) and the phoenix yin (female nature) symbolize the couple associated with the number 9, symbol of virile power squared (3×3).[7]

A fight between dragons represents the perpetual motion of the universe, the confrontation of apparently antagonistic forces which keep vital movement alive (in Nature as in man), the resolution of opposites (cf. the snakes in the caduceus).

People born under this fifth animal sign of the zodiac, associated with the east, spring rain, and bluish-green, are magnanimous, active, eccentric, self-centred, capricious and demanding.

The dragon brings luck and happiness. The Year of the Dragon favours grandiose projects, financial transactions, marriage, procreation, but is equally subject to setbacks.[118]

• As an archaic image of the most primitive of energies,

the dragon represents the unconscious 'as long as we have no bridge giving access to it'; it is in the unconscious that passions and complexes and hidden desires lead a primitive life. If we can 'explain ourselves to the full, using our mental powers' and fight the dragon, we can recoup part of our unconscious energies and use them to control our life.

'The fight with the dragon is a symbol of becoming truly adult. Then one can capture the treasure the dragon guards in almost every mythology: we can deliver our soul; symbolized by the virgin whom the dragon holds captive.'[24]

See also *Snake*, especially Amphisbaeno.

DREAM
key to personality

Dreams are produced by the unconscious. During sleep, reason and logic no longer exercise control over the conscious part of the mind, and give way to a substratum of thoughts, ideas, feelings and desires which during our waking hours have been buried in the unconscious. Now they rise freely.

This level of the mind obeys only its own logic and expresses itself in the incoherent language of the unconscious that the awakened brain can barely understand. It is a language made up of images, words, situations, gestures selected from ordinary everyday events. But the unconscious chooses from these those which are best suited to the actual state of mind or situation. The material of a dream, although expressed in an apparently irrational manner and without any logical progression, does in fact have a main theme: *archetypes* (ideas that have a universal cultural symbolism and that each of us carries within ourselves, inherited from successive generations – hero figures, giant, saint, witch, mother, father, God . . .) and *symbols* connected with our personal life – these are the true keys to our dreams and enable us to interpret them.

• Dreams help us towards self-knowledge. Jung wrote that dreams have both compensatory and complementary uses as far as the conscious is concerned: they transmit elements that the conscious lacks but needs, in order to understand a situation, or a state of the soul or mind. Dreams attempt to reestablish a psychic balance by accentuating the exaggerations or lacunae that are present in an individual's behaviour.

• A dream is a revelation of the dreamer's psychic state.

All the elements of a dream, however ludicrous or random they appear, relate uniquely to the dreamer himself, and represent aspects of his personality. They are the personification of his psychic functions, the expression of his desires, acknowledged or unacknowledged feelings, tendencies of the anima (the feminine side of a man) or that animus (the masculine side of a woman).

• To understand a dream, you must, first of all, remember it, so write it down as soon as you wake up; then think about it; analyse the meaning of the symbols as they apply to your personal situation in this particular period of your life, and, above all, try to be open and objective.

To decode dream material, you must separate out the general *atmosphere* of the dream, and its *structure*, which, depending on the whole, give the details a particular nuance. These interpret the symbols.

An enlightened, lucid interpretation of dreams is a rewarding activity, mentally, intellectually and morally, since it is the point of departure for a psychic appraisal which will lead to greater self-knowledge, and a more rational, tolerant attitude towards others.

• The first contact with the unconscious is generally painful, for it brings aspects of ourselves to light that we would rather not know, and give us no reason to be pleased with ourselves: this is why they have been buried in the depths of the unconscious where they provoke inappropriate attitudes, which in turn can cause suffering, problems in relationships and often neuroses. Once detected, these negative aspects can be demythified; bad behaviour can be explained and rectified. A more rational attitude will result.

Theories and Techniques of Interpretation

– Sigmund Freud (1870–1937). His theory is largely based on feelings of inferiority and how we compensate for them in daily life. He thought that dreams could ring into the open aggressive impulses and thus pave the way for successful social adaptation.

– Carl Gustave Jung (1875–1961). He established three levels of personality: the conscious, the personal unconscious and the collective unconscious which is of considerable importance in the interpretation of dreams. This collective unconscious is made up of ideas, basic inherited concepts common to all peoples throughout the world, expressed through themes that are eternal. They are the archetypes.[25, 18, 119]

Dreams in Ancient, Primitive Cultures

– The Sumerians thought that dreams were messages from the sun god Shamash (the soothsayer would translate the image, which was then deciphered by a priest). They interpreted dreams as prophecies of the future.

– The ancient Egyptians thought that night-time sleep was the dead time of creation, a time for return to primal chaos which put man in contact with all the beings and visions haunting the world of the uncreated, which were, however, a kind of premonition of the future.

Interpreters of dreams distinguished between the historic dream, the warrior's dream, in which a god appeared to encourage a Pharaoh who was anxious about a forthcoming battle, and the oracular dream which would offer a solution to a problem.

The techniques of interpretation were: the association of ideas, the opposite meaning to that expressed in the dream.

– In Israel dreams were by ancient tradition God's chosen method of manifesting his will. Ancient texts tell of dream-messages directly intelligible to the dreamer without the aid of an interpreter.

– In Islam divination by dreams was a true science and is mentioned in a number of sources. It coincided with religious beliefs, for Mohammed had used dreams to explain his doctrine. The Arabs attempted to understand symbols, particularly the archetypes.

– The Persians traditionally distinguished three types of dreams: dreams for interpretation or ordinary dreams conceived by the soul (*Nafs*), physiological dreams produced by the mind (*Ruh*), and truthful dreams which were produced when the nature of the dreamer is pacified. Dawn dreams had a greater value than night-time ones. Interpretation was based on commonsense or analogy.

– Brahmanism recognizes four states of mind or stages of consciousness: the state of being awake; the state of dreaming, an unstable state where the soul is moving around exploring domains inaccessible when one is awake; profound, dreamless sleep, a state of renewal when man returns to his centre, an early attempt at making himself into a united whole; and finally, there is the plunge into the

Absolute, the identification with Brahma, with the sleepless, wakeless, deathless, painless OM.[120]

The temporary vision of a dream is a reflection of unique reality which then becomes reabsorbed into the unique One.

In the Atharva Veda there are dreams that are seen as signs and a classification of dreams which identifies temperament:

– the *bilious* (ruled by fire, the moon and yellow) sees the forests in flames, bloody corpses, a red moon, flashes of lightning.

– the *phlegmatic* (ruled by water and white) sees forests of lotus, limpid rivers, enormous drifts of snow, gazelles, wild pigs, perfumed women, curdled milk.

– the *aerian* (under the air sign) sees mountains, windswept landscapes, darkened planets.
Dreams of the first awakening bear their fruit within the year; those of the second awakening in eight months; those of the third are already half-realized.[100]

– For the ancient Chinese a dream was an adventure lived by the soul, which left man's body while he slept and which also saw into the future. Dreams were sent by the gods, ancestors or ghosts and were a means of communicating with supernatural powers and the living. The Chinese were also interested in seeking out the cause of dreams, whether of a physical or pathological nature (suggested by an excess of yin or yang) or of a psychological nature.

The Taoists believed there were eight manifestations of the state of wakening or bodily connections (circumstances, actions, the act of receiving, mourning, grief, joy, birth and death) and six aspects of the dream (ordinary dreams which appear by themselves, dreams of fear provoked by a fright, thinking dreams that concern a subject that has been discussed or imagined the night before, dreams of waking, of joy, of fear).[120]

– In Japan there are treatises on the interpretation of dreams, borrowed from China, which make up the *ommyodo* or the way of yin and yang. Dreams were interpreted forwards or backwards (where they told the opposite). Dreams with bad predictions could be averted, however, by 'having a mythical beast eat them.' This was the *baku* whose picture was placed on the dreamer's pillow.[120]

DUCK
happiness for two

In China the mandarin duck (*yuan-yang*) is the traditional symbol of wedded bliss (they always swim in pairs).[75]

In everyday language mandarin ducks covered in dew symbolize an unmarried couple; the union of mandarin ducks is one of the thirty positions in lovemaking.[7]

DUST, ASHES
mourning

Like pollen or sperm, dust symbolizes the creative force.[1] Jews, however, associated it with death (like ashes) and covered their heads with dust as a sign of mourning.

• In popular language, it is associated with humility: 'to prostrate oneself in the dust, to kiss the dust of someone's feet.' It is also associated with the past: 'to shake the dust from one's feet' means a total break with the past.

• In China dust (*zhen*), just like smoke, signifies something ephemeral. 'A handful of dust' (*zen bing*) for Buddhists means a penis.

• A feather duster is the symbol of one of the eight immortals.[7]

DWARF
primitive urges

In legends and in Teutonic folklore, dwarves and gnomes were associated with grottoes and caverns, and were companions of fairies, working to extract metals from the depths of the earth; and so their symbolism is linked to metal's. They personify the primitive impulses stirring in the depths of our unconscious, and they often depict baser psychic functions that have been neglected or remain undeveloped.

These submerged forces, once brought out into the open, are a treasure the individual can share in.

• These undersized characters also symbolize pre-adolescence and the discovery of sexuality. And so Snow White's seven dwarves 'bring to mind phallic associations, and symbolize an immature and pre-individualistic form of existence that Snow White must transcend.' They depict pre-pubescence, the period in which sexuality in any form is relatively latent.[67]

• In contrast, the Nibelungen (literally sons of the mist) of the Norse sagas are immensely wealthy, but greedy and arrogant, and symbolize the need to dominate, megalomania and uncontrolled ambition.

EAGLE

light, conquest, power instinct, consciousness

Because its eyesight is so acute, the eagle is likened to an all-seeing eye, symbol of a watchful god, and Providence. In every civilization, the eagle is primarily a sun bird.

It is seen in many cultures as the firebird, a messenger between sun and earth, between gods and humankind, the companion or incarnation of all the greatest deities (Vishnu, Zeus–Jupiter whose thunderbolt he carries between his claws . . .) or of all the greatest heroes (Horus, the sun-god of the Egyptians with an eagle-head, St John the Baptist who dared look directly at heaven).

• Its wings bearing the sun-disk symbolize resurrection for the Chaldaeans, Syrians, Egyptians and the Indians of Yucatan.

• In Syria and Rome the eagle ascending became a psychopomp (a conductor of souls into the place of the dead), a messenger of resurrection, illustrating the descent of a part of divine consciousness into the individual and its return to God. This concept is illustrated by an eagle escaping from the top of the pyramidal bonfire where an effigy of Caesar is to be burnt, 'in order to take the soul of the newly deified direct to the home of the gods.' This would explain figures of eagles wearing crowns on monuments, as a promise of eternal life after the trials of earthly existence. This psychopomp-eagle symbolizes Christ raising souls and leading them into heaven.[3]

• The eagle descending is the light-bearer on earth (or, etymologically, Lucifer).

The eagle, the supreme sun bird in every civilization. Left, a head-dress; centre, a carved horn spoon; right, a rattle (all North American Indian)[142]

• The eagle plays an important role in Japanese, Asiatic and Amerindian mythology: the Zuni Indians place it beside the sun at its zenith, the fifth cardinal point, on the axis of the world. Its spreadeagled wings evoke fragmented streaks of lightning and the arms of the cross.

• In the *Bhagavad Gita*, the eagle is the divine word.

• In Western tradition it has been invested with the power of rejuvenation: the eagle basks in the sun until its plumage sparkles, then plunges into pure water and becomes young again, in an image of initiation and alchemy that implies passage through fire and water.

• In the specialized science of alchemy it represented

dematerialization, the flight of the soul, a defiance of gravity by an eagle devouring a lion.

• Because of its large size and power, powerful nations chose it as an emblem (the Roman, French, Austrian and German empires . . .)

• In dreams, it symbolizes elevated thoughts, but also, depending on its context, the will to power, all-consuming pride which can tear man away from his daily occupations and destroy what is of real value in his character.

EAR

receptivity, awakening

In Africa the ear symbolizes animality, while in China long ears symbolize wisdom and immortality and are the attributes of certain heroes and famous characters. But in Greek mythology, King Midas's ears were a symbol of stupidity and pride – 'excessive stupidity which led him to imagine that he could be better than others.'[36]

• The Gauls had a god of sleep with a deer's ear, symbolizing 'receptivity to the prayers of mortals . . . equal to the finest hearing of wild animals in light sleep.'[95]

• In Egypt the ear has associations with the future: a bull's ears represent hearing and a future thing or event.

• Ear piercing was once practised to mark an engagement – a slave's engagement – or a wish: some dervishes pierced one ear and wore an earring so he could be identified as such. Sailor's earrings were a sign of their engagement to the sea.

• As a passive organ of received communication, the ear indicates, through its size and shape, its owner's general attitude towards other people and his or her level of receptivity.

– small ears express shyness, and low self-esteem in relation to the environment;

– large ears reflect an extrovert attitude, and easy adaptation to new situations;

– ears that stick out belong to independent people who dislike tyranny and form their own opinion about things;

– flattened ears indicate submission, and a dependence on the environment.

• In dreams, the ear is a female symbol and ear-piercing is a symbol of defloration.[25]

EARTH
universal mother

Earth was worshipped as the mythical great mother because it bore fruit, was receptive and the origin of all life. Earth became the symbol of motherhood, and with the sky formed the primeval couple.

• Earth was a symbol of fertility and regeneration: for example, contact with telluric (earth or soil) forces gave one the power to recreate, give birth anew (from this came the custom of placing the corpse in the form of a foetus before burial, so that the earth mother could place it back on Earth a second time); the Mayas' human sacrifice at times of drought; and symbolic partial or total burial which has a similar religious value to baptismal immersion. The desire to return to the land of one's birth experienced by each of us sooner or later corresponds to a need for spiritual regeneration, to return to our roots.

• Earth is associated with fertility: farm work is identified with the act of procreation. Women have been likened to a furrow made by a plough, that is, the phallus. (In Old

English, *fuck* literally meant to plough a furrow.) Fallow land is compared to a barren woman in the *Videvdat*.[21]

According to Orphic tradition, earth is fertilized by the descending creator spirit manifested in ether and water.

• Earth, a female, passive element is contrasted with the sky, an active masculine element.

• In China, earth (*tu* or *di*), yin, is one of the five elements or forces of change, and corresponds to the centre, yellow, the number 2, sweet flavour, white millet, ox, and the naked animal (of which man is the prime example).

Sky and earth symbolize the entire world. Astronomers used the term branch of earth (*di-zhi*) to describe a collection of signs in series of twelve, arranged in a circle, which differs from the trunks of heaven (*tian-gan*), a cycle of signs in series of two.[7]

• The Chinese thought that the earth was square, and it is symbolized in the *Khwan* hexagram (complementary of *Khien*, sky), principle of passivity, receptivity, gentleness, the gift of self, female qualities of conception, energy, development, concord and diplomacy.[63]

• Earth is matrix, athanor (the philosopher's furnace), philosopher's egg, and, for Freemasons, the first element, the underground place of germination symbolized in the office of reflection, where, in French Freemasonry, the candidate is immured at the time of initiation.[109] It is there that in total isolation he will find himself in the presence of the heart of his individuality.

For the Hermetic philosophers, there was 'the ordeal of earth, symbolized poetically in the descent into hell, alluded to by the word VITRIOL whose initials stand for VISITA INTERIORA TERRAE RECTIFICANDO INVENIES OCCULTEM LAPIDUM: Visit the inner earth and in rectifying it you will find the hidden stone.'[18]

This idea is linked to the Chthonian (related to the Greek gods of the underworld in Orphic religion) mysteries celebrated in honour of the goddess Genes Chthonia, nocturnal earth.

• According to the Rosicrucian cosmology, the earth has nine layers, and a central core:

– mineral earth corresponds to the chemical region of the physical world;

– the fluid layer to the etheric region of the physical world;

– the vapour layer where life pulsates, associated with the world of desire which surrounds and penetrates the earth;

– the water layer where the archetypal forces are, a direct physical expression of the region of concrete thought;

– the seed layer where the original source of life lies, from which emerged the impulse that built every form on earth, this corresponds to abstract thought;

– the layer of fire, from which emanate feelings of pleasure, grief, sympathy and antipathy; this corresponds to the world of the vital spirit;

– the reflective layer, for reflection on the moral state of mankind, where the immoral forces known as the laws of Nature live, and which corresponds to the world of the divine spirit;

– the atomic layer, imbued with an extraordinary power of multiplication, an expression of the world of virgin spirits;

– the material expression of the spirit of the earth, closely related to the brain, heart and sexual organs of man; this corresponds to the world of God;

– finally the central core of the spirit of the earth, the ultimate, nourishing terrain of the earth, corresponding to the Absolute.[113]

EGG

growing life, the origin of conscious life, the future

The egg, containing the germ of everything that will be created in the future, is a symbol of growing life, and was one of the first religious symbols. It appeared as an ideogram of an embryo. The ancient Egyptians and Celts saw it as the very essence of living things. Druids wore a symbolic crystal egg about their necks.

• The egg contains all life, the germs of life and movement, although possessing neither itself, and for this reason it symbolized chaos which contained the seeds of everything and incubated them with his vital spirit/breath, and through his divine power they were able to detach themselves from inert matter.[83]

• This cosmic or mundane egg was seen as a sphere surrounding the earth, with the stars on its outer edge where universal life was hatched, and projected into the arena, as in ancient circular temples.[4]

• As a symbol of fertility and eternity, the egg played a role in festivities at the autumn and spring equinoxes. The passage of the sun was seen as the element that started life. In Libya, Scotland and France, eggs painted red (symbolizing life) were rolled from the top of a hill (to commemorate the ritual sacrifice on 25 March, or the vernal equinox), while Methraic priests sprinkled equinoxial bull's blood, which would later be replaced by the blood of a lamb.

• It was from this egg-rolling that the modern Easter egg originated 'which reminds us of the resurrection of the heavenly egg, that is to say, the spring sun',[25] while the feast of Easter celebrates the resurrection of Christ. And the egg painted the Hermetic colour of the sun also symbolized 'the springtime of life and fertilizing energy at its most potent.'[3]

• Numerous cosmologies have sprung from this cosmic egg. It is the seed of the manifestation (and therefore of the universe), enclosed in a cave, whose outer shell is the limit of the world in space. Its inner seed (the Vedic Golden Embryo) is a symbol of 'the inexhaustible dynamism of natural life.'

The cosmic egg is mentioned in the Egyptian *Book of the Dead* as 'the luminous egg laid by the celestial goose, and hatched in the East.' It is a symbol of synarchic wholeness, of microcosm and macrocosm,[10] and it has different shapes. This idea is similar to the Chinese concept of yin and yang, whose perpetual motion gives rise to Tao and the Hindu Samsara.

Sometimes the cosmic egg bursts, revealing the demiurge, the anthropomorphic personification of creative power, the living power of the Cabbalah.[66] Such was the Hindu golden egg from which Brahma sprang.

• The philosopher's egg, a symbol of the cosmic egg, is primal matter enclosed in the athanor (the alchemist's furnace) which served as an incubator for the philosopher's stone (or chick), symbolizing creation and fertility. Its counterpart in Freemasonry is the place in which the candidate is shut in order to reflect, at the time of his initiation: it is there that his past self dies and his new self emerges.

• The divine egg contains the 'harmonic architecture of the world. The firmament is its shell,' earth, the white membrane, 'water the albumen, fire the yolk. When we eat an egg, in all conscience we are absorbing the universe.'[80] The yolk suspended in the egg-white is also like the sun in the ether between the walls of the celestial vault.

• The Agnis on the Ivory Coast had the idea of an 'egg-limit' which was related to the concepts of property and intimacy, and symbolized the family and its unity.

'The egg is unique and the life it contains perfect,

protected and insured against all seeds of death. In its image, the family possesses a life protected by tutelary gods and a number of preventive medicines, and the protection acquired by the chiefs.'[139]

• Osiris's egg contained good and evil: inside it were twelve white pyramids, symbols of good, and twelve black pyramids, emblems of evil, introduced by Set or Typhon (Osiris' wicked brother).

• In dreams, the egg is a 'symbol of evolution complete with its own resources, and reserves for the future.' It has a positive meaning.

EIGHT
final equilibrium

As an even, female, passive number, and the first cubic number (2 × 2 × 2 = 8), eight represents the earth – not its surface, but its volume.

• In Babylon, Egypt and Arabia, it was a twice multiplied number (2 × 2 × 2) sacred to the sun: this is why the solar disk is decorated with an eight-armed cross.[107]

• The Egyptians saw 8 also as the number representing cosmic order; disciples of Thoth, Lord of the number 8, believed he had created four couples, the *Ogdoade*, who in turn created the cosmic egg from which Rê emerged, who organized the universe. (By creating eight other beings who established the unity of the cosmos, Rê was a primordial god.) Thoth was, in fact, patron of scribes, god of intellect who introduced writing, the concept of time and the calendar to the Egyptians, and, as a consequence, order and organization.

• The number 8's function of bringing equilibrium to the

cosmos is illustrated, in the East, by the eight spokes of the wheel of Buddhist law, the eight rules of behaviour in the *Shu-Ching*, the Chinese empire's eight ministers, the lotus's eight petals, Tao's eight paths, the eight basic trigrams, the eight pillars of Ming-Tang, Shiva's eight shapes (sometimes shown as eight lingams around a central lingam), Vishnu's eight arms, the eight guardians of space, the eight planets around the sun, the eight categories of Zoroastrian priests.

It was adopted by Christianity in the eight angels upholding the heavenly throne, the eight categories of the blest. In initiatory rituals: there are eight degrees or steps in the temple ritual.

• In China the octuple division, which was the basis of the arrangement of the world, appeared in many systems: other than the eight pillars of heaven connected to the eight cardinal points, there were eight cosmic mountains, eight doors making way for eight rain clouds and eight winds, and the eight trigrams. There are eight symbols of learned man (pearl, clinkstone, coin, rhombus, books, rhinoceros horn, artemisia leaf, pictures), eight of immortality (fan, sword, calabash, castanets, flower basket, bamboo cane, flute, lotus) eight of Confucianism (sea mollusc, parasol, baldaquin (a rich fabric), lotus, vase, poison, infinite know, wheel of law) and eight medical symptoms (external – *Piao*; internal – *Li*; cold – *Han*; hot – *Jo*; emptiness – *Hu*; plethora – *Che*; negative – *yin*; positive – *yang*).

• The eight divisions of the zodiac or the eight half-seasons can be transposed to an earthly level, identical to the eight 'places' of Manilius (the division of planets into active and passive signs), the eight divisions of the sky in Greek tradition.[4]

• Number 8 (*ba*) rules man's life: at eight months he has milk teeth; at eight years old he loses them; at 2 × 8 he is pubescent, and at 8 × 8 he is impotent.[7]

• The Japanese have adopted the Chinese system and for them 8 signifies multiplicity.

In Hiroshima, there is an octagonal building erected in 1932, displaying the statues of the eight sages of the world (Buddha, Confucius, Socrates, Jesus, Prince Shotoku, Kobo Daishi and two Japanese priests) to symbolize the innumerable forms of wisdom that direct spiritual effort and knowledge.

• In Japanese mythology, there are eight clouds, a sacred octuple mirror, a room measuring eight 'arms' (six-foot measures) in which the first couple gave birth to the earth and all who people it; a serpent with eight forked tongues, eight tails and eight heads, who has to eat eight daughters of the earthly gods, and who was finally vanquished by eight jars of saki refined eight times and poured into eight cups placed on eight platforms behind eight doors.[77]

• Eight is associated with the idea of resurrection, and rebirth, from which we get the octagonal form of the baptismal font: 'Four for the body, three for the soul and one for the divinity. It thus brings together the conditions necessary for the birth of a new life, whose whole being is purified in its waters.'[80]

According to Clement of Alexandria, Christ placed those whom he gave a second life under the sign of 8.

• For Cabbalists, 8 is the number of perfect harmony, of balance, of the world which is intermediary between the dome of the sky and the square earth, the final point of the manifestation;[30] of reaction and justice.[72] Some see it as the joining together of heavenly and earthly spheres.

• If the division into four symbolizes the earthly world and by extension everyone's work, the division into eight which also takes into account four intermediary points, symbolizes an intermediary world between heaven and earth, featuring the wholeness or completeness of the cosmic manifestation.[4]

This totality is final equilibrium as a result of evolution, that is to say, the state of freedom from the fatal repercussion of actions (samsara). Hence its importance in Buddhism and oriental traditions.

• In Greece, 8 was dedicated to Dionysos, in the eighth month of the year.

ELEMENTS
the expression of sacred forces

Natural phenomena were used as a basis for the occult, particularly astrology, in which the signs of the zodiac are divided up between the four elements:
Fire, symbol of instinctive biological and subconscious dynamism – Aries, Leo, Sagittarius;
Air, the ability of the conscious mind to be aware of itself – Gemini, Libra, Aquarius;
Earth, creative activity, the richness of the human subconscious – Taurus, Virgo, Capricorn;
Water, passivity and receptiveness – Cancer, Scorpio, Pisces.

Each sign is traditionally associated with a planet, a quality, a genie, an animal, a colour, a day, a precious stone, a flower and a part of the body (see Table, pp. 138–9).

The alchemists thought the occult elements, symbolized by the triangle, formed every substance in existence. They were intelligible abstractions that were paired in opposites: fire–water; air–earth.

The elements are distinguished by their elementary qualities of dryness, wetness, cold and heat.

Earth, which is cold and dry has the ox of St Luke as its symbol, or the zodiacal bull/Taurus of springtime. It is black and belongs to Saturn.

'In the warm, wet air, soars the eagle of St John, which is

also Jupiter's bird. It can be seen amidst the autumn constellations in the firmament. Blue, the colour of the atmosphere, is attributed to this element.

Water, which is cold and wet, flows from the urn of Aquarius, the water-carrier. It is a winter sign, and St Matthew represents this. Green is the colour associated with water and also with Venus.

Fire reflects the ardour of Mars and is hot and dry. It can be seen emerging from the red mane of the lion of St Mark, and is shown in mid-summer on the zodiac.'[18]

The elements are associated with parts of the human body: air is responsible for the breath of life in the chest; water is symbolized by body fluids that hold the key to energy; fire, a vital energy in itself and a source of heat and motor power, lives in the mind. Earth is bodily matter, the basis sustaining and containing the other elements. 'Each element is a *ligamentum*, a bond that God has created to bind the different aspects of nature together.'[80]

• The Chinese system of correspondences centres on five elements (earth, wood, metal, fire, water) which control every animate and inanimate being and thing in the natural world, in fact, all visible phenomena. They are linked through a cycle of subordination and control: wood is controlled by metal, metal by fire, fire by water.

• Hindu cosmology recognizes five elements that correspond to the five states of manifestation: air, fire, earth, water and ether.

• In Freemasonry, a man must be truly integrated into real life, and must participate in life around him until such time as he becomes an element of the cosmos. The more he accomplishes, the more expansive his communication with forms of life in the cosmos will become.

Elements

Signs	Elements	Elementary qualities	Planets	Genies
Aries	fire	dry-hot	Mars	Amon
Taurus	earth	dry-cold	Venus	Apis
Gemini	air	wet-hot	Mercury	Horus
Cancer	water	cold-wet	Moon	Hermanubis
Leo	fire	dry-hot	Sun	Momphta
Virgo	earth	dry-cold	Mercury	Isis
Libra	air	wet-hot	Venus	Omphta
Scorpio	water	cold-wet	Mars	Typhon
Sagittarius	fire	dry-hot	Jupiter	Nephte
Capricorn	earth	dry-cold	Saturn	Anubis
Aquarius	air	wet-hot	Saturn	Canopus
Pisces	water	cold-wet	Jupiter	Ichton

Animals	Colours	Days	Precious stones	Flowers and shrubs
sheep and small animals	red	Tuesday	amethyst	fern, hollyhock, primrose, carnation
large animals, bull	green	Friday	agate	lilies and lilac
monkeys	grey	Wednesday	beryl	verbena, balm
aquatic animals	white	Monday	emerald	lily of the valley, iris
wild beasts	yellow	Sunday	ruby	lavender, heliotrope
canines	grey	Wednesday	jasper	valerian, jasmine
winged creatures	pink	Friday	diamond	violet, rose, lily
voracious hunters	red	Tuesday	topaz	hawthorn, heather, mignonette
hunters and carnivores	purple	Thursday	carbuncle or garnet	wallflowers, mock orange
ruminants	black	Saturday	onyx	myrrh, coltsfoot, chalcedony
seafish	black	Saturday	sapphire, black pearl	incense, myrtle, rosemary
freshwater fish	blue	Thursday	chrysolite or coral	thyme, sainfoin, hay

ELEPHANT
intelligence, long life

In Greek mythology the elephant was synonymous with temperance, pity, sovereign power, eternity and public games. It was sacred to Pluto.

• In India, a white elephant is the incarnation of Ganesha, god of wisdom and discernment, and symbolizes control of the passions (Ganesha holds his trunk in his hand).

ELEVEN
the unknown in a new cycle

For Arabs the number 11 signifies the knowledge of God which passes through eleven stages:
will corresponding to self-control,
abstinence and music which lead to purification,
time, the stage of wandering between consciousness of self and God,
the image of God reflected in every creature,
the end of anxiety,
perfect tranquillity and permanent ecstasy,
stepping outside oneself,
the possibility of ascension towards God,
the loss of will,
return journey to God, and
permanent contemplation, empowering one to perform miracles.[4]

• In China it is the number that unites heaven (whose number is 6) and earth (whose number if 5); through this number, 'the Way (*Tao*) of heaven and earth is made perfect.'[8]

• In the eleventh arcana of the tarot, this number

combines the symbolic interpretations of the Pentagram[5] and Solomon's Seal.[6]

EMERALD

knowledge, chastity

The emerald was known as the magi's stone, and they looked upon it as a symbol of chastity, because it was supposed to break when its wearer behaved immorally. It was a secret stone. It was important in alchemy as keeper of the secret of the creation of life and cause of all things, and it promoted divination and prophetic dreams.

• In Central America, the emerald is linked with creation; and associated with spring, the east, femininity, the plant Venus and the Quetzalcoatl bird, a symbol of 'human reality in the era of movement',[48] of man created by the civilizing hero from 'bones wrenched from the kingdom of death and given life with his own blood.'

• Its divine origin is described in a Hindu legend in which it was born from the bile that Indra of the snakes spilt on the ground.[4]

• Sacred to Venus, it is said to encourage amorous enterprises.

• On the negative side, the emerald symbolizes the black arts and is associated with demons, against whom it can be turned, when used as a talisman.

EMERALD TABLET

wisdom

The *Emerald Tablet* symbolized revelation of the secret, and was originally an Egyptian document, attributed to

Hermes Trismegistus, and divided into twelve verses. It bears symbols that correspond to the signs of the zodiac, translating the natural development of things on all levels. It was a constant source of guidance and wisdom for alchemists in their researches.

EMPEROR
reason of state

The fourth major arcana of the tarot shows the Emperor sitting on a throne decorated with a heraldic eagle and brandishing the sceptre of authority. His rigid, severe demeanour is the very image of the master, the father, and moderation. He is a symbol of static power, order and conservatism, and the arcana emphasizes the influence of will, precision and calculation, but also reflects the callousness and despotism associated with the exercise of power. Antagonisms that can be reconciled through control and rectitude.[19]
Divinatory meaning: law, rigour, fixedness, unshakeable willpower. Materialism. Tenacious opposition, hostile posturing, tyranny; brutal masculinity indirectly subdued by female tenderness.[17]

EMPRESS
protection, fertility

The Empress is the third arcana in the tarot; she is the protective mother bringing together temporal and material energy (throne, colour, flesh), spiritual energy (golden sceptre), the wisdom of maturity (blue veil), and indulgence. This arcana, signifying fertility, invites us to reflect calmly, be of natural noble bearing, have patience and love.[79]

Divinatory meaning: charm, gentleness, affability, politeness, but also frivolity, vanity, seduction, affectation.[17]

ESOTERICISM
knowledge of the secret

Esotericism (from the Greek *esoterikos*, meaning reserved for followers, inner) is 'the inner meaning of everything' that can be fathomed through intuition. It also signifies 'the attitude of mind that will ask questions about the mystery, and question the mystery itself.'

EXCREMENT
psychic force

Faecal matter is associated with Tlazolteotl, the Aztec goddess of refuse, physical love, fertility, birth and confession; it symbolizes a sacred biological energy which is recoverable after evacuation.

• In dreams evacuation corresponds to psychic liberation, the elimination of feelings of guilt, repressions and inhibitions that are harmful to individual fulfilment and growth. In contrast, constipation reflects intoxication with oneself and reveals anal behaviour (such as greed).

EYE
vigilance and clairvoyance

The physical eye, as the organ of visual perception, is, by extension, the organ of intellectual perception.

In ancient cultures, the eye depicted Providence

watching over human life. And to emphasize the caring aspect of a god, they would place a third eye in the centre of his forehead. This frontal eye or third eye is in India an attribute of Shiva, the symbol of wisdom and intuitive perception. For Buddhists, it is the organ of inner vision, of clairvoyance, which enables one to see the reality behind the illusion.

• In Islam, the 'eye of the heart' is a projection of the heart, and eternity, and assures a vision of the present that 'transcends temporal polarizations of past and future, so that it is the "eternal present" that the eye of the heart discovers and not the present recognized by the brain . . . it is into the central and deep magnetic centre of the heart that the initiate must descend in order to realize his supreme identity.'

• The eye is the symbol of transcendency. The left eye is turned towards the past, the right towards the future.[85]

• Judaeo-Christian tradition made the eye (inscribed in a triangle) a symbol of Jehovah. At a human level, it is moral conscience.

• In ancient Egypt, the eye has a cosmogonical role: there is a myth that says that the eye of the sun left this star and fled into the desert, provoking a lack of harmony in the world and the end of humanity. Thoth, patron of sacred knowledge, succeeded in bringing it back to Egypt and reestablishing primordial order.[80] This may be the reason why Egyptians attach so much importance to vision and its organ, as is clearly shown in this line from the *Book of the Dead*: 'I see, therefore I exist.' This is an expression of their visual mentality.

The sun and moon are the eyes of heaven, and the eye symbolizes knowledge: in initiatory centres, the principle hierophant who possessed sacred knowledge acquired through his own sight was known as the great seer.[10]

'The burning eye of Rê', the sun-god, symbol of nature on fire, was represented by the uraeus, an erect snake with a dilated eye, symbolic of divinity, royalty, the two divisions of heaven, east and west, and Egypt (higher and lower).

Udjat: the winged eye[124]

The winged eye, or Udjat, was a manifestation of the god of war and retributive justice[10] and is found on numerous monuments. It was used as an amulet, or by itself, or in double or quadruple form, and was a sign of offering. ('Take this eye of Hor . . . said the text of the Pyramids XIX, 117').[19] This divine eye is also regarded as the emanation of this powerful, warring, vengeful deity.[10]

• Heraldry uses the eye as a symbol of vigilance, of the permanent awakening of consciousness in the coat of arms of Santeuil, a 'constellated face of eyes represents the spiritual completeness of the knight for whom heraldic art has become the art of thinking fairly.'

Beginning with Shiva's eyes, these innumerable eyes contemplate primordial reality, and this coat of arms is 'an admirable representation of universal man regenerated through the knight's quest.'[47]

• The one or all-seeing eye is sometimes attributed to a deity (Cyclops, shepherds identified as men-gods, guides of mankind and blacksmiths, makers of sceptres and shields and therefore builders of the new sun and the sun's heroes).[3] It also designates the sun-disk invoked by Prometheus on his rock.

Eye

• The eye is an aid to projection and guilt ('the eye was in the tomb and saw Cain') and it is also the antidote for it. The magic eye used to quell anguish and fear can be found in every tradition: on Byzantine amulets intended to ward off the evil eye in Babylon, and in Italy; the dried eye of a sheep that has had its throat slit on the anniversary of Abraham's sacrifice, contained in a glass bowl, was worn around the neck and in the hair by women and children in Persia, and as a bead with a black eye encircled with blue or yellow in Rhodes; the pentacle-eye fixed on to newly built houses; the wolf's eye engraved on an iron ring preserved the wearer from danger.[19]

• Eyes mirror the soul: they express every nuance of feelings, and exteriorize states of mind and mental processes. They are messengers offering invitations, signalling interest, indifference or anger.

• On a symbolic sexual level, the eye is the organ of vision that penetrates and takes possession, and therefore symbolizes the male organ . . . 'the look hardens: it points to its objective; implants itself, penetrates, pierces and transfixes; it throws out flashes of fire and lightning; it shoots and sparkles. The eye symbolically performs all the amorous tool's exploits.'[10]

It also symbolizes the female organ: it is receptive and allows itself to be penetrated by the look of another, captures and retains that look; it moistens itself when it sheds tears.

In dreams the eye is an organ of knowledge. To have clear, precise vision signifies recognition, admission, while blindness symbolizes psychic blindness (dreams of spectacles have the same meaning). See also *Peacock*.

FEATHER
truth

An ostrich feather was the attribute of the goddess Thmé, the Egyptian Themis of justice, and symbolized justice and truth. It was worn on the heads of happy souls who gathered the fruit from the heavenly trees 'watched over by the Lord of Joy' (the Hebrew for ostrich means song of joy).

• The head-dress of Amerindian chiefs is made up of feathers and is a symbol of spiritual authority.

• The Maya identified feathers with the sun's rays. The feather mantle worn by priests had the power 'to repel through magic all sorts of evil spells', like a star's luminous rays.[76]

FETISH, FETISHISM

A fetish is a venerated object imbued with divine energy and magical properties that exert a protective influence. There are collective fetishes (a tree, arrow, axe, stone, animal, palladium – such as the wooden statue of Pallas-Athene which protected the town of Troy – or Numas' shield, a fetish belonging to the Romans), and there are personal fetishes worn on the body (shells, bits of gold or other metal, sparkling stones, a coral hand, talisman or amulet).

Fetishes were thought to have active life and exert a special influence through the intermediary of a spirit; they had their own cults of worship.

A 'modern' fetish might be a part of the body (hair, feet, hands) or an object (a woman's shoe, underclothes, handkerchief, gloves) or a quality (a smell or a tactile sensation).

A classic description of a fetishist is someone who in his search for pleasure can be sexually aroused or ejaculate with the help of a fetish.[5]

According to one writer, K. Abraham, a fetishist sees 'a fellow human only in terms of the charm of the one part of his anatomy, with its overwhelming attraction.' The whole process is devalued, and one part of him is over-valued.

FIG TREE
knowledge

In Greece the fig tree was sacred to Athens and its sacred fruit could not be exported.

• Buddhists see it as a sacred tree, and as a symbol of immortality and superior knowledge; it was under a banyan or fig tree of the pagodas that Buddha ended his quest for knowledge and received enlightenment. The Hindus venerate the fig tree because Vishnu was born in its shade.

• In Rome, the fig was sacred to Priapus, because it fruited abundantly, and like the pomegranate and apricot had an erotic connotation.[83] Perhaps from this originated the

Egyptians' longstanding association of the fig tree with the sexual act and marriage.

FIRE
the vital cosmic force

Fire was primitive man's first achievement; it has been with us since civilization began. It was produced by rubbing two sticks together and the act of making fire this way has come to symbolize the sexual act in many folk tales and legends in different countries.

• Rituals involving an eternal flame, or everlasting fire can be traced back to prehistoric times, where they had a practical purpose (replacing the sun and fending off wild animals by night). At a later period, lighting a fire became a magico-religious rite: intended to prevent the death of the sun, to reinforce its vital energy, or assure its continual resurrection. There was the sacred fire of the vestal virgins which was never allowed to go out, and there were the rites associated with Mazda, the Persian god of light, which were linked to the worship of the sun.

These eternal flames, or ever-burning fires, became an image of immortal life, similar to evergreen leaves on conifers and hollies.

• Fire was the essence of divinity and dispenser of light; the Celts worshipped it under the name of Vulcan, with his double emblem of sun and moon; fire took the place of the sun in the centre of Orphic temples while the surrounding columns depicted subordinate parts of the universe.

• It symbolized a good God, and was thought of as a divine entity in its own right. It was worshipped by followers of Ahura-Mazda as the head of the world revealed in earthly fire and sun. Along with the preparation of *haoma* (a beverage similar to *soma*), the sacred ever-burning fire was the focal point of their religion.

The priest who lit the fire with the sacred sticks (*baresma*) wore a veil (the *panom*) over his mouth to prevent his breath sullying the sacred flame.[19]

The cult survives in Zoroastrianism among the Parsees and the Ghebers of India, for whom fire is still the essence of all active powers. A remnant also survives in sanctuary lamps throughout the entire world: temples, the tomb of the Unknown Soldier with its ever-burning flame, the torch at the Olympic Games – all bear witness to the eternal quality of the essential force of the creator's energetic principle.

• In ancient times it was thought of as a manifestation of God who was thus made visible and accessible to the human senses: disciples of Plato used images of light and fire to demonstrate God's way of acting.

• In Hinduism, fire belonged to Agni, god of fire, and had three purposes: as generator, purifier, and destroyer in heavenly, earthly, cosmic, magical and ritual fires . . . in the heat of anger and digestion.[50] Here fire represents intellectual enlightenment, the desire to conquer the destroying warrior.

• Thunder and lightning, the fire of heaven, are the attributes of Indra, god of war and agriculture, and the heat unleashed by fire is associated with Sarya.

• For the Maya, the flame of the fire in the hearth fulfilled the same function as Agni's flame: its light was a materialization of the divine spirit, 'just as the light of a candle represents the soul of the departed.'[76]

• By analogy with the heat of the sun's rays, it is a symbol of life; fire rids matter of impurities, throws up volcanic lava and is therefore an agent of regeneration and purification (tongues of flame descended on the heads of the Apostles at the feast of Pentecost).

• For Gnostics, fire was linked to generation; 'in man, fire, the source of all things, is at the heart of the human act of procreation. This fire, like primitive fire, is one entity, but is double in its effects: in man, it is the hot red blood changed into sperm; in woman, the blood is changed into milk.'[19]

• In Egypt, fire had two effective principles: generation and destruction, two antagonistic powers, especially ethereal fire concentrated in the sun, the creative one (incarnated by Osiris) moving perpetually through the world.[83]

• The ancient Greeks believed in a psychopomp, a medium between our present and future lives, in which fire could truly emancipate the soul, ridding it of all earthly blemishes (as the flail separates the wheat from the chaff and straw). And so the body had to be consumed by fire in order to separate the two principles, perception (thought and intuition) and sensation.[83] This is where the custom of cremation came from.

• For the Mexicans fire was a driving force of periodic regeneration, and was linked to forces from the underworld; it represented deep energy that 'enabled ascension from the depths.'[48] And so human sacrifices were offered to the god of fire residing in 'the navel of the earth', so that the sun's life would not be extinguished, and a new fire could reignite. The lighting of this fire (every fifty-two years, marking the coincidence of the two lunar and divinatory calendars, the moment when there was a risk of the sun disappearing) occasioned an exceptional ritual: after the sacrifice of a slave at midnight on the summit of a mountain, and the extinction of all the fires, a flame was lit by rubbing a stick against a wooden plank. From this, runners carried pine torches bearing the new flame to all the outlying villages, thus assuring the life of the sun and of the world for a further 52-year cycle.

This ritual has echoes in the feast of Prometheus in Athens, which also had runners, and in the festival of the new fire which took place in the temple at Kyoto at New Year, which was still practised until recently, a vestige of a magic ritual for the winter solstice.

• For Tantric Buddhists, fire is a male symbol, while the hearth is a female one.

Because it transforms what it burns from a gross, material state into a superior state, it is a metaphor for the ascension of the *kundalini*, the vital energy running along points in the vertebral column (*chakras*) which are consumed by the progressive transformation of seminal energy into spiritual energy.[30]

• In the West, by analogy, fire corresponds to Aries, in its dryness and heat, to the planet Mars in its red colour and masculinity and, spiritually, to joy (flames of joy). And in China, fire (*hio*) is one of the elements or states of mutation corresponding to the south, the colour red, bitter flavour, smell of burning, chickens and feathered fowl.

• Taoist alchemists have applied the heat produced by fire in contact with matter to the centre of the human heart, an interior crucible, anatomically localized in the solar plexus.[30]

• Since the heat of the sun's rays can be murderous, it can be compared to the fire of devouring passion and war. And smoke, which obscures and suffocates, symbolizes blindness and the obliteration of the conscious.

The outbreak of a fire, like firebrands and incendiary bombs, provokes panic and a desire to flee. And so fire becomes an instrument of punishment: Lucifer, bearer of light becomes the prince of eternal fire.

• Dreams about fire 'are never insignificant; they relate to great psychic powers . . . they reveal an intense, powerful life, but also indicate danger.' While a large bright fire expresses the birth of a new feeling, 'a blaze indicates that a destructive fire has been lit in the soul. The dreamer must live with the greatest prudence and scrupulously investigate where the smell of burning is coming from.'

FISH
fertility

The symbolism of fish, inseparable from that of water, signifies the universal renewal of Nature.

• It is associated with religious rebirths. The fish is a symbol of baptism: early Christians attributed the virtue of water in baptismal fonts to the invisible presence of Christ, and made the fish, which lives in water, a symbol of this sacrament. They also used it on monuments as a symbol of the Saviour offering food to his disciples.

• On amulets, portable objects and engraved stones, a fish is often portrayed with an anchor in the form of a cross, symbolizing the hope of God.

• The fish-phallus amulet was venerated by the ancient Egyptians in the form of Ab, the fish which swallowed Osiris's phallus when he was dismembered by Seth.[19]

• In China, the fish (*yu*) is a symbol of riches, life and fertility, because of its extraordinarily prolific reproductive capacity.

• The fish was part of the rain and spring rituals, in the course of which eight raw fishes were offered to the gods of the great waves[65] and to the god of riches; fish heads symbolize the beginning of fortune.

The carp symbolizes courage, perseverance and willpower, indispensable qualities for inner accomplishment, and also for a man who has passed his state examinations.[86]

In Buddhism, the *Matsya* or gold fish symbolized the freedom from constraint enjoyed by those who attain Buddahood.[90]

• A fish with a small child is a widely used symbol, meaning, 'may you have highly placed children in abundance,' while a fish with lotus flowers signifies, 'may you live in abundance from year to year.' A couple of fish symbolize harmony, sexual pleasure and possibilities of development. Goldfish (*yin yu*) in an ornamental pond mean, 'may your house be filled with gold and precious stones.'[7]

• In Egypt a fish was an unlucky symbol: it meant crime, fear and solicitude.

The Matsya, *gold fish, symbols of freedom*[90]

• In dreams a fish is an intermediary between the deepest layers of the mind and an aspect of the unconscious that has become accessible. Large fish or fish-shaped mammals (like a whale) symbolize the risk of conscious forces being swallowed up by energies deeply buried in the unconscious.

FISHERMAN
intuition

In the Egyptian *Book of the Dead* a fish symbolizes the silent, implacable battle waged ruthlessly in the next world. The deceased must behave like the spirit-fisherman who scans the depths for demons he must combat.

• The fisherman symbolizes the wise man who harvests his riches from the depths of his spirit, and by extension, the depths of the unconscious. In Christian tradition, the fisherman was the saviour of souls, the proselyte. He was Saint Peter saving souls from hell, the fish being infidels who must be converted.

• In China, a fisherman (*da yu-di*) is one of the basic occupations, like the woodcutter, peasant and scholar.

FIVE
balance, human perfection

The Etruscans and Romans held 5 to be a nuptial number (there were five torches to accompany the marriage ceremony) because it was the first number that came from adding the first female number to the first male number.[29]

Five is the number belonging to man 'seen as mediating between god and the universe.' As this, the human figure is inscribed in the pentagram, 'for the head dominates the four limbs, just as the spirit commands the quaternary of elements.'[17]

• Five is the number belonging to physical man, who has five senses at his disposal, five fingers on his hand, five extremities, and whose body is composed of five parts that are equal in length; the head, chest, pelvis, thigh, and leg; and equal across, with arms outstretched, the chest in the centre, and on either side, from the elbow to the shoulder, and from the hand to the elbow.

• In Hindu cosmology, 5 is also the number of the universe, with the five elements (fire, air, earth, water, ether), and five traditional planets beyond the two light-giving planets.

It is also the fifth cosmic element, the fifth essence or quintessence that perfects and accomplishes the quaternary, that must be separated from the four in order to discover the secret of the universe. 'It is called ether . . . or 'protyle'.[22]

• The Greek philosophers acknowledged five principles in man: body, animal soul, psyche, intelligence, and divine spirit; and after them Cabbalists thought that man had five principles: the body and four related elements.[22]

• In China 5 (*wu*) is a male number that brings good luck in correspondence with the five cardinal points (north, south, east, west, and centre), five colours, five smells, five flavours, five sounds, five costumes (for festivals, mourning, entertaining, the army, and good wishes), five poisonous animals, five animal varieties (furred, feathered, shelled, scaled and naked), and give relationships between men (prince and slave, father and son, older and younger brother, friends, and enemies).

• Chinese traditional medicine, astrology, geomancy and philosophy are all based on combinations of five.[7] And tombstones are covered with symbolic ornaments which describe the five felicities: happiness, long life, dignity, joy and riches.[6]

• According to Aepli, when 5, 'the number of life and nature appears in a dream, the face of the soul turns towards a calm, solid, unclouded life.'[24] While for Jung, this symbol of life and erotic love was an expression of irrational and amoral surges of yearning in life and love, and the number of revolt.[135]

FLINT
drought

In the Aztec zodiac, the flint sign (*tecpatl*) was a symbol of the north, and was linked to drought, cold, austerity, human sacrifices (the flint knife) and the number 18.

People born under this sign were courageous, resilient, had an imposing bearing and limited ideas. Women were remarkable for their cleverness and serious, domestic qualities.[125]

FLOWER
sun, beauty, femininity

A flower, which relies on earth and water for growth, is a symbol of the passive principle and of the manifestation coming from a passive substance. Its calyx is a receptacle for rain and dew and therefore for heavenly activity.

• In China, the flower (*hua*) is especially symbolic of the seasons: magnolia = spring; peony and lotus = summer; chrysanthemums = autumn; bamboo and plum tree = winter. The peony symbolizes wealth and honour. In the iconography, the association of an orchid, crab apple, peony and cinnamon tree flower symbolizes an aphorism.

In southern China, on the fifth day of the fifth lunar month, there is a battle of flowers, at the time of the summer solstice; when yang, the virile force, has attained its apogee and yin, the female force, begins its ascension. This symbolic battle is a kind of fertility ritual.[7]

• The Fleur-de-lis, an attribute of royalty which derived from the trident, symbolized both royal and religious power. It is still widely used today and found in the coats of arms of numerous towns both in Great Britain and abroad: Perth (Scotland), Turku (Finland), Paris (France), Lille

(Belgium), Florence (Italy) and Kosico (Czechoslovakia).[61]

The fleur-de-lis is also the flower of light, according to the Jewish etymology of its name, the flower of knowledge,

• A number of societies have used a flower in full bloom to symbolize the sun. The sun flower of the Assyrians, the daisy, as well as camomile (with its yellow heart and circle of white petals) in Persia were thought of as symbols of the divine word and its radiant light throughout the world.[121]

Sun flowers, used for divination and magic, were gathered at the summer solstice. From this sprang the custom of the flower of the feast of Saint John: the main flower used for this occasion was Saint John's Wort, which, according to J. G. Frazer, was hung from door and windows to protect the house against thunder, witches and evil spirits.

• In Christian iconography, the rose is the chalice which received the blood of Christ; it therefore symbolizes the Holy Grail, identified with Christ's heart, the origin of the emblem of the Rosicrucians who thought of it as a symbol of physical and spiritual purity.[113]

It was also the emblem of divine beauty which is present in every living thing.[47]

Ancient peoples saw it as a symbol of regeneration and placed it on tombs.

It is a symbol of life and initiations: in Islamic countries, the initiate receives a rose from the initiator (a transmission of the doctrine). The heraldic rose, the five-petalled dog rose, the equivalent of the pentagram, which was inscribed within an invisible circle, symbolizes the silence of the initiate, knight or candidate Freemason. The Freemasons communicate their symbolic secrets beneath a mystic rose (*sub rosa*) in the ceremony of the Rose Croix of Heredom (from *hieros domos* = holy house). The rose of silence decorated the ceiling of lovers' boudoirs, places of ritual, rooms where secret meetings took place. Lovers in tales of chivalry offered it to their ladies, as a sign of a secret understanding.[3]

• In India, the lotus (or water lily), emblem of fertility and water, and of purity, is the attribute of 'Brahms, who is shown holding a lotus in his hand and seated upon a lotus', of Vishnu, of Krishna, who bore the mark of this flower on each foot, and of Laskshmi, goddess of abundance. The pink lotus (*padma*) is a solar emblem and the blue lotus (*utpala*) a lunar one. The flowers of the mango tree were sacred to Kama, god of love.[62]

• For the Maya, flowers in general were symbols of beauty. The flowers of the plumerin (frangipani) symbolized sexual relations and were associated at one time with the moon and sun[60] because of the Maya's belief in the sacred marriage of the sun and moon.

• The Egyptians viewed flowers as symbols of joy and happiness, associating them with their daily life and with the worship of the gods and death.

The lily and lotus symbolized initiation or birth of the divine light; on some monuments the god Phré, the sun, is represented as born in a lotus chalice.[62]

Padma, *Buddhist symbol of purity*

The lotus which held Ré captive in its folded petals before creation was sacred to the sun and the emblem of Upper Egypt. Seeing it emerge from the water and open its petals each morning, and sink back into the water in the evening, the Egyptians supposed secret connections between this plant and the day star.[62]

• In Japan, the flower is the emblem of the plant cycle, and of *ikebana*, or flower arrangement, part of *furyu*, a concept that encompasses the art of living, gentleness and aesthetics.

An *ikebana* must always have an uneven number (to bring luck) of flowerless tree branches, shoots or flowers or fruit. Based on the triad of heaven, earth, man, the formal discipline of *ikebana* attempts to reflect as near-perfectly as possible man's communion with Nature.

Its three essential shapes are: *sin* (asymmetric), *so* (symmetric) and the intermediary way (*gyo*). *Yo* is the male style. If only a single branch is used, the main stem pointing upwards symbolizes heaven; a branch bent to the right represents man; and a low branch to the left symbolizes the earth.

The female style is based on a plant or flower: three different branches, placed very close to one another, represent the triad. And so a bamboo would symbolize the sky, a pine branch, man, and plum blossom, earth.[53]

It is the only living arrangement in which man is the mediator between heaven and earth.

• There is a language of flowers which was much used by the poets of antiquity and in medieval times, based on their colour (with shades varying their meaning).

Red flowers ardour. Pale: moderate capricious ardour. Bright: exalted violent, audacious ardour. Dark: a jealous ardour mingled with sadness.

Blue flowers tenderness. Pale: unavowed feelings of tenderness, shyness. Bright: passionate, declared tenderness. Dark: the painful tenderness of memory.

Purple flowers grief. Pale: a past, now calm grief. Bright: inconsolable grief. Dark: resignation, deep grief.

Green flowers hope. Pale: fragile nascent hope. Bright: robust hope, confidence. Dark: secret painful faded hope.

Yellow flowers happiness. Pale: tender joy, calm new-found happiness. Bright: ardent joy, constant complete happiness. Dark: a weak, secret joy; threatened, anxious happiness.

The flower symbolized the realization of latent possibilities. Lying open on the surface of a lake or in a garden it represents the development of the complete manifestation.[30]

• In dreams, a flower is a symbol of the soul, the spiritual centre, an archetypal symbol of the Self manifesting itself at the end of the process of individuation.

• Roses almost always signify something magnificent, but suffering, the opposite of happiness, is equally present.

'When flowers open out in a dream, when a coloured bouquet is presented to us, something positive is coming to us, it is a bouquet of feelings, harmonious in itself.'[24]

FOG
confusion

Fog illustrates indistinction: the lack of definition that preceded order in the creation of the world. In the Bible, fog precedes great revelations.

THE FOOL
super-ego

The character of the Fool in the tarot is an ambiguous one, since he has no number. He appears as a miserable wretch, having only a pathetic bundle of his belongings, symbolic of the unconscious, of irresponsibility, and abandonment of irrational impulses. His extravagant ideas are expressed in the rough blue stick over his right shoulder on to which

his bundle is tied; his poor appearance all too transparent in his wrinkled yellow stockings. But perhaps he is not so unaware as he appears, for facing him is the green crocodile on the overturned obelisk which symbolizes 'conscious lucidity and remorse'. Help is therefore at hand. More so, since the red flower signifies an active spirituality, and also that he is beyond appearances, beyond materiality, and has escaped from *maya* (illusion), from desire and illusory motivations and is directing his steps towards the infinity of possibilities.
Divinatory meaning: abandonment of blind instinct and passions. Irresponsibility, madness, slavery, loss of free will. Indifference, insensitivity, nonchalance.[17]

FOOT
presence

In old customs and in art, footprints and worn-out shoes symbolized real presence: there are many examples of old shoes featuring on African funerary pottery, representing hope in the resurrection of the deceased, who will get up to put on his shoes and take three steps towards a new incarnation: that is he will be 'born, live, and die'.

• Originally a footstep or an allegorical shoe marked the rebirth of the sun god in the winter solstice, and slippers left in front of the hearth (a place sacred to the sun through the fire that burnt there) are a survival of sun worship. They express the period of waiting for the resurrection of the new sun, which will take its first steps, that is, be born.

• Vishnu's three steps have the same symbolic significance. Traces of them can be found in myths and they always accompany Freemason's greetings.[121]

• Buddha's seven footprints symbolized the seven heavens in Hindu cosmology. His footprint alone is enough to depict Buddha in the iconography, for it is both the synthesis of his doctrine and the symbol of biological and spiritual fertility and creative power.

On the planetary vault is engraved a lotus, symbol of the life of the sun, the home of the sun. At its heel and on its toes are the two sexual symbols of the *lingham* and *yoni*, representing the opposed and complementary forces of creation, and swastikas, emblems of prosperity and happiness, and symbols of the movement of life.

• Feet are points of contact with the ground, good conductors of the magical or spiritual fluid with which a holy man is charged and which would disappear if in contact with the ground. And so it is forbidden for a divine person or a person who incarnates any god to touch the ground with their foot. Outside his palace, the king of Persia travelled only on horseback or in a chariot; outside the boundaries of where he lived the king of Uganda and his close family travelled astride the shoulders of their retinue.[66]

In the Sung dynasty in China, a whole folklore revolved around the foot and the shoe. A woman's tiny feet or 'golden lilies' were an essential attribute of female beauty. So much so that they came to be thought of as the most intimate part of the female body, the focus of her sex appeal, the symbol of femininity. Her feet were strictly taboo and were never openly displayed, and touched only as a preliminary to the sexual act.[75]

• According to Paul Diel, the foot is a symbol of moral strength, lack of which showed in Hephaistos' limp and in Achilles' heel.

It is also an infantile phallic symbol: in the story of Cinderella, the slipper is a female symbol and the foot a phallic one.

In dreams, in spite of their sexual connotations, feet are connected with possibilities of progress and movement in life.

FOOTWEAR
travel

As an indispensable item of dress in temperate regions, footwear is linked to physical comfort and is an indicator of social or financial status: such as poverty or limitations (in , for example, the phrase down-at-heel).

• Footwear is a symbol of travel and of the traveller: Hermes, the swift messenger of the gods, wore winged sandals.

• In China, slippers (*liu hang*) symbolized concord and harmony and a desire to have sons. In wedding ceremonies, the exchange of slippers between groom and bride expressed their wish for a long life together.

• A symbol in dreams, the shoe is linked to the phallic symbol of the foot, to which it must adapt.[25] Wearing children's shoes reveals childish or ill-adapted behaviour for one's situation or age.

FORD
crossing

The ford is a meeting point or limit, and is linked to the symbolism of passage, of water (symbol of rebirth), and signifies the struggle accompanying the passage from one stage, state or 'age' to another. It corresponds to the middle stage in the process of individuation or psychic evolution.

FOREST
the unconscious and its mysteries

In fairy tales, dragons, witches, ogres, and all sorts of threatening characters live in the heart of the forest. It is there that the princess gets lost before reaching the castle (security), and there that Theseus confronts the Minotaur, symbol of the passions and vices inhibiting development.

• If for the Celts the forest was a natural sanctuary, in China it was inhabited by the disquieting *tengu* (spirits), symbolizing unconscious aspects of the human personality, but the iconography always represents it as tamed, not wild, and surrounded by buildings, paths and people, and there are in it, as in Japan, a great number of sacred trees.

• There is an analogy between the forest, a symbolic place of learning for whoever can understand trees, and the labyrinth, the place of passions and instincts, where man loses himself, and which he must master before he can find the path, the way out, the light.

One can understand why carpenters used it as a place of initiation, and knights as a place for accomplishing their exploits.[80]

The deep forest is a mysterious, secret place where you dare not venture, with its invasive vegetation, symbolizing the active powers of the unconscious.

The wild, ferocious animals inhabiting it symbolize instincts and animal forces.

• In dreams, the forest 'features the unconscious and invisible life that is outside . . . in it are gathered what will one day emerge into the cultivated, bright field of our conscious.'[24]

It is a maternal archetype. When it is dark, it indicates danger, especially if one is lost in it.

FOUR
wholeness

The number 4 symbolizes organization. 'Four is a simple projection of unity, and the number of perfect rhythm. It is Jupiter's number, who symbolizes living law, is master of protection and justice, and organizer of everything that has been created.'[22]

Four is the number of order (the four directions of space were the earliest method of orientation known to man, on earth as on the sea, and became a symbol through sun worship. Originally, four represented the solstices and equinoxes, the seasons, the elements, the cardinal points, the phases of the moon, the winds in the heavens and the rivers of paradise.

Most states once had four provinces, and towns, divided into quarters, had entrances at four gates corresponding to the cardinal points (in China, Mexico, the Sudan).

These significances extended to royal titles: Lord of the Four Suns, Master of the Four Seas, Lord of the Four Quarters of the World, terms designating kings and chiefs, frequent in Sanskrit, in ancient Babylon, China and Peru.

• Four was the number of symmetry. It plays a significant role in the construction of the mandala 'which gives an impression of order and discipline'.[135]

• It is a symbol of wholeness: in initiations it was thought to be the root of everything. The pyramid, the earliest solid figure, is based on the quaternary.

It dominated the great religions, which have four sacred books: in Persia the books of Mahabad, who divided his people into four castes corresponding to the four elements.

• Buddhism has four Noble Truths, four awakenings of Mindfulness, four Spiritual Paths or bases of psychic power, and four Dwellings of Buddha related to the cardinal points whose characteristics and qualities they express.

• The Hindu sacred texts (Shastras) are divided into four classes: the Shrutis which come from direct divine revelations, containing the Puranas (mythological epics and stories) dealing with cosmology, theology, astronomy and physics; the Tantras (techniques and rituals concerned with the worship of the gods) which can lead to supernatural power; the four Vedas (collections of hymns and some of the Upanishads or treatises on philosophy, charms, liturgy and speculation). The latter are the very heart of Brahma, the soul of the world, his four faces and four heads, the four words issuing from his four mouths. And his doctrine is divided into four parts on a par with the four domains of the universe: space, worlds, light, senses.

• Christian tradition is regulated by the quaternary: God's name in Hebrew has four letters (YHVH); the cross has four arms. There are four evangelists, 'four meanings to the Scriptures: the literal one which teaches the facts; the allegorial one which must be believed; the moral one which must be carried out; the analogy, towards which we must strive' (Nicolas de Lyre). These four interpretations, represented by the four rivers of paradise, are symbolized in a pillar capital at Vézelay (in France) by four men wearing crowns, pouring out thirst-quenching streams for all who seek truth and life.[80] Four angels direct the four heavens: Michael, Raphael, Gabriel and Uriel.

• The quaternary can be found in the tetramorph (a composite figure combining the symbols of the four Evangelists – lion, eagle, calf, man – Mark, John, Luke and Matthew); the Assyrian karibu (from which the cherubim was derived); the Egyptian sphinx – head–body–paws–wings.

• In the Apocalypse, 4 symbolizes the 'universality of divine acts' in time and space: four horses bearing the four scourges, their colours corresponding to the colours of the cardinal points (which each of the walls of heavenly Jerusalem face), and to the colours of the day. There are four destroying angels in the four corners of the earth; four beasts (that are also in the Buddhist wheel of existence in the guise of an old man, a sick man, a corpse and an ascetic).

The spatial quaternary is extended in time with the four ages of mankind (gold, silver, bronze and iron) and of man (childhood, youth, maturity, old age) and the four parts of the day (morning, midday, evening, night) corresponding to the course of the sun.

• Pythagorians swore by this sacred number because if it is added to the numbers it contains it forms the sacred number 10 or the *tetraktis* (4 + 3 + 2 + 1 = 10).

They saw the quadrilateral supporting Hermes as a sign of infallible reason.[3]

• Four is the mystics' number: according to the Cabbalah, the fourth letter of the Hebrew alphabet, Daleth, symbolizes the physical existence of things animated by Ghimel and fed by the maternal waters, the origin of all life – Mem, forty.[115]

• The quaternary regulates man's biological life: Hippocrates distinguished four temperaments that Doctor Carton wrote down is his anatomical configuration of man: the nervous (head), sanguine (thorax), lymphatic (abdomen) and bilious (muscles). This classification was the basis of anatomical drawing.[117] This distinction is also found in the Cabbalah (the book of *Zohar*); Adam, modelled from clay, was the synthesis at the moment of creation.

These temperaments are determined by the four humours of the body, bile (bilious), atrabile or black bile (nervous), blood (sanguine), phlegm (lymphatic); and the four elementary instincts; material (lymphatic), vital (sanguine), psychic (nervous), motor (bilious).

The quaternary also regulates man's mind. C. G. Jung determined four psychological functions: thought, intuition, sensation and feeling. They 'reveal the four fundamental aspects of things in the four corners of our spiritual horizon.'[28]

Four is the number of strength, alchemists' tin, the warring planet Jupiter and the Huntress. Four is obligatory on pentacles that are intended to be used as a defence, and on arms.[190]

• In China, 4 (*si*) is a yin number, and corresponds to the west, death, the square and consequently earth which, according to tradition, is divided into squares.

The empire of Middle Earth was situated in the centre of four seas, surrounded by four barbarian peoples. The chief of the four mountains had to keep the peace among the four peoples. The four great kings protected the jade sovereign in the four regions of the world. In the gardens of the Taoists, there are four beneficial animals: phoenix, unicorn, tortoise and dragon.

The four learned arts are symbolized by the guitar, chessboard, book and painting. The four treasures of the office are Chinese ink, stone to rub the ink, paper and brush. The four books of Confucianism are the *Analects*, the *Men-zi*, the *Ta Hsueh* (great learning) and the *Chung Yung* (doctrine of the mean). Nowadays Chinese communism fights the four archaic traditions: ancient civilization, old habits, old customs, and the spiritual patrimony of the former régime.[7]

• Four is the number of initiation: the four journeys that Buddha made are symbolized by four doors. In Sufism, the candidate for initiation must pass through the same number of 'stations' as there are elements. The first is the *Shariat* (the word), at which he gathers knowledge of the book – this corresponds to air. The second, *Tariqat* (the book) corresponds to fire – here he will participate in the discipline of order. The third, *Marifet* (gnosis) relates to water, and gives access to mystic knowledge. At the fourth, *Haqiqat* (the plane of truth), which corresponds to earth, he becomes one with God.[115]

• In dreams four is a positive aspect of psychic development.[24]

FOX

cunning, long life, fertility

A medieval bestiary described the fox as a very deceitful animal, full of cunning and the incarnation of the devil. It compared it to human fornicators, murderers, thieves and liars.[27]

• In China the fox (*hu-li*) is a symbol of long life: in folklore it has a fertile vitality because it lives down holes and is therefore close to the earth's generative forces. At fifty it can turn itself into a woman, and at a hundred into a young girl, then acquiring supernatural vision (it will know what is happening a thousand miles away; it can change a man's mind, and reduce a person to a state of imbecility). When the fox is a thousand years old, it becomes the heavenly fox (*t'ien-hon*) which is particularly sensual. It possesses nine tails,[75] symbols of superior power.

• The fox also has the function of a siren: incubus foxes are endowed with supernatural powers and can change themselves into beautiful women to bewitch men or provoke sickness or disaster, then they are not playing tricks like the foxes in European folklore.[7]

• In Japan, it is thought that in addition to the attributes already mentioned, the fox (*kitsune* or *inari*) can be a wizard, take on human form and play tricks that may go on for several years. It is associated with Inari, goddess of plenty, and is a messenger of the gods. It stands at temple entrances with a key in its mouth, the key to the granary, and a bowl, symbolizing the spirit of food, or a roll of Buddhist sutras.[77]

• It also symbolizes spiritual aptitudes in man (wisdom, speculation, subtlety) which have lain dormant or undeveloped:[68] part of the elusive unknown that no analysis can ever capture.[80]

• In women's dreams, it is the incarnation of the animus.[68]

FROG

vital force, fertility

The symbolism of the frog is linked to the idea of rudimentary creation (and is related to that of the bear). The frog is generally featured as a result of involutional urges.

• The ancient Chinese thought of it as a lunar animal and, like the toad, associated it with water and rain. It corresponded to yin. An ancient text states that one of man's two souls resembles the frog (*wa*). When it croaks, it is claiming divine protection for all living creatures.[7]

• In Egypt it was thought of as the 'emblem of chaos, of primal matter, wet and unformed . . . the symbol of unformed man.'

• For the Jews, it represented man's larva stage, when he was as yet barely aware of himself and was beginning to convert towards wisdom; the neophyte who was not yet spiritually formed, but who was going to be or could be.

It is also the incarnation of indecision, for 'that also plunges into nothingness.'

It was symbolic of the 'brazen profanity' which, through false reasoning, claims to destroy wisdom; it is in this sense that the Apocalyse talks of three impure frog-like spirits.[9]

• In India, a frog is shown supporting the universe; in the Vedas, it is shown as the incarnation of the earth, made fertile by the first spring rain, and its cry is a thank you.[1]

• In fairy tales, because the frog metamorphoses, it represents the different stages of psychic development, the passage to a superior state. It is also symbolic of sexual relations (it predicts the conception of the Sleeping Beauty); 'the tale is addressed to the child's unconscious and helps it accept the form of sexuality which is suitable for its age, while sensitizing it to the idea that its sexuality must also undergo a metamorphosis.'

GAMES
initiation

Games, although a social ritual, originally had a sacred significance, assuring the victory of good over evil, and gods over demons. An Egyptian papyrus for the Year VII recounts a duelling game which used the *Book of Thoth* as a stake, and was played between a living person and a dead one, on a board divided into compartments on which pieces known as dogs or jackals were used.[136]

• In ancient Greece, the public games (fighting, racing, fisticuffs, chariot races, gladiator fights), celebrated in honour of the gods, also followed precise rules that recalled points of divine law. Chariot races in an oval ring, with twelve laps, symbolized the circular motion of the planets in the heavens.

• Numerous games are reenactments of the cosmogony with the aim of helping to sustain the cohesion of the universe. Teams carry the weight of the world on their shoulders, and the fate of the people, if not of humanity, depends on their performance.

The pole game and acrobatics of the Quiché in Central America dramatize an episode of the Popol-Vuh (a collection of their traditions) and is intimately linked with the creation myth. Young men perched (like birdmen) in a revolving drum fixed to the top of a pole are whizzed through space, describing larger and larger spirals until they touch the ground. 'The whole in full movement is a chronographic depiction of a moving wheel projecting from the cosmic framework and gravitating towards the axis of the universe, thus showing a schematic image of a circle around the world.'[76]

This game can be compared to the Mexican game of *voladores* (or flying men), intended to make the young shoots of maize grow.

• The Laotian *ti-khi*, forerunner of the game of pall-mall that was such a favourite of French kings, took place obligatorily on the fifteenth day of the twelfth month at the waxing of the moon, and its purpose was to guarantee peace and wealth to the country for the coming year.

• Since earliest times, the ball, made in the image of the sun, god the creator, was a sacred object: associated in ancient China and later in ancient Greece (under the name of *sphaera ourania* – heavenly sphere) with the games lovers play before marriage.

• The Aztec game of palms or *tlachtli*, played on an H-shaped pitch, consisted of passing a rubber ball without using hands or feet from one camp to another, across a stone circle set high up on a wall in the centre of the pitch.

The back-and-forth movement of the ball symbolized the sun's circuit, the players were powers of day and night, the game is a reenactment of the solar myth (the fight between Quetzalcoatl, the sun god, and Tzcatlipoca, the god of night, between life and death).

The pole of Cocagne, at the tip of which were hung victuals, is also similar to the conquest of the heavens, the pole symbolizing the axis of the cosmos, the cosmic tree, the Tree in the Middle of China, the central pillar joining heaven and earth, the shaman's route during his ascension.

• Similarly toys were sacred to the gods, and served as aids to magic rites or to divinations (knucklebones, rattles). The doll was derived from the menhir and baton, and once served to receive the soul of a dead person. Kites in the Far East were religious objects of the greatest importance, and symbolized the emperor's soul and its wanderings, and ghosts; and in Polynesia kites were linked to the myth of the conquest of the sky.[79]

In the Middle Ages, they practised a ritual called the flagellation of the allelujah to commemorate Christ's Passion: tops were spun in the choirs of churches and children chased them with whips.

• Tribal games are equally imbued with symbolism which goes back far into the past.

– Mexican *patolli*, a sort of snakes and ladders 'which has the plan of a cross divided into fifty-two squares, symbolized the number of years in the divinatory and solar cycle.'

– The African *awale*, reserved for warriors and priests, which is played on a table called the sacred ark, consists of making marbles go around twelve holes, similar to the path of the stars in the sky.

– The most famous game in the Far East, *go* or *wai k'i*, formerly one of four royal entertainments along with the harp, calligraphy and painting, is a microcosm: a draughtsboard like a grid for a crossword, on which pawns are pushed around, is similar to the heavenly *mappa mundi*; the 361 points of intersection symbolize the stars, the corners correspond to the four seasons, and the seventy-two intersections of the perimeter, to the duration of a human life. As a game of strategy centring on combinations of which the outcome is life or death of a territory, *go* offers an excellent way of bypassing world and personal conflicts by turning them into a peaceful confrontation that will determine the correct move.[79]

– Games using a supplementary diagram as an aid have a purpose similar to an initiation rite and are reminiscent of the Indian mandala, a symbol of the cosmos, which has tests to be passed along the course, similar to those in human life, and there is a requirement to follow rules.

Hopscotch, of which the design has scarcely changed over many centuries (names for the squares: rest, moon, sky, paradise), has a symbolism 'like the Minoan labyrinth; its signs are similar to elements in astronomy, and its simple structure symbolizes accomplishment at the end.'[3]

The game of hide and seek can be traced back to the myth of the Bacchantes' game of hide and seek with Dionysos.

• In India the swing was a symbol of the 'turning movement of the cosmos in the heart of which all living things were born and disappeared.' Used during an annual ceremony in which a priest helped the sun to rise, its trajectory, which linked heaven to earth, was associated with rain, fertility and the renewal of Nature.

GARDEN
paradise

The pleasure of gardens goes back into furthest antiquity. Hindu mythology mentions a garden of paradise, the centre of the cosmos, containing the tree that 'satisfied every desire'; the homes of the gods were surrounded by flowering gardens with lakes. Earthly gardens which had grottoes, natural lakes and artificial pools with fountains, swans and aquatic birds were intended for meditation.[62]

• Generally speaking, the garden is the centre of the cosmos, Eden, paradise, shown as the Islamic enclosed garden with a central fountain and running water, and as monastery cloisters.

• The Japanese garden is based on asymmetry, which 'suggests movement' and, in its incompleteness is 'a design that leaves a space in which the imagination of the spectator can expand.'[66]

• The heavenly garden (*iwasaka* or *shin-en*) in front of Japanese temples is a synthesis of the universe with its sacred tree of life (*himorogi*) which 'contains within itself the energy of the sun.' To reach it, one must pass through its three *torti* (doorways without doors made up of two beams held up by vertical uprights, symbolizing perches to commemorate the assistance given the gods by birds) and cross bridges that span the waterways. Between the entrance and the sanctuary you always pass in front of a small basis of clear water where you wash your hands and mouth, the water being a purifying agent which imparts an effective barrier against evil and impiety.

• The garden is an archetypal image of the soul, of innocence and happiness and, in dreams, 'it is a place of growth and the cultivation of vital inner phenomena. When it has a big tree or a fountain, this garden can be an allegory of the Self.'[24]

GEMINI
duality

This sector of the zodiac is traditionally symbolized in a couple holding hands, signifying duality, inner, antagonistic or complementary opposites.

Gemini
21 May–20 June

The third astrological sign. A male, airy, double sign. Planets: home of Mercury is exalted. Jupiter in exile, fall of Saturn.
Characteristics: duality, movement, moderation, thought, youth, ambivalence or synthesis.
Negative characteristics: mental overdiversification, confusion, lack of objectivity, duplicity.
Correspondences: air, heat, wet, positiveness, maleness, spring, multi-coloured, mercury (metal). Minerals: garnet, beryl.
In the body: lungs, arms, hands.[114, 122]
'The Gemini type takes pleasure in testing his or her own personality. He or she is an ambivalent individual who is aware of indulging in hero-worship[22] and, in a sort of introspective double-take, will observe him- or herself feeling, acting and living.'

GIANTS
excess

Giants (like monsters) are the incarnation of fears that tormented ancient tribes: 'faceless anonymous fears, fears of evil-doing spirits, of storms, of fire from the sky, of high tides, insecurity, bad luck, hunger and above all death.'[136]

As a defence against these redoubtable enemies were opposed magical protective figures equally formidable in appearance: these were the Assyrian *theraphim*, gigantic and horrible with hideous faces, batwings, a lizard's tail and an immense mouth; the Mesopotamian pentacular monster, fated to conquer the south-west winds, with a skull-like face and ram's horns, vulture's claws, a hairy bat's body; and the gigantic effigies displayed in villages in China at the time of prophylactic rituals.

These enormous figures survive in folk customs in numerous countries, for example, the giants of Flanders; immense figures carried in procession on Shrove Tuesday, Ash Wednesday and the first Sunday in Lent, destroyed after a mock trial or after a proclamation of the death sentence.[136]

• There were the earth giants of Greek mythology, like the Titans, born of Gaea, goddess of the earth, who rose up against Zeus and who symbolized immoderation, 'the crude forces of Nature, and subsequently natural desires in a state of revolt against the spirit.'

The vanquished giant, Atlas, condemned to carry the world on his shoulders, represents 'the symbolic fate of any exultation of desire.' Turned to stone by Medusa's head: 'the repression of open repentance.'[36]

• Giants can also symbolize uncontrolled passions, the irrational elements that encumber the mind and block a clear vision of reality; energies which, released and properly directed, could help towards a realization of personal goals.

GOAT

lasciviousness, the ambivalent power of the libido

Ancient peoples considered the billy goat the most lascivious creature of all, and a symbol of the creative power that fertilized and organized matter. Sometimes, like the snake and bull, it symbolized the power to procreate.[83]

From this the billy goat came to be associated with the idea of fertility: the harvest goat embodied the spirit of the wheat in fertility rites like the Libyan feast of the goat as opposed to the feast of the lamb which took place at the spring equinox.

• The Egyptians saw the goat as the incarnation of god, 'the vehicle through which he communicated his creative spirit to man.' It became personified in the god Pan, worshipped by the Greeks, who saw it as representing both fertility and universal order, and the primary element of love invoked in Orphic litany; or the 'creator incorporated into universal matter, thus creating the world.'[83]

The billy goat was associated with fauns and satyrs (the creator's symbolic emanations), and symbolized man and God's reciprocal incarnation embodied in universal matter; for God, being simultaneously male and female, is also both active and passive in the act of procreation.[83]

• In Vedic India, the goat is identified with the god of fire, Agni, whom it embodies. It symbolizes vitality, the sacrificial fire 'from which a new and holy life is engendered.'[1]

• In Judaeo-Christian mythology, it is simultaneously sacred (a symbol of virility in nature) and accursed: the scapegoat released into the desert to return to the wild the harmful power which the Jewish people had unburdened themselves of. (A common magical manoeuvre in order to protect oneself from the evil spell of a broken mirror was to throw the pieces into running water.)

• In Mexico and some regions of Africa, America, India and northern countries, the animal was substituted by pariahs: prisoners, slaves or prophets . . . previously deified. Through magic, all the evils and sins of the people were transferred on to them before they were stoned, hanged and cut to pieces or burnt at the stake. Later, disembowelling an animal at the end of a battle was preferred (an echo of this can still be found in bullfights).

Through these expiatory ritualized slaughters accompanied by all kinds of humiliations – swearing, spitting, whipping – the people were assured a saviour, at the same time as ridding themselves of any blemishes.

• Traditionally the billy goat was a symbol of lust, of exacerbated sexual desire, lubricity and the personification of the devil.

GOD
the great organizer of the cosmos

In myths, gods are symbolic personifications of laws regulating the controlled flow of forces issuing from the original source. They appear at the dawn of the world and disappear at the end of a cosmological cycle.[66]

According to ancient Greek theology, God or the primordial principle of love was produced by ether, time or eternity and necessity, acting in unison on inert matter; God creates eternally.

Known as the shining or splendid one, he dazzlingly reveals himself; this eternal light is his primordial, essential attribute, and like him is born of necessity and inert matter.

He is the magnificent one, the illuminated one, because the movement of his wings (symbol of the gentleness with which he enters into the world, and of the incubation that hatched the cosmic egg out of chaos) produces pure light. This explains the qualities of purity and holiness that the Greeks attributed to light.

He has a double personality: male and female, active and passive, and the whole of mankind participates in his divine emanation in various degrees.[83]

• In Orphic philosophy, God is the eternal father, time or eternity personified, a general pervading spirit without special form who fills infinity and eternity.

• For the Chaldaeans and Romans, the planets and constellations were simultaneously representations of cosmic forces and divinities. They are evidence of an existence parallel to the gods of the underworld, invoked through magic procedures.

• For Tantric Buddhists, divinities are 'symbols of various phenomena that are produced along the Way.'

GOLD
knowledge

Gold is the noblest of metals; it is incorruptible and precious. It has associations with the sun and the colour yellow, and is an attribute of the gods Horus, Mithras and Vishnu. The Church fathers made it a symbol of Jesus Christ, and of light, knowledge and the revelations made by priests to initiates. 'The sun, gold and yellow were symbols of human intelligence, illumined by divine revelation,' and in Christian symbolism they were emblems of faith.[32]

• In ancient times, gold was associated with beauty and perfection. The Golden Age corresponded to an era of happiness. Byzantine icons and Buddhist images are painted on a gold background to reflect the 'light from heaven'.

• In the knight's coat of arms, gold symbolized achievement, and the wisdom of a 'man who had been renewed through passing through the cauldron of resurrection,' who had undergone the trials of the world in order to know himself in God's image and shine out like a new sun.[47]

• Alchemists' gold symbolized the inner enlightenment brought about by the transformation, the evolution of materialism into spirituality: base metal (lead = an uncouth person dominated by instinctive urges) turned to gold (man transformed, freed from the yoke of materialism).

• The preparation of philosopher's gold, a symbol of individual perfection, went through several states which were symbolized by:

– astral gold with the sun as its centre; it penetrates everything that is sensitive, mineral or vegetable;

– elementary gold, corresponding to the moon, a pure portion of the elements, and the substances of which they are composed;

– common gold, perfect and incorruptible, the finest metal produced by Nature;

– the living gold of the philosophers, the true flame burning within all of us, without which no one could exist.

• Aztecs made gold a symbol of Nature's periodic renewal: Xipe Totec, god of spring rain and springtime was also god of goldsmiths; victims who were offered to him were scorched and priests covered their skin with yellow dye, the colour of gold leaf. This 'magical act symbolized the earth which had a new skin.'[93]

The Incas thought gold fragments of the sun turned to stone: and that gold was 'condensed light hidden in the shadows of the earth.'[138]

• In Greece, gold was associated with the sun and was a symbol of fertility, wealth and domination.

The Golden Fleece which Jason brought back symbolizes a precious treasure to be shared by everyone, acquired with effort, difficulty and danger.

• In dreams gold is the symbol of precious psychic energies. But it is an ambivalent treasure because of the feeling of power associated with it. Gold coins are, according to Paul Diel, the symbol of a dominating perversion and vanity,[36] and the golden apples of the garden of the Hesperides possess the power to sow discord.

GOLEM
robot man

The story of Golem, an artificial human being who was created through the power of the sacred word properly used, was related in all medieval Jewish communities. His fabrication is mentioned in the Book of Jeszirah, for his creation was thought to be the work of God.[19]

This living teraphim was a lump of unformed red clay awaiting completion (similar to the symbolism of the bear). All that was needed was to inscribe on his forehead the word 'life', so that he was endowed with speech and movement, and rapidly became a threatening giant. The magician was obliged to destroy everything immediately, so that he would return to dust.

GOOSE
alarm

In ancient Greece, sacred geese were the attribute of Priapus, god of fertility[83] and Juno. The geese on the Roman Capitol who served as watchdogs gave the alarm and so prevented an invasion by the Gauls, thus unexpectedly and indirectly contributing to an important event.

• In China, the wild goose (like the duck) is a symbol of fidelity in marriage, because of the regularity of its migrations. It was customary to offer a goose as an engagement present.[6]

• The goose is also the messenger between earth and heaven, as in ancient Egypt, where it was the attribute of Amun, god of the earth and known as 'the great cackler', because it produced the cosmic egg.[124]

• According to Portal, the Egyptians illustrated the idea of a son with a goose.[9]

GRAIL
the inner journey

The chalice which Christ used at the Last Supper with his disciples, and which was used to collect his blood at the Crucifixion was, according to an ancient tradition, carved from the emerald which fell from Lucifer's forehead at the time of his fall from heaven. As it endowed the wearer with eternal youth, it became the goal of knightly exploits and imaginary adventures (the legend of King Arthur and the knights of the Round Table).

This 'mystic chalice of the eternal resurrection' had a forerunner in the Celtic cauldron, which enabled initiates to be reborn: the 'birth of the new man after the ordeal.'[140] 'Possessing both the power of spiritual revelation and organic life, dogma and ritual,' the Grail became the chalice of the Mass and a homologue of the heart.

• The story of the quest for the Grail, by Merlin, Percival, Joseph of Arimathea – upon which the notion of chivalry is based – is the symbol of spiritual adventure, the search for God, the absolute, or, according to Jung, inner fulfilment which will come about through mastery of the senses. The adventure of the knight who made vows of poverty illustrated a type of 'ideal man . . . possessing three virtues: courage, fidelity, chastity.'[22]

GUARDIAN
individual conscience

The figures which guard the entrances to temples and sacred places (dragons, lions, threatening demons, winged bulls) are the guardians of the threshold who watch over and hunt 'those who are not capable of confronting the more elevated inner silences. These are the personifications of the presence.' They signify the metamorphosis undergone by whoever passes through the temple doorway.[66]

• On an individual level, in dreams, the guardian (policeman, etc.) symbolizes the conscience, prohibitions which prevent the interference of dangerous desires and immoral acts.

GUIDE
psychic help

In fairy tales a guide is the bearer of supernatural aid. He could be a dwarf, wizard, hermit, shepherd or blacksmith who at the critical moment dispenses amulets or necessary advice.

• In myth the guide is the ferryman, the psychopomp; Hermes–Mercury, Thoth, the god with the head of an ibis; the Holy Spirit.

• In dreams, the image of a guide is seen at difficult moments and announces a new period, a new stage, in the course of life: old values become obsolete, familiar occupations seem to become vain.[66]

This supernatural principle, which is protective and formidable, maternal and paternal at the same time, protects and directs, and brings together all the ambiguities of the unconscious.[66]

HAIR

animal nature

The virtues and properties of an individual are concentrated in his hair (and nails) which are associated with a man's vital power and strength: hence the cult of saints' relics and the custom of keeping a lock of hair as a memento of a loved one, or a child's first milk teeth.

- Hair symbolizes physical strength, virility (Samson depends upon it for his prodigious strength).

- As a symbol of instinctive forces, it is an incontestable part of female seductions and physical attraction: the voluntary sacrifice of hair, a sort of symbolic castration, represents the sublimation of these instincts, the renunciation of worldly values. In female religious orders, novices' hair is shaved off at the time they make their vows. Women of ill repute used to have their heads shaved as a form of punishment. Monks and Hindu ascetics have their heads shaved.

- In ancient times, hair was a symbol of freedom: slaves and criminals had their heads shaved (a custom still followed in some prisons).

- It was sometimes a mark of belonging to a group or sect: in Japan, a Samurai was recognized by his privileged hairstyle – the loss of his topknot was the worst dishonour he could undergo.

In Japan, hair is intimately linked with the symbolism of the comb which holds the hairstyle in place and symbolizes man's power, his nobility, his links with God, 'all that is thought of as the most precious and the most characteristic element of his personality': it holds the personality together, while the comb's teeth preserve the individuality of its different parts.[77]

Moslems reserve a tuft of hair on their shaven heads to guarantee a link with God at the moment of death – so that Mohammed can grasp it and pull the deceased into paradise.

• In myths, total baldness signifies sterility.

• A hairstyle expresses the persona; it reflects the individual's attitude to instinctive drives. Whether women wear their hair long or short, up or down, reveals availability or reserve, whether they show or hide it, a desire to please, or get themselves noticed, or avoid being noticed or lusted after (such as the puritan with hair scragged back).[101]

• According to Aeppli, both 'hair and whiskers reflect the animal element of human nature. Whether have hair in abundance, or a lack of it, whether we groom it or leave it untidy are all indicators of this.'

In dreams, if we meet a hairdresser, 'it also indicates that it is time to pay attention to our animal nature; it is time to train unruly hair, civilize what on the one hand is too virile and crude and on the other too feminine and delicate. We must adapt to more conventional ways.'[24]

HALO
sun crown

The halo, as pictured by the Persians, symbolized the total power of the god Ahura-Mazda. This golden circle is a variant of the sun crown and is also linked to the symbolism of gold. It is the hieroglyph of the supreme being and the psychic forces emanating from him.

It simultaneously represents the identification with solar divinity and a power takeover.[3]

• When it surrounds a saint's face, it indicates holiness, sacredness, a radiance of solar origin.

• The elliptical halo symbolizes the light of the spirit.

• The round halo is an emanation of central spiritual energy of the soul, and it symbolism is linked to the circle's. In Byzantine art, it was reserved for the dead who had earned a place in heaven through their exemplary life on earth.

HAND
vital tool

The hand is a unique, inimitable part of the body that has fascinated man since prehistoric times for all its range of inherent possibilities: gestures to communicate with, its creative potential.

• It was seen as a symbol of God the Father: the raised right hand is a sign of power and command; the extended right hand, or with fingers extended at the tip of the sun's rays was a sign of the presence of divinity, of a vigilant god, a providential god, of his protection and inherent goodness. It can be seen in the gesture of blessing of the great Cretan goddess in Aegean art, with her hands dispensing blessings at the ends of the rays emanating from the face of the sun god.

• Moslems view the hand as a symbol of providence; the hand is also a synthesis of the Prophet's faith.

Hands dispensing grace at the tips of the rays from the sun-disk[121]

The five fingers correspond to the five dogmas or fundamental precepts. On the fourteen phalanxes (twenty-eight for both hands) are written the twenty-eight letters of the alphabet (*huruf*): the fourteen sources of light on the right hand are linked to the south; and the fourteen sources of darkness on the left hand linked to the north. Just as fingers rely on the unity of the hand as a base, so the dogmas have their source in the unity of God.

• The hand transmits knowledge. In the rite of initiation, the master proceeds by taking one hand; he puts his left hand over the candidate's right hand which has been placed in his while the sacred formulas were being recited.

This ritual, which reproduces the pact made between Mohammed and his companions on the road from Medina to Mecca, is symbolic of a 'spiritual decanting from one receptacle to another, itself symbolized in the arrangement or reordering of potential letters written on the hand.'

• The right hand is a symbol of spiritual authority, of the way of heaven, of YHVH's (Jehovah's) clemency. All light, all blessings emanate from the saint's right hand.

• The left hand symbolizes temporal power, the way of royalty, of warriors, the rigour of Elohim.[85]

• The hand of justice (ivory left hand with fingers raised, symbolic of judicial power, the principal power of royalty) was 'God the judge's instrument for dividing time, that is to say, for separating day from night, the hot, living season from the cold, dead season, the state of waking from the state of sleeping, and by extension, good from bad, life from death, the just from the unjust.'

In ancient art, sculptors attempting to show this idea of decline or renewal would mutilate statues to illustrate the evening or morning of life, dawn or dusk, month or year. An armless statue symbolized flight beyond time, that is, sleep or death.

• The hand is associated with activity and control: in Egypt it signified strength, power, vigour. Joined hands, as potential bearers of letters, became the bearers of sacred names. 'The Pope's hand offering a blessing is a symbol of the Almighty himself. His blessings extend like the joints of the fingers from the palm of the hand. The palm itself symbolizes divine essence.'[85] This explains the ritual of blessing given in the Cabbalah.

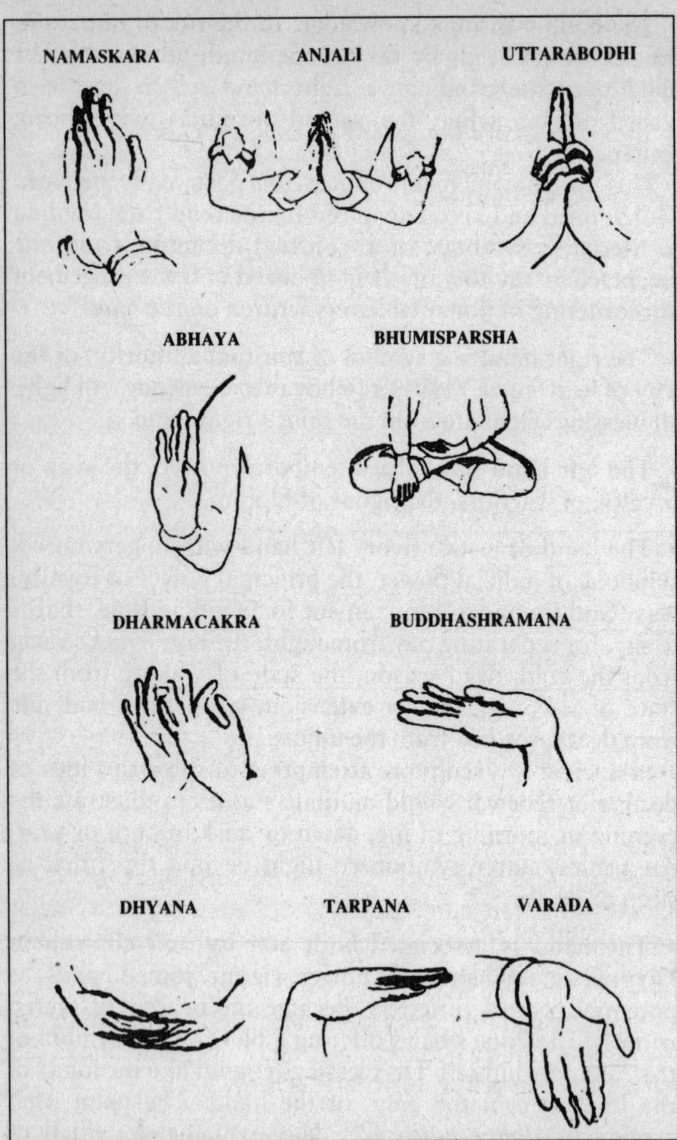

The ritual hand gestures of Hinduism and Buddhism

• Joined hands are found in the three *mudra*, the ritual hand gestures of Hinduism and Buddhism, that symbolize spiritual attitudes:

– the *namaskara-mudra* of homage or prayer: hands together and raised to chest level, fingers straight and opposite one another.

– the *anjali-mudra* of offering and worship: hands joined, fingers outstretched or pointing upwards in front of the chest or forehead, or above the head.

– the *uttarabodhi-mudra* of perfection: hands together pointing upwards with the index fingers, but thumbs and remaining fingers interlocked.

The other gestures are as follows:

– the *abbaya-mudra* of safety, protection: right hand raised, palm facing forward, fingers straight.

– the *bhumisparsha-mudra* of touching the ground or taking the earth as witness: the right hand hanging down, palm face down, fingers straight, touching the ground, left hand on lap.

– the *buddhashramana-mudra* of greeting: right hand raised to shoulder level, fingers straight, palm facing up, parallel with the ground.

– the *dharmachakra-mudra* of teaching or turning the wheel of law: right hand vertical in front of chest, palms facing front; left hand horizontal or vertical, palm facing inwards, thumb and index finger touching, and touching those of right hand.

– the *dhyana* or *samadhi-mudra* of meditation or concentration: two hands on lap, one palm above the other, the one below, thumbs touching.

– the *tarpana-mudra* of homage: hand extended horizontally at shoulder level with palm facing down.

– the *varada-mudra* of giving or favour: open hand hanging down, palm outwards.

– the *vitarka-mudra* of argument: hand raised with palm facing forward, thumb and index touching at tip.[90]

This symbolism of the *mudra* forms the basis of Asiatic ritual dancing, which is a real dialogue with the gods.

• With such potential, the hand is a religion in miniature, and, as far as Moslems are concerned, has remained an infallible protection against the evil eye. When invoking God, says the Koran, 'show him the inside of your hands and not the outside; when you have finished, run both your hands over your face.'

In Islamic countries, a drawing or carving of a hand painted black or red with outstretched fingers is placed inside or outside a house. The five fingers of the right hand are levelled at people who might possess the evil eye.

The hand of Fatima is the most widespread amulet in the Islamic world. For the Shi'ites it also symbolizes five sacred people: Mohammed, Ali, Fatima, Hassan and Hassein.[19]

• In Babylon there was a tower known as the Zida Tower, capped with a right hand, sacred to Anu, and known as the tower of the right hand.[19]

• The phallic hand (fist clenched, with thumb pointing out between the index and medius fingers, or with the medius erect, and other fingers clenched) is a phallic symbol, a talisman against evil influences, which in antiquity was used as a decoration.

This gesture, later known as the 'fig', had an erotic connotation, and using it was (and still is) considered one of the most contemptuous of all insults.[83]

• The propitiatory hand-amulet, in bronze used by Jews, was a concentration of spiritual and magical influences emitted by names written on the fingers: Adam on the phalanx of the thumb; Abel on the joint; Eve on the index; Cain on the medius; Seth on the ring finger; Noah on the little finger; El (God) on the creases of the palm, and *Haya* (life) on the palm; *Sar Tsebaoth* (prince of heavenly powers), *Ain-Soph* (infinity) on the ball of the thumb.[19]

• The number of fingers was linked to the number of senses, and in the iconography those who have a sixth sense have a sixth finger: saints in Byzantine frescoes, Fatima's hand . . .

• In palmistry, the left hand is the seat of predestination. It corresponds to the past, the passive, and reveals temperament, an individual's inner leanings, his physical and psychic tendencies.

The right hand corresponds to the active, the future; it registers experiences, modifications exerted by willpower and individual initiative. Its configuration is therefore changing constantly; that is why in palmistry both hands must be analysed together and periodically redone.

THE HANGED MAN

The accomplishment of the Great Work within oneself

The twelfth arcana of the tarot shows a young man, with arms bound, hanging upside-down from a dark green gibbet which is held up by two yellow trees (the two columns on either side of the initiate, symbolizing 'sentimental aspirations which tend to shield man from gross materialism') planted on mounds bearing green plants. His arms behind his back (a symbol of acceptance) are holding sacks of gold and silver coins (spiritual treasures accumulated by the adept who has enriched himself intellectually and with good feelings and good will). His hair hangs down towards the ground, indicating inhibition of animality.

The Hanged Man reminds us of the ancient Egyptian guardian of the *arrit* (the seven massive doors that give access to the seven mansions of *duat* (the dwelling-place of the gods, or the underworld) – the 'Being-of-many-aspects-hanging-head-first.'[10]

This arcana encourages us to abandon our ego in order to attain greater knowledge and a greater flowering of spirit and soul.

Divinatory meaning: abnegation, moral perfection, being less self-conscious. Enthusiasm fed by illusion. Unrealizable plans. Generous but sterile desires. Unshared love.[17]

HARE, RABBIT
fertility

Their incredible capacity to reproduce makes the hare and rabbit symbols of fertility and the moon's power to fertilize and rule over vegetation, water and the menstrual cycle.[25]

• The hare was the animal form adopted by the Egyptian moon god, Osiris, and 'a symbol of the enlightenment neophytes received regarding morals; it also signified the contemplation of divinity.'[9]

• In some regions of Africa Bantu, Niger) the hare is one of the most important characters in the golden legend of animals and in mythology. His adventures and metamorphoses are legion: in black magic, turning into a sorcerer and vice versa. There are hare masks with stylized ears and trembling nostrils, and dances 'which imitate the frenetic course it follows when trying to escape.'[138]

• Sexuality and incontinence are equally important in the

symbolic interpretation of these hot-blooded creatures; in the Aztec calendar, the *totchli* (rabbit) years and days are ruled by Mayahuel, goddess of Maguey, of the Pulc and fertility.[82]

• In ancient China the hare (*tu-ze*) was a symbol of long life and linked to the moon; it represented the everlasting cyclical renewal of life and Nature. It was the emblem of long life for Chinese alchemists and the fourth sign of the zodiac, the most propitious of all, conferring on the natives of this sign, charm, grace, wisdom, gentleness and reserve.

The Year of the Hare favours diplomatic relations and leads to a certain relaxation in the social order, and a tendency for *joie de vivre* and indolence to dominate individual preoccupations.

• The appearance of a rabbit or hare in dreams indicates 'a sort of short springtime. Something very alive, not necessarily precious, has been fertilized in the dreamer.'[24]

It must be remembered that this symbol stands for quantity, often to the detriment of quality.

HELL
the unconscious, shortening days

Hell was associated with darkness, with the origin of life, and was a symbol of night and the terrors that cold, darkness and loneliness inspired in primitive man.

The descent into hell mentioned in myths corresponds to those early days that prelude winter, when the hours of daylight grow shorter, in contrast to the Ascension which falls between the first longer day following the spring equinox and the 24th of June.

On the esoteric level, hell symbolizes allegorical death, as when in French Compagnonnage (the equivalent of Freemasonry) in the ordeal of the Master Mason, the candidate 'purifies his heart of every baneful and malignant passion' in the dark office of masonic reflection, the transition from black to white in alchemy. This is reminiscent of the myth of the black lamb gradually turning into the white Paschal lamb.[3]

• Although ancient peoples had their own varied ideas of hell, most imagined it as a mysterious frightening subterranean place, where the souls of the dead underwent unspeakable suffering, as a punishment for crimes committed on earth, this after attending a tribunal, a symbolic image of the conscious, of the super-ego.

• The Koran attributes hell with seven doors (or seven steps) reserved for: worshippers of the true god who have sinned (*Gehennem*), Christians (*Ladha*), Jews (*Hodhama*), followers of the Queen of Sheba (*Sair*), the magi (*Sacar*), idolators (*Gehin*), and hypocrites (*Haoviat*).

• Hell is generally associated with fierce flames that consume and destroy and symbolize remorse, the torments of moral suffering or jealousy, while the Catholic hell symbolizes despair, a hardening to a life of sin and error through a total, definition incapacity to improve.

• Hell symbolizes 'the nocturnal sea of the unconscious' which must be crossed in order to reach the other bank, 'leaving behind a more and more restricted conscious life.' Here we have the process of individuation which begins by descending into one's own inner depths, a regression, turning in on oneself (it is in this calm and silence that man can find himself).

Elsewhere, hell is the home of Pluto–Hades, a symbol of repression, according to Paul Diel, but also god of fertility, the father of riches who is featured holding a horn of plenty in his hand. Hell therefore contains within it 'all the creative values, but poorly shared and distributed',[80] the creative values of the unconscious, brought to light by plumbing one's own depths.

HEN
mother of the cosmic egg

In southern China, the hen (*ji*) fulfils the role of a demiurge (a maker of the world): a black hen and a white hen each lay nine eggs, from which evil and good men respectively emerge. The blood of black hens had the power to fend off spirits.

• In Rome, a hen was used for divination: they used to interpret the way these sacred hens ate.

HERMAPHRODITE
integration

The myth of the son of Aphrodite and Hermes has echoes in Plato's myth concerning an androgyne: man originally possessed both male and female characteristics, but then the gods separated the sexes because they were jealous of such a concentration of power.

• The androgyne is sometimes shown with wings to symbolize spiritual or heavenly union, the integration of matter and spirit.[68]

HERO
guide

In ancient Greece a hero was the son of a god or goddess and a mortal (Heracles, Dionysos, Achilles, the Dioscuros, Aeneas, Helen), and as such the subject of a cult: every city, every tribe honoured a hero endowed with an attribute, offered him or her sacrifices and celebrated their feast day in sanctuaries known as *heroon*.

Hero

• The hero of myths, tales and legends is the one who has 'succeeded in surpassing historical and geographical limitations and becomes a figure of universal significance, a figure who corresponds to man's true condition.'

A hero is the eternal man whose ideas and aspirations are in touch with 'the very sources of life and human thought, and express the inexhaustible spring that is present at the birth of society.'[66]

His quest is the same as God's. He is therefore the 'symbol of the divine image, creator and redeemer, hidden in every one of us, only awaiting recognition to bring him back to life.'

The hero of myth is given a task and his adventures follow a prescribed course: virgin birth, abandonment of the world, quest and initiation through confrontation with mythical forces, return. He is victorious on a universal, macrocosmic, historical scale, and has the means of regenerating whole societies (Jesus, Mohammed, Buddha) or in the case of tribal or local heroes, a whole race (Moses, or the Aztec Tezcatlipoca).

The hero's victory in a fairy tale, on the other hand, is on a smaller, more familiar level and is over personal oppressors.

• Certain heroes are spiritual guides who direct us along the right path towards the light, such as Prometheus bringing back a spark stolen from the sun's chariot in order to save mankind.

• Others are civilizing heroes, founders of cities, carriers of the cosmic force (the Aztec plumed serpent, Quetzalcoatl; Huang-Ti in China).

• The image of the hero can appear in dreams at all stages of psychic development in the guise of a leader, a guide in touch with the future, someone bringing about a change that is indispensable to civilization.

HEXAGRAM
the conjunction of opposites

The hexagram is a universal symbol, composed of two superimposed equilateral triangles (one upright, the other upside down) to form a six-pointed star (see *Star*).

• For the Hindus, the hexagram symbolized primordial energy, the source of all creation, and expressed the penetration of the *yoni* by the *lingam* or the union of male and female principles.[16]

• The sixty-four Chinese hexagrams or *Koua*, which are derived from the eight trigrams, are geometric figures formed by combining yang and yin characteristics, which make up the *I-Ching* or Book of Changes.

The point of departure is the second month of the winter solstice, when the yang succeeds the yin: the hexagram *Fou*.

These diagrams correspond to a number, an element, a colour, a direction, a planet, a part of the body, an animal, a period. Each has a special symbol and together they are used for divination.

Here are their divinatory meanings:

1 *Khien* – success through work rather than luck;
2 *Khwan* – need to show oneself to be receptive;
3 *Kun* – promising beginning, then slowing down, insecurity;
4 *Mang* – casts doubt on the consultant's frankness;
5 *Hsu* – lack of self-confidence, health needs to be attended to;
6 *Sung* – competition, court case. Compromise preferred;
7 *Sze* – bad pregnancy;
8 *Pi* – gathering;
9 *Hsiao Khu* – short stop;
10 *Li* – difficult period, but no fatal consequences;

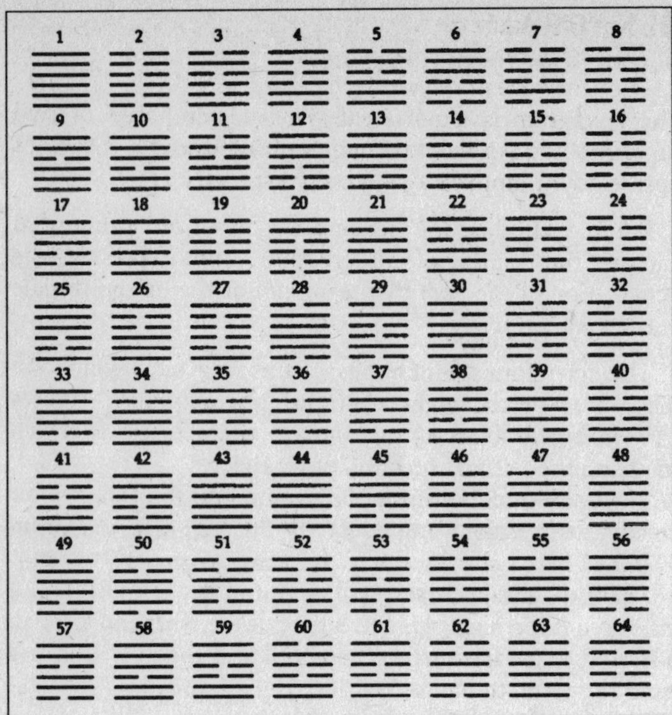

The sixty-four hexagrams of the I Ching

11 *Thai* – peace, prosperity, success;
12 *Phi* – foretells decadence, beware;
13 *Thung Zan* – brotherly gathering;
14 *Ta Yu* – great freedom of action, heightened situation;
15 *Khien* – caring from those around you;
16 *Yu* – avoid excesses that might compromise the situation;
17 *Sui* – avoid ill-considered acts;
18 *Ky* – a decision must be made immediately;
19 *Lin* – unstable situation. Temporary amelioration;
20 *Kwan* – act objectively;

21 *Shi Ho* – court case;
22 *Pi* – beware of appearances;
23 *Po* – beware of those around you;
24 *Fu* – better days will soon return;
25 *Wu Wang* – success through perseverance;
26 *Ta Khu* – stop, reorganization necessary;
27 *I* – act with moderation;
28 *Ta Kuo* – perilous situation;
29 *Khan* – danger, imprisonment;
30 *Li* – need to act correctly;
31 *Hsien* – engagement;
32 *Hang* – marriage stability;
33 *Thun* – a need to make tests discreetly;
34 *Ta Kwang* – success through diplomacy;
35 *Tsin* – social and spiritual progression;
36 *Ming I* (symbol of the cosmic fall for Taoists) – accident, serious wounding or imprisonment;
37 *Kia Zan* – behaviour of a profitable woman;
38 *Khwei* – disagreement, falling out;
39 *Kien* – stop sign, ambushes, obstacles, difficulties;
40 *Kieh* – disappearance of worries;
41 *Sun* – need to balance budget and conduct;
42 *Yi* – journey and success in enterprises;
43 *Kwai* – avoid using force;
44 *Kau* – inopportune encounters, *liaisons amoureuses*;
45 *Tsui* – political meeting;
46 *Shang* – rapid success, acquisition of favours;
47 *Khwan* – difficult period, trickery and bad luck;
48 *Tsing* – a need to bow to circumstances;
49 *Ko* – change of tastes, ideas;
50 *Ting* – worries will disappear. Female successes;
51 *Kan* – war troubles bringing about an enforced retreat;
52 *Kan* – a rest is necessary in order to regain strength;
53 *Kien* – a need to act prudently. Good luck;
54 *Kwei Mei* – bad marriage;
55 *Fang* – a difficult period that could last three years;
56 *Lu* – journeys, homelessness, emigration;

57 *Sun* – hypocrisy;
58 *Tui* – short period of calm;
59 *Hwan* – great journey or declaration of war;
60 *Kieh* – a need to act firmly;
61 *Kung Fu* – act confidently on something;
62 *Hsiao Kwo* – impossibility of achieving great things;
63 *Ki Tsi* – setbacks due to subordinates' lack of awareness;
64 *Wei Tsi* – need for a radical change.[69, 70, 71]

THE HIGH PRIESTESS

initiation

The eleventh major arcana of the tarot shows a motionless impenetrable High Priestess, in a dark blue mantle (secrets), her right foot resting on a cushion (the lowly baggage of positive notions that we can acquire in the domain of the mysteries). Her open book and her veils enclose an unknown but accessible truth.

This hieratic character, similar to the Sphinx, is inviting us to live reality divested of illusions instead of dreaming it, and discover the true meaning of our life.

Divinatory meaning: inhibition, restriction, punishment, Priestliness, knowledge. Certainty, affability, kindliness. Duty that confers prestige. Medicine for the soul.

Negative meaning: immorality; faults instead of qualities.

HIND

femininity, the anima

The hind is a symbol of spiritual beatitude; does nuzzled Buddha's face when he enlightened his followers with his teachings.

• According to Paul Diel, the myth of the hind with brazen hooves, hunted by Heracles for a whole year, symbolizes the 'quality of soul as opposed to dominant aggression, patience and the difficulty and effort required in attaining finesse and sublime sensitivity. The brazen hooves add vigour untinged by the least sentimentality or weakness.'

• For the Celts, hunting the hind symbolized the pursuit of wisdom.

• In literature and folk tales, the hind (like the gazelle or antelope) symbolized gentleness, vulnerability and, to a certain extent, passivity.

• The appearance of a hind in dreams reveals anxiety provoked by a hostile environment or painful living conditions, the need for tenderness and gentleness.

HORSE

universal energy, libido

The horse was a totem of the Germanic nations and a solar symbol; in horse races which symbolized the course of the stars, it represented the sun.

• In the Bible, it was a symbol of intelligence, signifying that man must master his instincts, as the rider masters his horse. 'Come and gather yourselves together unto the supper of the great God; That ye may eat the flesh of horses, and of them that sit on them.' (Revelation 19: 17, 18) means that one must make use of the intelligence in divine truths; the horseman symbolizes the wisdom that directs intelligence (the chariot being religious doctrine).

'[The Lord] delighteth not in the strength of the horse' (Psalms 147: 10) refers to intelligence that is not backed by wisdom.

Horse

'Be ye not as the horse, or as the mule which have no understanding' (Psalms 32: 9) refers to man's intelligence which has been brutalized by lowering himself to a material level.[9]

• According to the colour of its coat, in Revelation, the horse is a symbol of victory (a white horse) or destruction (fiery-red).

Black or pale, it is linked to the moon and water, and is the incarnation of the devil or the damned. White and winged (spirituality), it symbolizes self-mastery: the unicorn can only be captured by a virgin, and is endowed with a strength and power so miraculous that the Christian church made it a symbol of religion, purity and physical virginity. Pegasus is a winged vital force and his hooves spark with the lightning of intuition, of poetic inspiration. A white horse carried the Holy Scriptures from India to Tibet. A luminous horse bore Mohammed into heaven.[25]

• The horse is a maternal archetype in stories and legends, and represents life that is purely animal and physical. It is also the image of the heart of the family. The Trojan horse led to the fall of Troy because it carried the enemy within it.

• A symbol of (solar) life, the horse is also an underworld figure, an image or incarnation of death in numerous myths associated with all the cosmic forces; with the earthly feminine element and the spiritual masculine element (Diomedes' cannibalistic horses devouring travellers), the incarnation of pride and the need to dominate – opposed to any form of spirituality (the centaurs, the red horse in the New Testament Book of Revelation).

• The horse was associated with lust in medieval bestiaries and held to be a universal symbol of psychic energy in the service of human passions, and sexual passion in particular, which, if unmastered, would lead man to his own destruction.

It also symbolizes impulsiveness, the impetuosity of desire, the instinctive impulses that motivate man. Formerly it was sacred to Neptune–Poseidon, god of the sea and storms, and associated with the impetuous Phaeton who dared confront Zeus.

This association of the horse with darker human drives, such as virility and sexuality, has been resented by numerous writers (Nietzsche made Zarathustra say: 'My foot is a horse's hoof. It trots and gallops in spite of obstacles to left and right, and its swift pace gives me a fiendish pleasure'[23]).

• In dreams, the horse is a psychic animal; an expression of all the characteristics it has in myths. It symbolizes the 'disciplined and productive aspects of the instinctive drives that enable the dreamer to achieve his natural goals.

Here the black horse of death and destruction is synonymous with misery; it incarnates the perverted, negative libido. The white horse betrays a lack of realism or can be linked to death.[24]

When a horse rears, snorts, breaks loose, and gallops off, it is interpreted as psychic derangement in the dreamer's erotic life.

• As the seventh sign in the Chinese zodiac, the horse (*ma*) describes a lively, charming nature, but one given to irritability, changeability and stubbornness. The year of the Horse is hectic and adventurous, favourable to daring enterprises, overwork, and tension in diplomatic and political circles.[118]

HORSE AND CARRIAGE

libido

The horse and carriage is an archetype encountered in every esoteric tradition. Its three elements: coachman, horse and carriage, have a special symbolism. The horse is a motor force and represents the *libido*, animating energy, passion, and a powerful motivation for man to act; the coachman is man's *spiritual nature*, an image of intelligence, helping man avoid pitfalls: and *will*, which maintains the balance of the carriage – symbol of harmonized relations between these forces, helping things to run smoothly.

HOUSE

cosmic axis

The house is a centre of the world, as are the city, temple, palace, mountain, primitive hut, replicas of the cosmic mountain, world tree or central pillar supporting the layers of the cosmos.

The house is linked, then, to the idea of sacred space, developing around a hearth or axis of the world, and made sacred by its walls. Beyond the entrance stretches profane space.

• The house is an image of the universe, a link between heaven and earth, and its orientation follows the directions of space; its construction is a repetition of the cosmos. Assyro-Babylonian palaces depicted the world moving round the king's throne, like the Omphalos, the central mountain, the star around which the world revolves.

Originally all dwellings, all palaces were constructed round this world axis that linked the three levels of existence: the infernal underworld, earth and the air of heaven.

• The Navajo Indian hut or hogan (New Mexico and Arizona) faithfully reproduces the plan of the cosmos: open to the east, with eight sides symbolizing the cardinal points, every joist, every beam incarnating an element of the giant hogan of earth and sky.

For the Indian this hut symbolizes 'the basic harmony of man and world, and reminds him of the hidden road to perfection that he must follow throughout his life.'[66]

• The Sioux tepee is conical like the leaves of the sacred cotton tree, and their lodge where the dance-that-looks-at-the-sun takes place is an 'image of the world . . . the fire at its centre . . . is Wakan-Tanka [an all-powerful and invisible being] in the world.' The twenty-eight pillars surrounding it bring to mind the monthly lunar cycle.[13]

• The Aztec house was constructed around a hearth, the image and incarnation of the 'old God, the god of fire.' The three stones in the centre of which the fire burnt were sacred, for they sheltered the mysterious presence of God.[93]

• The traditional Chinese house, the imperial palace, the city, whose square base symbolized the earth, and whose round roof symbolized the heavens, was linked by columns to its square foundations, which in turn were linked to the eight directions of the compass, eight mountains, etc.

The square and cupola can be seen again in mosques, mausoleums and Arab houses set around a garden in which there is a fountain, a reminder of paradise.

• The House (*Calli*) is a sign in the Aztec zodiac associated with the west, tradition and the number 3.

People born under this sign had a tendency to be extravagant, tricksters, and were lured by lust. The women were scandalmongers, lazy and clumsy.[125]

• A house in a dream with its storeys and rooms is often compared to the human body. It depicts the layers of the mind especially: the façade is the persona, role, social function or mask that is worn from day to day.

The bedroom is linked to our intimate life; the floors symbolize various parts of the body and states of mind. The roof and upper floors relate to the head and conscious functions; the loft to childhood memories; the kitchen is the place of psychic transformation – it is one of the symbols of initiation; the cellar represents the unconscious. The lavatory alludes to the need for deliverance and order. Empty rooms correspond to baser psychic functions that are asking to be developed. Stairs serve as a link between the different levels of the personality.[24]

THE HOUSE OF GOD or THE TOWER STRUCK BY LIGHTNING

victory of the spirit

In the sixteenth arcana of the tarot, the Tower Struck by Lightning which is falling down (a symbol of punishment) is a replica of the Tower of Babel and has a further origin in the Bible, in the account of Jacob's dream. Jacob slept with his head on a stone which he afterwards set up as a pillar and called Bethel, or the House of God, a term signifying the continuing, eternal quality of holy places as reservoirs of telluric forces that are in direct communication with heaven.

This tower symbolizes human society and the individual; the arcana puts us on our guard against the ego's emotional demands and fanciful enterprises, for 'things that are unreasonable condemn themselves by disintegrating.'[17] The tower of our material possessions is quite fragile, and life is full of surprises.

Divinatory meaning: materialism, presumption, pursuit of chimaeras, megalomania, narrow dogmatism.[17]

I

For the Greeks, the letter I symbolized the day star and according to Plato it could explain delicate things, the smallest detail. Plato gave it a meaning of mystery.

INDIVIDUATION

In Jungian psychology 'individuation' means the long process leading to the full and entire realization of the individual, the integration of the contents of the unconscious into the conscious, ending in the enlargement of the conscious. This psychic transformation is accompanied by archetypal symbols:

- In the beginning: a cosmic catastrophe (flood, earth tremor): some animals (lion, snake, bird, horse, bull), water, the sea, a cave, cavern, arms, instruments, cross.
- The middle stage is symbolized by a frog, a dangerous passage (ford, bridge), a tree, the act of flying, hovering being suspended in the air.
- The final state: the symbols of Self: the isosceles cross, a circle, square, flower (in particular, a rose), wheel, star, egg, sun, child. Images of the hero and adolescent can equally be revealed during other stages.

INITIATION
rebirth

Initiation is indissociable from the ancient mysteries and the mystery that surrounds the rituals and ceremonies that accompany the passing from childhood into adulthood.

It is the death of the unconscious, irresponsible being, and the birth of a new being, aware of his responsibilities and of the role he must fulfil in life, when passing through a series of more or less painful, even dangerous ordeals. 'The mystagogue (teacher of mystical doctrines) – the elder or substitute father – must only confide the symbols of his role to a youth who has truly rid himself of every vestige of childish inadequacy. Ideally the person who is inducted is divested of his normal appearance and takes on the aspect of an impersonal cosmic force. He is reborn, he becomes the elder. And consequently he is capable of assuming the role of initiator or guide himself; he can become the sun-bearer through whom the childish illusions of "good" and "evil" pass into an experience of the majesty of cosmic law.'

• Circumcision (considered by psychoanalysts as a mild form of castration linked to Oedipal aggression) and excision are initiation rites.[66]

• Initiation is comparable to the process of individuation, because, according to Jung, it has always been imagined as a route, as a descent into the cave, where lie 'the mass of secrets into which one is going to be initiated',[28] and where lie the mass of forces to be brought into daylight and used in everyday life.

INSECTS
bad luck

The insect is a symbol of greed, sensual pleasure, a multiplicity of desires, and the need for renewal: all characteristics linked to the Freudian pleasure principle. It represents the individual who 'accepts neither the deep truth about himself nor his artificial justification', who refuses to do any soul-searching and fritters away his energy.

• In fairy stories, insects often symbolize precision, meticulousness: their services are called upon for impossible tasks such as separating sand from seed. In this context they have similarities to the spirit of differentiation of the individual (separation of the conscious and unconscious contents of the mind).

• In dreams they are associated with organic irregularities and often reveal problems of the adenoids. The ant is linked to the sympathetic nervous system; the wasp is a sign of anguish; the coleopteran (beetles and weevils) reveal nervous excitement; the cockchafer is associated with jollity and relaxation.

IRON

Iron comes from the chthonian underworld and symbolizes hardness and solidity. In the chronology of the ancient world, the Iron Age corresponded to mankind's misfortunes, and to drought in the natural world; it was a symbol of materiality, of giving in to instinct and brutality.

• In ancient Egypt it was identified with Seth, the personification of drought, evil and perversity, whose attribute was the primordial knife, an instrument of dismemberment and death.

• It is linked to the symbolism of the forge and blacksmiths.

ISLAND
spiritual centre

The island 'which emerged from the primal waters on the first day of creation'[80] could be called the centre and axis of the world, a spiritual centre.

• An island is a haven of peace, far from the crowds and bustle of city life; it symbolizes the ideal of our aspirations and inaccessible desires – like Atlantis, the lost paradise for which each of us has within him an unconscious nostalgia.

• The islands of paradise, the paradise where the Taoist immortals fly to, represents the centre of the personality; the Self in the Jungian sense, 'our psychic wholeness, made up of the conscious, and the infinite ocean of the soul on which it floats . . . My soul and my conscious, that is what my Self is, and I am part of it like an island in the midst of the waves, like a star in the sky.'[28]

JADE
perfection

Jade was venerated in western Asia, Mesopotamia and especially in China, where this noble substance was used in astrological and plant rituals: jade tigers and dragons marked periods of growth and decline in the natural world, and symbolized the two great astral constellations that ruled the two halves of the Chinese year – yang and yin.

• Jade symbolized the sky and the elements:

– The jade *Pi*, a symbol of perfection and purity, was a circular disk, representing heaven; its central hole symbolized the threshold of celestial influences.

– the *Ts'ung*, a yellow jade cylinder, round on the inside and square on the outside, was the symbol of earth and served as a channel for the heavenly and earthy influences of yang and yin. It was also a votive object, often decorated with the *Kona*, an imperial symbol that was placed on the abdomen of dead emperors.

– The *Kuei*, a jade rectangle (symbol of the female *yari*, yin) ending in a triangle (the ancient lance, the family home, the *lingam*), when associated with the *Pi*, symbolized sexual union. It was used as a stellar pentacle, as an insignia of an initiatic dignitary, and later of nobility; the *Kuei* has the seven stars of the Great Bear engraved on it.

– *Chang* was a tablet of red jade, symbolizing the fire used in rituals of the sun.

– Metal was represented by a white jade tiger, corresponding to the west, autumn and Orion.

– *Huang* was the sixth cultural instrument in black jade, similar in shape to the *Pi*, cut into two or three, and used in black magic.

These six instruments were buried with the emperor.

• They also blocked the nine orifices of the corpse along with other jade amulets, as symbols of immortality, and to prevent putrefaction.[19]

• A symbol of life, the *K'in-pao* (piece of jade) was embedded in the forehead of the phoenix, the most vital point of the seven-stringed lute, considered to be a replica of a living human being.

• Jade is closely linked to the sexual act: 'playing with jade' signifies 'making love'; jade liquid means either man's sperm or female secretions, jade door or jade wall means the vagina, and jade stalk is the penis.

• Green jade, which is reminiscent of the colour of the sacred quetzal bird, is sacred in Central America: as the Mayan precious stone of grace, it was a symbol of fertilizing rain (and by extension blood); for the Aztecs, it was a symbol of plant life and water – the goddess of lakes, seas and watercourses was Chalchiuhtlicue, whose name signified 'jade skirt'.

• In India, it was attributed with miraculous properties: it could soothe kidney pain, eliminate kidney stones, cure epilepsy, and cure poisonous animal bites.

JAGUAR
fierceness, pleasure

The jaguar is an important part of the Meso-American pantheon, associated with the Aztec-Earth goddess, and shown as a pregnant woman whose mouth is armed with canine teeth and hands with jaguar's claws. Sentinel jaguars watch over the four pathways of the world and the four paths that lead into the villages.[76]

• For the Maya, it was an underworld divinity connected with the secret forces of the earth, and the Aztecs assimilated it into Tezcatlipoca, god of night, represented by a jaguar whose spotted coat resembled the night sky,[36] showing the nocturnal course of the sun.

• In dreams, this jungle animal symbolizes ferocious instinctive leanings that have become dangerous: a need for power, and sexual pleasure.

JASPER
enemy of witches

In antiquity, jasper was used as an amulet against snake bites and headaches (Dioscorides); against fever and dropsy (Marbode); to fend off epilepsy and stop toothache (Greek tradition); against bleeding and to strengthen the pulse (Jerôme Cardan) and to help the digestion (Renodaens).

• It governs the sixth hour of the day, according to the Egyptians. According to Gregory the Great, it was the attribute of the angelic hierarchy of Thrones. In Ireland it was the enemy of witches.[19]

• In astrology, it is in harmony with Aquarius.

JEWEL
talisman

The origin of jewellery dates back as far as the origin of man: prehistoric tombs have yielded thousands of pieces made from shells, intaglios, ivory, teeth, and later metal (iron, bronze, silver and gold) in combination with precious stones.

• Before they were used for adornment, or as a symbol of wealth, jewels had a religious, ritualistic purpose, and were also talismans to ward off bad luck or sickness.

• They were symbols of temporal or spiritual power and worn by magi, priests and chieftains, and very precise rules were followed in their manufacture. The shape, metal and colour of stone were chosen for their symbolic value, and they bore well-defined motifs, such as the phallus, sparrowhawk, scarab or lotus. Chain-link shaped in a figure of eight symbolized infinity.

• Jewels made of gold – which came from underground and therefore contained cosmic energy, as well as being a stable metal, matter 'developed' by alchemists – and jewels made from sparkling gems symbolized esoteric knowledge and endowed the wearer with primordial energy. Masonic jewellery is indicative of rank or function: square and compasses intertwined for the 'Master', cross, rose or pelican between the legs of a compass for the 'Rosy-cross'.

• Freemasons are taught that there are six jewels in the lodge: three 'mobile' – the square, spirit level and plumbline – and three 'immobile' – rough rock, cubic stone, and tracing board.

• On a psychological level, jewels symbolize the passions, such as love, but also greed.

JOURNEY
spiritual adventure

In myth, a journey symbolizes the call of fate, the transfer of the hero's centre of gravity from his habitual milieu to an unknown zone, full of dangers, or treasures, a faraway land, the underworld, or a heavenly kingdom, forest, lost isle, mountain.

• The symbolic journey is a spiritual adventure, the descent into oneself, to meet the Self, crowded with hindrances and small victories, sufferings and joy, until serenity is achieved, in the form of the central void.

This process of individuation leading to the discovery of hidden forces in the unconscious and the annihilation of the ego has three stages, each of which have archetypal images:

1 In the initial stage, the 'call' from the depths is manifested by cosmic catastrophe; (earthquake, flood); by animals: (lion, horse, bull, snake, bird); by a grotto, the sea, arms, the crucifix, or instruments.

2 The symbols of the intermediary stage are: a frog, ford (dangerous crossing), tree, flight, swimming, being hanged. They often symbolize the anguish that is inseparable from spiritual development, and which accompanies every crossing of the limits of the personality and enlargement of vision.

3 At the end of the process, when masks are removed, barriers crossed, limited horizons removed, the symbols of the Self (the centre of the personality) appear, demonstrating that the individual has entered new spheres of wider awareness. The symbols are: circle, cross, square, flower, especially rose, wheel, star, egg, sun, child. The hero and adolescent are manifested in the three stages.

• Whoever undertakes the quest for the Holy Grail or for the elixir of immortality has as physical and mental support, yoga, the mandala, techniques of meditation, the interpretation of dreams or the advice of a guru. This quest is illustrated in Freemasonry through the symbolic journeys that help the initiate to cross from material life, philosophy and religion to reach pure initiation.[109]

Initiation to the degree of Companion or Fellow Craft comprises five journeys in the course of which the candidate discovers his five senses, the four orders of architecture, Nature, humanity and work.[109]

JUDGEMENT
discernment

The twentieth major arcana of the tarot shows a flaxen-haired angel playing the trumpet (could it be of the Last Judgement?), a symbol of discernment and of separation of good from evil. The people praying cannot see the angel; only the man being awakened by the sound of the trumpet can.

This arcana illustrates initiation, and the new horizons that it makes available, the prospect of discoveries, a change of existence, a metamorphosis. But, whatever path you choose, you will always be judged by your deeds.

Divinatory meaning: reestablishment, moral and intellectual freedom. Reputation, upheaval. Drunkenness, Dionysian ecstasy.[17]

JUSTICE
fate

The eight arcana of the tarot shows Themis, Justice, actively participating in our fate, meting out reward or punishment, depending on how we behave, as indicated by the sword she holds in one hand, an instrument of death, and the scales she holds in the other, with which she weighs our merits and defects.

This arcana is linked to the letter I (*Yod* in the Hebrew alphabet) meaning 'hand', and is ruled by the number 8, a symbol of conscience; it counsels vigilance and a need to maintain inner balance and harmony, to act impartially and with integrity; in other words, a need to establish discipline in our lives.

Divinatory meaning: impartiality, integrity, honouring of customs and conventions. Decision, method, meticulousness. Routine. Someone who is subordinate and obedient but incapable of initiative.[17]

K

In Greece, a person who had been struck by lightning was made to wear the letter *kappa*, and was considered impure and harmful.

KA'ABA
the sacred centre

The Ka'aba is the sacred centre of the Islamic world, the throne of the khalif of God on earth. It is a cubic stone building which stands in the centre of a courtyard, in the centre of the Great Mosque in Mecca. It is built in such a way that the four lines running from the centre of the corners correspond to the four cardinal points.

The Ka'aba was originally built by Semitic tribes who practised camel sacrifice, and was a temple sacred to the seven planets and the 360 astral gods (days of the year) that the tribes carried with them on camel-back (as the Jews did the Ark of the Covenant). Worship consisted of swearing oaths to the accompaniment of tambourines and sexual rituals, all of which were banned by Mohammed.

The Ka'aba is covered by the *Kiswa*, a black brocade cloth brought solemnly from Egypt and replaced every year. It has only one entrance, which faces north-east. Inside, the roof is supported by three columns, and embedded in the corner facing east is the black stone or *al hadjar alaswad*. On its south-east side is another sacred stone, the *al hadjar al asaad* (the happy one).

The Ka'aba also contains other sacred objects: the *makam Ibrahim*, the stone on which Abraham rested while the monument was being built; the well of *Zanzam* opposite the black stone, surmounted by the *Kubba*.[19]

• Every Moslem has a duty to make the pilgrimage to Mecca at least once in his lifetime. He then becomes a *Hadji*.

KARMA
action

An Eastern belief. Karma is the sum of our actions, good and bad, from our previous existences.

The worthy karma (made up of good deeds) leads to reincarnation in the world of gods, demigods and man. The unworthy karma leads to reincarnation in the inferior regions of animals, *pretas* and hell. The *achala karma* or invariable karma leads to reincarnation in the superior worlds of forms and formlessness.

Karma and illusion are the true causes of suffering and of samsara, the chain of successive reincarnations.[141]

KEY
access to secrets

The key has a double symbolism: locking away (what is hidden, captive, secret) and opening up (a means of reaching this secret, and freedom).

• As a symbol of wisdom the key is like the stick in being an attribute of Janus, the two-faced god of the doors of the sun, which he opens and closes for the solstices. Janus fulfils the function of a guide (symbolized by the stick), opening up the initiatory path.

• As a phallic symbol, the key given back to his wife by Bluebeard opens the door of the forbidden room and denotes the male sexual organ.[67] It represents temptation. The key is also a symbol of the mystery about to be penetrated, the enigma about to be solved, a stage on the road to discovery and, by extension, to enlightenment.

KING
mediator

In medieval society, the king was a manifest symbol which belonged to everyone, somewhere between a god and a man, a guarantee of harmony which, without him, could not exist.

He acceded to his power only after a complex coronation ceremony, then donned the mantle (symbol of heaven), the hand of justice and the sceptre (symbol of righteousness).

As a synthesis of the entire society, he was a person of responsibility, the first and last, chief and servant: on Maundy Thursday he would wash the feet of the poor, repeating Christ's gesture.[80]

• In China, the sovereign was the heart of the empire, the intermediary between heaven and earth, the cosmic and social regulator. An identical function was attributed to him in India, where he turned the wheel of the world like Buddha or Manou, the universal legislator. He was responsible for justice and peace, and guaranteed the harmony and balance of the world.

KISS
love

In Christian religion, the kiss is a sign of love. The holy kiss, administered by the bishop, is part of the ceremony of the Eucharist, and sometimes at the end of certain prayers, the faithful kiss each other in a gesture of congratulation.

• In China a kiss symbolizes sexual union.

KNOT
protection, defence

The knot was once a sacred symbol, and signified the concealment or secrecy surrounding sacred mysteries: only those who created the knot knew how to untie it because they possessed the secret.

• In India, it was a symbol of arrest. Everything that exists in the universe as in human life is linked by invisible threads, tied and knotted by the gods, who make real or imaginary knots, snares and bonds and use them as magic weapons.

These gods of bondage are gods of sickness and death; they are the gods in the Vedas (Varuna, Yama, Nirrti) whose purpose is to 'tie up' the guilty, dam water, or provoke illnesses (snares) or death (the supreme bondage). These bonds can be unknotted by a tutelary (protecting) god.[92]

• Magic bonds used in witchcraft and war possess the power to disturb the natural order of things, prevent happiness, or affect the victim's health. In imitative magic they are symbolized in a physical object that corresponds to an identical obstacle in the organism. In Babylon, sorcerers claimed they could strangle their victims by remote control, by tying knots in a rope to the accompaniment of incantations; Pliny went so far as to denounce postures that looked like knots, such as crossing the legs or joining hands while the legs were crossed. The opposite procedure of cutting the bonds could release the victim.[136, 92]

These preventative charms and all sorts of images using rope or cord were formerly part of a witch's or sorcerer's repertoire and in fact still are today.[136]

• But the knot is ambivalent and can cure the wrongdoing it has caused. Beneficial knots become protective symbols, and are similar to the symbolism of the plait, cable and interlacing, methods of defence against enemies, wild animals, spells, demons, sickness and death. The Herculean knot was adopted by brides in ancient Greece as a fastening to their girdles which only the bridegroom was allowed to untie. Although an evil knot could also prevent the consummation of marriage. Doctors, in ancient times, would bind the sick part of a body, and amulets made of knots would be worn.

The Buddhists' endless knot; symbol of love and devotion[90]

• The floor of the Masonic lodge has a carpet with a tessellated border with tassels at each corner, a survival of the Gordian knot; this forms a symbolic protective wall signifying the union of a brotherhood, the unbreakable chain formed by men who have reached perfection. Its rope-like tessellation symbolizes the secrecy that surrounds their mysteries. [108, 3, 92]

• For Buddhists, the endless knot is one of the eight symbols of long life and happiness in their iconography.

• In the Upanishads, untying a knot of the heart means attaining immortality. In Egypt Isis' knot was a sign of life and immortality.

• As a symbol of difficulties, the seven or nine knots in the Taoist's red stick symbolize the degrees of initiation and the internal orifices that must be opened before gaining enlightenment.

LABYRINTH

wandering

We know of the ancient Egyptian labyrinth which was built on a square foundation and was made up of twelve large parallel rooms and an enormous number of smaller rooms, of which 1,500 were underground and served as tombs for kings and sacred crocodiles.

But the most famous labyrinth is on Crete, and was built by Daedalus (a symbol of intellect and intelligence) on the orders of King Minos, to serve as a lair for the Minotaur, a monster with a man's body, and head and rear end of a bull. His terrible nocturnal appearance was an ancient representation of the incarnation of the sun god and divine king.[66]

• The labyrinth has come to mean a place where it is easy to get lost and become dispirited; it conjures up the despair of wandering aimlessly, without having heard the inner call to spirituality, and lacking any external belief. It also stands for complication, difficulties, and initiatory ordeals that every individual must undergo in his quest for Self, the centre of his personality, where the process of regeneration will take place. Traditionally, the labyrinth had three passages: one which had a dead end (in the tarot, a symbol of the Fool's wanderings and the unconscious); the second passage has many false side passages to get lost in (symbolic of the superfluous burdens we have to bear); and finally there is the third passage which leads directly to the outside, a symbol of full consciousness.

• At an individual level, the Minotaur in the labyrinth represents the harmful aspects of our personality: repressed buried instincts that have become paralysing complexes, scruples. All this exhausting muddle must be destroyed if we are to find the third path paved with hope, leading to freedom and total self-realization. All we have to do is follow Ariadne's thread (in the myth, Ariadne helped Theseus find his way out of the labyrinth after he had killed the monster, by giving him a reel of thread – symbolic of the imagination). 'Where we think we will find a monster is where we will find a god; where we think we will kill someone, it will be our own ego that we sacrifice; where we think we will find our way to the outside world is where we will attain the centre of our existence; where we think we are alone is where we will be in the company of the whole world.'[66]

• The labyrinth is a similar idea to the spiral and the mandala, the elaborate diagram surrounding a centre, which the initiate must reach.

LADDER or STAIRCASE

the levels of consciousness between man and the cosmos, between heaven and earth

Like the giant tree, the giant ladder is a path of communication between heaven and earth.

• The ladder is a symbol of progressive ascension and self-actualization, and represents the passage from one level to the next and the spiritual itinerary involving different states of consciousness, symbolized by steps connecting each initiation: an ascension which begins in the material world (at the bottom) and moves towards spirituality (at the top).

This dates as far back as the ladder in Sumerian writing, the ideogram *litu*, translated as 'victory' and 'strength' in historical texts.[47]

• Jacob's ladder established contact between man and God, but symbolized conscious man, the intermediary between heaven and earth, 'capable of perceiving divine magic through the acquisition of wisdom.'

• The philosophical ladder is one of the symbols in the esoteric doctrine of the Persians: it has 'seven doors plus an eighth; each door being of a different metal connected with the sun, moon and planets.'[136]

• Mesopotamian ziggurats were known as heavenly ladders.

• The ladder used at the ritual of the fifth degree in French Freemasonry (known in France as the Scottish ritual) represents a programme of learning identical to that taught in medieval universities where degrees were known as the seven arts. It consists of seven rungs which the candidate must climb: grammar, rhetoric, dialectics, arithmetic, music, geometry and astronomy.[136]

• In medieval coats of arms, the ladder signifies the power required to attack cities: the knight who wishes to penetrate divine law and make it respected on earth 'must know how to ascend the rungs of a ladder and how to descend as well.'[47]

• In the cosmological sense, it symbolizes the path that links the underworld, earth and heaven. Its vertical sides symbolize the duality of the tree of knowledge, and correspond to the two columns of the sephirotic tree in the Cabbalah.

• The staircase features in numerous initiation rites. A spiral staircase is related to the spiral revolving round the cosmic axis.

• In ancient Egyptian sanctuaries, the lunar cycle was symbolized by a staircase with fourteen steps, symbols of the lunar houses and of each phase of enlightenment which served equally in the ascent towards 'the full moon (the fullness of the eye)' as in the descent. These steps led to a terrace which sheltered the 'left eye of heaven,' likened to Atoum, the sun setting in the west. The ascendant phase with the growing moon represented the 'filling of the eye' until full moon.[91]

LAMB
sacrifice

A lamb symbolizes the solar, virile, luminous, positive principle at its full strength, and its symbolism is connected with the seasons.

• A Libyan legend has a lamb born black at the winter solstice and growing whiter as it increases in size, until it becomes an immaculate white at the spring equinox, when night and day are the same length. It is then called the pure lamb.

• In Utica, near Carthage, the lamb was worshipped under the name of *Kar*, a symbol of light, as opposed to the kid, *This*, a symbol of darkness and of the feminine, dark, passive principle, or the waning of the year between summer and winter solstices.

These two elements (light–dark) have an equal share of the circle of the year from one solstice to the next, from 25 December, the solar god's birthday, to 24 June, the day of the summer solstice, then from 25 June to 24 December.

During their ascendancies, these two elements reach an equinox, in which fertility rites take place. The festival of the lamb's equinox is Easter, and the kid's (which became a billy goat) is harvest festival.[121]

Later, in Jewish, Islamic and Christian tradition, the lamb became the sacrificial victim of Easter and Ramadan (and it can be found in Vedic India as Agni, the fire god). In Christian tradition, the lamb represents the Messiah, the Word of God: 'Behold the Lamb of God, which taketh away the sin of the world' (John 1: 29), John the Baptist cries as he sees Jesus coming towards him.[9]

LAME MAN
suffering, the shadow

Lameness is an abnormality generally caused by debility. In every mythology, the god of the underworld, of the forge, of smithies, is symbolized by a limp, the price of knowledge acquired by offending a god.

• symbolically, limping signifies 'being feeble, an ending or a beginning': the lame god, Hephaistos, in his underground smithy, is the 'symbol of the winter sun accomplishing the greater part of its course below the horizon.' In myths, a lame man personifies the sun at the end or the beginning of the year.[121]

• In dreams, lameness symbolizes exclusion and solitude, but also the Jungian shadow, the unusual, ill-adapted elements of our character which have a negative influence on our behaviour.

LARK
happiness

The lark is an attribute of Ceres, Mother Earth, and is the sacred bird of the Gauls.

In popular French belief it brings good luck. Because it climbs so high in the sky, then falls rapidly, it symbolizes the union of heaven and earth. Its soaring flight in early morning evokes the ardour of youth, man's yearning for joy.

• Theologians consider its song as a joyful prayer to God enthroned.

LAUREL
victory

Laurel is the symbol of victory earned by one's own efforts, and of the productive peace that follows; or of victory over ignorance and fanaticism. In Masonry at the initiation ceremony to the fourth degree of Secret Master, a crown of laurel and olive branches is placed on the altar.

• Laurel is a symbol of divinatory power, the plant of prophets and soothsayers who burnt or chewed it before proclaiming the oracle.[12]

LEAD
heaviness

Lead is associated with Saturn and heaviness.

• The Masons link it to the skull, skeletons, the scythe and the hourglass, all attributes of Saturn.

• It has a place in initiation and 'symbolizes the death of

the profane which will be reborn into a life of the spirit, the transformation of base lead into gold.'[109]

• In the Mithraic mysteries, the first rung on the ceremonial ladder was made of lead and corresponded to Saturn's heaven.[92]

Leo
21 July–21 August

A fixed, fiery sign. Leo is in the house of the sun. Neptune exalts, Uranus is in exile, and Saturn is falling.
Correspondences: heat, dryness, sterility, day, positive, summer, king. Christ, golden yellow. Metal: gold. Mineral: ruby, jacinth. Parts of the body: back, heart.
Characteristics: generosity, light, power, will, flame, energy, strength.
Negative characteristics: pride, vanity, autocracy, tyranny, an inflated sense of self-importance, jealousy. Uses other people.[114]

LETTERS
catalysts

In Jewish, Islamic and Far Eastern traditions, letters of the alphabet have had magical, sacred powers.

When they were linked with planets and included in protective pentacles, they were supposed to have released planetary fluxes and attracted 'forces wandering around the fluid generator which they had created.'[19]

The Gnostics, who claimed to possess an occult

knowledge of the secrets of the universe, used the seven vowels of the Greek alphabet as a vocal notation and as a sacred syllable. Each vowel was associated with a sphere, a planet and one of the seven notes of the Greek lyre, the heptachord, which was played at their ceremonies.

• Cabbalists, who had developed a science of letters, thought that the letters of the Hebrew alphabet contained a creative force and established a system of analogies with the twenty-two currents or moving forces, analogous to those in nature, that man followed or diverted,'[81] and with the major arcanas of the tarot, astrology, the zodiac, and the planets.

Here are the correspondences, and the divinatory meaning of each set:

Aleph – 1 – The Magician – Neptune = the arrival of mysterious things; providential protection; signpost, creation of original works, embarking on new business.

Beth – 2 – The High Priestess – the Moon = formulated projects, the beginning of self-realization; steps, pregnancy, birth of things; expression of things through writing; twins; passive acceptance.

Gimel – 3 – The Empress – Venus = unexpected protection, possibilities of initiation; visits, conversations, frequent contacts, locks, roof, coat, furs, anything that protects; inheritance, contracts, promises.

Daleth – 4 – The Emperor – Jupiter – imagining, formulating, expressing, acting in a desired direction, moving towards success; finished work, difficulties overcome.

He – 5 – The Pope – Mars – Aries = power of the *lingam*, the creator, production of shape: modelling, painting, drawing, moulding; farmwork; setting things in train.

Vav – 6 – The Lover – Moon – Taurus = choice of action in life, honesty, lack of reaction, indecision, allowing oneself to be influenced, healthy decisions, provocation, accidents through inertia.

Zayin – 7 – The Chariot – Sun – Pisces - self-control, need for advice, astrology, geomancy, victory in every field, specialists, lawyers.

Cheth – 8 – Justice – Venus – Cancer = result of action, expiation, rewards; mirages and obsessions; pregnancy.

Teth – 9 – The Hermit – Sun – Leo = research, prudence, patient discreet work, hidden blemishes or vices, confidential missions, night journeys. Thief.

Yod – 10 – The Wheel of Fortune – Mercury – Virgo = ascension, changeover, good and bad luck; pride, accidents from lifts, planes, falls, a healthy balanced body.

Caph – 11 – Strength – Saturn – Aries = strength of power and money, strength of soul; capitalization, saving, publicity, daring speculation; danger from large animals.

Lamed – 12 – The Hanged Man – Moon – Libra = remorse, guilty thoughts, chains, desire to unburden oneself, suffering, trials and tribulations.

Mem – 13 – Death – Uranus = changes, loss of fortune or reputation; grief, social and worldwide upheaval; happiness after unhappiness.

Nun – 14 – Temperance – Sun – Scorpio = individual regeneration, and renewal of things, procreative union, illnesses, cures, transplants; meetings, fleeting loves; associations.

Samekh – 15 – The Devil – Saturn – Sagittarius = obstacles, pessimism, temptations; love of luxury, vengeance, procuring; expiation.

Ayin – The House of God – Jupiter – Capricorn = punishment, failure, bad luck; loss of situation; court case, cataclysms, fall on Stock Exchange.

Pe – 17 – The Star – Mercury = inspiration, understanding, discovery; hidden letters, secrets unveiled; prosperity.

Tzaddi – 18 – The Moon – Venus – Aquarius = falseness, lies, bad business, denouncements, accidents, ignorance.

Ooph – 19 – The Sun – Jupiter – Gemini = balance, tranquility, union, understanding.

Resh – 20 – Judgement – Saturn = renovation, return, cure, spiritual awakening; change of situation.

Shin – 21 – The World – Sun = chance, success, renown, beneficial unexpected events.
Tau – 22 – The Fool – Earth = ignorance, error, danger of sickness or accident.

While most experts maintain that ABRACADABRA is a meaningless word, claims have been made that in Jewish tradition, its four Hebrew letters set out in an inverted triangle make up a magic formula signifying: MAY YOUR LIGHTNING BE BANISHED UNTIL DEATH.

A B R A C A D A B R A
A B R A C A D A B R
A B R A C A D A B
A B R A C A D A
A B R A C A D
A B R A C A
A B R A C
A B R A
A B R
A B
A

Abracadabra

When *Aleph* is repeated seven times on an amulet, the amulet possesses a magic power.

• Sacred letters fulfil a religious and mystical role; the names they form possess an irresistible magic power. There is also a mysterious link between them and the things or beings they designate.

And so God's name, kept secret and part of his unlimited power, is endowed with such singular, special properties that a 'special hypostasis was formed for it.'[19] This tetragram made reference to the tribes of Israel and the months of the year (the table is taken from *Amulets, Talismans* and *Pentacles*, Marques-Rivière).

The name of God

Letters	Tribes	Jewish months	Signs of the zodiac
Y	Judah	Nisan	Aries
	Issachar	Iyyar	Taurus
	Zebulon	Sivan	Gemini
H	Reuben	Tammuz	Cancer
	Simeon	Ab	Leo
	Gad	Elul	Virgo
W	Ephraim	Tishri	Libra
	Manesseh	Marshesvan	Scorpio
	Benjamin	Kislev	Sagittarius
H	Dan	Tebeth	Capricorn
	Asher	Schevat	Aquarius
	Nephteli	Adar	Pisces

• The name of Solomon, 'grand master of the magic science of plants', whose wisdom surpassed that of 'all the sons of the East and all the wisdom of Egypt', was used as a talisman against epilepsy, rabies and fever and to conjure up help from demons.

• In Islamic tradition, letters symbolized the mystery of human life, man's link with divinity and his complex make-up that is the result of innumerable realizable combinations. The twenty-eight letters of the Arabic alphabet are therefore the essence of things. They have a secret relationship with the universe, the heavenly spheres, the signs of the zodiac and the four elements;

they correspond to the twenty-eight houses of the moon.

• The science of letters attributes a numerical value to letters. And in the making of pentacles, the letters are transformed by calculating the numbers corresponding to them. The resulting combinations are a subject of serious study for learned Moslems.

Certain verses in the Koran are particularly well known for their magic power – the *bismila* that begins the sacred text 'bimi Llahi Rah'mani r Rah'im (In the name of the clement, merciful God) are used as a magical and religious incantation, which is sun, murmured or written.

The basic formula or *Shahadah* (witness) of Islam is: 'La ilaha ill'allah' or 'Muhammadun rasulu'Llah', separated into two parts, which apply to the two aspects of the macrocosm and microcosm in Arab esoterism, 'Muhammadun being universal man, the affirmative aspect of a human being.'[19]

Incantations that include God's name have a conspiratorial value and are controlled by the *Kitaba*, the science of magic writing. Note that the seven letters which are not found in the seven verses of the first *Sura* (chapter) of the Koran are endowed with special magic virtues. Equally used is Hebrew 'spectacle' writing, which has great protective properties.

• In the Sanskrit alphabet, each letter corresponds to one of the five states of manifestation in Hindu cosmology: air, fire, earth, water, ether.

Letters make up the mantra, a ritualistic formula based on the forty-six letters of the Sanskrit alphabet, animated by 'an informed energy . . . The fundamental human sound is the great Hindu mantra OM, the Pranava.'[19]

The mantra is inscribed within a geometric figure or *yantra* which can be in the form of a circle or a complex combination of lines.

The recitation of the mantra is a sort of communion with the cosmos, a direct participation in the immense vibration of the universe, giving the reciter of the prayer a corresponding spiritual energy.

• Tibetans frequently use the mystic phrase, 'Om Mani Padme Hum', whose magic power is sometimes used as a prophylactic aid: it is inscribed on an amulet which is dowsed in water and the resulting coloured liquid is then drunk.[19]

• Chinese monosyllabic ideograms are a living language, possessing an immediately accessible mystical power (there is no need to create a science of living letters such as the Moslems have). These are real, moving forces that are associated with the planets, with the directions of the cardinal points, with trigrams, etc., according to the law of correspondences which dominates Chinese philosophy.

The characters are engraved on a peachwood seal to make talismans or reproduced on the doors and walls of houses to ensure their protection.

Libra
22 September–23 October

A masculine, cardinal, airy sign, a symbol of analysis and discernment. Diurnal house of Venus. Saturn is exalted in Libra, Mars is in exile, the sun falls.

Characteristics: a sense of justice, harmony. Courteous, observant, practical.

Negative aspects: lack of moderation, self-centredness.

Correspondences: warmth, humidity, autumn, sterility. Bronze, diamond, quartz.

In the body: kidneys, internal genital organs.

LIGHT
conscious life

According to ancient Greek theology, light, God's essential primordial attribute, which was co-eternal with him and emerged with him out of inert matter, is pure and holy.[83] this idea is expressed in myths, in the preconscious unity that preceded the separation of the darkness of primal chaos from light. Evidence of the duality can be seen in the opposites of day/night, waking/sleeping, conscious/unconscious, the Chinese yin–yang, etc.

• Light is generated by the sun, and the ancient sages imagined this solar light or animating movement of the cosmos as a 'radiation coming from a centre and spreading continually in all directions across space.'

• For the Hermetic philosophers, astral light was the magical agent of universal life. According to the Cabbalah, it is a latent force which animates and fertilizes the worlds, whose radiance created space 'like a reverberating command from chaos: what Genesis explains with the divine "And let there be light", the appearance of light that announces the Word at the beginning of the Gospel according to St John.'[30]

And so light from the sun is identified with the spirit, with direct knowledge, as opposed to light from the moon which is a reflection of the sun's rays.

• Freemasonry, whose goal is progress through regeneration, depicts the Redeemer by inner light or *logos*, the thought process of reasoning, spiritual illumination, which is the object of initiation, or the conquest of light. The expression 'to see the light' signifies admittance into the mysteries of Freemasonry.

• Whatever the aspect under which it appears in dreams, be it a lamp, night light, candle, a ray of light in a dark room, light from the sun or dazzling light, light is the expression of spiritual or vital energies. It is a symbol of the Self, centre of the personality, a translation of a state of mind which has overcome the subjection of the individual ego.

LIGHTNING
revelation

In India, a storm signifies the powerful unleashing of creative energy.[21] Heavenly fire is an attribute and an arm of Indra, Vedic god of the atmosphere, who, like Vishnu under the name of *Chakra* (wheel), is the symbol of divine creative and destructive power, and is featured in the twin-bladed axe.

• The Maya also identify the polished stone axe with lightning: the Chacs (rain gods) belonging to the cardinal points direct their axes towards the earth to produce thunder.

• A flash of lightning is symbolized in the arrow of the archer, Krishna (Vishnu's avatar) and the trident (*trisula*), attribute of Rudra, the violent and terrible Mighty One of the Sky, god of the storm

• In ancient Greece, thunder was compared to the bellowing of a bull, and during the feasts of Dionysos the sacrifice of a ram was accompanied by a sacred song, the origin of tragedy, called 'the Ram's song'. As an attribute of Jupiter, thunder was used as a means of divination to foretell the nation's fate.

• All the ancient traditions (on every continent) make something of the magical virtues of the thunderball, meteorites that they believed came from thunder, which were used as pentacular aids against lightning and sickness. Two stone hatchets called thunderballs formed part of six precious objects bearing good luck, mentioned by the Chinese *Feng-Shui mo* (1588), along with the jade seal, white coral, red jewel and precious pearl.[19]

The trident[90]

• In the *I Ching*, thunder corresponds to the trigram *Tchen* (awakening man), to the reed, movement, dragon, vehemence, agitation, feet, shaking, drum, to the return to life, to whatever is strong.[63] 'It is the noise of fire and heaven's laughter.'[7]

• One of the major symbols of Buddhist inconography, lightning (*vajra*), indicates the 'spiritual power of the Buddha (indestructible enlightenment) which pricks the illusory realities of the world.' It is the symbol of the method, the male principle and eternity. Accompanied by a bell, it is the enlightened mind, whose note is the sound of eternity, perceptible throughout creation to the pure in mind.[66]

It is also the diamond, the weapon of knowledge, the instrument of the word, of the intellect.

Vajra, *lightning*

• Jupiter's lightning is featured in a great gun which shoots out zigzag darts.

• In dreams, the lightning flash is an image of sudden and terrible events, symbols of intuition, of sudden revelation and impetuosity.

LILITH
the obscure impulses of the unconscious

In the Cabbalah Lilith is the moon goddess, a nocturnal harmful power (in contrast to Venus), mistress of debauchery, prostitute, wife of the serpent-demon who, according to the *Zohar*, seduced the first woman.

Jewish midwives would attempt to ward off this devourer of new-born babies by writing an inscription on the walls of the room where a woman was in labour, ADIM CHANAH CHOUTS LILITH 'May Lilith keep her distance.'[19]

• She ruled over Friday and was depicted as a naked woman with a fish's tail. A direct echo of the Siren, Lilith is the personification of blind, sovereign sexual lust, and of the shadow (in Jungian psychology).

LINGAM
the principle of creation

The *lingam*, or *linga*, is the male sexual organ, which in Hinduism serves as a symbol depicting the creative power of the divinity. This power was primitively shown in the union of the two sexes: one raised cylindrical column (phallus, male principle) in the centre of a square receptacle, with channels and a spout called the *yoni* (vulva, the passive female principle); sometimes a snake was entwined around the base, 'a symbol of time constantly turning back upon itself.'[83]

The whole symbolized the union of Shiva and his creative power, Shakti, his wife. This ouroboros is similar to the Chinese monad and the spiral.

The erect *lingam* was associated with a divinity to symbolize his procreative powers: Osiris in Egypt, Pan, the Greek's universal principle (Priapus for the Romans) were sometimes equipped with a sexual organ to signify 'the application of creative power to sensitive, rational beings.'[83]

• For Buddhists, the *linga sharira* is the astral or etheric body, the knot of our personality, on which everything has a bearing, made up of the fusion of body and soul, the third principle that constitutes the individual.[18]

LION
psychic force

In ancient symbolism, the lion represented the destructive power of the sun, which was as necessary for the maintenance of harmony in the universe as its generative power. When the lion was linked to a divinity, it endowed that divinity with destructive power.[83]

• In Egypt there was a close connection between the sun god and the lion, a symbol of strength, the soul, and incandescence. Also, because it closed its eyes when it was awake and opened its eyes as it slept, its head symbolized vigilance and guardianship; 'it was for that reason that lions were placed as guardians at the entrances to temples.'[9]

• Medieval bestiaries took it as a symbol of prudence because its firmness was in its head, its courage in its breast, and its face and tail expressed its feelings.

• In the West, kings' thrones were decorated with lions to symbolize royal justice, and church doorways to represent ecclesiastical justice.

• On coats of arms, it personified courage and generosity, nobility and strength.

• It symbolizes the force of divine energy and spiritual power. Buddha is the Lion of Mankind; his throne is the Samhasana, the throne of lions, supported by four or eight lions; Vishnu could change himself into a lion; Krishna and Christ have been compared to this king of animals.

• In China, the lion (*Shi-ze*) is a celestial animal which serves as mount to Mansjuri, Boddhisativa of wisdom. The red lion is alchemist's gold.

• In its nocturnal aspect, the lion represents the power of the libido, hotheadedness, aggression, a brutal need to dominate, susceptibility and selfishness. But, as an ambivalent symbol of powerful, active strength, it represents moral strength, 'in our lion's den, at the heart of our uncontrolled instincts, we must daily test our ability to tame them through the influence of our thoughts.'[80]

This self-control is illustrated in Strength, the eleventh arcana of the tarot, which shows the lion, a savage beast, capable of devouring and destroying, the incarnation of selfishness, passion, undisciplined hotheadedness, as capable of rendering immense service, an image of self-control by dint of will and intelligence.

This is the interpretation of the lion given by Aeppli when it appears in dreams: an untamed psychic energy, 'the presence of impetuous energy which is trying to forge a path towards a new personality with more disciplined instincts.'[24]

In psychological tests, the image of the lion symbolizes pride, the need to create. A symbol of virility and an expression of the father-image.[23]

LOTUS, WATER LILY

resurrection

The lotus or water lily is a plant that lives in water and is self-propagating, growing entirely by itself, without any sustenance from soil; as a consequence it was thought of as a symbol of water's generative power brought about by the creator-god instilling matter with life and nourishment.[83]

Buddhists and Hindus placed sacred pictures on this vehicle of energy, power and procreative power.

• The lotus was shown as the creator-gods' marriage-bed and the place where gods were born: this was true of Isis and Osiris in Egypt; Bhava, the generative sun, and Bhavani in India; the god Phré was depicted being born in the calyx of a lotus.[9]

• From birth, the image extends to rebirth or birth into celestial light after initiation, which makes the lotus the matrix symbol of every resurrection: of worlds after chaos, of souls in a new body. (Any presents to the deceased in the hope of resurrection were in the form of a lotus flower, along with the ankh (looped cross) or other symbols of resurrection).[139]

Egyptian Lotus[124]

• For Taoists, the lotus not only symbolizes female beauty and purity, but joins together the elements and the three cosmic levels: its roots plunge into the mud, its stem passes through stagnant water, its flower opens in the sunlight.

It carries within it the image of man's spiritual development in the world: its root symbolizes insolubility; its stem, the umbilical cord; its flower, blossoming, realization through light.

It also features the triple aspect of time: the past through its buds; the present through its flower; the future in its seeds.

It symbolizes wholeness because it reconciles the yin of water with the yang of light.

Since it intrinsically balances the forces of yin and yang, it stands as a symbol of perfection and enlightenment; since it is self-propagating and exists by itself, it symbolizes Tao itself (the nameless, unchanging essence and source of heaven and earth).[86]

• It has an identical significance for Tibetans: the iconography depicts the lotus bud as the cradle of Buddha's emanations of enlightenment coming from the void.

In the expression *Om mani padme hum* (the jewel in the

lotus), *padme* = lotus, and signifies spiritual flowering which in turn gives access to the jewel (*mani*).

It also symbolizes dharma, the principle of universal stability, a fundamental harmonic balance 'presiding in the cosmos, in nature, society and the individual'[50] and the jewel symbolizes the truth contained in the lotus.

• In India, a distinction is made between the pink lotus (*padma*) (a solar emblem and a symbol of prosperity), the white lotus (reserved for the Buddha of compassion, *Avalo kiteshvara*), and the blue lotus or *utpala* (a lunar emblem sacred to Tara and Shiva).

LOVE
spiritual youth

Love features in most cultures as a naked child with wings, symbolizing the eternal youth of deep love, and associating it with a certain irresponsibility. With its weapons of bow, quiver and torch, he hunts, blinds or enflames. his sovereign power is depicted by a globe which he sometimes holds in his hands.

Love's symbolic mediums are:

• Eros or Cupid, the Greek god, featuring, according to Paul Diel, 'sexuality in a form as banal as it is sublime.' Eros' power extends to everything, and he encourages humans and things to unite and create life. Eros therefore personifies loving desire.

The union of male and female opposites lasts only if this bond is solid, that is if it goes beyond sexuality and combines sensitivity and spirituality.

This process is symbolized in the myth (explained well by Paul Diel) of Psyche (the soul) seduced by Cupid (sexuality), in a perverse disguise (a monster). Cupid imprisons Psyche in a palace (prisoner of luxury), only visits her at night so that she cannot see how ugly he is (repression, prohibitions, taboo). One night Psyche disobeys him, and lights a lamp to look at him (the awakening of the conscious and foresight). Seeing himself discovered, Cupid flees (guilt) to his mother Aphrodite's house (regression). Mad with grief, Psyche wanders far and wide in search of him, before calling upon Aphrodite for help, who makes her work extremely hard (initiation, purification) until Cupid escapes from his mother's palace and reappears in his true guise (true vision of love, the conscious, sublimation of instinct). Zeus (the spirit) then gives him and Psyche permission to unite (spiritual union).

• In contrast to Cupid (love of sexual pleasure), are, on the one hand, Pathos, idealized love, associated with the myth of the hero in search of the inaccessible (Prometheus, Ulysses, Jason), and in the myths of Samothrace, personifying eternal youth; and, on the other hand, Thanatos, messenger of death, who inhabits the underworld (the unconscious). Man's life evolves between these two extremes.

THE LOVER

temptation, doubt, deliberation

The sixth major arcana of the tarot symbolizes the uncertainty so characteristic of adolescence. It shows a young man hesitating between Virtue, dressed in red and blue (energetic action and spirituality) and symbol of a difficult life, and Sloth whose yellow and green veils (symbolizing materiality and passivity) represent ease and surrender to instinctive impulses.

This card highlights the angelic/demonic duality present in every personality, the need for awareness that leads to self-knowledge and the resolution of conflicts.

Divinatory meaning: determinism, desires. Deliberations, responsibilities. Trials to be undergone, dangerous temptation. Debauchery, weakness.[17]

LOZENGE

happiness, femininity

The diamond or lozenge shape (*ling-xing*) is one of the eight Chinese symbols for happiness, and depicts the well being of the state. It can also be an emblem of victory.

The double lozenge shape (*fang-sheng*), two overlapping diamonds, is, as in the West, a defensive magic.

• The Maya established a symbolic link between the rhombus or diamond shape and the jaguar (both containing the idea of femininity): it guarded the rhombus-shaped fields and everyone within the perimeter of the gigantic rhomboid figure, which reproduced the shape of the world guarded by jaguars.

The diamond shape or lozenge is found on tortoiseshell, a symbol of the earth-moon goddess.[76]

THE MAGICIAN

the beginning of initiation

As the first arcana of the tarot, the Magician is shown as an agile, clever conjurer with an intelligent, smiling, but impassive face.

Symbols: the three-legged table (pillars of the objective world), on which there is a cup (knowledge, wisdom), a sword (courage, the word which drives away the ghosts of error), a wand (will), a coin (a necessary base for operations/actions). His hat symbolizes infinity, the active emanations of his mind; his multi-coloured costume symbolizes multiple activity; the five buttons, the quintessence; the rosebud, the beginning of initiation. This arcana corresponds to *Kether*, the first sephira at the top of the middle pillar of the tree of life (according to the Cabbalah).

The Magician symbolizes the 'threshold of the unconscious', and the element of self-creation. He is the 'personification of the ego, the conscious element, the point of departure for any initiative.' He symbolizes the mind's potential waiting to be revealed. He also stands for the power of the imagination, inviting us to discover the truth hidden behind appearances.

Divinatory meaning: the beginning. Initiative, autonomy, discernment. Cleverness, diplomatic finesse. Lack of scruples. Exploitation of human candour.[17]

MAN
microcosm

The myth of cosmic man was used in all traditional civilizations to represent universal life. The Veda conceived of man as carrying the universe (like Atlas in the Greek legend), as a cosmic pillar, supporting heaven and earth.

• Cosmic man was the size of the universe, he had existed since all life began; he was God the Architect and his spreading out through the world produced the diversification of natural kingdoms: human, animal, plant, mineral.

• This cosmic or universal man 'who contains within him all the stages of creation' is found in the nine matrix points of the knight's shield.

The upper part corresponds to the head, the 'highest point of the human body, a reflection of the heavenly world which contains the organs of orientation and directions', through which man can direct himself and find his way through ambushes.

The neck, narrow corridor joining the head to the trunk, is 'the place of honour, decorated with necklaces for ceremonial occasions.'

The heart or abyss, 'the primordial ocean' is 'the place of every possibility . . . where human existence becomes conscious, the symbol of intuitive thought.'

The navel is situated in the middle.

The legs are at the base of the shield, symbols of constancy and steadfastness when faced with happy or unhappy events.

• Man (*nan*) is, in Chinese tradition, integral to yang. Literature distinguishes between two fundamental types of man: the unpolished, crude, courageous military man, and the civil servant characterized by his gentleness, his lack of aggression and his passivity.

The organism forms a harmonious unity, a microcosm implanted in the macrocosm, a truth expressed in the *Nei-king* (a medical treatise dating from 475–221 BC). Man is placed between the active and passive creative principles of heaven and earth, and constantly submits to their influence.

In the system of correspondences which dominates the Chinese way of thinking, the intestines are associated with the five elements (earth, wood, metal, fire and water), which regulate all animate and inanimate beings in Nature; 'all the phenomena of the invisible world.'

– the liver and its vessels, the bile duct, sight, corresponding to wood, and the east;

– the movement of limbs, spleen, kidneys, bladder, to water, rain and the north;

– the lungs, large intestine, gall and hearing, to metal and the west;

– speech, small intestine, the envelope of the heart, to fire and the south;

– will, the stomach, the heart, to earth and the centre.[143]

MANA
source of energy

The Maori see mana (a supernatural or magical power) as a general source of life and energy, supporting every individual life and every kind of authority.

• For American Indians this energy activating the universe is a sort of 'impersonal power which is inevitable and present all around us'; it is sacred, magical, supernatural, strange, marvellous. The sun is rich in mana, 'as are the winds and the sea. Stars, clouds, and breezes also possess it, but in smaller quantities.'

Anyone who comes into contact with this power momentarily takes on supernatural powers and is endowed with *Wakan* (according to the Indians of the plains), *Orenda* (Iroquois) or *Manitou* (Algonquins).[12]

• The seeds of life floating in the air which man inhales are the equivalent of mana, as is the subtle substance absorbed by Hindu yogi who practise methods of breathing similar to those used by Taoist Buddhists. These assist in concentrating the intellect and allow the spirit to traverse individual consciousness to immerse itself in the soul of the world.

In these methods 'there are links between the atmosphere and the human organism which appears to absorb life from it, and consequently consciousness itself.'[98]

MANDALA
the journey in search of the Self

The mandala (Sanskrit for sacred circle) is a cosmogram, a geometric diagram of the universe. It depicts the universe 'not only as inert space, but also as a revolution of time, the one and the other seen as a vital process developing from an essential principle, turning around the central axis of Mount Meru, the axis of the world which supports the heavens, and whose foundations plunge down into the mysterious regions of the underworld.'[12]

Here, once again, is the symbolism of the Babylonian ziggurat, the Chinese and Persian imperial city: images of the world at whose centre man is linked to universal forces from which he assimilates his psychic power.

• The mandala serves as a visual aid to meditation, and is essential in the process of initiation into different Tantric cycles. Whether the mandala is drawn on the ground with rice powder or different coloured sands, or painted on silk, its construction follows certain immutable rituals. Each detail has a symbolic significance and helps the person meditating to concentrate and channel currents of feeling and mental energy into a spiritual perspective that gradually narrows until it reaches his centre, his true Self.

• The mandala is composed of a square, surrounded by a circle in three parts. The first, outer circle is the circle of flames (the mountain of fire) and is made up of five colours that form a barrier to the uninitiated; it symbolizes the elements and knowledge which must burn away ignorance and lead the meditator to a state of refined knowledge.

The second circle is the belt of diamonds or *vajra*, symbolizing supreme consciousness or *bodhi*, the state of enlightenment that, once acquired, remains unchanging, like a diamond.

The third circle is composed of lotus petals, symbolizing the state of purity that enables the harmonious development of mediation. Inside it is drawn the mandala or palace, a square divided into four triangles, each bearing a projection facing one of the cardinal points, symbolizing a door, and protected by one of the four cosmic guardians and crowned with a half-*vajra*.

The perimeter is made up of a wall in the five primary colours.

The centre of the mandala is identified with Mount Meru, the axis of the world. It is surrounded by a circle or *vajra* and resembles a lotus flower with eight petals symbolizing the divinities; the central divinity is shown in the form of a bud, the place from which flow the enlightened emanations of the Buddhas and their symbols, as rays from the void.

Mandala

The meditator must seize the mystical relationship between the elements of the earthly world and the divine world, and progressively master the parts of the mandala. When he reaches the central figure, symbolic of the Absolute, he becomes identified with divine vision, and 'regains unity of consciousness.'[12]

• Hindus endow these diagrams with life, as they do statues of their divinities before worshipping them in the Pranapratishtha ritual, which attempts to transmit energy from the adept to the inanimate object, through psychic waves.[19]

• Navajo and Pueblo Indian sand paintings replicate the mandala, and fulfil a propitiatory, therapeutic magical function. They use sand in symbolic colours that are rich in cosmic energy and supernatural forces, made from powdered stones, chalk, charcoal, ochre, etc.; at the cardinal points are mythical figures, symbols of sacred elements (sun, moon, lightning, rainbow, stars, lake, clouds, birds) surrounded by a protective rainbow.[12]

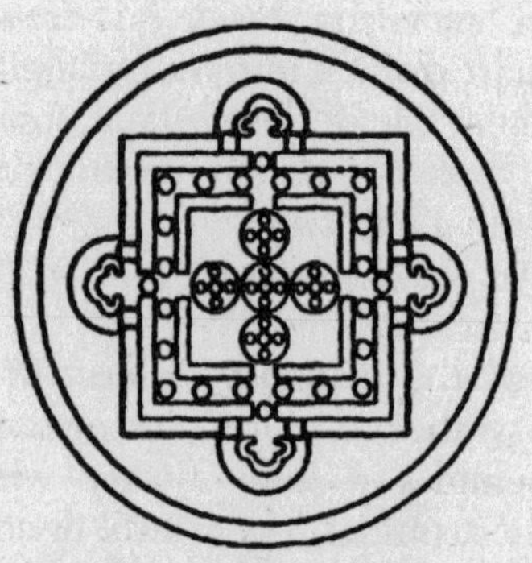

Plan of a mandala[132]

Hopi Indian initiation ceremonies used mosaics of coloured powder that have the same symbolic function: one of them represents the sun radiating feathered rays like arrows; a piece of feathered quartz is placed in the centre of the diagram to symbolize the heart of the sun.

These symbolic figures, a kind of written ritual, form the basic design of 'carpets and Islamic embroidery, and were once essential objects in magic rituals.'

• An identical principle to the mandala can be found in temple construction: at the entrance, the faithful enter into a holy place, a place of mystery. By visiting a sanctuary following the prescribed rules, or the ritual of circumambulation, he retraces the mechanism of the universe, and when he arrives at the mystic centre of the sacred building, he is transfigured and identified with primordial unity; 'the hidden principle of his own life, his own mysterious essence, the luminous point of his consciousness from which his psychic faculties radiate.'

• Adepts of certain Tantric schools have recourse to interiorized mandalas: mental visualization or identification with the mandala in his own body, through reanimating the *chakras*: 'points of intersection between cosmic life and mental life', equivalent to the initiate's penetration into the centre of the mandala.[92]

MARRIAGE
unity and duality

Marriage is a symbol of union and loving understanding between a man and a woman; it is also a reconstitution of the primordial couple before the Fall, and, through this, a reclamation of a new world of regained unity.

The Greeks symbolized it with oregano, dedicated to Hymen who lost his life on his wedding day.

• The marriage of gods symbolizes the union of divine principles, which in turn give birth to emanations: the union of Zeus-Jupiter (power) and Themis (justice) = Eirene (peace), Eunomia (discipline) and Dikte (law).[1]

• In alchemy, the philosopher's marriage is the combination of sulphur and mercury transformed into the quintessence of the elements (that is, gold); it is symbolized as a body with the two crowned heads of a man and a woman, representing the union of virile energy and female sensitivity.

It is the *Rebis* (re-bis = two things, the two bodies of *prima materia*) corresponding to the matter prepared for the definitive work (in alchemy), to the Freemason worthy of being elevated to Master, to the adept who has mastered his instinctive tendencies, overcome his animal nature, 'distanced himself from everything that prevents him from becoming a complete man.'[18]

• In traditional civilizations like India, marriage has taken the place of initiation for women, and the ceremony takes place in front of the sacred fire, the mill for grinding grain and the goblet of water, an indispensable element for the *avahana* or descent of divine essence which takes place during religious ceremonies (the forces of the universe are concentrated in the goblet).

MARS
war

Mars (Ares in ancient Greece) was originally called Mars Silvanus, god of agriculture, regulator of the seasons. He was worshipped by the Romans under the name of Mars Gravidus as god of war, father of Romulus, and under the name of Mars Quirinus, as ancestor of the Romans and protector of Rome. Among his followers were the allegorical divinities of Pallor (pallor), Pavor (fear), Virtus (courage), Honos (honour), Securitas (safety), Victoria (victory) and Pax (peace), symbolizing the god's attributes.

Mars was variously depicted as a wolf, a horse, a green woodpecker, a lance and an oak tree.

• The month of March was dedicated to him and corresponded to the passage of the sun in the constellation of Aries (governed by Mars and linked to germination and hatching). During this month, feasts were celebrated, dedicated to Mars Grandirus (*grandire* = to grow).

• In astrology, the planet Mars characterizes instinctive dynamism, willpower and courage, brutality or violence, individuality, fighting and opposition.

MASK
persona

The mask originated in fancy dress worn at Dionysian feasts. In antiquity, there were masks for tragedy and comedy before they were worn for religious or profane ceremonies: masks for dance, theatre, ceremonies and carnivals. This almost extinct tradition remains in only a few rare traditions whose initially profound meaning is long forgotten: for example the Fashings in Germany, or the giants of Flanders.

In essence Dionysian, the mask used in ancient Greek drama was a permanent fixed expression of an emotion, perhaps 'fear of the soul when faced with fate, or free gaiety of spirit tinged with a sense of the ridiculous . . . or an expression of deep distraction.' Its aim was to 'impose the feeling of fate on the audience. This was the basis of ancient tragedy.'

The expression on the comic mask is jovial and presents an 'image of an inverted world. After the distraught fear of being confronted with fate comes a gross malicious irony and between them they offer us the enigma of existence.'[138]

• Oriental masks are concerned with the superficial aspects of human nature, illusory appearance adopted by man: piebald, violently decorated faces in Hindu drama, instruments for the incarnation of gods; Chinese caricatures of human shortcomings; traditional dramatic or comic types of the Japanese No or Gogaku theatre . . . Or the distracted, infantile, or placid, comical expressions of the Incas.

All have detail: symbolic ornament, colour or motif which indicates for whom they are intended, or the circumstances in which they are to be used.

They also seem to give out a message, contain an impersonal impalpable significance, 'which leaps out like an involuntary oath . . . the revelation of instinct, of its ever-present lusts, and especially of dreams of the life beyond; this sort of frantic, diffuse immense perception of something that we cannot discern and that this eyeless face seems to see inside itself, in the depths of life.'[153]

• The message transmitted by the mask is expressed through its appearance (its shape, the addition of feathers, wings, necklaces, jewels, tattoos, etc.), the expression of its soul, and its comical expression, a visible transcription of its profound meaning.

– The god-mask is the permanent dwelling-place of a divinity or an ancestor: masks made of papier mâché or gold brocade in performances of the Hindi epic, *Ramayana*, where the heavily made-up, painted faces of the Kathakali actors combine with the expressive movements of the dancers and the choice of colours to symbolize the multiple power of demons as well as the kindness of the benevolent gods.

– The warrior's mask is invested with magic power that

assures invulnerability and confers supernatural powers; it transforms a mere mortal into a hero: a reminder of the prestige conferred by wearing a uniform even today.

– The shaman's mask is intended to frighten off evil forces.

– The funeral mask, which has links with worship of the dead, and in which the dead person is reincarnated, exerts a protective influence against evil spirits and preserves the dead person's image. Its destruction will condemn the dead person to wander eternally. Often this mask represented the deceased at the time of the funeral ceremony.

A door opening onto the Absolute, the Egyptian mask forming the outer casing of the mummy took the form of a portrait of the deceased and an ideal depiction of his 'double'. This supernatural portrait 'with its dazzling ochre and purple, silver and gold lustres, indicated his new personality.' Rigid lines gave the face a definite framework and marked a geometric limit 'which directed the face towards a fixed contemplation of eternal truths, and maintained it thus exposed for ever to the rays of the sun god and to the god of death.'[138]

• Wearing a mask is a means of identification with what it represents. In primitive civilizations, the identification is total; the mask has the same virtue as the animal skin that the sorcerer wears: whoever wears it *is* the creature whose skin or mask is being worn. 'Consequently, in ceremonies and ritual dances, actors don their masks and often also wear a costume and ornaments to complete the transformation – they become, *ipso facto*, beings whose masks are symbols and representations.'[39]

The Sioux shaman dressed in a godlike mask is totally identified with the spirit who is incarnated in it: his bearing, his voice, his gestures are modified through the magical power present in the components of the mask, which are all charged with meaning. The cosmos is shown on it through the use of colour: north – yellow; south – red; west – blue; east – white; zenith – rainbow; nadir – black.[12]

• The mask is an effective means of metamorphosis; it empowers its wearer to change his face, and, by extension, his personality. Make-up, false eyelashes and other artifices – wigs, hairstyles, face-lifts – all form a mask of the face, transforming it into a magic face that reveals a desire to please and seduce, something which is by no means just the privilege of women.

The French poet Charles Baudelaire listed many of the female masks: 'their charming appearances which go to make up feminine beauty are: the blasé look, the bored, distant, impudent, cold, inward-looking, dominating, wilful, wicked, sick, feline, childish looks, the look of nonchalance mixed with a touch of malice.'[138]

• Dressing up reveals the persona, the ideal image we wish for ourselves that we can then pass off as the Self. At the same time, it has a protective role, and its anonymity allows us to shed inhibitions and fears.

Because it can transform reality through imagination, the mask enables projection and the choice of a borrowed personality has its deepest roots in the unconscious.

'Through choosing the personality we would like to be, wearing a mask we like most, with all its aspects of evasion and freedom, we reveal hidden tendencies which would otherwise be difficult to express in normal everyday life.'[94]

MAY
vital growth

The month of May, once sacred to Apollo who personified spring in the myth of Bacchus (representing autumn), symbolizes hatching and renewal.

May 1st was symbolic of vegetative energy forcing its

way through barriers. In Rome, the festival of new leaves, when the young went out into the woods searching for spring buds, was an occasion for debauchery to celebrate the rising sap. This tradition has lingered on in France in the custom of giving lily of the valley on May Day.

• There was an old tradition that made it a day to respect authority; workers vowed fidelity to their master. French peasants also planted a tree, called the May tree, near the doors of their houses – see *Tree.*

METAL
secret energy

Metals symbolize condensed cosmic energy. Their symbolism is linked to Pluto, the underworld god of riches, hidden treasure and rare metals, as opposed to the planets which are heavenly metals.

• Alchemists distinguished seven metals, all derived from a single element and formed under the influence of the planets. Each metal was attributed with a god and a basic colour, and they were divided into 'pure or perfect metals, and impure, imperfect metals.'
Gold, incorruptible, formed by the sun, corresponded to Apollo, red, and the pure spirit from which everything that is within us emerges. 'The spiritual sun symbolizes the divine light that continually illuminates our personality, more especially the anima.'
Silver, a perfect metal, corresponds to the moon, Diana, blue, the ethereal soul, which forms our feelings and our images of the ideal.
Mercury, imperfect, corresponds to the planet Mercury, white, the etheric body, 'the knot of our personality.'
Tin, imperfect, the lightest of metals, corresponds to the planet Jupiter, Juno, purple, and the spiritual soul or

anima.

Iron, imperfect, corresponds to both the planet and god Mars, orange, and the animus 'which gives rise to vehement, sometimes ferocious impulses that stimulate motivity, the power of initiating motion.'

Copper, imperfect, corresponds to the planet and goddess Venus, green, the animus that 'aims to control the vitality protected by sensitivity.'

Lead, imperfect, corresponds to the planet and god Saturn, yellow, the material body, basis of the vital edifice 'without which no work would be done.'[18]

When Solomon's Temple was built, the use of metal tools, particularly iron ones, was forbidden, because of the impure quality of metals. It was believed by some that iron represented the first state of metallic matter which was then transformed into copper. In the perfection process, this was changed to lead, then mercury, then silver, then gold. Here we can recognize a process similar to alchemy.

• The manufacture of the first metal alloys (bronze) marked the transition from man's uncivilized era to his civilized one, from prehistory to history.

Primitive metallurgy was linked to fire worship, for fire was the only possible means of extracting metals from minerals and forging them.

Metal-working had both a military and a magical purpose at that time: the sword, which was wrought with fire and forge, and the metallic mirror, which reflected the sun's fire, are essential elements in Japanese myth.

• Heraldry uses two metals: gold or sol: 'symbol of man renewed after he has passed through the cauldron of resurrections', and silver or argent: 'expression of true simplicity, that is, when we are divested of everything that is not divine in us.'[47]

• In China, according to the law of correspondences, metal is one of the five elements linked to the west, the colour white, the lungs, hearing, the nose, cold, and sadness. It is extracted from rock with fire and produces water (since it liquefies).

• Metals were used to create pentacles, in particular lead which was sacred to the gods of the underworld through its association with Saturn–Kronos, god of hatred and vengeance. Bronze (an alloy of several metals with a copper base) was a powerful counter-charm, which on malefic nights (Lemuria) was beaten to drive away demons.[19]

MILK
abundance

In the Vedas, sacred cow's milk is the elixir of eternal life, the food, the ambrosia of the gods, linked to immortality and knowledge.

In the *Ramayana*, the Titans churned the sea of milk of eternal life in order to make ghee from which beings of concentrated power would spring: these beings were the Asparas (nymphs), Lakshmi, goddess of fortune, and thirteen gods, the last holding the moon in his hand, a cup of the nectar of life.

The ghee or nectar of immortality is the *ghrita* of sacrifice. It is a symbol of clarity which can manifest itself on three levels: the level of sensation, which, liberated can lead to beatitude; the mental level – thinking that can lead to illumination and intuition; and truth.

These levels correspond to Soma, Indra and Surya.[44]

• For Tantric Buddhists, milk signifies illumination, luminous consciousness or *bodhicitta.*

• For the Celts, Greeks and Egyptians, this symbol of life, abundance and fertility procured immortality.

MIMOSA
certainty

Mimosa symbolizes safety, and means, 'No one knows that I love you.'

MIRROR
the world's and God's reflections

Traditionally in China, a mirror was used to repel evil, 'for if evil sees itself in the mirror and observes its own ugliness, it will be seized with fear.' On a social level, the mirror symbolizes loyalty, and, on a spiritual level, it is the attribute of a wise man who 'uses his intelligence in the same way as a mirror.'[86]

• In Japan a mirror (*yata-no-kagami*) is one of three imperial treasures that are handed down, along with the throne, sword and three jewels, symbols of the three virtues of *chi* (knowledge), *yu* (bravery) and *jin* (kindness, charity).

In Shinto tradition the octuple mirror is linked to the symbolism of metal and to the cosmic period of Amaterasu, the sun goddess, who had to emerge from the cave in order to return light to the world. 'The mirror reflected the goddess and tore her from the august repose of divine non-manifestation, and is the symbol of the world, and space, in which its image is reflected.' The mirror therefore produced an act of manifestation or creation.[66]

• The mirror is linked to the number 8, which signifies wholeness, and is a symbol of divine perfection.[77]

• The mirror is a moon symbol: like the moon, it sends back an indirect image. The cult of Shiva explains *abhasas* or appearances by using the analogy of a reflection in a mirror. 'Just as a reflection in a mirror is in no way different from the mirror but appears as something different, so the *abhasas* are no different from Shiva, even though they appear different. Just as in a mirror, a village, a tree, a river appear as different from a mirror, but are not, strictly speaking, in any way different from it, so the world reflected in universal consciousness is in no way different from it.'[96]

When associated with water, a mirror becomes magical and is used for divination by the Bambara tribe in Zaïre, and in Asia. The medium sees the spirit appear in the glass of water or ice.

• In the Middle Ages, the mirror was thought to be a reflection of the divine word and the medium through which it was understood. As it says in the theological work by Vincent de Beauvais, *The Great Mirror* or *Speculum majus*, a book that was very much admired at the time: 'To speculate is to use a mirror which will reflect the divine laws and make them known to us. It means observing the stars and learning the laws of the universe. The righteous man,' according to Vincent de Beauvais, 'is a mirror of the cosmos, in whom the invisible is reflected. Through speculation, we can achieve a state of creativity.' Good works are mirrors that reflect the Light, and a mirror is a reflection of inner life.

MISTLETOE
vitality

Mistletoe which grows on oak trees, is the only plant to bear new leaves in winter, and is the king of the winter solstice (people kiss under the mistletoe).

For the Celts, it was symbolic of the creative principle

and could only be cut with a golden sickle, gold being symbolic of the sun.[107]

The druids solemnly performed this harvest on the sixth day of the moon after the winter solstice, a magic ritual intended to take the water from the oak, that is to say, its vitality and strength, which it had hidden during the summer, and protected for its leaves.

When the branches of mistletoe were collected, they were not allowed to touch the ground. A white sheet was spread out to catch them and thus preserve its magic power. Its distribution was equally solemn and was followed by the sacrifice of two young white bulls, then the druid would cry out: 'O ghel an heu', which meant 'May the corn grow.'

• Mistletoe only grows on oak trees, which symbolize long life, knowledge and strength. Mistletoe became a phallic symbol of vigour and regeneration 'probably because of the spermatic viscosity of its fruit, the sperm being the life-bearer.'[107]

• Because of its berries' round translucid appearance, mistletoe was associated with night and the moon (reinforcing the idea of fertility).

MITHRAS
protector

Mithras (meaning 'friend' in Parsee) is a great Persian god, the creator, born on 25 December, the day which celebrated the birth of the sun, after the winter solstice.

He is the god of created light, truth, good faith and justice, invoked as a guarantee for the given word and contracts; he is the clear-sighted judge of human behaviour. As a personification of light, Mithras was revered as the mediator between two opposite worlds (the luminous world above and the shadowy world below), between man and supreme divinity.

His worship was based on the doctrine of resurrection symbolizing psychic and physical regeneration through the power of blood and divine energy from the sun. His followers worshipped purity and truth. Rituals took place in caves around a permanently lighted lamp, and consisted of sacraments (which involved a baptism through blood, a baptism in pure water, sprinkling of lustral water, anointing with honey, a distribution of sacred bread and wine), seven grades of initiation, with ordeals reminiscent of those in Freemasonry, and seven classes of priest. Members of Mithraic communities were known as 'brothers' and called their chief 'father'.

MONKEY, BABOON

cleverness, cunning

The monkey was a symbol of time. For man, it was the first clock. The Egyptians discovered twenty-five centuries ago that monkeys urinated with an astronomical regularity twenty-four times a day. The baboon was worshipped in Egypt under the name of *Bais* and was patron of the arts and music.[121]

• A large white baboon was the incarnation of the god Thoth (Hermes and Mercury) and was a symbol of knowledge and wisdom. It was patron of learned men, a divine scribe who wrote down the words of Ptah, God the creator, and Anubis' verdict at the time of weighing souls.

• In India the monkey was a symbol of the soul. The monkey-god Hanuman was venerated there. He was known for his knowledge, agility, speed, physical strength and fidelity to Rama, whom he protected in his flight from the giants, a symbol of the painful labours of regeneration.[32]

• In heraldic art, the chained monkey symbolizes 'the artificial world of mental excitement' that the knight must control in order to give place to intelligence.[47]

The chained monkey

• The monkey (*hou*) was once worshipped as the ancestor of all Tibetans and was the ninth sign in the Chinese zodiac, associated with summer and metal; it symbolized ingenuity, optimism, diplomacy, perseverance and a taste for speculation.

Years of the Monkey are exciting and amusing periods of progress, and favourable to impossible enterprises and improvisations.[118]

• The monkey (*ozomatli*) is patron of a day in the Aztec divinatory calendar, and associated with the god of games. It symbolizes gaiety, humour, *joie de vivre*, good sense and insolence.[125]

The Maya, on the other hand, considered it as a symbol of harsh feelings, barbarity and vices (laziness), characteristics belonging to the third age in the Mayan cosmogony.[76]

MOON
femininity, collective unconscious

Through its power over the sea, the moon was seen by Indians as ruler of the nutritive element. 'Its gentle rays accompanied by cool night breezes and gentle morning dew have made it appear to the inhabitants of those hot countries as a conciliator and restorer of the earth.'[83]

Sunlight, moonlight and fire were considered to be one unique entity emanating from the supreme being; supremacy was given to the sun.

• Egyptian priests chose the moon as a symbol of faith which reflected unveiled truths, because it was 'lit up by the sun and received its vital force from it.'[9]

• The moon was also regarded as the mother of the world impregnated with the sun's fertile principles, which she sowed in the air. People attributed passive and active generating powers to it, the same in essence though different in form.

• The waxing of the moon in the first fourteen days of each lunar month was associated by analogy with the growth of living things; from this came the custom of sowing and cutting trees during this period and harvesting during the moon's waning period. Its influence was extended to human enterprises, which were considered more likely to have favourable outcomes during the waxing of the moon than during its waning.

• Since dew is much more copious on clear nights, agricultural societies deduced that moisture came from the moon; this became the cold and wet principle that produced rain, which explains why in hot dry regions the worship of the moon supplanted sun worship. This occurred in America and in Egypt in Ur, an oasis on the edge of the desert where an abundance of water was felt to be a benediction. From this stemmed the duality of moon/sun; wet power emanating from the moon, as opposed to dry power from the sun.

• Because of its change in size and the speed of its trajectory, the moon is the symbol of fertility. The worship of *Mater Magna* (the earth mother) in Egypt and Chaldaea came as a result of drawing parallels between the moist fertile earth and the human womb, and it found its expression in the growing moon and the principle of moisture.

It is easy to understand the affinities existing between the moon and the goddesses of these countries, who were sources and symbols of life and protectresses of plant life, and who, like the moon, were born and faded away.

In fact moon gods and goddesses are legion in agrarian societies. There is Sin, father of the sun god Shamash, master of the plant kingdom; the Aztec Quetzelcoatl, son of the sun who, as he drew close to the sun, sacrificed himself like the Son of God in order to save mankind; In India, Chandra, who valued the intoxication of the *soma* ritual and possessed twenty-eight wives, symbolic of the house traversed by the moon each month, and the terrifying Kali, avid for blood; the Egyptian goddess Isis, symbolic of femaleness in Nature, wearing a disk on her head and cow's horns (signifying power and fertility); Astarte the Phoenician; Ishtar the Babylonian . . . Or the goddesses of Greece and Rome; Silene symbolizing the polarities of day and night, Nature–mind, male will and female passivity; Hera, the full moon, symbol of maternity and female dignity in marriage; Diana–Artemis, symbol of the 'strong impulses of the mind, uncontrolled by reason', whose attribute is an ideogram in the form of a sickle, the growing moon, transferred to the Virgin Mary by Christian artists (the Madonna and Child standing on the horns of the moon and crushing the head of a snake).

• The waxing moon features on numerous Egyptian and

Babylonian monuments and documents; the divine barque was in the shape of a crescent moon (like Noah's Ark and the ship of the Argonauts).[89] The Church is compared to the moon: it watches over children like a mother, storing and transmitting light.[89]

• The main lunar symbols are: the rabbit or hare in a receptacle full of water (Pre-Columbian, Chinese, Hindu), 'The snail and the tortoise because they withdraw into their house for several days, the frog for it was believed to have fallen with the dew, and horned animals – bulls and cows made sacred as lunar divinities.'[89]

• The moon is sometimes referred to as a symbol of renewal because of its periodic reappearance; and as a symbol of dependence and indirect knowledge because it reflects light received from the sun.

Its weak light forms an intermediary between sunlight and darkness, between the conscious mind and the nocturnal unconscious.

• The moon is the incarnation of the anima, the female, maternal passive principle, the shadow (in Jungian psychology) and the unconscious, the mistakes committed before reaching the light of the conscious, symbolized by the sun.

In astrology, it is the symbol of the soul, and its position in the horoscope reveals the way a subject reacts, his receptivity and capacity for reflection and adaptation to the exigencies of daily life. The thin sliver of a crescent moon through which it is depicted symbolizes the old moon detaching itself from the embraces of the sun; so that it can be transformed into the new moon, charged with energy.

These phases correspond to the periods of development in a woman.

The new moon is a symbol of infancy, the crescent moon of youth, adolescence, of universal indiscriminate receptivity which attracts everything towards it, childish impulses, attachment to the mother, traditions; it corresponds to the extravert type.

The full moon corresponds to maturity, pregnancy, childbirth.

The waning moon, the left hemisphere of the shining star, symbolizes the decline of life and represents the introvert, directed towards an inner life, sleep, presentiment, fantasy, the collective unconscious, in which is found the seething mass of human archetypes.

It is this last phase of the waning moon in the lunar cycle that alchemists called the balsamic moon, because at the end of the life cycle, man's spiritual experience rises, like sacrificial incense (balsam) towards the kingdom of the spirit.[89]

As for the black moon (the period of three to four days when the moon is invisible), this symbolizes the inaccessible, personified by Lilith and Hecate, goddesses of night, acting insidiously in the depths of the unconscious, and symbolizes the powerful psychic forces that escape beyond the conscious's control.

• In antiquity, lunar astrology was symbolized by Osiris who ruled for twenty-eight years, and 'whose body was torn into fourteen pieces (the number of houses through which the waxing or waning moon passes) before being dismembered by Typhon at the time of the full moon (image of the moon losing a piece of itself every day for fourteen days which constitutes the second half of the lunar month).[91]

• The moon is an essential pivot of eastern astrology which distinguishes twenty-eight lunar houses, known in China as *sieu* (places to spend the night). These constellations crossed by the moon during the twenty-eight days of its cycle correspond to ancient feudal states and are associated with an animal.

• Hindu astrologers localized the solar–lunar zodiac in the human body. They thought that during life in the womb the individual developed around two centres of force or *chakras*: the *Pingala* – the cardiac twelve-petalled lotus, a microcosmic transposition of the solar zodiac, and the *Ina*, human locations of the lunar zodiac with its twenty-eight houses or *nakchtras*. And so *Pingala* and *Ina*, centres of the forces of development of the human foetus, symbolized the microcosm.[91]

The following list shows the significance of the lunar houses in the West:

1st house (Aries) = our enemy's ruin
2nd house (Aries) = reconciliation, short illness
3rd house (Aries) = prosperity, good luck
4th house (Taurus) = enmity, vengeance, deception
5th house (Taurus) = favours from important people
6th house (Gemini) = love affairs and good marriage
7th house (Gemini) = good for acquisitions
8th house (Cancer) = victory in battle
9th house (Cancer) = fatal illness
10th house (Leo) = riches
11th house (Leo = fear of death
12th house (Leo) = deprived of admiration
13th house (Virgo) = peace and marriage
14th house (Virgo) = divorce
15th house (Libra) = acquisition of friends
16th house (Libra) = money-making in commerce
17th house (Scorpio) = theft, robbery
18th house (Scorpio) = illnesses, death
19th house (Scorpio) = cure
20th house (Sagittarius) = hunts
21st house (Sagittarius) = calamity and affliction
22nd house (Capricorn) = flight and banishment
23rd house (Capricorn) = destruction and ruin
24th house (Capricorn) = mass fertility
25th house (Aquarius) = affluence and prosperity
26th house (Aquarius) = desire doubtfully accomplished
27th house (Pisces) = illnesses and death
28th house (Pisces) = pain then death [91]

THE MOON IN THE TAROT
chimaeras

The eighteenth arcana of the tarot shows the moon exuding inverted dewdrops (symbolizing a tendency to take without giving in return) on to parched yellow ground (materiality), between two towers (warning the reader to be on his guard against bad behaviour that may endanger mental balance or physical health), above a lake with a crayfish (emblematic of Cancer and symbolizing the past, concealment, complexes, immobility, but also regeneration).

There are two dogs (attributes of Diana, the moon goddess, the huntress, and Hecate, goddess of the underworld), and they are barking (signifying desolation).

This arcana symbolizes *maya* (which in Hindu Vedanta thought means the magical power of creating illusion or deceit), which can lead man to his doom. The arcana urges us to lead a rational life, and not abandon ourselves to fantasy and credulity.

Divinatory meaning: extravagant fantasies, crazes, fads, indiscreet inquisitiveness, intellectual passivity, pitfalls, flattery.

MOTHER
childhood, security

A mother is a bearer of life; like the primal waters, she is the matrix, the womb in which the living world was conceived. She appears under many guises in every tradition, from virgin mother to wicked stepmother.

Myths use the idea of the universal mother to confer the female characteristics of nurse and protectress, encountered in early life, on to the cosmos.

Five thousand years ago a considerable part of the civilized world worshipped innumerable mother-goddesses. They were almost all agrarian goddesses, fertility symbols: the Celts and Gauls venerated them as symbols of Nature and Mother Earth, the creative force of all living things. They were shown holding baskets of fruit and cornucopia as emblems of earthly prosperity; they were depicted as mothers of mankind with a child in swaddling clothes on their lap. 'People placed themselves under their motherly protection, and the goddesses watched over the community or region. When the people, and especially their children, fell sick, they quite naturally asked these mother-goddesses for a cure.'[95]

• In Hinduism, the cosmic mother was incarnated in Kali, the maternal archetype, who had two different sides to her character: one was terrifying, the other kindly. Kali depicted cosmic power, 'the totality of the universe, through the perfect alliance of terror and absolute destruction, and impersonal, though maternal, powers of consolation. She created, protected and destroyed.'[66]

• The mother symbolizes life and also death: birth from the womb; death – return to the earth-mother.

• In Shiva worship, Uma/Shakti (the personification of divine power and energy conceived as a woman) is the goddess of cereals, symbol of 'the way Nature creates and maintains life,' but under the wild guise of Kali she is also the destroyer; she is the 'great ambivalent mother'.[50]

• A mother suckling a baby generally symbolizes divine maternity. This virgin mother is encountered in numerous myths; she is the divine mother, a symbol of love.

• According to Jung, the maternal archetype symbolizes origin, nature, passive creation, and, consequently, material nature, the womb, the body, and instinctive, impulsive, physiological aspects.

Mother

The mother is an incarnation of the vegetative role, the unconscious, the home of consciousness, but also nocturnal darkness full of anguish, the Chinese yin.[28]

In her guise of nursing mother, she is the symbol of satiation, security, tenderness and love, of warmth and understanding. She is the protection and refuge we long for in the storms of life.

She is the child's first love object, and also its first ideal. This double unity, symbolized in the Madonna and Child, is later retained as the unconscious basis of every image of happiness, truth, beauty and perfection.[66]

In the female psyche, a maternal image is linked to the unconscious, and a prolonged attachment to the mother is the basis for the Oedipus complex: love and a desire to regain the paradise that has been lost, opposed to the death instinct (aroused by an unconscious hatred of the father).

According to Aeppli, frequent appearances of a mother in our dreams betrays a lack of autonomy in the way we manage our lives.

In men's dreams, negative aspects of the mother archetype are condensed into images of 'witches, horses (the physical, animal side), water, moon, dragon, whale, any animal that embraces, tombs, deep water, nightmares and childish fear of females.'[24, 25]

All these feature the 'devouring mother' with her excessive authority, and include the aggression naturally reserved for wicked or absent mothers. These monsters clearly indicate to the dreamer a need to free himself from the all-powerful presence of his mother in order to become a man.

In the female psyche, the mother symbolizes her conscious life, her youth and the carefree happy life of childhood.

Maternal images are, according to Jung, the grandmother, nurse, governess, goddess, Virgin Mary. And, in a wider sense, with deliverance as their purpose, the church, university, town, country, sky, earth, forest, sea, and stagnant water; matter, the underworld. In a more restricted sense as a place of procreation and birth: field, garden, rock, grotto, tree, spring. In an even more limited sense of womb: any hollow place, oven, saucepan. On the animal level, a cow and any domestic animal.[24]

MOUNTAIN
axis of the world

Every country has a sacred mountain in answer to a need for providential protection: there is the Potala in Tibet, the Hindu Mount Meru, the Celts' White Mountain, the Jews' Mount Tabor, the Moslems' Qaf, the Chinese K'uen-luen, the Christians' Golgotha (summit of the cosmic mountain and Adam's tomb).

• In flat countries the mountain had a substitute, such as a cairn (a heap of stones sheltering Celtic tombs in Gaul and Great Britain), a tumulus, a pyramid, a monument (the Buddhist stupa, the Islamic Kuba, an Arab building made up of a cubic base and covered by a dome built over the tomb of a venerated person), the Omphalos at Delphos, a menhir (erect stone), or baetyl (a sacred meteoric stone). The belfry or clocktower in a village is a modern equivalent of the cosmic mountain. Temples and towns were assimilated into the cosmic mountain: the Temple of Barabudur built in the form of a mountain, the Babylonian ziggurat (see *Ziggurat*), the Buddhist nine-storied pagoda in China.

• The summit of the cosmic mountain is also the starting point of creation, the navel of the world in which the first man was created. 'Paradise where Adam was created from mud was, of course, the centre of the cosmos, and, according to Syrian tradition, was on a mountain that was higher than any other, and where he was also buried, that is to say, on Golgotha, where the blood of the Saviour would redeem him.'[97] Generally the mountain forms a real link between heaven and the underworld.

• The mountain is simultaneously the centre and axis of the universe and as such is thought to contain divine inspiration. Its summit is the centre of the world, the junction between heaven and earth. As the pilgrim climbs it, he grows closer to the centre of the world, and as he reaches higher ground he enters a new level, transcending profane, heterogeneous space, and entering a pure land.[21] And so the mountain is a symbol of transcendency, the culminating point of ascension and spiritual elevation.

It is on a mountain summit that the prophet enters into communication with divinity (Moses received the Ten Commandments on Mount Sinai).

• In ancient China, mountains 'guaranteed the solid permanence of the universe' and symbolized immutability (a mountain landslide is an infallible sign of the end of a dynasty, the presence and proximity of the gods).

Worship of the five mountains situated between the five cardinal points was practised. The five mountains were dominated by a Taoist temple, refuge of the immortals, who thus found themselves nearer to heaven, and it was from here that they flew to the isles of paradise. It was on these mountains that 'the ten thousand things [an infinite number] have their origin and yin and yang alternated.'

• Mountains cause clouds and rain: in the iconography, a mountain encircled by clouds symbolizes the earth.[7]

• In dreams a high mountain symbolizes danger or a perilous situation. Climbing a mountain depicts inner elevation.

MOUTH
the word

In ancient Egypt, the mouth symbolized a door and also the idea of a part, portion and chapter.[9]

• The mouth, tongue and larynx were 'organs of the magic Word (that is, language), the perfected instrument bequeathed by Thoth (the lunar god) as the supreme weapon of the dead.' Opening the mouth with an iron instrument called the sacred crook was a highly efficacious magical ceremony, for it communicated the power of language to the dead'[10] in the life beyond, so that the dead man could justify his actions.

This resurrection ritual is a theme that has been used in medieval sculpture to symbolize the initiated, 'the man reborn who acquires the gift of speech; the Word becomes capable of transmitting the experience lived beyond words.'[80]

• The mouth is also the organ for breathing and symbolizes 'a high degree of consciousness, an ability to organize through the use of reason.'[1]

• But, as an organ of communication and transmission, it is also an aid to the aggressive instinct, through which man can inflict verbal wounds, and make others suffer.

MUD
inertia, potential

As a mixture of earth and dynamic life-giving water, mud was, according to the Scriptures, the raw material from which God created man and the animal kingdom.

• Mud, the very source of life itself, must therefore hold the secret of creation and, by extension, it symbolizes the very beginning of evolution, or a cycle, or a world of possibilities.

• In a negative sense, it symbolizes decomposition and degradation, and is associated with the baser instincts, the lower levels of human nature.

MYSTERY
secret of the gods

Mysteries (doctrines of faith involving difficulties which human reason is incapable of solving) are widespread all around the eastern Mediterranean (there are the mysteries of the Cabiri in Samothrace, of Zeus in Crete, of Demeter, Hecate, Proserpine and Ceres at Eleusis, Attis and Adonis in Asia Minor and Syria, Dionysos in Greece and Osiris and the cult of Isis in Egypt). They all have the same fundamental rituals: purifications through fire and water (Baptism, mystical immersion), a supper, prophetic utterances and esoteric teachings presented in dramatic form, frightening or reassuring symbolic dramas, journeys to hell or a cave, return to the light and resurrection. It is the immolation of a god which saves the world, the passion of Osiris, his death and resurrection, images such as wheat (see *Death*), 'which are metaphors of the resurrection and immortality of the human soul.' Such mysteries were made known only to those who had undergone initiation.

The growth of a new plant after sowing seed symbolized a prelude, and was an analogy of the human soul's resurrection and immortality.[89] The early beginnings of Christian doctrine were inspired by these rituals.

NAME
identity

The names of God have an important role in every religion (see *Letters*).

The Chaldaeans gave a divine name, Schem, to properties that were so special that they came to be worshipped. In Jewish magic, everyone's name becomes part of their essence: uttering a name is enough to ensnare the person whose name it is. To name someone is to make them come; to make them come is to make them obey.

This belief is common in most ancient civilizations that consider someone's name part of his personality. In initiation rites, the initiate is given different names at each stage of the ceremony.

The name is also often kept secret, because to reveal it would be to give others a certain power over oneself.

In rabbinical Judaism there is a belief in the absolute power of the secret name of God. The name of Yahweh (Jehovah) could only be uttered in the temple on certain occasions, and so equivalents were substituted: the Almighty, the Eternal One, the Holy One, as well as tetragrams signifying Adonai, Ehieh, Ha-Schem (the name).[19]

This tradition also existed among the early fathers of the Christian Church, who specified that 'names are not given to things for pure convenience, as Aristotle believed, but . . . are a deep and mysterious link with the things themselves. Just as there are potent names, like the ones used by the sages of Egypt, the magi of Persia, the pontiffs of Asia, magic names must be used cautiously and with prudence.'[19]

• The science of names originated among learned Jews. The most secret name, the tetragram YHWH expressed the essence of God and was associated with the twelve tribes of Israel, the twelve months of the years and the twelve signs of the zodiac.

• Other names were invested with a particular power: names formed by the first three sephiroth (a Hebrew word used in the Cabbalah for the vessels through which the light of God is emanated down to man) that priests murmured as they blessed the people; a name of forty-two letters, the holiest of mysteries, was taught to initiates and contained the names of the ten sephiroth; and there was a name of seventy-two letters, beginning with *Ain Soph* (meaning the infinite state) and ending with the word *Kadosh* (meaning holy) repeated three times.

• It was the same for Moslems: the written name of Allah is a symbol of the universal being and unites the essential principle (the point) and the substantial principle (the circumference), whose coexistence 'achieves the union of complementaries . . . The name of Allah is the complete symbol of Being, it includes the active and passive principles, the essence and the substance . . . it is peace and contemplation; it is inscribed in the eternal present',[85] and can be used as an aid to meditation.

• In China, children are given a nickname at birth (for example, Little Lion). The official symbolic name, corresponding to the personality or expressing a wish on the part of the father for the child's future, is known only to those close to the family, and will be given the child only when he reaches the age of about ten. Chinese names therefore reveal the personality of their owner.[7]

• To hear oneself called by one's name in a dream is an invitation to see oneself as one really is. To change one's name corresponds to psychic transformation. To forget one's name is to lose one's individuality.[25]

NARCISSUS

self-love

In Asia, the narcissus is a symbol of happiness, the incarnation of the god Narcissus who was remarkably beautiful but whose indifference drove nymphs to despair: he became a symbol of frigidity.

According to G. Bachelard, Narcissus' contemplation of himself in the mirror of water is 'sublimation for the sake of an idea, fatally linked to hope.'[46] This is why the goddess of the underworld wears a crown of narcissi; in the kingdom of the dead, sublimation of the ego occurs in those who were unable to free themselves on earth.[114]

• In China, the narcissus (*shui-xian*) or everlasting water flower symbolizes the couple (like the orchid) and, if it flowers in time, happiness for the New Year.

• In the language of flowers, it symbolizes transient lovers; it corresponds to white, and means, 'You have no heart.'

NEPTUNE
fertility and tumult

Neptune–Poseidon is the god of earthquakes and the sea. He has the power to stir up and calm storms by shouting or striking the waves with his trident, a symbol of water's active manifestation, the equivalent of lightning from heaven. (In India, lightning is depicted with three prongs representing the past, present and future and the three levels of universal manifestation; it has become known as Buddhism's triple jewel).

Neptune was often seen as an agrarian god because he helped to fertilize the fields by distributing rain.

• In astrology, Neptune is a planet which influences the group rather than the individual and incarnates plasticity. It acts on the imagination, intuition, the power of the medium or in psychic disturbances.

It governs the subconscious, and, according to G. Holley, is the 'symbol of unity, towards which every being consciously strives, with whatever faculties he possesses depending on the stage of development he has reached.'[14] At birth, it exerts a magnetic fascination, inciting the subject to excel himself, but also predisposes him to illusions, idealism, unrealistic ideas.

J. Gerson-Lacroix describes the Neptune type as a person who is practical, ponderous, methodical, persevering, endowed with insatiable curiosity, clever at exploiting circumstances, sometimes having unlimited greed and a plethora of plans.

He will be a speculator or pioneer with a taste for mystification, who often deliberately adopts an air of mystery. Equally frequently the Neptune type will have a taste for travel, will be a studious youth and will have unhoped-for material success 'in spite of a difficult or mediocre beginning, and a very full love life.'[100]

NIGHT
ignorance, potential

Night is the oldest allegorical divinity in Greek mythology, she is the daughter of Chaos who coupled with Erebus to give birth to Ether and Day. She also gave birth to abstractions, some of which were unfavourable to humans: these were Discord, Cunning, Lamentation, Old Age, Vengeance and Death, Fraud, etc.; others were beneficial, such as Dreams and Sleep.

• The night-time was once associated with the goddess, and a religious cult was devoted to her, especially among the Orphic fraternities, who performed rituals by night because of the inherent holiness they attributed to it, for it 'had the blessing of the gods.' They immolated animals with dark colours: black sheep, cockerels, owls.

• Night was a symbol of pregnancy and germination of every possible kind; it was the 'spring of everything'. It fed the lights in the sky and produce from the ground, by 'the productive power that it truly possesses,' for it was thought that plants and animals grew more during the night than in daytime.[83]

Ancient civilizations counted in nights because lunar months and phases were observed by night: in the Rig-Veda, *kshapâ* (night) is often synonymous with day (*râtri*); Sanskrit uses the word *dacharatrâ*, which means ten nights, for ten days. And numerous cosmologies and mythologies see the darkness of night as the origin of things, before the appearance of light. Also, for certain peoples night marks the beginning of the day (the Moslems' official day begins at sunset).

• The symbolism of night is coupled with darkness and black, with ignorance, the unconscious and unconsciousness and all their possibilities.

NINE
hierarchy

Nine is an uneven, male, active number, and the first squared uneven number. The ancients thought that the earth plus the seven planets plus the sphere of fixed stars, made nine concentric spheres.

• Nine is the number of hierarchy: Hesiod listed nine muses. This spiritual hierarchy also appears in the nine choirs of angels (corresponding to the Gnostics' nine heavenly spheres).

• Nine is the number of harmony, and symbolizes the perfection of ideas. It is the Virgin Mary's number and expresses absolute divine perfection.

• Nine as a number represents a crowd and, according to Parmenides, was associated with absolute entities, and was the symbol of the totality of being.

In this respect, Orphism defines nine symbolic aspects of the universe, divided into three triads: (1) night, heaven, time; (2) the ether, light, the stars; (3) the sun, moon and Nature.

• In China the number 9 (*jiu*) is a yang number and corresponds to bitter flavour, autumn, and metal. It is associated with the cosmology. The Chinese world was divided into nine regions of symbolic space, depicted as nine planes and 9,999 corners. The tree-axis of the world had nine roots, which plunged into nine springs, resting places of the dead; its branches stretched out towards nine heavens.

• The Aztecs thought there were nine underworlds.[73]

• In astrology, the ninth house is that of philosophical or religious thought, of abstract, spiritual flights into the upper regions.

• The Hermit is the ninth major arcana in the tarot and symbolizes initiation and the synthesis of potentialities.[17]

NIRVANA
perfect peace

In Buddhism, nirvana is the supreme goal, Buddha's promised reward for the faithful, the state of 'perfect beatitude awaited after death, the state of divine union, permanent ecstasy'.[5]

It is symbolized in the sudden appearance of the moon in the night sky, and corresponds to *sahasrara* in Tantric yoga, whose 'thousand petals surround the centre of enlightenment,' which 'encloses the existential void, whose rays are the nectar of immortality.'[102]

The state of nirvana is the final stage of spiritual ascension, the deliverance from karma (the endless chain of reincarnations). 'When the Bodhisattva gains enlightenment, becomes a Buddha and enters into nirvana, he is *nivta*. The presence of the psyche is eliminated for ever, the Bodhisattva is on another plane, the plane of the unconditional, which transcends *avidya* (ignorance, complacent abandonment to life), *maya* (the mind's power to create illusions in the subconscious, in contrast to enlightened consciousness) and karma (death and rebirth).'[11]

NOSE
sexual vitality

In ancient China, the nose (*bi ze*) was the orifice corresponding to the lungs. The line between nose and mouth, or the body's centre, symbolized the joys of sex.

A short nose is a sign of sexual vivacity, and, in Turkey, 'to bite off someone's nose' signifies jealousy.[7]

• While in the West this protuberance is considered a symbol of lucidity or discernment, it is, more than anything, a phallic symbol, which through its sense of smell is associated with sensuality and the sexual organs.

It commonly symbolizes the male organ, and their respective lengths are often thought to be in ratio. 'It is sometimes instructive to observe individual behaviour, focusing on the nose. Blowing the nose briskly, sniffing endlessly, examining the contents of one's handkerchief in public betray a naïve sexual vanity in the male. The man is proud of his organ and shamelessly flaunts its symbolic manifestations.'[101]

NUDITY
inferiority or truth

In Christian tradition, nakedness is the symbol of original sin, the Fall, and, in the Bible, it signifies humiliation and spiritual poverty. For Gnostics, its symbolized the ideal we strive for.

• Nakedness forms part of some initiation rites: 'to be divested of clothes and false ideas,' the initiate 'dies like an old man, to be born anew.'[80]

In ancient China, nudity was part of the magic ritual of rain-making. 'A magical way of producing rain was to draw up two battle lines, with men on one side and women on the other, both with no clothes on, and then fling themselves against each other.'[7]

• Nakedness in dreams reveals inhibitions that the dreamer is suffering from, which are obstructing his development. It is usually a question of shame, inferiority, or lack of adaptation to an environment.

NUMBER

cosmic harmony

All societies have attached great importance to numbers, their properties and significance. For Pythagoras 'everything' was 'a number' and the number was divine; it was 'the force that maintains the eternal permanence of the cosmos.' Since law and order and music had numbers, it followed that everything in the world was regulated, ordered and musical.

• Followers of Pythagoras saw numbers as points, so that they could prove at a glance that 'the sum of unequal numbers is equal to the square of the middle number':

$$1 + 3 = 2^2 \qquad 1 + 3 + 5 = 3^2 \qquad 1 + 3 + 5 + 7 = 4^2$$

• Every number therefore possesses an individuality, a personality that expresses the relationship of the part to the whole, to the inner harmony, of the individual to being, of the multiple to One and All.

And numbers have substance, matter and the element of movement that human beings and the natural world have; they are 'the source and root of everything.'[29]

Each number has its own shape (3 has a triangle, 4, a square, 5, a pentagon, 6, a hexagon, etc.) and possesses its own meaning, a derived meaning and an allegorical meaning. The cardinal numbers indicate quantity, and the ordinal numbers quality.

• Numbers are links between the macrocosm and the human microcosm, and are attributed with a potency related to the forces of the universe, from which man can extract magic power and exploit those forces to his profit.

• Alchemists and Cabbalists also believed in the power of numbers and their occult influence. The doctrine of the Cabbalah relies on the symbolism of numbers, geometrical figures and the Hebrew alphabet. Through this system that is based on combinations of these factors, 'one can glimpse fundamental laws and predict truths that would otherwise be impossible to see.' (See under *Sephiroth*, *One*, *Two*, *Three*, *Four*, *Five*, *Six*, *Seven*, *Eight*, *Nine*, *Ten*, *Zero*).

In the sephirotic tree of life, there are five primary numbers that can be divided only by themselves and by one, the unity of which they are manifestations. Each represents a force which derives from the primal force. (They correspond to the five primordial currents of Prâna in Hinduism.) These numbers are also used in onomancy (divination from the letters of a name). This is based on the name of a person, the numerical equivalents of the letters in the name, and the combination of letters and therefore of their equivalent numbers.

• Thirty-six is the number of the Great Tetraktis of the Pythagoreans, and is obtained by adding the sum of the first four unequal numbers ($1 + 3 + 5 + 7 = 16$) and the sum of the first four equal numbers ($2 + 4 + 6 + 8 = 20$), making $20 + 16 = 36$, which is also the sum of the cubes of the first three numbers:

$$1(1 \times 1 \times 1) + 8(2 \times 2 \times 2) + 27(3 \times 3 \times 3) = 36$$

• The golden number or divine proportion is an essential feature of architectural harmony. It is 'that mysterious number in which mathematical logic, divine logos, the creator of the cosmos and the innate sense of beauty in man come together in a revelation.'[22]

It is related to the number 5 and features the invariable connection between the side of the pentagon and its large segment, or between the diagonal and the side of a regular pentagon, which is always equivalent to the large segment. Its value, is 1·618 and its mathematical formula is:

$$\frac{1 + \sqrt{5}}{2} = 1{\cdot}618$$

The aesthetic values of beauty of the human face in ancient Greece were based on this golden number, as were a great many of the temples that were built, such as the Parthenon, as well as Strasbourg Cathedral, and the pyramid of Cheops. The laws of music and metaphysics were also based on it.

• In ancient China, numbers were used to work out the arrangement of the world. Numerology, based on the belief in the two antagonistic yet complementary forces of yin and yang, on the trinity of sky–earth–man, the square, the five elements and the eight trigrams, regulated occult speculations.

• The systems based on numbers are:
Astrology, founded on the system of the 'ten divisions of the heavens,' and the 'twelve branches of earth' which examine the 'order of the twenty-eight constellations, the movements of the five planets, the sun and moon in such a way as to consign good or bad-omened scenarios.' The emperor used this as a basis for his rule.

Astrologers saw four groups of seven constellations, that is to say, twenty-eight asterisms; seventy-two malevolent terrestrial stars and thirty-six benign heavenly stars used in the making of pentacles. They added up to the sacred number of 108, that can be found all over Asia: there are 108 beads in the Buddhist or Shaiva rosary, the Chinese rosary of Tantric or Buddhist origin has 1,080, 108, 54 or 24 beads; 108 lamps in 12 rows, with wicks in the colours of the five elements.[19]

The calendar. 'This establishes the order of the four seasons, adjusts periods of equinox and solstice, notes the concordance of periods of the sun, moon and the five planets, and forecasts periods of cold and heat, death and birth. This is why the Supreme Sovereign must keep the numbers of the calendar in good order, in the same way that he keeps his ceremonial dress and colours according to the system of the Three Rules.'

The popular calendar, which is always printed, is an almanac that gives useful information for everyday life: favourable days for cutting wood, repairing houses, cutting hair, marriage, setting out on journeys, etc. It has chapters on medicine, the interpretation of dreams and forecasts.

The five elements. These are the material essences of the five permanent virtues.

Different methods are: divining stalks and the tortoise, the interpretation of dreams, the method of forms, which takes into account the number of men and of the six domestic animals.

The I Ching or Book of Changes, which, in conjunction with divining stalks, is used for divination, and also has a chapter on numbers, which sets out the emblematic figures: uneven ones for heaven, 1, 3, 5, 7, 9, which add up to 25; and even numbers for earth, 2, 4, 6, 8, 10, which add up to 30.

It also demonstrates that divinatory numbers are capable of summoning up the universe, the total number of which exceeds 10,000. This number was obtained by studying the 64 hexagrams: 64 hexagrams of six lines make a total of 384 lines, that is, 192 lines of uneven numbers (for strong undivided lines) and 192 lines of even numbers (for weak divided lines). The even numbers or yin are equal to two rows of uneven numbers. The compilers of the I-Ching had decided that there were 24 hexagrams of 192 even numbered lines, giving a total of 4,608 female essences. They did not multiply the lines that had uneven numbers by the remaining 40 hexagrams (64 – 20), but by 36, so obtaining the sum of 6,912 male essences, which, added to the female essences, gave a total of 11,250, a number that exceeds 10,000, evoking the number of all things.[69]

• The symbolism of numbers is a vast field, by virtue of the law of correspondences.

It forms the basis of Chinese music, which was considered a means of communicating with the spiritual hierarchies, and, combined with ritual, puts man in touch with the invisible.[69]

The five rudimentary notes (corresponding to doh, ray, me, soh, lah), when combined with numbers, correspond to the five planets and five colours, the four seasons and the centre, and can be placed in a square which reproduces the arrangement of the Chinese cosmos. These notes were used by diviners who practised the compass-card method.[65] Later on, the Chinese adopted twelve notes (seven tones and five semi-tones), corresponding to the twelve months of the year and the signs of the zodiac.

The symbolism of numbers regulated ceremonial at court: each dynasty had its own number, and, with each change of dynasty, the colours of court dress were changed, along with the range of the pieces of court music.

• Favourable numbers are: 6, which is linked to long life; 2, a symbol of ease; 3, associated with childbirth; 8, with prosperity, and 9, with eternity.[103]

• When numbers appear in dreams, they are usually linked to personal events. When they are small numbers, the dreamer must ask himself what has happened that many years ago or when he was the corresponding age.

Uneven numbers are male and even numbers are essentially female.

NUT, HAZEL
knowledge, science

In medieval symbolism the nut is Christ; the shell, the sacrificial cross; its outer husk the body which, correctly nourished, is capable of undergoing ordeals. It contains three virtues and three benefits; unction, light and the gift of vital energy. At the heart of the nut is the divine truth which is within reach of anyone who chooses to seek it.[80]

• In China, the nut (*hu-tao*) is a symbol of a flirt.

• The hazlenut is the fruit of knowledge and the hazel bush was used by druids as an aid to incantation; in Greek tradition, the walnut was associated with the gift of prophecy.

• Dreaming of a nut can be connected with a problem that is hard to crack. But the nut is frequently a symbol of female genitalia.[24]

OAK

wisdom and strength

As sacred to Zeus, Jupiter and Heracles, the oak played an important role in Greek mythology. Priests uttered their oracles under the sacred oak trees surrounding Zeus' sanctuary.

- It was a symbol of moral and physical strength and long life; and it is said that early man fed off its acorns.

- It had an important role in Celtic religion, which used it as an emblem of endurance and triumph (it flowered at the time of the summer solstice). The oak was attributed to D (Duir) in the tree alphabet and gave its name to a month (10 June–7 July).[107]

- The Gauls, who worshipped tress and plants, saw it as the axis of the world. Only the druids, who possessed wisdom and strength, could be present at the symbolic cutting of the mistletoe which grew on it.

OGHAM

Ogham was the secret alphabet used by druids in Britain and Ireland before the Roman alphabet was introduced. It can be seen in inscriptions on stones. It had twenty letters, and could also be expressed by gesture, like a sign language.

OLIVE TREE

peace, wisdom

In Greece the olive tree was sacred to Athena, and a symbol of peace and wealth.

- In Islam it symbolizes man.
- The olive tree gave its name (Oliver) and its virtues to the hero of the Carolingian legend, *The Song of Roland*, in which he was a friend of the hot-tempered, irrational Roland, whom he complements with his wisdom and moderation.

OM or AUM

wholeness, enlightenment

This sacred monosyllable, that precedes the recitation of Buddhist and Brahmanic hymns and prayers, is made up of three Sanskrit letters, A, U and M, initials of the basic triad: three gods, Brahma–Vishnu–Shiva; three Vedas, Rig–Yajur–Sama; three states of being, awake–dreaming–sleep; three levels of man, physical–verbal–spiritual; three worlds, heaven–earth–hell; three elements, fire–sun–wind.

Om's symbol is the conch, a shell used as a musical

instrument or as a scentholder, which is also the attribute of Lakshmi, the fertile goddess of primal waters.[102]

Om is a primordial sound, the creator-sound, representing the whole of sound and by extension the whole of existence, the manifestation, followed by the non-manifestation, provoked by the pulsating cosmic cycle, in the silence of the unknown.

The syllable is God, creator–saviour–destroyer, the silence is eternal, regardless of the pulsating semibreve.

The A sound symbolizes the consciousness of the awakened state, the U sound the consciousness of dreaming, the M sound dreamless sleep. The silence surrounding the syllable is the unknown or fourth state, the non-manifested transcendency.

• This syllable appears in numerous yantra (see *Yantra*) as the symbol of spiritual realization. Repeated inwardly with faith and concentration it enables the person meditating to reach perfection 'and consequently reabsorption that enables contemplation of God in the three great characteristic attributes he embodies: namely, creation, conservation and dissolution.'

• The mark or point which indicates the high-pitched sound of OM is known in the Sanskrit alphabet as infinite potential, wholeness, the synthesis of creation, 'God's mystic seed, white as autumn lotus springing from the immaculate moon disk.'[12] It is the nut that contains potential enlightenment, 'the truth of the void'.[90]

• The formula OM MANI PADME HUM is a mystical interjection addressed to Bodhisattva Padmapani.

MANI means jewel, the non-substance assimilated into the *vajra* (diamond, lightning) that is contained in the lotus (PADME), symbol of *dharma* (Law), the spiritual development that gives access to the jewel: the 'jewel of eternity is in the lotus of birth and death.'[66]

The three syllables of OM, AH, HUM, placed

respectively on the adept's head, throat and heart at the initiation of the mandala, are the three diamond beads which help the divine essence to enter into the adept. 'At that moment, a transfiguration is accomplished, a change of personality: this is the essential goal of Indian liturgy.'[11]

OMPHALOS
central axis

The omphalos was a great sacred stone, on which Pitthea's trivet was placed in the Delphic underworld. It symbolized the fertility of the earth and linked the three worlds of heaven, earth and underworld, and the three levels of existence.

There were quite a number of societies who imagined the birth of the world as emerging from a navel: the Greeks' omphalos had a replica in India in Vishnu's navel as he lay on the primal ocean from which sprang the lotus of the manifested universe.

• Like the cosmic tree, the Pole Star around which the sky seemed to rotate, the baetyl (a sacred meteoric stone), mountain, cosmic pillar, obelisk, clock tower and pyramid, the navel is the central axis uniting heaven and earth; it is also a spiritual centre.

• In yoga, the navel is where the *manipura-chakra* is situated, presiding over the return to the centre of the personality.

ONE
basis, scale

The most appropriate symbol of unity is the imperceptible mathematical point which is arbitrarily situated at the intersection of two lines or in the centre of a circle, and which, through being displaced in space, begins a line, or creates a surface, or gives an idea of a third dimension. 'A point is ONE on the verge of generating everything.'[22]

• In ancient times totality was likened to the hub of a wheel: 'its reality was like a motionless motor; while perceptible realities were like the spokes and rim of the wheel.' These realities are permanently dependent on one another, and so, according to the philosophers, 'Unity rules time and space, while multiple entities are thrust out into the flow of the future and the expanse of space.'[26]

Numerous civilizations (Meso-American, Chaldaean, Assyrian, Egyptian) have symbolized unity in a winged wheel.

• For Cabbalists, *yod* (shown in Hebrew script as an apostrophe), the first letter of God's name YHVH, symbolized 'the primal and ultimate unity of beings and things.'[5] The Greek letter *alpha* is the beginning of everything, as is the first letter of the Hebrew alphabet, *aleph*, the breath of the creator-spirit. The magician, the first major arcana in the tarot, signifies creation.

• Greek alchemists symbolized totality as a circle (the ouroboros – see entry), an image of the global unity of everything that exists and can be conceived.

Their speculations led them away from unity and unfailingly back again, to use it as a basis on which to assess the value of things.

'One, primal matter, makes one think of alum, *the* basic substance that was analogous to ether, and which was seen as constituting the intimate essence of things, their subtle weft divested of all distinguishing characteristics, the substratus of all materiality.'[18]

• Unity is therefore the point of departure, a symbol of absolute origin and absolute end (universe means 'turned towards one'), a symbol of a personal god, the first in a hierarchy of authority, or of power (the one God of Christian symbolism), of the creator, and of the cosmos.

But one, originally an androgyne, encloses the germ of duality.

• The number 1 symbolizes man, erect, a standing stone, phallus, pillar, a vertical stick.

• The Chinese symbolized unity in the T'ai-chi or monad, a circle encapsulating the positive and negative currents of yin and yang. One (*yi*) is perfection, totality, and the ancient philosophers stated that 'one, the greatest' was born and grew to 'the greatest and most supreme nobility', and was then metamorphosed into the two basic principles of yin and yang, from which sprang the five elements or states of change (fire, water, earth, metal, wood) which, in turn, generated 'the 10,000 things' (*wan won*, that is, an infinite number).[7]

ONION
levels of personality

In China the onion is a symbol of intelligence.[7]

• Its successive layers depict the different layers of the personality or habits which are obstacles to personal development, and which the individual would like to rid himself of, one after the other, in order to attain the centre of his Self (Jung's process of individuation). This explains Ramakrishna's comparison of onion layers to the structure of the ego, progressively losing its leaves through spiritual experience until it is void and reaches a state of fusion with Buddha (see *Nirvana*).

ORANGE
love

In China an orange (*ju-zi*) is a good-luck fruit and is always eaten on the second day of the festival of New Year.

Pictures of two oranges and two fish in a basket are sent to wish 'Good luck for the New Year'.

But bitter (Seville) oranges symbolize fate, and death.

• As a fruit with pips the orange is a symbol of fertility and has a very positive meaning in dreams: to be given one in your hand means that you will acquire 'the perfect fruit of love, full of sunshine: just as if it had been picked fresh from the tree of life in all its golden beauty.'[24]

ORCHID
ambition

The orchid symbolizes beauty and love. In the language of flowers, it is an emblem of fervour. White orchids symbolize pure love; spotted orchids symbolize ambitious love.

• In China, the 'golden orchid bond' (*lan*) symbolizes a close emotional relationship between two people, while the breath of a beautiful woman is compared to the scent of an orchid.[7]

ORGY
liberation, participation

Orgiastic rituals were part of the cult of Dionysos and Bacchus. Originally they symbolized total oblivion, and the fusion of mankind with the cosmos 'through drunkenness caused by the spirit making contact with the divine.' This really meant 'loss of consciousness and supreme ecstasy.'

It was only later, when the symbol had degenerated, that this drunkenness was attributable to wine, and that Dionysos became a symbol of exaggerated extroversion and sexual licence.[22]

Dionysian rites practised at the time of initiation indicated self-abandon to animal instincts in order to participate in Mother Earth's acts of fertility. Wine provided the intoxication necessary to transmit Nature's secrets, whose essence was expressed through the sexual union of Dionysos and Ariadne, his companion in the sacred ceremony of marriage.

Seen in this perspective the orgy was on the one hand a means of getting in touch with life's elementary forces again, and on the other a return to chaos, through debauchery, lust, self-abandon and fancy dress.

Traces of this can be found in the giants and monsters of the carnival, and harvest festivals that are celebrated all over the world and express a need for liberation and relaxation after the hard labour of cultivating the crops.

• Mystical orgies exist in Vedic religion. Here *soma*, an enlivening potion which aids longevity, fulfils a function of renewal. Through mystical drunkenness it facilitates the descent of the divine into the human.

Soma is a libation *par excellence* and a drink dear to the gods. It is an alcoholic potion that is poured on the sacred fire during sacrifices to feed and strengthen it. The *soma* ritual has the purpose of mediation: the absorption of alcohol makes the person making the sacrifice into a new man. '*Soma* is the immortal pleasure of existence secretly hidden in the sap of plants.'[44] So important is it that it becomes the incarnation of a divinity, the third in the triad of Agni–Indra–Soma.

ORPHEUS, ORPHEISM

sun worship

Orpheus was a legendary character whose powers of seduction and songs could tame wild animals. He founded the Eleusian mysteries by taking the mysteries of Osiris as his inspiration.

Upon the death of his wife, Eurydice, he obtained permission to lead her back to earth from the underworld, on condition that he made no attempt to look at her face before returning to earth. But at the crucial moment of reaching the world of the living, he turned round, and Eurydice vanished for ever. Mad with grief, Orpheus disdained the love of women, in particular the Maenads, who tore him to pieces.

• Orpheus is the mythical personification of a secret doctrine, according to which the planets gravitated around the sun, in the centre of the universe. Through its powers of attraction, the sun was the cause of harmony and cohesion of the whole world and, through its fluxes and rays, it caused the movement of parts of the universe. Followers of Orpheism attributed the creation of the universe (from an egg) to love and time, and the universe was one in which Zeus or Zagreos represented the universal force, the sun.

• The myth of the primordial engenderer of love symbolizes immortality and the migration of souls. In fact Orphic teaching was based on the mythical story that

Dionysos' divine substance was reincarnated around his heart by his father, Zeus, after he had been torn to pieces by the Titans.

• Orpheus' inability to save his wife also made him a symbol of human weakness (which was the cause of his failure at the moment of crossing the fatal threshold) and of the tragic aspect of life.

According to Orphic doctrine, the immortal soul inhabits a mortal body; after death, it stays in the underworld to purify itself for a while, and then is reincarnated in another human envelope, or in the body of an animal, enriched by experiences acquired during its successive transformations.[83]

But those initiated into the mysteries knew the magic formulas which brought about the metempsychosis and could claim their soul's definitive salvation.

• Orpheism has dogmas, mysteries, philosophical principles, an initiation into the mysteries with a baptism in goat's milk, to prepare the soul for eternal life, while leaving the initiate its free arbiter between good and evil, a sacred banquet in which the raw flesh of a bull was eaten (omophagy) in memory of Dionysos (see *Orgy*). The initiates practised abstinence of the flesh and wore white linen clothes, symbolic of purity.

OUROBOROS
eternity

The ouroboros, or circular snake swallowing its tail, is an incarnation of the perpetual movement of the universe, a symbol of unity and infinity, with no beginning and no end, and identical to the Chinese monad, which features yin and yang (see *T'ai-chi*), the cycle of night and day, the seasons, life and death, the eternal return, the union of opposites, heaven–earth, and good–evil.

The ouroboros, endlessly turning on itself, without the ability to raise itself to a superior spiritual level, also reminds us of samsara, the Buddhist wheel of existence, the endless chain of rebirth.

OX

physical work, sacrifice

The ox symbolizes obedience, unhurried, straight ploughing, renunciation and sacrifice. The Greeks, who made the ox sacred to gods such as Apollo, slaughtered it for sacrifice. In Hindu mythology the cow represented fertility.

• In China, the ox (*nion*) symbolized spring because spring work began with ploughing. It was also associated with water: dead oxen were used to shore up dykes which threatened to break.[7]

The Chinese venerated the patron of oxen, a learned man who lived at the end of the Sung Dynasty and who became a ploughman when the Yuan succeeded the Sung.[6]

• As second animal in the Chinese zodiac, the ox confers strength of character, patience, and a sense of method. The year it rules is marked by trials and tribulations that call for unrelenting toil.

• For Christians, the ox symbolized Saint Luke because it was a sacrificial animal and the Gospel according to St Luke opens with Zacharius' sacrifice. It also symbolizes Christ's own sacrifice and renunciation.[5]

• As a sacrificial animal, the ox replaced the messenger-ox of early Eastern religions, when wild buffalo were lassoed to be sacrificed to the gods at the spring equinox. This ritual slaughter or expiatory sacrifice, the origin of the bullfight, was thought to be an insurance against illness. (see *Goat*.)

PALACE
centre of the universe

A palace, a sovereign's home, is associated with wealth and secrecy, and symbolizes the inaccessible, what is beyond the reach of ordinary man.

• It is always thought of as the centre of the world by the sovereign's own people, and it connects the three levels of heaven, earth and underworld, the three classes of society and the three duties.

• In China, it was built according to the rules of yin and yang and geomancy (*Feng Shiu*)

On a psychological level, a palace symbolizes the three levels of the psyche: the super-ego, the ego and the unconscious.

PALM TREE
early clock

For early Egyptian farmers, a palm tree symbolized time, and it was used to calculate the months of the year, because it grew a certain amount every month. The palm tree branch represented the year. In the iconography, the god Thoth is shown writing the number of years of a human life on a palm leaf.

• In esoteric terms, a palm tree was a symbol of truth, integrity and justice. 'And the righteous shall flourish like the palm tree' (Psalm 92: 12). In the Apocalypse the righteous carry palms on their heads.[9]

• In Babylon the palm was the tree of life and also symbolized the birth of the Middle East, because it grew at the edge of the sea, and the sea was regarded as the universal mother.[107]

• Clement of Alexandria associated the palm tree with the clock as a symbol of astrology.

PAN
all life

Pan was the god of flocks and shepherds. He was deformed, horned, and had cloven hooves. He took park in Dionysos' procession playing the syrinx (shepherd's flute). His name meant 'all' and he was the oldest and most revered of the gods in Arcadia.

• Pan is the principle of universal order, invoked in Orphic litany as the first principle of love, or creator, incorporated in universal matter and thus shaping the world.

He is the unique source and origin of all living matter animated by the divine spirit: his limbs are made of sky, earth, water and fire. His horns symbolized his domination of the universe.[83]

Pan is the divine essence of light embodied in universal matter. When the position of the earth's axis shifted and the Hyperborean Isle, situated in the extreme north yet enjoying a subtropical climate (which earned it the name of earthly paradise), grew cold and dark for six months of the year, its inhabitants cried out in the darkness: 'Pan is dead'; green vegetation and animal life were killed by the cold and darkness, and the people were truly afraid. They then 'perceived that they were naked' (because they were cold), and this caused a panic flight to the south. This terror gave rise to sun worship, to cults of the dying, absent sun and to Bacchic rites, etc.[4]

• Pan engendered an assortment of creatures; satyrs, fauns, human incarnations of emanations from the creator. Together with the billy goat they represent the reciprocal incarnation of man and God incorporated in matter.

Depictions of Pan sometimes show him with an enormous sexual organ, indicating the application of creative power to the procreation of sensitive rational beings.[83]

• Pan was also the god of divination identified in astrology with Capricorn.

PANSY
affectionate thought

Because of its (five) petals, the pansy is a symbol of man and signifies meditation. In the language of flowers is means; 'All my thoughts are for you.'

PARADISE
happiness

The word 'paradise' originally meant an orchard. The myth of an earthly paradise, with its spring and rivers flowing in four directions and fertilizing the whole earth, is common to most ancient peoples.

Mohammed crossing a garden of Paradise (Persian miniature from a manuscript in the Bibliothèque Nationale, Paris)

Paradise is the home of the immortals, the heart of the universe, the earliest spiritual centre, the link between heaven and mankind. It is identified with the Indian Mount Meru, the highest mountain on earth, which rises into heaven, the Moslem Qaf, the Taoist isles of paradise, and Eden (which in Hebrew means pleasure, sensual delight), the 'garden eastward in Eden' in the Book of Genesis, in which God placed Adam and Eve.

This idyllic place where man, plants and animals grew in harmony side by side is a symbol of happiness, peace and harmony. There is always a lake there, a fountain or central spring, the origin of life and knowledge, animals roaming freely yet under man's control – a symbol of the spirit's and intellect's domination over instinctive urges.

And the nostalgia for this happy place symbolizes an aspiration for a state of simplicity and purity that existed in the original Eden.

• The Chinese paradise (*Xi-wang-mu*) symbolizes the happy age and the age of innocence: 'where there is neither love of life, nor hatred of death . . . nor self-love nor the distancing of others, nor clouds nor mist, nor thunder nor lightning.'[8]

PARTRIDGE
lasciviousness

According to Aristotle and Pliny, the partridge, like the quail, was sacred to the goddess of love, because of its reputation for sexual ardour.

• In Christian tradition, it was an incarnation of the devil, and in the Book of Ecclesiastes, a partridge in a cage (used to lure other birds) symbolizes 'the heart of the proud; and like as a spy watcheth he for thy fall. For he lieth in wait and turneth good to evil; and in things worthy of praise will lay blame upon these.'[107]

• In China, the partridge (*zhe-gu*) symbolizes mutual attraction.

PEACE PIPE
the centre, the soul

The long-stemmed pipe used by North American Indians is a sacred emblem belonging to Wakan-Tanka, master of the universe. In Sioux religion, it symbolizes the axis which unites man to the supernatural powers.

The sacred pipe contains all living things in the universe, is a vital part of every event of their lives and assures them inviolable protection.

• The ritual of the peace pipe had three phases: *purification* with the smoke from the ritual plant; the *transfer* of the universe into the pipe, and the *sacrifice* in the fire, representing Wakan-Tanka's presence in the world.[13]

The peace pipe is also invested with a cosmic dimension: the universe, represented by the offerings to the powers of the six directions (sky, earth, and the four winds), is concentrated in its bowl of red stone, the pipe's heart. The grains of tobacco symbolize all created things. All kinds of contacts take place in its hollow stem.[12] It represents all growing things on earth. The feathers which hang from it come from the speckled eagle and represent all the winged creatures in the sky.

• The peace pipe is simultaneously macrocosm and microcosm. The Indian becomes identified with it as he fills it, and 'actualizes not only the centre of the world, but also his own centre.'[13]

• Its decoration varies according to the occasion: peace (blue stem and feathers from a female eagle), war (red stem, feathers from a male eagle), grief, victory, etc.

• The peace pipe is also the focal point of culture, and the soul of the Indian people, and symbolizes the continuity of the race: 'As long as the peace pipe lasts, our people will survive; but as soon as it is forgotten, our people will no longer have a centre and will perish.'[13]

PEACH TREE
immortality

In China the peach tree or *p'an t'ao* symbolizes spring, renewal, fertility, and also marriage. It represents the third month of the year and its festival is celebrated on the third day of that moon.

It is the most frequent symbol of longevity. In the Paradise of the West, the cultivated peach tree of the fairy queen, Hsi-wang-mon, produced the immortal peach whose fruits ripened every three or 9,000 years.

• Peachwood is associated with fertility and possesses a power to ward off evil influences. Pentacular tablets are made from it that are hung in doorways on New Year's Day (it is the origin of the doorway gods in China).[75] People suffering from fever are struck with a peachwood stick as a cure.[6]

• In antiquity, the peach was used as a symbol of female genitalia,[75] and in everyday talk peach blossom is a synonym for lovemaking. Young girls' complexions are compared to a peach, and so are women of easy virtue. A lovers' secret rendezvous is known as 'the green flowers of the peach tree,' and 'peach blossom delirium' is used to describe the problems of puberty. 'Eyes like peach blossom' is an expression used to describe the magnetic appeal of male actors playing female roles in the theatre.

PEACOCK
appearance

The peacock was an attribute of Hera–Juno (the goddess wife of Zeus–Jupiter) and of Argus who had 100 eyes and only closed 50 when he slept. In antiquity, it symbolized heavenly splendour and divine glory.

• Because its fanned tail was similar to the wheel of the sun and also an image of the starry sky, it was a symbol of immortality

• In the second century bc the Romans engraved peacocks on stones to signify eternal beatitude.

• In Burma it symbolizes the dynasty, and in Cambodia it is identified with the sun, the mount for the god of battles and the goddess of poetry; in India it is Indra's throne.

• The peacock is thought to absorb poison from snakes and thus destroy them, and also owes the beauty of its plumage to them; for these reasons it symbolizes the power of spontaneous transformation.

• Its gaudy plumage signifies multiplicity and creation (which is linked with colour in numerous myths).

• In China the peacock (*Kong-quiao*) symbolizes dignity and beauty. In Manchuria the feathers were used to indicate a dignitory's rank.

• In Buddhism, the peacock is a metaphor for worldly values and renouncing those values of outward appearance for awareness.[23]

• In Middle Eastern imagery, this 'animal with a hundred eyes' features on either side of the tree of life and symbolizes the incorruptibility of the soul and man's psychic duality.

• As a cosmic symbol, its fanned tail symbolizes the universe in Islam, and the starlit sky in Christian tradition.

Three peacock feathers, a divine attribute of Buddhism[90]

• It was considered a noble bird in the Middle Ages, its meat reserved for valiant knights, for whom it became the gauge of sincerity and courage. At feasts the knight would swear the peacock's vow or the vow of courage or love: with his hand on the dish, he would swear to be the first to plant his standard in the town he intended to lay siege to. Failure to carry out that vow would stain his reputation.

• Because of the jewels in its tail and its magnificent plumage, the peacock always symbolizes, on the one hand, the beauty of existence, on the other, narcissism, vanity, feelings of power and its inevitable corollary, isolation.

PEAR, PEAR TREE

fragility

In China, the pear fruit and tree are symbols of long life, and pear blossom is used as a symbol of mourning and fragility.

• In dreams a pear is a 'typically erotic symbol full of sensuality . . . its sweet taste, abundant juice and shape all suggest femininity.'[24]

PEARL
incorruptibility, perfection

Pearls are found in shells and their appearance resembles drops of sperm or dew from heaven. These factors, together with their dull lustre, make them moon symbols: of transcendental reality, of reproductive forces and cosmic energy. This is why the pearl was used in rebirth rituals and funerals (pearls were placed in the mouths of the dead).

• The oyster from which the pearl comes was associated with the moon and water in Pre-Columbian America (the Codex Dresdensis shows water flowing from oyster shells) and in China (oysters are full at a full moon). The Chinese used the pearl as a symbol of the sun, fertility and magic power.[75]

• The pearl is also a symbol of long life, and 'gives its wearer access to the very sources of energy, fecundity and universal fertility.'[92]

• The pearl became a talisman: in India young Brahmins wore one around the neck as a protection against all kinds of evil, anguish, 'acts of gods and demons,' and to give themselves vigour and energy 'for a long life, the life of a hundred autumns.'[19]

• The pearl is one of the golden names praised in the Vedas: 'Born of the wind, air, thunder, light, the shell born of gold grows the pearl to defend us from fear. It is the jewel that prolongs life.'

• In Persia it was a symbol of the Saviour, the 'image of the inexpressible Light which is the Lord,' the symbol of Christ the King and his descendant – the Christian.

• For Gnostics, the quest of the pearl defended by serpent monsters 'symbolized the spiritual drama of man's fall and his salvation . . . the mystery of the transcendent made visible, the manifestation of God in the cosmos.'[92]

• In Greece, India and many other countries, the pearl is a symbol of marriage and love. In China, the pearl (*zhu*) has the power to grant wishes. It is one of the eight jewels of Confucianism, along with phonolite, a coin, the rhombus, books, pictures, rhinoceros horn and yarrow leaves.

It is yin and symbolizes woman as creator, but also 'the sun, fertility and magic power'.[75]

• The pearl was created from the tears of the Hindu god of the moon, and was an emblem of the generating energy of water and therefore associated with eroticism. It is endowed with tonic, fertilizing, gynaecological and aphrodisiac powers, which are still claimed for it today in Indian medicine.

• Because of its association with the snake (it was thought to have fallen from the head of a snake, or be contained in a dragon's gullet) it was listed in the English pharmacopoeia until the seventeenth century as a cure for eye troubles and as an antidote.

• Chinese doctors use only 'virgin pearl' (pearl which have not been perforated) for eye troubles, epilepsy and depression.

PELICAN

secret energy

In ancient Egyptian legend, the pelican fed its young with the blood from its breast, and symbolized the birth of the seventh vital energy, or the soul emanating from the Most High, born of the virgin goddess Neith. (The Egyptians thought there were seven souls, six of which existed before human life began.)

• The Hermetic philosophers used the pelican as a symbol of charity and absolute devotion to the master, which extended to self-sacrifice, without which 'everything to do with initiation would remain totally in vain.'[18]

The pelican then became one of the main symbols of Rosicrucian philosophy, signifying love 'without which the most knowledgeable and powerful of men could only be "as sounding brass or a tinkling cymbal", according to Saint Paul.'[18]

• In coats of arms, it symbolizes piety.

PENTACLE
macrocosm

The pentacle or pantacle (from Pan meaning all; an object that comprises everything, a synthesis of the macrocosm) is the most developed form of talisman. It is a fluid emitter of universal essence. It protects like an amulet; and like a talisman it radiates a magical, holy force, but acts in harmony with the powers of the cosmos.

It is recognized as having the power to counteract the influence of evil spirits and demons that are responsible for epidemics, catastrophes and all kinds of disasters.

In short, the pentacle's purpose is to conquer fear and 'spirit away collective terrors',[136] a purpose similar to that of great monuments or enormous figures that are always accompanied by inscriptions (magic words in capital letters) which are nothing more in fact than giant pentacles.

This condenser of waves ranges from the hand of glory (the pickled hand of a hanged criminal) used in medieval magic ritual to the great dynamic metal or stone pentacle, a radiant heaven in itself, corresponding to the vibrations of the universe – like the Jewish high priest's breastplate.

• The making of a pentacle follows precise rules that take symbolic and magical values into account:

– numbers, Arabic, Cabbalistic or Hebrew letters, words that are written in them (names of angels and demons associated with planets);[19]

– its shape and the shape of the figures in it (magic square or triangle, five-pointed star, Jewish symbols of the constellations, geomantic signs).

Equally important are:

– the time when it is made up;

– the preparation of the person making it.

• The personal pentacle, made of metal, silk or parchment, is calculated by beginning with the value of the radiation of the person who is being put into contact with a supernatural force, whether star, planetary system or divinity.

• The planetary pentacle is a centre of attraction for the magnetic influence emitted by the star ruling one's birth. It is engraved on the metal that corresponds to the time when the star is in a favourable position, and the day when its influence is at its most powerful.

• There are beneficial pentacles – teraphims from *rafa* meaning to cure – and evil, necromantic ones, and pentacles for dreams and divination.

There are other forms of pentacles. Phylacteries are rolls of parchment bearing passages from the Old Testament which are hung near the door of a house; the palladium is a protective statue in a town to protect it from the plague; the Hindu *yantra*, the *kavac* or *mantra* is enclosed in a tube and has an esoteric, magical or protective purpose.

PENTAGRAM
microcosm

A pentagram can either be pentagonal or star-shaped, and is associated with the symbolism of the number five, the symbol of man: the human figure is drawn inside the pentagram, with the head dominating, and the four limbs in each of the other star-points (the spirit ruling the four elements).

Inverted pentagram with a goat's head, symbolizing the devil

The pentagram is the star of the microcosm, or pentacle of magic willpower, used as a symbol of magic and appropriation.

• It is also a symbol of marriage and accomplishment, the five branches representing the fertile union of 3 (the male principle) and 2 (the female principle).

• Inscribed within an invisible circle, the pentagram symbolized the Pythagoreans' 'silence of the initiate': the five points, representing the five years of silence and study preceding initiation.

• Along similar lines, the blazing star used in Freemasonry and presented to the Mason symbolizes the 'personality which has obtained enlightenment, the quintessence' or essence of the Self, released through work in depth on the Self,[48] and free thought, free of all preconceptions and superstitions.[121]

• Upside-down (i.e., a star with two points at the top), the pentagram is a symbol of destruction; of the devil (a goat's head), of ardent lust and the grosser instincts.[18]

PEONY
sincerity

The peony was Pluto's flower, a symbol of fertility and also an expression of sincerity. A pink peony means, 'Don't count on me.' a red one, 'My love is watching over you', and a white one, 'Look after yourself.'

• In China, the red peony (*mu-dan*) is associated with the phoenix and the Taoist's drug of immortality. A peony is slang for a bewitching woman, and is a symbol of the female sex organs: 'A peony opens when it tastes the dew' (sperm).

• In Imagery, a peony with a chrysanthemum and a plum tree represent the four seasons; the peony symbolizes spring.

• It is a symbol of consideration, and, with hibiscus, expresses a wish for prosperity and consideration; with the peach tree it expresses a wish for a long life, riches and consideration.[7]

PERFUME
offering

The use of perfumes (resins and balms) was once reserved for the cult of the dead (the Egyptians used aromatics to embalm the dead and preserve mummies); later on it was introduced into religious ceremonies as one of the elements of sacrificial offering.

• Incense was reserved as a privilege of the gods, and Arabs had to be perfectly chaste before they collected it.

• Incense smoke, which can be found in every temple of every deity throughout history, was sacrificial smoke. The Maya associated it with clouds 'because they are all emanations of the divine spirit.'[76]

• This scented smoke was a vehicle for the spirit: by absorbing the sacred smoke from tobacco, 'the perfume of grace', the Sioux 'exhaled themselves with it towards the unlimited, and spread themselves supernaturally in divine space.'[13]

• Perfume, like colour and light, is a vibration that we pick up, and in each of us it provokes reactions of sympathy or antipathy. It can exert a calming or stimulating influence on the organism, produce a sensation of wellbeing and euphoria, or just the opposite. Some scents decompose on the skin of some women and are accentuated on others, according to a law of affinities.

• Traditionally perfumes are associated with planetary influences, and it is recommended that you should use perfume on yourself that corresponds to the planet that governs your date of birth. Heliotrope perfume corresponds to the Sun; Iris to the Moon; Juniper to Mercury; Verbena to Venus; Heather to Mars; Mint to Jupiter; poppy to Saturn.

• Perfumes also correspond to signs of the zodiac: Aries –

Fern; Taurus – Lily of the valley; Gemini – lavender; Cancer – lilies of thyme; Leo – forget-me-not; Virgo – cyclamen; Libra – thyme or laurel; Scorpio – hyacinth; Sagittarius – carnation, jasmine; Aquarius – heliotrope; Pisces – jasmine.[78]

• When pentacles are being made, perfume is used as a bond, since it creates a balance between planetary magnetic forces and personal magnetism.

By burning perfume, a mystical ambience is created similar to the heavy vapour created in churches, and perfume then serves as a wave-carrier.[78]

– To make a Sun pentacle, a perfume is used that is composed of saffron, aloes, balm of laurel, cloves, myrrh, incense, musk and ambergris.

– A Moon pentacle requires a mixture of white poppy, benzoin and camphor powder;

– Mars, gentian and incense;

– Mercury, juniper and incense;

– Jupiter, benzoin and incense;

– Saturn, black poppy, henbane seeds, myrrh;

– Venus, musk, ambergris, aloes, crimson rose, powdered coral, red pepper.

PHALLUS

the power to reproduce

The phallus was worshipped as 'a source of life and libido, as creator and miracle-worker', Jung wrote. It was the emblem of Priapus, god of vines, navigation and procreation, who was symbolized in an outsize organ, personifying virility, physical love and the power to reproduce.

Gods such as Osiris and Priapus were shown with an erect phallus to express their prolific reproductive powers. In India, the *lingam* (the male sexual organ) and the *yoni* (the female organ) are emblems of the active and passive powers of procreation. The sexual act symbolizes the gods' creative power.

However, the use of the male organ as a symbol of creative Nature was not limited to Priapus worship. It was common in all the religions of the East as in the West: the cults of Chronos, Apollo, Heres, Aphrodite, Demeter, Dionysos/Bacchus. The phallus, guardian of the original principles of religion, was 'solemnly processed at the celebration of the mysteries.'[83]

This cult was practised until the fourteenth century, and the priapic figure played a protective role: it was painted on the façades of houses, and worn as an amulet against the evil eye or other pernicious influences (the *fascinum* was worn by Roman children around their necks and by women as necklaces).[83]

• Along with the phallus, the male principle shares its symbolism with everything that is erect in relation to everything that is horizontal: Moses' rod, Mercury's staff, the royal sceptre, Parsifal's lance, the fool's bauble, the cross, column, post, key, erect stones.

The phallus can also be in the form of a sword held erect.

PHOENIX
the immortal soul

The phoenix was a mythical bird with scarlet plumage, of unparalleled beauty, which, having lived for several centuries, burnt itself to death in a bonfire and was reborn from the ashes. In the Middle Ages if was a symbol of immortality and resurrection, Christ's resurrection.

• It was associated with philosopher's sulphide and the number 4 (the four elements of physical stone and the four stages in alchemical transformation). It 'represents the living human being's endurance of continual death, a source of spontaneous rebirths.' The image of this legendary bird encourages us 'to burn our inadequacies and be reborn from the ashes of the old man.'[80]

• In Egypt the phoenix was a symbol of the sun's revolutions and a manifestation of the sun god Rê's soul. It was associated with Heliopolis, the initiatic centre, sacred to the worship of Rê.

• In China, the phoenix (*feng-huang*) is the second of four mythical sacred or spiritual animals, uniting yin and yang.[86] Its body represents the five human qualities: its head, virtue; its wings, duty; its back, correct behaviour during rituals; its breast, the virtue of humanity; its stomach, reliability.

• The taoists called it the cinnabar bird, because of its colour (cinnabar is the bright red mineral form of mercuric sulphide used in the process of alchemy). It served as a mount for the immortals, as did the crane.

• In iconography, the male phoenix symbolizes happiness: the female, the empress. Together they express hope for a happy marriage.

PIG, SOW
lust, full maternity

In Islam, the pig is viewed as an unclean animal, and symbolizes evil tendencies, ignorance, voracity, and lust. Moslems are forbidden to eat its meat, a rule shared by Egyptians and Jews.

• Because a pig loves wallowing in mud and swill, it

became, in medieval times, an image of the devil, lust and worldly pleasures. But in medieval imagery, a pig is sometimes portrayed lying at the foot of a saint (in particular Saint Antony) indicating victory over animal nature.

• The pig (*zhu*) has been rehabilitated by the Chinese. It is the last of the twelve animals in the zodiac and symbolizes virile energy[7] and abundance (from which comes our piggy bank).

• In dreams, the appearance of a pig, especially a sow, is a favourable indication. The sow, once sacred to Demeter, goddess of the earth, is a symbol of happy, mature maternity; a boar, however, signifies bad luck.[24]

PINE
life in its imperishable form

The pine is a needle-bearing tree sacred to Cybele, Attis, Artemis, Demeter, Poseidon, Pan, and Sylvanus. It symbolizes the permanence of plant life, the changing seasons and Nature's resurrection.

In the mystical drama of Attis, the Phrygian god of vegetation, celebrated at the spring equinox, the Romans used to bring a pine tree wrapped in a shroud and garlanded with violets into the Palatine temple, to represent the dead Attis. The following day, on 24 March, the day of blood, fasting and mourning, the faithful would lament; on the 3rd day, the high priest would bleed himself in the arm and present his blood as an offering to Attis, the saviour who had been crucified and had risen from the dead, and the god's resurrection would be solemnly announced and celebrated in sumptuous banquets and masquerades. There were dances to the music of cymbals, flutes and drums, and people used to sprinkle their blood on the tree and altar, ending with a procession.[3]

• The pine tree was one of the seven noble, or chief, trees in medieval Ireland.[107]

• In the language of flowers, the pine cone is a phallic fruit and symbolizes 'the vain desires of worms and spectres, and says "I haunt what I cannot possess".'[99]

• In China, the pine (*song*) is a symbol of long life and permanence because it endures the winter cold without shedding its needles. The Taoist immortals fed themselves on pine nuts and its resin. As a tree with a double needle it sometimes symbolized married happiness.[7]

• Pines and cedars symbolize self-control. In the iconography, a pine and a crane represent the final years of a long life. A pine, a bamboo and a plum tree are the 'three friends in winter.'

• In Japan, Shinto temples and ritual instruments are made from pine, a symbol of immortality. In order to ensure the protection of the *kami* (gods), a pine tree is placed on either side of the entrance to houses, and encircled with a *shimenawa* (a sacred rope made of rice straw and plaited to form a crown, which is linked to the symbolism of the circle.[77] Pine is one of the most eloquent sun symbols in Shinto ritual, meaning the 'miraculous grace of the return to light.' At New Year, it is hung at temple entrances or in garlands along the streets and symbolizes 'the resurrection . . . the renewal of the world'.[66]

• In the iconography, the pine is a symbol of vital power and also the unshakeable strength developed throughout a life full of difficulties.

Pisces
19 February–20 March

Pisces is a changeable, female water sign, in the house of Neptune. Venus exalts, Jupiter is in exile, Mercury falling.
Correspondences: cold, wet, night, silence, sleep. Minerals: rocks, pumice stone, coral. Body parts: the feet.
Characteristics: evasion, fusion, fraud or ecstasy, pity, tenderness, split personality, divination.
Negative characteristics: ambivalence, idealism, duality, instability, lack of willpower, method or wisdom.[114]

PLAIT
protective rope

Ornaments in the form of a plait, cable and interlacing around buildings, vases, urns, etc. can be traced back to early Chaldaean history. Now they are used in decorative art, but then these motifs were a physical form of protective magic: for example, the plait used as an ornament on shields in ancient Greek and Roman times, such as Athena's snake coils bordering her shield or around her neck.

• This motif is a symbol of the protection of the magic ritual rope, the chain of defence forming a barrier around a place or object, the closed circuit having the power to ward off evil influences and perhaps enemies.

The double plait with a central point links the symbolism of the plait with the eye, emblem of the second entity of the solar trinity (the watching, protective god, the good eye). This plaited rope has become the rope belt worn by monks, the Arab headband and cord on military headgear.

Ropes and cables are symbolic of the protection of the magic rope or chain of defence [121]

Chain of defence around Solomon's seal (the Star of David)[19]

PLANTS
psychic growth

Plants are both manifestations and symbols of solar energy, and synthesize the symbolism of water, earth and air. They are a manifestation of the cosmos (like the lotus), and in the Vedas, they are seen as deities.

• Traditionally they are associated with the planets: the root is in harmony with Saturn; the stalk with Mars; leaves with the Moon; flowers with Venus; bark and seeds with Mercury; fruit with Gemini.

• In magic, there are basic plants that possess special properties: a buttercup, corresponding to the Sun, is the plant of loving ardour; cinquefoil, associated with Mercury, provides security; verbena, Venus' plant, provides knowledge; henbane, an attribute of Jupiter, favours wisdom; fern, Saturn's plant, engenders serenity.

• Properties of secondary plants are as follows: aloes, as a decoration, helps to ease childbirth; angelica is worn as a protective agent; artemisia, worn, brings serenity; heather as a perfume develops intuition, and balm inspiration; heliotrope favours sight; clover, worn, brings gains; a red rose, worn, is the flower of conception.

• Dreams involving plants are connected with psychic growth. Whether flowers are vigorous or wilting reflects our normal or stagnant mental development.

PLUM, PLUM TREE
fertility

In the Far East, a plum tree (*mei*) is a symbol of fertility and creative power, because its knotty branches, which appear to be dry of sap, produce flowery clusters in spring and make one think of the 'vital essence that is renewed after the winter.'

By extension it comes to mean sexual pleasure and young girls: they call venereal diseases *mei-ton*.[75]

Its flower's five petals symbolize the five gods of happiness.

A picture composed of a plum tree, a pine and bamboo and children playing symbolizes three friends in the cold season, that is, in adversity.

PLUTO
evolution

Hades–Pluto was originally an agricultural deity who played a role in the Eleusinian mysteries. (The word Pluto, meaning rich, was first an epithet for Hades, before designating an underworld god.) He personified the earth's fertility and guaranteed abundant harvests.

• In the Orphic tradition, Pluto, life-giver and destroyer, ruled as much over creation and conservation as over disintegration, over the living as much as over the dead.[83]

• In astrology Pluto is the slowest of all the known planets: it takes 235 years to travel the 360 degrees of the zodiac.

It is a 'collective' planet and presides over great transformations and mutations (the conquest of space, laser, the world of the atom) and rules the ultra-modern sciences such as information technology, television, antibiotics . . .

Pluto is the planet of evolution and rings unutilized forces into the open; shortly after its discovery in 1930, scientists succeeded in splitting the atom, unleashing immense energy.

Pluto is the great reformer which destroys in order to rebuild in a better way, which subjects everything to scrutiny, abolishes customs to replace them with more efficient ones, recycles.

People under its sign are the most adept at discovering these human energies.[112]

This is the influence it exerts: it introduces the notion of discovery of energies, the possibility of surprising revelations and primal forces that remain unintegrated.[14]

Its subjects are sociable people, possessing an acute sense of the future, of transformations of organisms, of ideas and of the suitability of judgements and discrimination. They are generally penetrating critics, good psychologists, sensible observers and impartial witnesses, who lack passion.[100]

POINT

centre, point of departure

Every manifestation begins with a point. A point is the principle element of every dimension, the beginning of a line, the central link of a cross, and the centre of a circle. For Taoists it is the Inevitable Centre, for Moslems the Divine Station which reconciles contrasts and antagonisms, the Holy Palace in the Jewish Cabbalah.

• Although fixed and motionless, it produces a movement, like the hub of a wheel.

• According to the Cabbalah, the primordial point is unity, God, the centre of the world of space and time: 'the heart of the universe, from which the endless extent of space stretches above, below, to right and left, in front and behind.' (In Hindu tradition these lines extending in all directions are shown as Shiva's hair.)

• The primordial point is beyond comprehension; it is the

non-manifested One, which divides into three: a symbol of the beginning, middle and end, assimilated into the three elements of the mystic syllable AUM (OM). Joined together, they make up the Hebrew letter Yod ['], the hidden point which represents the Principle, from which all the other letters of the Hebrew alphabet are formed, and which is in itself a symbol of the manifested world.

• The point is the centre of the Self: when a wise man attained his central point he had attained peace, the divine presence symbolized in the heart.

• In Koranic mysticism, the point within a circle which is used above the name of Allah is 'the Name, and is a representation of the Principle. 'The point and circumference are joined in a Point, which is the Name . . . This junction corresponds to a 'coalescing' process of the multiple into One, meaning deification.'[85]

POMEGRANATE

fertility

A pomegranate flower symbolizes perfect friendship because its fruit which is so full of seeds signifies union and fertility.[114]

• Pomegranates were sacred to Attis as well as Adonis–Dionysos, whose cult was absorbed into Jehovah's in Jerusalem.[107]

• In ancient China, a pomegranate (*shi-liu*) was a metaphor for the vulva and symbolized fertility because of the resemblance of the red pulp surrounding the seeds.

THE POPE
wisdom, experience

The fifth arcana of the tarot shows a pope with a pleasant, jovial face, dressed in blue and crimson (idealism and spirituality), seated between the two posts of his throne (the opposite poles of the domain of faith). He is the symbol of the wisdom of the spiritual master of the souls that he guides towards supreme knowledge (his white beard symbolizes intelligence and lucidity); he is the conciliator of marital disputes, the fair mediator, the Way of Tao.

His white gloves, symbolic of purity, have a blue cross on them, the colour of fidelity to the faith on three levels, as is indicated by the three crowns in his tiara (symbol of his supreme authority) and the three crossbars on his pontifical cross, emblem of his spiritual power.

This arcana encourages us to meditate to help us listen to our inner self, and urges tolerance and compassion.

Divinatory meaning: respect for holy things, resignation. Dissimulation, inertia, fantasy.[17]

POPLAR
double polarity

Because its leaves have two colours, the poplar symbolizes man's duality.

• In Celtic tradition, the poplar is one of the five magic trees that symbolize times of the year – in this case the autumn equinox and old age.[107]

POPPY
oblivion

The poppy was an attribute of Demeter, goddess of fertility and harvests, who found her daughter, Persephone, again in the underworld. It symbolizes Nature's eternal cycle of death and rebirth.

• The philosopher's poppy is the perfect stone, alchemist's red in colour.

• Because of its heavy scent, the poppy also symbolizes the oblivion and ecstasy that can be obtained through the morphine contained in its seed heads.

• In the language of flowers it signifies the time of day: white for morning; coloured for evening.

PYRAMID
divine ethereal essence

There are Assyrian, Etruscan and Mexican pyramids. They can be found in Iran and Thailand. The most famous are in Egypt. They derive from quadrangular *mastaba*-tombs, the earliest form of royal tomb built by sovereigns of the third dynasty who wanted to prove their power through the size of their eternal abode.[115] But the pyramid's magnificence is far outweighed by its significance. It is probable that the pyramids were also intended for esoteric initiation.

The great pyramid of Gizah, situated at thirty degrees north latitude, guarded by the great Sphinx, contained mathematical messages, astronomical and geographical lines and markers, the mathematical symbol pi, the exact calculation of the dimensions concealed a prophetic message (the measurement of the corridors corresponded to dates and events). These were symbolic messages guarded by the Sphinx with its impassive, majestic mask.[5]

The pyramid is a 'block enclosing for ever the dead monarch, yet containing an open door to the world of beyond and its infinite possibilities, a geometrical and astronomical résumé of creation, whose function appears to have been to put the spirit of the deceased sovereign in touch with the universe, by giving him the measure of all things.'[138]

• It was a symbol of fire through which the final emancipation of the soul was accomplished: 'the Greeks and Celts burnt their dead bodies as the Hindus still do, while the Egyptians, for whom cremation was rare, placed them in pyramids.'[83]

• In its exterior shape, a pyramid is also a symbol of ascension and had the quaternary as a base, the ternary for its sides, while its summit synthesizes unity, union with the Word.

QUYIT

magic gesture

The quyit was a magic ritual in ancient China in which magicians traced intersecting vertical and horizontal lines in the air with incense sticks. These grills were intended to fend off evil spirits.[136]

RAIN
drops of truth

As a fertilizing agent of the earth, rain symbolizes the beneficial influences of heaven, the fertility of the earth, Nature and the spirit.

• To produce or prevent rain, the Chinese practised a ritual associated with the dragon and the frog, and carried out a succession of identical symbolic operations adapted to the time of year, according to the law of correspondences. In spring and winter, 8 and 6 would be the master number of animals sacrificed or dancers, since they were even numbers, they corresponded to yin; in summer, the final month of summer and autumn, the master number would be 7, 5 or 9, uneven numbers corresponding to yang. In spring, the colour would be green, in summer, red, at the end of summer, yellow, and in winter, white. Similarly there would be corresponding cardinal points.

The ceremony took place around the effigy of a large dragon and five frogs were thrown into a pool of water.[65]

• In Greek mythology the legend of the Danae, whom Zeus fertilized when disguised as golden rain, symbolized both sperm and the cycle of plant life which needs water to reproduce.

• Rain, which is produced by cloud and storms, brings together the symbolism of water and fire (lightning).

• The Maya, who compared rain to blood and divine essence, showed it as ropes in their manuscripts and as small columns on monuments or in the image of a bird falling from a roof into a real tennis court, which symbolized 'the spirit of rain that animates and guides the clouds across the universe.'[76]

During periods of drought, they sprinkled the ground with 'virgin water' to attract rain through a sort of imitative magic.

Among the Maya-Chorti, the four watering gods, monsters which were half-man, half-snake and associated with the cardinal points, announced rain through the croakings of their frog servants; they threw their stone axes on the ground provoking thunderbolts and flashes of lightning; they shook their calabashes filled with water to make the rain fall.[60]

• For the Sioux, the west wind brought thunder and rain, symbols of revelation and grace: *Wakinyan-Tanka*, the thunderbird, who is also patron of water, lives in the west and protects the earth and vegetation against drought and death; he sends out forked lightning through his eyes and produces thunder with his wings.[13] He is symbolized in a whistle made from eagle bones.[12]

• The Aztecs associated rain with fire: Tlaloc is the lord of the waters, the god of the rain of fire (lightning, heavenly sperm). His attributes are the rings around his eyes (a stylization of the butterfly, a hieroglyph of flame) and an arrow (a magical instrument belonging to the rainmaker).[76, 48]

Rain (*quiauitl*) is the name of a day and a sign of the Aztec zodiac, associated with the east and the number 19. It indicates an impetuous, stormy temperament and a predisposition to rheumatism and skin problems.[125]

• The Egyptians established a link between the early rain which helps to germinate plants and instruction which prepares man for intellectual life: rain (or dew) symbolized teaching the virtues of faith.[9]

RAINBOW
heavenly bridge

In every tradition the rainbow is a means of communication between heaven and earth: a stairway of seven colours used by Buddha, the Celtic *bifrost* (trembling bridge) in three colours, with the red on fire to discourage the mountain giants from using it to climb into heaven.

• It is generally a good-luck sign, but in China it also presages disturbances in the harmony of the universe.

• In ancient India the rainbow belonged to Indra, god of the sky, and symbolized heavenly activity, for Indra dispensed rain and lightning.

• In Islam, the rainbow's colours reflect divine qualities, while in the West it announces the return of the sun after rain, and is considered a good sign; it alludes to the covenant God made with Noah in the Book of Genesis, in which he announced that neither he nor any living creature would ever have their land destroyed through flood.

RAM
ardour, sexual vitality

The ram is a symbol in numerous myths. It symbolizes 'Nature's wild and creative forces', the instinct for procreation which assures the continuity of life, aggressive impulses. In Egypt, Khemu, god of creation and fertility, is shown with a ram's head, and was thought to be the potter-god who had fashioned gods and man. Certain hieroglyphs show him with four ram's heads, representing the elements. He was identified with the Nile, the source of life.

RAT
obsessions

This elusive, frightening, nocturnal creature belongs to the dark underground world of caves, drains, wet places, dungeons and wells. Stories about rats are similar to those about spiders, toads, lizards and worms.

The rat is a distasteful creature and symbolizes anything that slowly but surely gnaws, wears down, eats away and destroys. The ancient Egyptians saw it as a symbol of destruction, but also linked it to the idea of the soul undergoing judgement.[9]

• In the West it is associated with both poverty and greed. In ancient Egypt it was the god of the plague, and in China, the rat (*da-shu*) is the first animal in the zodiac and is a symbol of prosperity. Those born under its sign have brilliant personalities, a sense of economy and a tendency to meddle in other people's affairs.

Years of the Rat are times of plenty, good luck and growth, marked by happy speculation, discussions and fruitless quarrelling.[118]

• Because it moves silently, and is destructively greedy, its appearance in dreams indicates the presence of exhausting, obsessive ideas.[23] Alternatively, it can be connected with death: the disappearance of one aspect of the personality, worn away by the teeth of time.[25] It can symbolize disappointments, confused or hidden worries that are gnawing away at our vital energy.[24]

REBIS
the initiate

The *rebis* is a figure used in pentacles, mentioned by J. D. Mylius and Basile Valentin in the seventeenth century, and used by the Hermetic philosophers as an emblem of the 'royal art', that is, alchemy.

It appeared as an androgyne above the dragon (a symbol of instinctive life), over which it has triumphed as an initiate of the second degree, and master of the four elements.

The sun and moon adjacent to its double face represent reason and imagination. The star of Mercury placed between the planets symbolizes intelligence, knowledge and gnosis.

The duality is symbolized in Mars (iron, linked to the right arm which has a mallet ready to strike, or execute), Venus (copper) on its right (activity), and Saturn (tin and lead – soft metals) on its left (passivity).

The circle, cross, triangle and square are basic ideograms in Hermetism and linked to Pythagorean ideas of unity, binary, ternary and quaternary.

The oval figure of the *rebis* has echoes of the cosmic egg and the alchemists' philosopher's egg, which corresponds to 'matter prepared for the definitive work [i.e., alchemy], in other words, for the Companion who has rendered himself worthy of being raised to Worshipful Master.'[18]

REED
fertilization

In ancient Egypt the reed was a symbol of royalty, irrigation and the fertilization of everything.

• The Aztecs made the reed (*acatl*) a sign of the zodiac, linked to the east, riches, light, tradition and knowledge, and it gave those born under its sign an intellectual, contemplative temperament, the faculty of concentration, a certain aridity of feeling, and a predisposition to meditation.[125]

RETURN
repetition of the cosmic myth

A return to the beginning or centre is common in spiritual processes and rituals that have cosmic symbolism

• In traditional societies, the whole of life is a return: 'all responsible activity that pursues a well-defined goal' is a ritual; rituals which dominate religious, profane or agricultural activities are not simple reflexes, but a repetition of acts linked to cosmology.

• All dances are a repetition or imitation of sacred dances, originally revealed through a god or hero; they reproduce the movements of a symbolic animal, and are enacted as a means of procuring food or maintaining the harmony of the cosmos, at the time of an initiation or marriage, for example.

• The coronation ceremony of an Indian king is a down-to-earth repetition of the ancient consecration of Varuna, the first sovereign.

• Using the magical or medicinal properties of a plant, and its ritual gathering, are activities that repeat its first gathering by a god.

• Territories, temples, towns had their heavenly prototypes: in Egypt the names of places were chosen after identifying the celestial fields; the tabernacle was built after the heavenly model described to Moses by Jehovah; Babylonian cities had their archetype in the constellations; heavenly Jerusalem in the Apocalypse was to serve as a model for Jerusalem on earth; royal Indian towns reproduced the celestial city, home of the Universal Sovereign of the Golden Age. These sacred cities were thought of as centres of the world where the act of creation was repeated, the passage from chaos to the cosmos realized from a centre.[97]

On a psychic level, this return to the centre can take place through the mandala and the labyrinth (processes of reintegration into the centre of consciousness). It is realized completely by the Bodhisattva who, having obtained enlightenment, a seat on the Diamond Throne, the ideal centre of the world and the plane of the Absolute, becomes as one with the essence of consciousness.

• In myths, the return of the hero after his victory over fearsome enemies is similar to the theme of the resurrection and deliverance, and symbolizes man's success.

• The Hermetic philosophers expressed the idea of the eternal return through the serpent biting its tail, the ouroboros, a symbol of cosmic unity, of the perpetual cycle of emergence from chaos and disappearance back into it, whose equivalent is alum, salt of salts and substance of substances, 'which is only emptiness, but an animated emptiness, although of shadows and chaotic essence.'[17]

• On an individual level, a study of your dreams can be, like meditation, a return to the Self and 'revelatory', ending in a discovery of the Self and wholeness of the personality.

RIGHT
the future

In the symbolism of space, right has always stood for what is 'positive, male and favourable', and symbolizes strength, success, the future, fatherhood, projects. While left (*sinister* in Latin) is a bad omen, associated with femininity, weakness, the past, motherhood, regrets, nostalgia.

In politics, the right corresponds to 'order, stability, authority, hierarchy, tradition, relative self-satisfaction', while the left represents dissatisfaction, protest, movement, a concern for justice and progress, freedom, innovation and risk.[1]

RING
the double bind, domination and submission

The ring forms part of the solar symbolism of the circle (see *Circle*). It is a symbol of power, the supreme power of the sun god, the divine power of pharaohs, kings and the ecclesiastical hierarchy, and it provides concrete proof of their power and spiritual, material or intellectual domination.

• It is linked with magic circles, and is by nature female and negative, capable of repelling harmful influences.

• As a general rule, it originates from the symbolism of the tied knot (a ring with no breaks) which creates limitations, raises barriers, expresses an embargo, a hindrance, subjection, restraint (the wedding ring is a limiting factor; the novice's ring is an emblem of submission.

• The wedding ring also demonstrates the idea of unity, the recreation of the primordial couple who existed before the Fall, of a new world of regained unity. Its origin goes back to the Chinese harem: a silver ring was placed on a courtesan's finger (on the left hand) when she approached the emperor's bed. After completing her duty, she would wear it on her right hand. The gold ring was reserved for those who were pregnant, in the month before their confinement.

• In antiquity, rings, bracelets, and necklaces were

stabilizers, and were worn to preserve the link between body and soul, by keeping the soul within the material body. They were removed to facilitate their separation at the moment of death, or during a mystic ceremony (which would explain why so many soldiers wore bracelets).

• For early Christians, the ring served as a sign of recognition.

• In China, the ring is the symbol of the indefinite cycle that corresponds to the trigram *li*, and to fire and the sun.

The jade ring, *Pi*, a hieratic sign of royal and imperial dignity, was made up of a flat jade disk with a central hole, the dimensions of which varied, but which preserved the same proportions between the circular ring and the central hole (its diameter was twice the width of the hold). *Pi* symbolized heaven, and the central hole the threshold of heavenly influences. A ritual offering of *Pi* would be made to the gods at the solstices.

The same symbolism is expressed in the carving of a soup bowl that can be seen on the capital of a pillar at Louviers, depicting a man holding a bowl pierced by a central hole, featuring 'the circle of the bottomless, unfathomable universe, which can nevertheless be "held in the hand" by those who practise the craft.'[80]

• In dreams the ring has no connection with the circle. It is highlighting a desire for power, which can be exercised either equitably or tyrannically.

• The necklace has the same symbolism as the ring; in Egypt it was a mark of dependency and slavery and symbolized a closed circle (the necklace wearer was a slave attached to a master).[3]

RITUAL
participation

A ritual is a collection of rules that must be observed in religious, traditional or magic ceremonies: it consists of words to say, attitudes to adopt, precise gestures to be performed, clothes to wear and certain procedures that must be followed.

Rituals are the result of socializing collective activities that have magical implications: dances, songs, different kinds of ceremonies become established almost unconsciously, and once they become established, they become a dogma.

Originally rituals evolved from natural laws; consequently, all rituals are only repetitions of corresponding rituals that have taken place in earlier times. This explains how there are parallels between Roman Catholic and Orphic ritual, why Christmas has echoes of the winter solstice or New Sun (Noël), why giving lily-of-the-valley on 1st May in France can be traced back to the Greek custom of looking for new leaves on 1st May. (This coincided with the festivities of the spring equinox and summer solstice, which was pushed back to this date by changes in the calendar.)

• When a ritual loses its primitive substance and its original meaning, it degenerates or is transformed into a superstition or game.[114]

RIVER
the river of life

Rivers, made sacred by the Greeks, have often been depicted as bearded old men, with long hair entwined with aquatic plants, and holding a rudder and an urn, or with bull's horns, to express their power of fertility.

• In Chinese mythology, the river is part of evolution; it is to Yu the Great, 'who rules the waters and the waves', that the horse-dragon emerging from the Yellow River gives the magic square, and to whom the tortoise from the River Luo imparts Luoshu writing.[7]

• In stories, legends and myths, crossing a river symbolizes the need to surmount an obstacle in order to reach the other bank, or another state of mind or other thoughts. The current flowing downstream towards the sea features the return to a lack of differentiation, access to non-being, Nirvana; and going upstream, return to the Principle, or divine source.

• The rivers of hell, Acheron, Styx, Cocytus, Phlegethon and Lethe, carry the dead souls to torture, burning, lamentation, horror and oblivion.

• A river or water course in a dream is the symbol of the flow of life, the paternal wave. We say for example, 'Father Thames'.[28]

ROSACE

image of the sun

In early art where every detail had a spiritual language and symbolic value, the rosace, or rose window, a stylization of the rose, represented the sun-disk (when it had eight open petals), and sometimes the moon-disk (when the rosace was a helix.)

It evolved from the symbolism of the circle, rose, sun flowers (rose, daisy, chamomile, sunflower), star and solar cross.

As a stained-glass masterpiece the rosace 'reveals how light is generated in the mysterious rose . . . it illuminates two essential movements of thought: the movement from the periphery to the centre, and the movement from the centre to the periphery. Its immobility is only appearance; in reality, it is always moving, in harmony with the eternal cycles of the cosmos.'[80]

ROSE
star or sun

The rose is to the West what the lotus is to the East.

When it is open it symbolizes the sun. The heraldic rose with five petals is linked to the symbolism of the five-pointed star or pentagram, or the Freemasons' blazing star.

The Rosy Cross[113]

• It was once a symbol of the first step in regeneration and initiation into the mysteries,[32] an image of the death of the flesh: in ancient times, every year in May people would scatter roses on graves in a ceremony called Rosalia and offer the spirits of the dead a meal of roses.[32]

• It also signifies the silence demanded in initiation, free thinking, removed from prejudices and superstitions, a symbolism common to all the roses carved on the vaulted roofs of churches which, in a stylized way, become ceiling rosaces.[121] The rose can also be found as an emblem of a political party.

• In India it is a symbol of the divine word, and in the Bible it has a meaning similar to dew, but while the rosebush is an image of what has been regenerated, dew is one of regeneration.

• Christian iconography uses it to symbolize the chalice which received Christ's blood, an evocation of the Holy Grail, and Rosicrucians place it in the centre of their cross, the place of Christ's heart or the Sacred Heart.

The white rose was the symbol of monastic wisdom and of renunciation of the world; the red rose, initiation into divine love.[32]

• For the Greeks, the rose was a symbol of wisdom and love, sacred to Minerva and Venus. The five-petalled rose encircling the head of Hecate, Roman goddess of death symbolized the beginning of a new state.[32]

• In heraldic art it was the symbol of the mysteries of spiritual life.[47]

• In the language of flowers, a rose is used to speak of love: white, for aspiring love; pink, for swearing love; tea, gallantry; bright red, ardent love, a sign of beauty.

• The rose is a symbol of the Self which appears at the end of a process of psychic transformation and announces great spirituality.

In dreams, 'if roses almost always announce something magnificent . . . we must not forget the thorns reminding us of the presence of the Cross and suffering, the opposite of happiness.'[24]

SABBATH
night of the week

The Sabbath (Hebrew *Schabbat* meaning rest) is linked to the symbolism of the week.

Established as Saturday, the seventh day of the week and devoted to Jehovah, for Jews the Sabbath is a day of total rest, a replica of the seventh day of Creation. The second commandment gives as a reason the need to regain strength after six days of labour. As a sacred time and feast day, the Sabbath gives the believer time to recover his soul. It is forbidden to do any chores which involve more physical than mental work.

It is also the end of a cycle or the night of the week.

• Originally the Sabbath in demonology and witchcraft was linked to the cycles of the moon, fertility rites and the symbolism of the night. As Saturday is the night of the week, Sabbath is the great night. It is a feast of the full moon held on top of a mountain or hill, or in the solitude of a wood. It is said that the devil is present in the form of a snake or billy goat.

• In the Middle Ages, there were 'small' Sabbaths, during which the efficacy of magic powders (halluncinogens), aphrodisiac unguents, and all alcoholic drinks were tried. Bacchus was celebrated just as in the Saturnalia. At dawn everyone would rapidly disappear, stupefied and full to bursting. The great Sabbath became an extension of these small ones.[114]

SACRIFICE
gift of self

Sacrifice symbolizes renunciation, and implies the exchange of material goods for spiritual ones. In antiquity its aim was to ensure health and return innocence to a people who had rid themselves of their sins by projecting them on to a victim, who or which was then ritually slaughtered, along with their sins.

• Sacrifice is a symbol of expiation, purification and intercession, and is often encountered as ritual murder accompanied by swearing, whipping, and spitting on the condemned who thus becomes the scapegoat, bearing away all the sins of a community or a people. This is what happened in ancient Libya, when, each year at the spring equinox, they held crucifixions, hangings, or abandoned their victims to bulls, whose horns symbolized the moon (the cult of Astarte), or tortures involving rolling them in or on an object whose shape symbolized the sun – a wheel or chariot (cult of the goddesses Bobat and Tanit, linked to the principles of light).

The first ritual victims were anthropophagic Blacks reduced to slavery, some of whom offered themselves for sacrifice, then the Christians.

• These sacrifices were a source of inspiration for ancient mythologies: the myth of Theseus offering to fight the Minotaur, of Attis who was hanged, of Bel or Indra crucified, of Osiris chopped to pieces . . . Until the time when they opted to put an animal to death instead (the myth of Adonis, of Actaeon), an occasion for people to watch an enthralling fight, thirsty for suffering and blood.[121]

• But sacrifice could also be a symbol of love, like the Roman Galles, priests of Cybele, who at the time of the feast of blood on 24 March, sacrificed their virility to her in sacred drunkenness.

Their organs were then collected, embalmed and kept in a jar, and placed in the goddess Thalame's nuptial chamber.

Mayan human sacrifice

• Human sacrifice among the Amerindians had, as an end goal, the magic fertilization of the land, through the action of the sun. These sacrifices were inseparable from agriculture and agrarian rites. 'Spilling blood was indispensable in order that the earth, thus fertilized, could produce its fruits.' When the inviolability of human life was proclaimed, they replaced human sacrifices with animals ones.[76]

• This concept is similar to the one in the Vedas which also believed in the efficacy of blood in sustaining life.

Sacrifice fulfilled a dual role: it increased the vital force of the gods and helped them continue to exert their beneficial influences on earth, while at the same time it strengthened the men who participated in the cult against the forces of destruction, by giving them a new lease of vital power.

The Vedic sacrifice used to have five victims: a man, a horse, a bull, a goat and a sheep;[98] now it consists only in lighting the divine flame, offering ghee (clarified butter) and *soma* wine while chanting the sacred words.

The adept makes a gift of what he possesses in himself to divine nature and, in exchange, benefits from an enrichment of his human nature, through the gods' generosity. Parallel to this, the gods grow, develop mentally and physically, and create, beyond heaven and earth, other levels or superior worlds.

Seen in this light, sacrifice is a progression towards the truth, light and happiness, on condition that man has 'recourse of thought to divine will and wisdom, represented by Agni, through submission, worship and the gift of the self.'[44]

Sagittarius
23 November–20 December

Sagittarius is a double, masculine, fiery sign and the ninth sign of the zodiac, in the house of Jupiter. Mercury is in exile. It is the sign of wisdom, philosophy and the general ideas of a legislator.

Characteristics and qualities: optimism, taste for travel and exploration, intrepidness, enthusiasm, daring, judgement, sense of honour and joviality.

Negative characteristics: feverish impatience, fanaticism with little objectivity, presumption, blind confidence and enthusiasm, lack of realism.

In the body: thighs, buttocks, arteries and arterial circulation.[122]
Correspondence: tin, turquoise, autumn.

SALT
wisdom

Salt is a primal substance. Baptismal salt (used in the Roman Catholic Church) is a symbol of spiritual food and incorruptibility.

• For alchemists it was the basis of everything that took shape. Combined with sulphur and mercury, its action produced everything that was created.

• As a stabilizing element in the body, salt is therefore a symbol of wisdom and levelheadedness. Its crystallized substance became the body of the philosopher's stone, and the Hermetic philosophers made it sacred to the heavenly Virgin who fertilized the spirit.[18]

• Arabs and Greeks made it a symbol of friendship, hospitality and the given word (along with the breaking of bread).

• In Japan salt (*shio*) is an essential element of worship, and is thought of as a powerful purifying agent because Izanagi bathed in the sea to purify himself after contemplating Izanami's corpse.

Nowadays it is used as a protection against evil in front of the house, morning and evening, or after a visit by a beggar, at restaurant doors, and is sprinkled on returning home after a funeral service.

Before proceeding in the *misogi* (purification exercises), salt is thrown into the bathroom.

Several sanctuaries are sacred to the kami (god) of salt, of which one is Okama-jinja, a temple built on the place where the kami mined salt for the first time, which contains four round cauldrons full of sea water whose colour is said to change when a catastrophe threatens the country.

• Sea bathing is one of the traditional forms of purification.[77]

SAMSARA
eternal beginning

The word of samsara refers to a belief in the transmigration of souls. It means endless reincarnation in a cycle of different existences. Indian religions attempt to deliver the soul from this relentless cycle by interrupting it.[37]

Ignorance, they preach, is the cause of these successive reincarnations into new worlds of suffering. Between these worlds there are twelve links or causes (*nidanas*) corresponding to the signs of the zodiac and to states of consciousness, in ascending order. These states are no more than extensions of the four cardinal principles: moral rules, control of the senses, self-control and learning to be content.

• This 'unending future of causes and effects'[98] is symbolized in the wheel which turns inexorably (as does the wheel of the zodiac), and in the Hindu god Yama, who is also the incarnation of love, for 'love and death are joined, the one feeding the other.'[12]

SATURN
fatal ticking

Originally Saturn was a rustic god; he was shown armed with a vine-grower's pruning knife, and he taught the art of gardening. As the creator-god linked to the creative power of Rhea, he symbolized progress, the principle that regulated vital production. When he was chased from Olympus he took refuge in Italy, where he continued the good deeds of the Golden Age begun by Janus.

• He became a symbol of time and, with the scythe and hourglass as attributes, he became identified with the Greek god Chronos (who had eaten his father and killed his children so that he would not have to undergo the same fate).

• For the Hermetic philosophers, involved in alchemy, Saturn symbolized lead, the basis of their art, a base metal containing the potential of gold; the colour black, which came at the end and beginning of a cycle, if the work of transformation had been effective; arrest, decline, dematerialization, decay, maturity, experience and death.[18]

• In astrology Saturn is the incarnation of scrutiny, fatality, rigour, and the preservation principle, from which comes foresight, seriousness, mental maturity, willpower and reflection.

On an individual level, he appears as an intellectual element ruling memory, and inhibition. Saturn also slows down reflexes.[100]

Negatively, Saturn is associated with weaning and severance and their consequences: fear of life, boredom, lack of adaptation, slowness, laziness, evasion of responsibilities, moroseness, introversion, harking back to the past, solitude, sadness. 'Saturn's rule is that of inhibition and its affective climate of loss, deprivation, frustrations and finally of renunciation and detachment. The type of events associated with Saturn are delays, hindrances, hiatuses, limitations, abandonments, separations, losses, sacrifices. Saturn is especially associated with misery and poverty.'[123]

Correspondences

Body: bones, teeth, cartilage, liver, right ear; becoming cold, lesion of the nervous system, paralysis, weakness in the legs, constipation, deafness.
Moral: greed, mistrust, misanthropy.
General: ruined buildings, cold, fog, hail.
Animal: camel, bear, donkey, rat, mole, bat, owl, crow, tortoise, toad, scarab, spider.
Plant: cypress, ash, hellebore, narcotic plants.
Mineral: lead, sulphur, hard rocks, black stones and earth.
Sites and various: arid, desolate spaces, moorland, desert, cemetery, prison, dungeon, cave, agricultural tool.

SCARAB
eternal return

In ancient Egypt the scarab was a sacred beetle, symbolizing self-creation: its appearance in the mud of the Nile was associated with the phenomenon of spontaneous generation, without recourse to a female.

Having been created from its own matter, just like the sun every morning,[124] it became the symbol of the demiurge (creator of the universe) Khepara who presided over the future of the cosmos. 'When it wants to reproduce, it forms a ball out of cowdung in the shape of the earth, which it rolls with its back legs from east to west . . . and buries this ball in the earth for twenty-eight days, and on the twenty-ninth pushes it into the water.' Here one can see the image of the lunar cycle and, by extension, the drama of initiation: death and new birth at the same time as the resurrection of the dead, according to the Egyptians' beliefs.

• On coffins, the scarab is seen with outstretched wings, rolling the ball of the world in its feet; it symbolizes death and the new birth of the heavenly neophyte.

Scarab with wings spread[124]

• The scarab was a symbol of the world it had fashioned, and also of man, the 'small world' (microcosm) which is mentioned in the mysteries, just as the world is the 'great man'.

• This ball was also thought of as a symbol of the sun, source of life, rolling across the sky, the god 'who embraces the heart and illumines the mind.'[9]

The scarab was intimately linked to life events; it became the psychopomp accompanying mummies as a guarantee of resurrection; and as an agent of protection it was worn as an amulet to attract Khepara's patronage.[124]

SCEPTRE
authority

The symbolism of the sceptre is similar to that of the stick and its derivatives (pillar, column, sword, arrow, obelisk, phallus), attributes of the son god–creator and symbols of God the Father, whose rays fertilize the earth, and of the human father when the symbol is used on a lower level. In popular symbolism, the ideograms have a phallic meaning which conforms to the esoteric symbolism, of creating and giving life.

• The sceptre was associated with the Athenians' sacred circle: the heads of large families, known as sons of Zeus, carried a special sceptre when they went to the *agora* to sit in the sacred circle.

• The sceptre is an extension of the arm and hand and the symbol of active authority and power.

• The Egyptian triple sceptre is made up of a whip, symbolizing domination over matter, a staff, control of feelings, and a stick, domination of thought.[5]

• As 'an indication of royal dignity . . . the sceptre belongs to the group of male symbols'[25] linked to the symbolism of the stick and staff. It is the symbol of the central axis, like the king himself, the intermediary between God and his subjects, a guarantee of peace and justice.

• In China, the sceptre (*ru-yi*) is a sort of good-luck talisman carved in wood or jade. In the iconography, when it is associated with a paintbrush, it symbolizes a cultivated man; if a silver slipper is added, representing money, the picture expresses a hope for success in a profession or business. Formerly, at weddings, the groom's family would place a sceptre alongside that of the bride's family.[7]

Scorpio
23 October–22 November

Scorpio is the eighth sign of the zodiac, a fixed, feminine fertile watery sign, ruled by Mars, a receptive female energy.

Correspondence: cold, heat, night, obedience, crawling, Metal: iron. Mineral: topaz, magnet. Physical: sexual organs. Venom, viruses, infections.[122]

Characteristics: perseverance, tenacity, energy, jealousy, enormous capacity for work.

Negative characteristics: envy, cruelty, hatred, self-destruction or destruction of others.

SCORPION
secret

In Egypt the scorpion was sacred to the goddess Selket, associated with death and the companions of Isis in his wanderings. The Egyptians believed that it would never attack women.[124]

• Because it spent most of its life underground, the scorpion, like the snake, symbolized mystery.

• It has a purifying role, because 'it absorbs poisons from the earth, thus making the earth welcoming, and registers negative forces that the magician can turn into positive ones.'[80]

SEASONS
rhythm of the universe

The Arabs and Greeks once had only three seasons – spring, summer and winter – while Northern peoples only had winter and summer; then the Greeks established autumn, followed by the Romans and Gauls.

• The whole of Nature is subject to the universal rhythm of the seasons, identical to the diurnal cycles divided into three visible parts – sunrise, noon, sunset – and a fourth invisible one – midnight. There is also a cycle of the four ages of man – infancy, development, maturity, decrepitude.

• Each season corresponds to an element: winter – earth, spring – air, summer – water, autumn – fire.

In stories and legends winter is symbolized by a princess being kept in a dungeon, a well, a dark place, or in a prolonged sleep, from which she emerges through the intervention of a Prince Charming, symbol of the new sun; by lame, one-armed crippled gods leaning on a stick (one-legged Priapus); by the masonic grade of Apprentice; by the Hindu caste of Pariah; in tree worship by the root; and in Celtic mythology by Granus, the peasant, the seed of society.

• The symbols of spring are departures on a journey, and flights to escape a persecutor or the love of a god; a white animal (a colt) that escapes, linked to the birth of the sun; winged genii, symbols of alleviation and freedom, the god Vulcan, symbol of springtime sun; the wandering Jew, synthesis of all flight and all travel; the clog-wearers in legends; Goeffrin, the character in chivalric romance; the Masonic grade of Companion or Fellow Craft; in tree worship, the trunk; the Hindu caste of Shudras (serfs); in the theatre, Pulchinello.

• Summer corresponds to aquatic myths of god-fish, bathing, immersions (Vishnu walking on the waters), Lethe's waves of oblivion, symbolism translated in folklore by manikins thrown into rivers; in the initiatic rites, through immersion, a test to ensure the energy of the candidate and to detach him from his past (it survives in the ordeal that is undergone by passengers when they first cross the equator by sea); by Mars, image of a burning sun; soldiers; everything that is rich and has panache; the Hindu caste of Kshatrias (warriors); the Masonic grade of Master Mason; in society, nobility; in chivalry, the characters of Galbinus, Galvaing and Guvin; in tree worship, the ripe golden fruit.

• Autumn corresponds to myths of fire destroying everything before total renewal: the myth of Hephaistos who forged shields, swords and arrows, the body and members of the new sun; Argos and the spies of fairy tales, from the wizard to the pedlar; everybody who wears a mask (Harlequin); the Hindu caste of Brahman (the highest caste); the Masonic grade of Purple (in France); in tree worship, the root.

• In ancient China there were five seasons corresponding to the elements, colours, etc., the fifth being very brief and following summer. Whereas in the West the seasons begin only shortly after the equinoxes and solstices, in China they began one or two months later. And so when they talk of plum tree blossom in winter, they would be really talking about April or May.

The seasons correspond to a colour and a plant: spring – green, peony; summer – lotus; autumn – white, chrysanthemum; winter – plum tree.

Man's life, which begins at conception (a new-born baby is already a year old), is compared to that of the four seasons: spring lasts until fifteen, summer from sixteen to twenty-nine; autumn from thirty to thirty-nine; winter from forty to fifty or sixty.[7]

SEPHIROTH
creation mysteries

The tree of the ten sephiroth (*sephira* (sing.) = numeration) or the tree of life is a fundamental part of Cabbalistic teaching and is an attempt to explain the mysteries of creation through numbers. It is a synthesis that applies to everything, every idea in the divine, intellectual, affective and material plan, a universal logic helping us to glimpse worlds situated beyond our normal horizons, and approach truths which human intelligence can barely grasp.

The sephiroth are the simple numbers from 1 to 10, 10 being a return to unity. These numbers are divine attributes or manifestations of the divine substance: *Ain Soph*.

Each of them is associated with ideas, images, analogies, and knowledge.

• One, Kather, is the point of departure for everything, the first manifestation of the Absolute, the philosopher's 0; 10 represents the world, the betrothed in the Bible, or the created universe; the intermediary numbers symbolize the process of creation or the universe nearing completion.

• The sephiroth are divided into three groups of three.

– 1, 2 and 3 form a triangle pointing upwards, a symbol of the spiritual trinity, of the world of archetypes containing the Principle of things that have the potential to create, *Olam Atsilus*. It rules the abyss.

– 4, 5 and 6 form an inverted triangle, symbol of the world of creation, *Olam Briath*, containing concrete ideas of things which have the potential to create.

– 7, 8 and 9 form a third (inverted) triangle, the world of forms, *Olam Yetsirah*, the astral world containing exact images of things nearing materialization, according to the law of the Emerald Tablet of Hermes Trismegistus: 'Everything that is on high is as it is below.'

The Tree of Life is summarized in the formula YHVH.

• Here are the correspondences of the sephiroth:

0 nothingness: ouroboros – non-manifested God – possibilities – camphor.

1 Kaether: the crown, principle of all principles – awakening of consciousness – Neptune – inspiration, mental creation – projects. White – space. Heaven of fire – phallus, eagle, almond flower, diamond, ambergris, swan (ecstasy).

2 Cochma: highest wisdom, creative thought: logos – air and breath – female principle – passivity – word – support in enterprises – obedience – reconciliation. Infra-red – grey – musk – aramanthus flower. Movement – yoni, sperm, turquoise, ruby.

3 Binah: intelligence or spirit, comprehension, conception of ideas. Water – Holy Spirit – Chronos – material of things – breath of life – vital force – time – water – sea – illusion. Process of realization – childbirth – genius – knowledge – union of the sexes. Opium – myrrh. Saturn – lily, starred sapphire, pearl, lead.

4 Chesed: associated with fire: grace, mercy. Power to give and spread life – Jupiter. Order – solidity. Materialization – ministers – prelates. Buildings – monuments. Olive tree – cedar – pine. Blue – sapphire, amethyst. Chamois. Jupiter – ostrich feather, horse, thunder, sceptre.

5 Pechard: associated with the zenith: strength, rigour, severity; corresponds to duty. Creative power – realization of hopes – heartbeats – novelties – new affairs – dissipation of fortune – armed robbery. The five currents of Prâna – surgical operations. Nettles – insect stings or snake bites. Red. Mars – eagle – sword, dagger – oak – tobacco – iron.

6 Tipheroth: associated with the nadir: beauty, connected with sensitivity: sun – vine. Abundant vitality –

renaissance. Heat – affection – abundance. Oliban. Yellow diamond. Sun – lamp, rays, yellow diamond and gold, acacia, vine, raisin grape, orange.

7 Nizah: associated with the East: victory, firmness; reliance on the coordinating principle governing the world: completed cycle – sexual strength – attraction – return to lost things. Success – production. Restitution. Green. Venus – pink – rosebush. Emerald – frankincese – sandalwood. Copper.

8 Hod: corresponding to the west: honour, glory; the immutable law of things: the caduceus, Mercury. Writings – words – knowledge – astrology. Medicine: sympathetic and vague sensitivity – sensation. Businessmen – thieves – writers. Loss of objects. Instability. Business papers – messengers – light yellow – multi-colours. Opal. Mercury.

9 Yesod: midday, foundation, basis, latent energies and their future: water – mirror. Diana. Clairvoyance – reflection – dreams – stability through change. Good fortune from a mysterious source – remunerative journeys. Photographs. Light blue – quartz. Jasmine – ginseng – silver – moon.

10 Malcuth: North, kingdom, reign, thought, will, action: earth. Persephone. Sphinx – preparation for return to unity. Completed work – harvest – old age – fertility – consequences of deeds completed irremediably. Materialism – heaviness – people of limited vision – ivy – willow – lily – rock crystal – earth.

• As in every symbolic representation of the world, this planetary ladder is continued in the dark kingdom of the *Qliphots*, in the black sephiroth and the tree of death situated in the underworld.[81, 4, 17]

SEVEN
harmony

From ancient times, the number 7 has symbolized the manifestation of cosmic order and organization.

• As a solar number, it is featured on ancient monuments as a crown with seven rays related to the seven heavens of Zoroaster, the seven oxen drawing the sun's chariot in Nordic legends, and above all the seven planets made into gods by the Babylonians who named the days of the week after them.

These divinities were symbolized in seven stars, seven crosses, seven busts, seven flaming altars, seven knives planted in the ground or seven trees.[121]

• The planets corresponded to seven planets described by Hermes Trismegistus: the Sun – horsetail, Venus – verbena, Mercury – cinquefoil, Mars – plantain, Jupiter – sugar, Saturn – asphodel, the Moon – honeysuckle.

• In the Scriptures, the number 7, which ruled time and space, is a complete number signifying all or the entirety of the thing to which it is applied.

• The summer solstice takes place when the sun passes the seventh zodiacal sign, the winter solstice when it has completed seven signs after that. There are seven signs between one equinox and another, which together make up the whole solar cycle.

• Seven is a symbol of abundance and an expression of divine wholeness. It is linked to the Jewish cultural past: the Jewish year begins in the joy of the new moon in the seventh month, the Day of Trumpets. Every seven years, they celebrate the Year of the Sabbath which is also known as the Year of Dispensation: slaves were freed and land was left fallow.

At the end of forty-nine lunar years (7 × 7) they celebrated Jubilee Year. The candlestick had seven branches; there were seven seals, seven trumpets, seven scourges, etc.

• Seven is the number of order and organization in space: the seven wandering stars gave rise to the concept of seven heavens crossed by the soul on its return to the eternal, unique principle and organizer of the world, symbolized in the seven storeys of the ziggurat, the Babylonian temple uniting heaven with earth.

• The seven stars of the Great and Little Bear, the seven oxen or *septem*triones which have given us the word septentrion.

• In ancient times, these seven planets under their different aspects incarnated all possible aspects of divinity and the secret forces of Nature and the unknown.[4]

• But 7 is also the number of sin (the seven cardinal sins) and, in the Old Testament, 7 is the number of expiation and vengeance (Cain would be avenged seven times; Lamech, his descendant, seventy-seven times). Lamech lived to be 777 years old.[135]

• This ambivalance applied to number 7 dominates the Revelation of St John the Divine, where 7 is both a symbol of divine abundance and punishment.

• In the West man's life is ruled by multiples of seven: after seven months in the womb, a foetus is viable. Seven marks the periods in a life: infancy until 7, the age of reason 7 × 2 = 14 which is the end of childhood; 7 × 3 = 21, coming of age, end of adolescence; 7 × 4 = 28 youth; 7 × 5 = 35 adulthood; 7 × 6 = 42 maturity, followed by a decline in strength.[73]

• In China, 7 (*qi*), a yang number is associated with woman, yin, whose rhythm of development it rules: at seven months, the appearance of milk teeth, which will be lost at seven years. At 7 × 2 = 14, the 'path of yin' opens (the appearance of menstruation), which finishes at 7 × 7 = 49 with the menopause. After death, the soul is progressively separated from the world and its family, over a period of seven days. The seventh day is given over to precise rituals and offerings. On the forty-ninth day, the dead person passes into another world.[7]

• In Egypt, 7 was a symbol of eternal life, and gods, like the dead, were subject to the septenary rhythm: at the seventh hour of the night, Rê's barque confronted the serpent Apophis; the dead had to cross 'seven chambers' and 'seven doors' before reaching the elevated spheres of Amenti. Seven was also a creative number. Osiris spent seven months in the bosom of his mother Nut, and in certain temples his statue was left for seven days on the branches of a sycamore tree (one of Nut's attributes); in early Christian belief, the Virgin Mary gave birth after seven months of pregnancy.[4]

• In Persia it was a sacred number. There were seven initiatory degrees in the Mithraic cult: Crow – Griffon – Soldier – Lion – Persian – Heliodrome (sun's messenger) – Father.

• In Greece, the seventh day was sacred to Apollo, born on the seventh day of the month, the seventh god, of the seventh door, who played a lyre with seven strings (the heptachord). Pan's flute had seven reeds, a symbol of celestial harmony. In mythology, there are the seven Hesperides, the seven children of Niobe, seven Cyclops, seven daughters of Astarte, and seven doors and circles of hell.

• Seven is also the number of female initiation. In the legend of the Holy Grail, the hero, Sir Galahad sees seven virgins defended by seven knights: an image indicating to the knight that he 'must free the seven in order to give back indispensable spiritual illumination to man's life.'[47]

Seven is also found in the seven great rites of the Sioux:

guarding the soul, purification ritual, vision quest, sundance, rites of puberty, rites of marriage, and the ball game.[12]

• Seven is the number of virginity, which Pythagoreans linked to Minerva, who was born from Jupiter's head, and was therefore without a mother, and always the virgin goddess of reason.

• Seven is the number of accomplishment, expressed in the Chariot of the tarot and the seventh sephira Netzah, meaning victory.

• Seven symbolizing the perfection of fullness is a common feature in all religions: Mesopotamian, Sumerian, Jewish, Greek, Persian, Arab, Christian, Chinese, Hindu, etc. Egypt had seven gods of light and seven of darkness, prototypes of the seven spirits of the presence and the seven devils of the Christians.

• Seven is the number of purification, of penitence (seven years for each sin, freeing slaves in the seventh year, mourning lasting seven days).

• Seven is the agent of evolution: creation took place in seven days, there are seven patriarchies in the Book of Revelation, seven candlesticks, seven stars, seven spirits, etc. Number 7 is mentioned 700 times in the Old and New Testaments; it contains the secret of the true cross which has arms in six directions (plus the centre), extending endlessly up, down, to right, left, in front and behind. 'Directing its gaze towards these six extends us towards a number which is always equal, it completes the world; it is the beginning and the end; in it the six phases of time are completed and it is from time that it receives their unending extension: that is the secret of the number 7.'

• In Islam there are seven heavens, seven earths, seven hells, seven gates to paradise, seven prophets that the Sufis link to the seven subtle prophets and to a colour: Adam – matt black, Noah – blue, Abraham – red, Moses – white, David – yellow, Jesus – luminous black, Mohammed – green.[116]

On pilgrimages to Mecca, the Ka'aba is circumambulated seven times, and the distance between Mounts Cafa and Marnia is walked seven times. The souls of the dead live near their tomb for seven days. The newly born are given their name on the seventh day.[73]

• In Hinduism, 7 is a number obtained by adding the three divine principles to the three principles of the universe and inserting a seventh principle of union, that of consciousness of the truth. It plays an important role in the Vedic system which has seven delights (*sapta ratnani*), seven fires of Agni (*sapta archishah*), seven rays (*sapta gavah*) seven rivers, seven cows or nursing mothers.[44]

SHADOW
imperfections

Shadow and light are the Chinese yin and yang. Shadows were once thought to be the souls of the departed leading a semi-material existence and able to intervene in human affairs: this was the reason for funeral rites and sacrifices intended to help the dead.

• The shadow of a person is sometimes identified with his soul: whoever sells his soul to the devil loses his shadow. In certain cultures, to step on a shadow is a mortal offence. Midday is the most dangerous time when 'to diminish a shadow is equivalent to a death threat.'[28]

• In the Jungian sense, the shadow is the semi-conscious negative part of the psyche, rejected on moral or rational grounds as not appearing sensible or acceptable, or the individual simply refuses to acknowledge it. It consists of residues of paralysing childish complexes that we drag along with us, and which Paul Diel calls 'false motivations'.

These obscure triggers of bad behaviour, repeated mistakes and nasty, selfish attitudes are often revealed in or superimposed on so-called high-minded motives.[105]

In as much as we live on this side of the veil it cannot be torn from us;[66] for the integration of this *alter ego* is the beginning of awareness, leading to an objective attitude to our personality.

• In dreams, the shadow is sombrely disguised as monsters, or clumsy, badly dressed or inept people, who appear during the process of individuation or psychic maturation, inviting us to criticize severely our behaviour and ourselves.

SHEEP
susceptibility

The sheep (*yang*) is the eighth sign in the Chinese zodiac. Those born under this sign will have a timid, gentle, sincere and compassionate personality, capable of creativity, but easily overwhelmed by emotion and pessimism.

During the Year of the Sheep, there will be calm, slow development on both a world and personal level. But relationships risk disruption through hypersensitivity and irritability.[118]

SHIELD
protection

In the mythology of the sun, the shield and sword symbolize respectively the solar disk and its rays, god as father and god as judge, or boundary or partition spirit, and it represents the meridian dividing the circle of the equator into two equal parts, east and west. This in turn marks the exact point where the sun begins its daily course around the globe (in primitive believe, the sun revolved around the earth).

• The shield can be found as a decoration on ritual vases, protecting chapels, trees and sacred animals. Numa placed Rome under the protection of twelve consecrated shields based on a model 'sent from heaven'; in other words, it imitated the solar disk. At the beginning of the year, priests used shields in their sacred dances.

• The shield was the earliest kind of setting for a ring and is still in use today on signet rings.

SILVER
fidelity, purity or corruptibility

Silver is associated symbolically with the moon; and in the same way that the planet darkens during daylight hours, this metal tarnishes and must be polished. In its harmful aspect, it can symbolize the corruptibility of man who must constantly fight his negative tendencies if he wishes to develop.

• It is also associated with femininity, and those who are attracted by it often need to find or accept forces of the anima within themselves which they have neglected or repressed.

• Because of its shiny light colour, polished silver symbolizes purity, frankness, fidelity, correctness; its opposite is black.

• In Christian symbolism it is identified with divine wisdom.

SISTRUM
celestial music

The sistrum (a musical instrument, made of an oval frame supporting metal rods threaded through metal disks, which makes a strident noise when shaken) was used in the worship of Isis to chase away demons.

The curve at the top symbolized the moon's orbit from which the goddess exerted her power 'by shaking the four elements symbolized in the four rattles below.'

Buddhists' ritual sistrum[90]

The central ornament is the 'symbol of the star, which, through its influence on women's health, presides over childbirth.'

• The shaking of the rattles and the resultant noise, recognized as a symbol of the 'movement and mingling of the fundamental elements of everything' gave rise to the symbolism of sound: the tinkling of bells, the clashing of metal cymbals accompanying sacrifices, etc. Even today, the sistrum continues to ring in the shape of the small bell that accompanies the division of Mass in the Catholic Church.[83]

SIX
beauty

Six is the number of perfection and beauty: the sixth sephira of the Cabbalah, Tipheroth, signifies beauty and ornament (symbolized in the planet Venus); there are six colours (three primary, blue, yellow and red, and three derivatives, green, orange and purple).[30]

The sixth major arcana of the tarot, the Lovers, is associated with Venus-Ishtar, the warrior-lover, morning star as well as the star of the setting sun.[17]

• Six is a symbol of stability and balance, and according to Cabbalists the number of union and fertilization.

According to the Persians' *Avesta*, the macrocosm was created in six periods: (1) heaven in forty-five days, (2) water in sixty days, (3) earth in seventy-five days, (4) vegetation in thirty days, (5) animals in eighty days, (6) man in seventy-five days (total = 365 days). From this came the idea of the six days of creation by Jehovah for the Jews and by Allah for the Arabs.

• Six symbolizes universality and harmony: it is the number of the hexagon and of Solomon's seal, the king who built his temple on six steps, and whose throne was elevated on six steps. It is also the number of arms on the spatial cross which extend in six directions.

Six is also found in the six-pointed star enclosing the four elements, each characterized by two qualities (fire (heat and dryness), air (heat and moistness), water (moistness and cold), earth (cold and dry)).

• In the Apocalypse, 666 is the number of the Beast, incarnation of the spirit of evil.

SIXTEEN
accomplishment

Sixteen is 4 squared and indicates the accomplishment of material power.[1]

It is also the sum of the first four uneven numbers, 1 + 3 + 5 + 7 = 16, which, through theosophical addition, gives 1 + 6 = 7, a sacred number. Some cathedral rose windows (for example Strasbourg) have sixteen sections.

• In antiquity, there were sixteen sacred plants: catnip (vitality), centaury (spells), celandine (triumph), mistletoe (health), heliotrope (sincerity), henbane (death), hound's tongue (sympathy), lily (manifestation), balm (comfort), nettle (bravery), periwinkle (fidelity), rose (initiation), sage (life), snakeroot (fluids), verbena (love) and virgo pastoris (fertility).

SNAKE, REPTILE
life or death

Snake symbols appear in every ancient civilization, but with varying meanings.

• The snake is a symbol of life and vigour because it is able to shed its skin and regain an appearance of youth, and in myths it is an attribute of gods of health. Aesculapius, god of healing, the incarnation of inner, psychic life and a symbol of the perpetual renewal of life, had as an attribute two snakes entwined around the caduceus to symbolize the ascending and descending currents of the universal force.

• Playing a protective role is the *uraeus* (cobra), incarnation of the goddess Butto of Lower Egypt, who spat fire to defend anyone who held her. She is seen accompanied by a vulture (symbol of Upper Egypt) on the pharaoh's double crown, encircling the winged sun wheel as a symbol of creative force.

• The snake also served as a psychopomp, protecting the dead against their enemies as it led them on their journey into the Beyond.

• The snake is also present in the cycles of universal manifestation: in the *Pistis Sophia* (attributed to Valentinus), the body of a Gnostic snake was divided up like a zodiac.[4]

• A reptile also appears as a death symbol, and a symbol of Satan, who is found joined to his opponent, the serpent of life, in the *amphisbaena* (a reptile, sometimes depicted as a dragon, with a head at each end, and able to move in both directions). One of its heads is white, winged, and wearing a crown, which symbolizes 'the unity that results from attention to self-improvement, and that unleashes the volatile from the static, conquers the baser instincts and releases the bonds' that are symbolized in the reptile's black half. The central knot in its body represents suffering that is an integral part of this obstinate search for spirituality.[136]

• In heraldic art, the image of a crowned snake giving birth to a child is used to symbolize the revelation that comes after initiation, or the true dignity that comes with initiation.

Reptiles also symbolize the hidden forces of the underworld which, if procured, 'give the knight invincible strength'.[47]

• In the Egyptian *Book of the Dead*, the snake is seen as a symbol of earth, while among the Maya-Chortis, it was linked to creation: the coupling of heaven and earth from which the Maya-Quiche race was born is symbolized in the bird-serpent (or plumed serpent) Quetzalcoatl, shown in the iconography as a snake whose blood was extracted to form a human body.[76]

The Aztecs worshipped the snake as a symbol of supreme power and of the unique spirit which impregnates all forms of life in the universe.[5]

• It was part of the process of creation surrounding the cosmic egg (chaos), where it symbolized fertilization by the vital divine spirit found in the sperm of every living thing, thus releasing inert matter through its divine power.[83]

• A reptile appears a a symbol of immortality, entwined around the tree bearing the golden apples in the garden of the Hesperides and the sacred oak in the forest at Colchis on which the Golden Fleece was hung.[35] A snake encircled the omphalos or cosmic mountain (axis of the world) to symbolize the 'collection of cycles of universal manifestation,'[35] the samsara, man's enchainment to the endless cycle of rebirths.

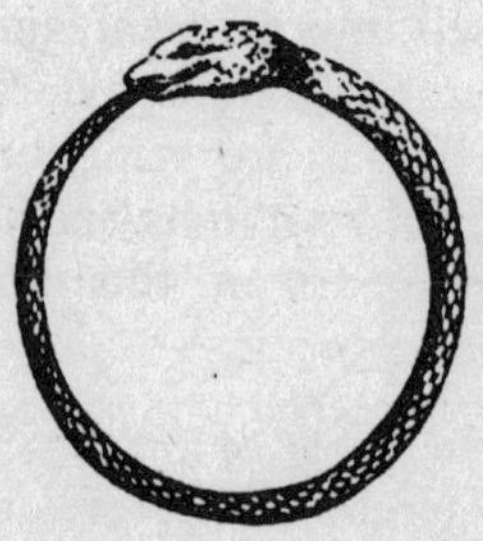

The ouroboros, the snake swallowing its tail[47]

The snake also forms the ouroboros, the vicious circle, the unendingness of a cycle which, seen in isolation by man who lives in the presence of time, seems like a life sentence lived over and over again.

• The serpent in the Garden of Eden symbolizes dangerous knowledge (the discovery of sexuality). And developing from this the snake has become a phallic, sexual symbol. The snake is a tempter-snake who is the bearer of dangerous and malefic forces, and whose weapon lies in Eve's seductive powers (the anima).

• The *kundalini*-snake of hatha yoga symbolizes cosmic and sexual energy, the vital power of libido, asleep in the *chakra* of the pubis, which must be awakened, revitalized and directed towards the chakra on the crown of the head (sublimation of the libido, union in God), passing through the vital intermediary centres. Sublimation is full of pitfalls and hindrances.

• The reddish-brown snake in the centre of the Buddhist Wheel of Existence symbolizes hatred.

• In India, Vasuki, king of snakes, is a symbol of knowledge and intelligence. In the epics, serpents are descended from gods, and the snake, Cesa, who in mythology upholds the earth, is similar to Ananta, the snake stretched on the waters, a personification of eternity which, with Vishnu Narayana (who rests upon it) forms the triple manifestation of cosmic energy, unique and imperishable.

Under the name of *nag*, reptiles are still the focus of worship in a cult that relies on the fear and fascination they provoke, and on the impression of mystery and strangeness they give. The iconography shows them as polycephalic (many-headed) creatures with a cobra's hood.

• In China, the snake (*sue*) is one of four poisonous animals and the fifth sign of the zodiac associated with the south, spring and fire. It symbolizes cunning, wrongdoing and stealth.

The Snake Years are characterized by contrasts, and are favourable to shrewd negotiations, commerce and industry, the settlement of conflicts, and romance, but also to *coups d'état*, scandals, calamities and surprises of all sorts.

In the collective unconscious, snakes and reptiles symbolize aggression at a lower level, and power and wisdom at a higher one.[5]

The snake symbolizes the unconscious where all the rejected, hidden, unknown or misunderstood factors accumulate, as well as the possibilities latent within us.

It is these very primitive forces, clustered together, that make the snake appear in dreams, where it is a manifestation of a dormant psychic energy ready to become active in either a positive or negative way – for the symbolism of this cold-blooded creature is ambivalent, capable of evil (fear, anguish) or good (healing).

SOLOMON'S SEAL
macrocosm

Solomon's seal is made up of two interlocking equilateral triangles, one white, one black, forming a star hexagram. In both Jewish and alchemical traditions, this symbol is an image of the world, the Star of the Macrocosm or the Great World, the sum of Hermetic thought.

• There are ideograms of the elements contained in it: fire is the white triangle with its point at the top, water the inverted black triangle, air the white triangle intersected by the base of the black triangle, and earth the black triangle intersected by the base of the white triangle.

The white triangle also symbolizes God, or the forces of evolution; the black triangle, which is both opposite and complementary to it, symbolizes involution and earthly forces.

• Some occultists see the triangle as a symbol of the Cabbalists's solar Christ, and upside-down it is the 'ideogram of the sun's shadow' or 'Satan's fall from spirituality', which makes the seal the image of the 'true sun containing good and bad influences.'[4]

• The seal is a symbol of the philosopher's stone, the ultimate goal of alchemy's great work, which consists in transforming and purifying imperfect metals into perfection in order to create the union of the human microcosm with the macrocosm. The seal symbolizes the seven metals of the royal art and the seven planets which are the sum of heaven: silver – moon – top point, lead – Saturn – bottom point, iron – Mars – top left point, Venus – copper – top right point, Jupiter – tin – bottom left point, Mercury – mercury – bottom right point, gold – sun – centre, place of unique perfection.

• In (French) Masonic symbolism, the seal represents the Officers: the Worshipful Master and Superintendents who are in charge of the lodge form the ascendant white triangle, while the descending black triangle features the Speaker, Secretary and Tylers.

• Placed near the seal, the Masons' square and compasses suggest infinity, spirit and matter.[109]

SOMA
sacred drunkenness

In India, the preparation of *soma* as an oblation is a vital part of Vedic sacrifice, and follows a complicated ritual; it takes place on a sacred site replicating the configuration of the universe.

The presence of seven officiants is required, and there must be three fires (the ever-burning fire, and, to its right, the fire of oblations, and the south fire, associated with the spirits) fed by *soma*.

The plant (*asclepius acida*) undergoes three poundings, in the morning, at midday and in the evening, using a sacred stone pestle and mortar. The juice is then filtered and poured into cups, mixed with water, milk, soured milk and flour. It is then sprinkled on the south fire. Meanwhile the participants also drink the sacred liquid to become an integral part of the divine intoxication.

Soma is Indra's soul, and the divine being or spirit of the pounded, plant, which is truly present in the sacred beverage, renews the life of the world, of man and gods, and transfers a magical power to Indra, enabling him to accomplish deeds and be victorious. This is the drink of heroes.

It is also the drink of immortality, an intermediary between man and gods, and corresponds to the heavenly drink brought down to mankind by Indra's eagle: 'liquid fire', associated with the sun. Its oblation has a cosmic power that extends over the entire universe.

It is recognized as having healing and magical properties: restoring sight to the blind, movement to the paralysed, assuring prosperity and a long life.

• This ritual is closely linked to the ritual of *Haoma*, the focus of sacrifice in the worship of Ahura Mazda in ancient Persia; according to the *Avesta* scriptures, *Haoma* also has healing powers, and offers strength, long life, prosperity, wisdom and immortality.[129]

SOUL

the centre of energy, the manifestation of invisible reality in man

According to primitive belief, every living body is made up of visible matter and an invisible spirit, the soul.

• The Egyptian *Book of the Dead* sees man as made up of several components.

– *Ka*, the immortal spiritual element, a basis for life after death, life's etheric double (which must be preserved so that the dead body's members can be held together and its integrity maintained – from which stemmed the practice of embalming). *Ka* is depicted by an egret-ibis, or by two raised arms.

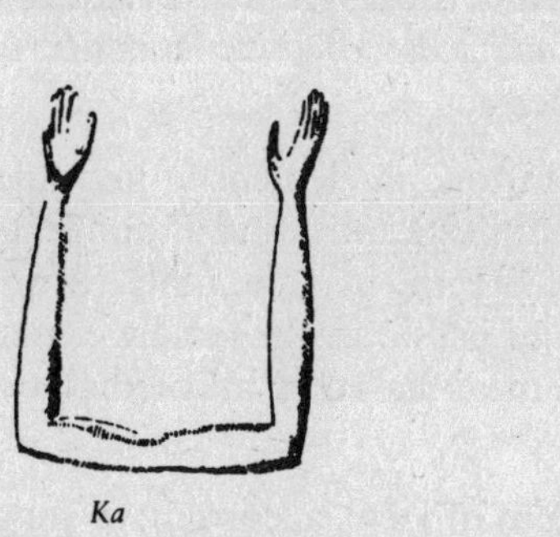

Ka

Ba

Two components of the soul; two raised arms, Ka, *and a bird with a human head,* Ba

– *Khaibit* or shade (elementary instinct, animal passions, vices . . .) reveals itself in the form of a ghost (the Cabbalist's outer skin).

– *Ba* is the emotional element twinned with the heart (*Ib*) and is depicted by a bird with a human head, capable of making judgements and decisions.

• The Chinese distinguish two souls: *po* which animates man and lives for a long time after death near his tomb, and *hun*, which determines personality.[7]

• The Canadian Naskapi Indians depict the soul as a small flame coming from the mouth.

• Saint Paul made a distinction between the soul (*psyche*) which animates man's body (*soma*) and the immortal spirit (*pneuma*), under the influence of the Holy Spirit, shining through the psyche on to the complete man, so that he might live and be made whole again after the resurrection.

• Scholars have distinguished three levels in the human soul: the vegetative soul which governs elementary functions (nutrition, reproduction); the sensitive soul which governs the sense organs; the rational soul governing the intellectual and affective functions that differentiate man from beast.

• The soul is vital inspiration, an element of invisible life, of which we see only manifestations, and is connected to the symbolism of air, of breath. It is the male element or animus, seat of desires and passions, the female element or anima, concerned with the inhalation and exhalation of air.

• From an analytical point of view, according to Jung, the soul 'denotes a link with the unconscious . . . a personification of the contents of the unconscious . . . belonging both to the individual but also to the world of spirits.'

For Jung, the anima is the female element in the male psyche, and the animus is the male element in the female psyche.

The animal has four stages of development: the first,

symbolized by Eve, is the instinctive, biological level; the second stage is on an aesthetic and romantic level but retains the sexual elements; in the third, love is taken to an elevated plane of spirituality and devotion, as depicted by the Virgin Mary; the fourth stage is represented by wisdom. The human soul must pass through all these stages before it attains spirituality.

SPACE
totality

The symbolism of space is based on the compass card: East – right, West – left, North – top, South – bottom, a means of orienting oneself that places man at the centre of the universe.

• Above him is the sky and North, corresponding to spirituality, intellectuality, moral and spiritual ascension and ambition.

It is also the starting-point for alchemy: 'they met at the small north doro to embark upon the Great Work. Uncreated light is regenerated in the North.'[80]

• The area below man is linked to the underworld of hidden powers, sombre pictures, decadence, instincts, the unconscious, everything that is hidden and repressed.

• To man's left, the West is associated with the idea of origin, and thus of childhood, the mother, the past, conservatism, unhappiness, clumsiness and, by extension, introversion, a turning-in on oneself, passivity.

Left (in myths, dance, statuary) is associated with matriarchy, lunar religions, the past, the mother.

Everything that is found or which happens on the left is bad: the underworld had two roads, the one on the left led to the place where the wicked were punished, where 'the

Last Judgement took place, where we come face to face with our Number, with the truth that we have gleaned or failed to glean from our existence.'

Japan is the exception to this rule. In their mythology and ritual, the left (*hidari*) is linked to the sun, the male element. The goddess of the sun, Ameterasu, principal kami (god) of the Shinto pantheon, merged from Izanagi's left eye.[77]

• The right corresponds to the East where light dawns each morning, 'where the creative impulse rises', the father, the future, action, progress, evolution, goals to be achieved, extroversion, an opening-up to others, to happiness.

In myths, everything that takes place on the right is good; in hell, the right road led to where the happy souls lived.

But in Shinto tradition, the right (*migi*) was connected with *mizu*, water, the female element. The goddess of the moon, Tsukiyomi, emerged from Izanagi's right eye.[77]

• The four cardinal points are significant only in relation to the centre which created them, a symbol of the affective ego that intervenes in daily life and is constantly receiving impressions from the four orientations.

• This symbolism has penetrated deep into twentieth-century man's life, and his gestures, writing, superstitions and folklore are all tangible manifestations of this.

SPHERE

universe, divine power

In ancient civilizations, the sphere was a symbol of the universe, of the extreme limits of every direction of the supreme God's power (for example, the sphere carried by Atlas).

• In the centre, primordial ether was symbolized by Yod, the tenth letter of the Hebrew alphabet (in writing Yod is like an apostrophe). In India Yod and the sphere were symbolized by the lotus flower floating on the mother-waters, whose petals enclosed the totality of lives yet to be born in all the kingdoms of Nature.[136] This symbolism has been projected on to the ball (*sphaera ourania*) and bowl, symbols of life, and the apple.

• For the Stoics, Pythagoreans and Neo-Platonists, the perfect soul, once freed from the body, took the form of a sphere.[121]

• When the sphere is cut through by two crossbands, decorated with a crescent moon and seven stars, or cut diagonally into two intersecting circles, and by the disk around the sign of the zodiac, it symbolizes divine intelligence.

• The upper hemisphere (*dome*) symbolizes religious aspiration, and the lower hemisphere is a receptacle with a symbolism similar to the chalice, cup or vase.[78]

• In ancient Egypt, the sphere (winged globe) represented sublimated matter.[17]

SPHINX
guardian

Tetramorphs, that is, hybrids made up of the head of a man (*androsphinx*), hawk (*hierocephalus*), or ox (*criosphinx*), are found among Assyrian, Egyptian, Persian, Hittite, Phoenician and other cultures, and are sun gods. In fact, the animals from which they are made (lion, eagle, bull) and the angel symbolize the cardinal points in Indo-European sun worship.[121]

In these figures the bull is generally positioned in the

lower regions 'to show that creative strength is the basic support of all his attributes.'[83]

In ancient Egypt, sphinxes, masters of the secret, were positioned at entrances to sanctuaries. 'They guarded the mysteries by warning those entering to conceal the knowledge from profane people. They had the significance of masters or lords who, like gods, were hidden from public view.'[9]

• Here is Dr P. Carton's interpretation of the tetramorph's symbolic meaning:

> The bull's flanks represent the physical body, abdominal nutrition, lymph, the inertia of water . . . the vice of sensuality, in short, the lymphatic temperament.
>
> The eagle's wings represent the vital force, thoracic nutrition, blood, the movement of air, all the exaggerated passions we feel, in other words, the sanguine temperament.
>
> The man's head represents the immaterial spirit and the seat of thought, earthly knowledge, earth, in other words, the nervous temperament.
>
> The lion's claws and limbs represent devouring flames, active vigour and unifying energy, which adds intensity to instincts and voluntary action, in other words, the bilious temperament.
>
> The ancients in their wisdom drew the four fundamental rules of human conduct from the enigma of the sphinx: learn with the intelligence of the human brain; desire with the vigour of a lion; dare to rise with the audacious power of eagle's wings; be silent with the massive, concentrated power of the bull.[5]

• The sphinx (KRVB) is the ancestor of the cherubim (derived from KERUB) and is an example of the translation of sun symbols into Christian tradition.

The original symbolism of the cherubim, shown in a vision to Ezekiel is exactly similar to that of the tetramorph. 'They four had the face of a man, and the face of a lion, on the right side; and they four had the face of an ox on the left side; and they four also had the face of an eagle.' Each of these figures was accompanied by a gigantic luminous wheel, representing the sun at the times of the solstices and equinoxes.

• The KRVB is also the griffon in sun worship, seen vigilantly guarding treasure, and a symbol of the god of heaven, Phoebus Apollo.[121]

• The sphinx of myth was a kind of monster, half female, half lion and is, according to P. Diel, 'a symbol of debauchery, the domination of perversity, and the imagined exaltation of desire . . . in its active form it becomes stirred up into a danger that ravages the world and can only be controlled through the intellect.'[36]

• For the visitor of every age, the sphinx remains a mask, the symbol of unfathomable mystery, as Georges Buraud wrote: the sphinx is 'the essential mask, because as a transposition of the human face (or rather a combination of beast and man) it is devoid of any individuality . . . the monster of Gizeh survives for every because it looks out across time, and will forever remain the eternal idea (in the Platonic sense) of a simulacrum of the human face.'[138]

SPIDER
anguish, depression

The spider's symbolism is partly related to the Greek myth of Arachne, who challenged Athene, Zeus' daughter, to a weaving contest, and hanged herself when the goddess destroyed her web. Athene then changed her into a spider, condemned for eternity to hang at the end of her thread: an example of the danger of excessive ambition.

• The spider spins its thread, weaves its web, and once it has finished, cuts the thread: such was the image of human destiny, revealed by the Fates in ancient Roman religion. From this sprang the idea of the spider having the power of creation, and of the web as an endlessly complicated network, symbolizing the cosmos and the mysterious motives for existence.

• There are legends in West Africa that attribute the creation of the sun to the spider. And in various parts of the world it is thought to possess the power of divination, which give it cosmic significance.

• In folk tales of the Agni (Ivory Coast), the spider symbolizes 'man disturbed by short-lived vain conquests, which fade away the moment they have been achieved, so that improving his situation in any decisive way is impossible.'[139]

• The Jungian interpretation of the spider, motionless in the centre of its web and repellent to most people, is that it is a symbol of anguish and associated with narcissism, excessive love of oneself.

• In dreams, a spider reveals hidden terrors, a state of mental confusion, introversion and difficulty in communicating.

SPIRAL

evolution or involution

The spiral is frequently found in the natural world and has been widespread from earliest times. Spirals formed by the movement of water, a sacred maternal element, were manifestations of the life of the universe and seen as 'living things', and were therefore images of life. They also symbolized breath and perhaps fire (solar rosaces had a spiral in the centre, and barleycorn columns are another example).[121]

• The spiral cycle symbolizes the form evolution follows. Each spiral is a cycle that merges into the next. 'Each cycle completes the one preceding it and forms the beginning of the next, which could not be perfect without it.'[113]

• The spiral has the same movement as a whirlwind and is consequently the symbol of the evolution of a state, a force of perpetual change. Its symbolism is like that of the shell and also of water, moon and woman (fertility, birth and regeneration, love and marriage).

Representation of the spiral (New Guinea)[142]

• In its flat form, the spiral is related to the labyrinth: evolution and involution (a return to the centre). A double spiral is symbolized in the snakes of the caduceus, the double helix wound around the Brahminic baton, the two subtle channels around each side of the *susumna*, symbolizing polarized fluids, antagonistic forces, the alternative rhythm of movement, of life, the yang and the yin.

• The spiral staircase in medieval cathedrals 'is the path climbing invisibly around the walls of a church' through which we know, without seeing, the secret of the spiritual building, revealed only to those who have ascended into heaven.[47]

SQUARE
perfection

The square is a cosmic symbol, an 'emblem of the world and Nature. It assumes the symbolism of the number 4 and symbolizes order.'[15]

• In ancient China the sacred square guaranteed order in the world and symbolized the empire in its totality.[8] The cosmos was based on the square: the earth was square and divided into squares, fields and camps were also square, and the altar of the earth was a square mound. All Chinese towns were built according to a cosmographical model of the earth, space and the house of the calendar, or *Ming-t'ang*. The mandala (a mystic or cosmic diagram, which served as an aid to Tantric Buddhists' meditation) is surrounded by a square border with four doors opening on to the four cardinal points, representing the earth.

• In Christian tradition the square was also a symbol of the cosmos, and was used as the basic structure for numerous churches, to symbolize a firm foundation in which to interiorize. The square is, in fact, a perfect shape, evoking stability and solidity.

• 'As matter controlled in all four directions, the perfect square has an inherent idea of balance. It symbolizes the cubic stone, that is to say, the perfectly balanced individual, in full possession of himself, whose body has adapted rigorously in every way to the demands of the spirit.'[18]

• For Jung it symbolized matter, body, reality.

• In dreams the square is a symbol of unity, wholeness; it represents a balance between the four psychic functions (thought, sensation, intuition, feeling). A square in the form of a rectangular town, the foundations of a house or the floor of a room often indicates the unconscious female drive in man.[24]

• The square is often combined with a circle to express the dualism of heaven and earth.

• In a negative sense, in astrology, the square represents an angle of 90 degrees formed by two planets, and symbolizes difficulty, effort, struggle.

• Each planet has its own square, constructed by squaring the number which is associated with it: 9 for Saturn, 16 for Jupiter, 36 for the Sun, 49 for Venus, 64 for Mercury, 81 for the Moon. The law of correspondence determines which metal is used for making the pentacle, the propitious time, and the part of the body where it is to be worn. The seven squares of the seven planets, brought together on an ascending system of Saturn to the Moon, or a descending system of the Moon to Saturn, form a powerful, protective pentacle.

• Magic squares (in which the sum of the numbers in the vertical columns equals that in the horizontal columns) are condensers of energy, endowed with a power transmitted by the sacred name or number with which they begin.

Used as talismans, they have a prophylactic and esoteric value. For example, the *ouifk* of 15, the *badouh* (the Aramaic–Persian name for Venus), became, in popular belief, a djinn or genie, associated with the planet Saturn, and was used as a talisman against physical pain, sexual impotence, difficult childbirth, and as an instrument of divination.

4	9	2
3	5	7
8	1	6

Magic square

• There are also numerical squares of air, fire, earth and water, or squares formed by the sum total of the numerical value of the letters in the Koran; these squares' construction begins with a sacred name, which can be beneficial or harmful (such as the names given to the moon).[19]

• In China, arithmetical squares reproduce the arrangement of the Chinese *Lo chu*, an image of the world presented to the mythical Emperor Yu by the god with the body of a tortoise; this image had to be reproduced in the *Ming-t'ang* (house of calendars).[8]

• The cube is a symbol of solidification, of arrest. The sacred centre of Islam in Mecca, the Ka'aba is a cubic stone building, built in such a way that the four lines from the centre to the four cardinal points end in the four right-angled corners.[19] This cube is the central point of the Islamic world, mother of the holy saints, the throne of the khalif of God on earth.

STAG

complacency

The stag is a symbol of long life. For the Egyptians it represented someone who succumbed easily to flattery, because it allowed itself to be seduced by the sound of the flute.[114]

• In China, the stag (*lu*) symbolizes both longevity and riches.[7]

STAR

a ray of light in the night of the unconscious

The star symbol can be traced back to ancient Babylon, where three stars formed a triangle to represent the triad of Sin, Shamsh and Ishtar, that is, the Moon, Sun and Venus.

• The star (the typographical asterisk is derived from it) was the ideogram chosen to express the words 'god' and 'heaven', and it is this many-rayed emblem of heaven that tops the Christmas tree, which, with its flames, candles, spheres (gold and silver balls) and garlands, is the synthesis of heaven.

In early Judaism, each star had a guardian angel, and in Chinese religion, every individual had their own star in the sky to which he had to make an offering at New Year.[7]

The Pole Star, around which the firmament revolves, has always been though of as the prime mover, the symbol of preeminence. In China, it was 'the centre of the world, the solar pillar'.[30]

• The star in the East announcing Christ's birth was Sirius, the dog star, in the constellation of Canis Major, the traveller's guide, symbolized by the god Anubis–Hermes who had a dog's head (the ancestor of St Christopher who retained these attributes of the dog, palm tree and military dress).

It appears in legend and history.

1 In the Egyptian ceremony that accompanies the flooding of the Nile at the spring equinox, the priests would observe its rise and could predict the future height of the river's waters which actually began to rise as the star rose; it was on this event that the fertility of the year's harvest depended.

2 In the legend of Buddha's birth (five centuries before Christ), it was perceived in a dream by Buddha's mother.

3 In the legend of the birth of Christ, it was seen by the magi.

The magi's star

• Common in all traditional civilizations is the drawing of a five-pointed star (the magi's star) or pentagram, the matrix of cosmic man; a figurative design of man with his universal measurements, with arms and legs outstretched, microcosm of humanity.[47]

The fiery star of the Hermetic philosophers has 'five points which correspond to man's four members and head.' Since the head gives instructions to the limbs, the pentagram is also the sign of sovereign will, which nothing can resist, provided it is steadfast, judicious and disinterested.[18] In Freemasonry this star is placed between the square, which measures the earth, and the compass, which measures the sky, and symbolizes regenerated man, the complete brother in the brotherhood of Freemasons.[30]

The fiery or flaming star[18]

The pentagram corresponds to Pythagoras' golden number, to Leonardo da Vinci's divine proportion which defines the idea canon of man, 'whose navel divides the body according to the same golden section, and determines a logarithmic spiral of growth, according to which living beings develop without any modification to their shape.'[30]

• Upside down (with a point at its base), the star becomes a satanic sign belonging to the Prince of Darkness, and symbolizes 'gross instincts, the lascivious ardour that dominates the animal world.'[18]

• The star which is the emblem of Judaism and shown on the official flag of Israel as a sign of peace and harmony is the *exalpha*, a six-pointed star or shield of David. This is formed by imposing two triangles one on top of the other, and was formerly a battle talisman.[3] It is thought to represent strength in movement, and is the emblem of wisdom. It is Solomon's seal, one of the expressions of the alchemists' philosopher's stone, the ultimate aim of the Great Work, 'through which the microcosm of humanity is in touch with the macrocosm of the universe.'[47]

• For the Egyptians the eight-pointed star was a divine sign, and for the Babylonians it was a solar symbol. It was associated with the idea of influence and contained the solar circle (its circumference), the cross of the solstices and equinoxes and the cardinal points.

It was the wheel of crowned Cybele–Demeter, the Indian wheel, the Pre-Columbian octopod. It was pictured on the shield of the Knights Templar.

• The eight-rayed star can be found among the other stars in the middle of the seventeenth arcana of the tarot. This card shows a young girl pouring water from two pitchers into a lake (symbol of the perpetual motion of the course of life). The butterfly, withered rose and acacia recall the enlightenment that comes with initiation, and hope.
Divinatory meaning: Valour joyfully supporting the miseries of life. Sensitivity, music, the arts. An easy character. Candour, naïveté, youth, charm, seduction. Resignation, indiscreet curiosity.

• In dreams, the star is an archetypal symbol of psychic transformation, 'the traveller's immortal guide to holy places, the ever-present light for the knight in his quest for initiation. Now, inside, at the heart of every star, a smaller star is born. This determines three indissociable centres of the spiral; and so one emerges from the world of duality and immobility; and enters into the world of movement and evolution.'[47]

STICK
support, defence, guided, power

In primitive societies, the short stick, baton, cane and pylon (wooden cylinder) were symbols of activity and of a human being; in ceremonies, they could signify past activity (connected with an ancestor), present activity (active adult), or future activity (associated with the newly born), and, by extension, power (sometimes posthumous power of the person concerned).[136] From this stemmed a group of sticks (*fasces*); used in Roman auguries; the laurel branch said to inspire the epic bards; the mace, associated with the president of the Bar, diplomats, and marshals; orchestral conductors' batons; crosses and sceptres of every age and country, symbolizing some special type of activity.

• The Egyptians added moderation to the idea of power; the *pedum* (inaugural stick) and the whip between the pharaoh's knees, accompanied the emblems of royalty as symbols of moderation.[9]

• The stick (or sceptre), symbol of authority and temporal and spiritual power in the hands of the gods, kings and chiefs reflects their function of spiritual guides.

The bishop's cross, replica of the pharaoh's sceptre, is used 'to guide man magically along the road to God'[80] and is perpetuated in the Freemason's mace. As an incarnation of the master, it guides the footsteps of the initiate–apprentice, 'it marks the rhythm of the walk along the narrow path of knowledge.' Its size, shape, and flexibility correspond to sacred measurements.

• This insignia if power is primarily a magic instrument invested with occult power, a reservoir of power, of *mana* which it transmits through contact or by fluxes escaping from its point: Moses' rod, fairies' wands, and witches' broomsticks which they ride,[19] the pilgrim's stave or shepherd's crook, descendants of the cross, the sticks of the master builders of the cathedrals, used as condensers of cosmic forces.

• An idea of ascension is associated with the Taoists' red stick which has seven to nine notches corresponding to the degrees of initiation and to the internal orifices that must be opened after death, before the deceased can ascend into heaven.[19]

• The stick and its derivatives (pillar, sword, arrow, obelisk, phallus, sceptre) were regarded as attributes of the creative solar divinity, symbols of the father, God the Father, when he made the earth fertile through solar radiation, and the human father when it was a question of producing offspring. These are phallic symbols, incarnations of strength and virile power.

• Another magic stick was the cane that belonged to Jizo (a god in the Buddhist pantheon), the *shakujo*, in Sanskrit *khalkara* and in Tibetan *hkhargsil*, made by the person who carried it, whose vital essence resided in its head in the form of a ring cut into two and always made of iron.

This voice-carrying stick is one of sixteen indispensable objects used by the Bonze (a type of monk) magician, who, by planting it in the ground, transforms it into a magic rampart.[19]

In Japan considerable importance is given to this flat wooden sceptre carried by priests. Its use is regulated by rigorous ritual: 'to hold the *shaku* is a purification in itself and the priest is transformed by it.' The *shaku* symbolizes both macrocosm and microcosm: its upper part symbolizes heaven and man's head; the lower part, earth and man's foot.[77]

• The stick in the middle of the caduceus symbolizes an axis of the world and of life. It is an evocation of the Tantric *sushamna*, the vertebral column around which circulate two opposite currents (the snakes of the caduceus) of cosmic energy, and on a human level, of vital energy, an aid to the mind's sensory, emotional and intellectual activities.

• The stick stuck in the ground evokes ideas of stability, material security, conservation of physical vigour, and erotico-sexual vitality: these are the stakes, pegs, hut posts, and poles of traditional societies.[136]

• The stick is linked to the circle and forms part of coupled symbols, emblems of generation: the phallus–female organ, the *lingam–yoni*, the sword and sheath, the sceptre and crown, attributes of royal, formerly divine power, the cross–tonsure, the flute–drum, accessories sacred to the mystery of Attis, and hung from a pine tree, a column–vault substitute for the god.[121]

• The negative aspect of the symbol is shown in medieval batons: war weapons, arquebuses, partisans, pikes . . . and in the Roman cane, which was a symbol of vengeance and brutality and which, in France in the Middle Ages, was used for punishment, notably on the Pont-Neuf. Some of its victims were famous: Malherbe, Molière, and later writers like Racine, Boileau, J. J. Rousseau, Voltaire, in spite of their genius.

• In heraldry the stick–club is used to depict instinctive, savage forces that man must tame.

STONE
immovability, hardness

Early man was deeply impressed with stones because of their hardness, permanence, splendid shapes and often huge size; he worshipped them, and vestiges of this cult can still be seen in dolmens, menhirs, sacred stones that stand out in the symbolic landscape of humanity.

Stone

• Originally the menhir (or standing stone), situated next to a flat stone, symbolized the new sun's moment of birth or winter solstice. These stones were incarnations of gods. The Arabic Druse called the standing stone a *hirmen* and the large flat ones lying on the ground *saul*, while their gods were called Hiram and Salomon (and were turned into Irmin Sul by the Gauls). These names were drawn in hieroglyphics as the trunk of a tree and its leaves.[121]

• The menhir (symbol of the male spring and energy) standing next to a flat stone (the female principle, matter) is the oldest symbol of androgyny,[136] and, in common with most primitive civilizations, is found in India with the *lingam* or upright stone.

• Standing stones, and by extension columns, obelisks, the forerunners of the spires of Gothic churches, were sacred to the sun 'whose rays are represented in their shape'.[83] Perhaps this symbolism can be attributed to the gigantic megalithic groups of standing and flat stones found all over the world, the thousands of menhirs and dolmens (Breton for tables) grouped in circles or straight lines as at Carnac in Brittany, Stonehenge, Easter Island, and Malta. Some people view them as a gigantic almanac, a religious calendar and a sundial, since the stones are so arranged that they successively capture the sun's rays at the equinoxes and solstices. Others believe them to be signs of the existence of a 'great ancestor' who gave the human group an identity, and they remembered him in these monuments. Some of the tombs have been emptied then refilled, some burnt, as if to mark the end of their use after a period, before they were used again.[110]

• These stones contain a protective, fertilizing energy as symbols of the presence of the god and support from spirit influences: in Greece protective stones or *herma* are situated along roads. (These became the *hermes*, images of the god of the same name.) Cities were guarded by a palladium: the Ark of the Covenant was held up by a sacred stone; the altar in Christian churches is a stone.

Pierced stone which is said to have curative powers (Courgenay, France)

• Stones are said to contain divine influences and cosmic energy. They possess a spiritual strength and are consequently endowed with curative powers. As a result of this belief they came to be used in religious and magic ritual: the stone knife for circumcision; the Egyptian embalmer's flints; stone daggers sacred to the Knights Templar; prehistoric axes, sacred tools occasionally made of precious stones (agate, chalcedony, emerald); coral, home of the Maori god Varuga, lord of good and evil, consecrated by the shaman, which becomes alive and acquires a supernatural power; the moonstone which, when worn, is said to have a diuretic effect and help lymphatic exchanges and cellular drainage; the flint which, according to the Maya, had the power to ward off evil spells and help in childbirth.[76]

• The worship of white and black stones, practised in the East in antiquity, and by Arabs, Romans and Gauls, has a direct bearing on the worship of light, the separation of light and shade, and, by extension, good and evil.

• The black stone (black = female, negative, shadow) is generally an incarnation of a goddess personifying ever-virgin and fertile Nature: the black aerolite at Cybele, the Magna Mater Deum Ida of the palatine in Rome, the Ka'aba at Mecca which pilgrims have to circumambulate seven times divested of any jewellery or cosmetics, the omphalos at Delphi, a fertility symbol. A black stone gave birth to Mithras among the shepherds and their flocks.[121]

• Some stones were associated with water: the stone of the Porta Capena in Rome was solemnly carried in procession to ask for rain. Some were associated with sacrifice: the black stone of Emessa in Syria, said to have come from a meteorite, was the object of bloody worship.

• Because of their hardness and usefulness, stone and rock became a symbol of a solid, stable foundation of faith and truth: Christ called Simon, Peter (= Petra = rock), so that he could stand as a symbol of the foundation of the Church.[9]

• In the Middle Ages, the stones that were used to build cathedrals were considered to be living and symbolized 'members of the Christian community who thus became an integral part of the edifice of faith.' According to St Bernard, they were held together by knowledge and love. These stone walls formed a magic enclosure that ensured peace between men, each incarnating an indispensable virtue along the path to initiation: 'charity which organized the divine palace, humility predisposed to heavenly treasures, patience which illumined our inwardness, purity which guaranteed the requisite rectitude'.[80]

• Some stones are invested with creative power, such as fertility stones and love stones on which sterile women would rub themselves to make themselves conceive, and on which young married couples would rub their bellies on the first few nights after they were married.[21]

This brings to mind the black stone of Cybele, a symbol of the earth-mother, the eternal mother, the sacred stone of certain Oceanic tribes which would open up for a tree to emerge which, in turn, would burst open to give birth to man.

These sacred stones, star-stones, moon-stones and famine-stones, could influence the elements and provoke famines[2] or even petrify the souls of ancestors, as in New Caledonia where they were regarded as the 'petrified spirits of ancestors'.[136]

• In every tradition, the solid, immoveable stone has been seen as the crystallization of magic forces and has been used for divination and making talismans and curing the sick: from thunderballs which were thought to have been produced through the transformation of clouds into crystal by the action of fire and thunder, to fossilized sea urchins which sweated when it was going to rain, and via corals and bezoars (concretions found in the bodies of some animals) to precious stones.

A bezoar was once an all-powerful talisman and a remedy against thirst (for example, the alectorian stone found in the maws of the partridge capon), or against quarrels (the chalydony stone of swallows), against cobra bites (stones which come from snakes and centipedes), or as a means of divination (tortoise shell).

• The Annamites swallowed concretions of powdered pearl to attract health and prosperity.

• Bezoars were used as aids in sympathetic magic: the

Stone

Javaro Indians painted designs on their faces with concretions from the stomach of a toucan (*jukka*) and wild turkey (*misha*) before hunting, because it gave them the power to attract these birds through sympathetic magic.

• In Italy, red coral was once used in amulets to deter the evil eye, and to make menstruation regular. Witches' or stellar stone – fossilized mandrepore with spotted surfaces – have always been used there against evil spells, and have been 'Christianized by turning the stone into the form of crosses and pious figures.'

• Meteors were worn in talismanic necklaces in the Middle Ages and as *gougad-patereu* (Celtic for necklets of secret beads), which have been discovered in Brittany. In Britain, there were hag stones, naturally perforated flints used against witches and the evil eye, hung on bedposts or on the key of an outer door.

• For Moslems, the most sacred object in the world is the black stone set in the Ka'aba, the *al hadjar alaswad* which is the pardoning stone. It is a group of three great stones of blackish-red with red and yellow spots, assembled in a ring of chiselled stone in a silver circle 30 cm thick.

Tradition has it that it was originally white, when Ibraham/Abraham received it from God as a reward for his firmness when confronted with tempting demons. Just embracing this stone is sufficient to be forgiven for one's sins, and over the centuries it has become as black as night through being burdened with the sins of millions of believers. On the day of the Resurrection, the Right Hand of God, as it is called, will testify on behalf of all the faithful who have made the pilgrimage.

• In China, stone (*shi*) is a symbol of long life and is illustrated in pictures offered to elderly people. On the tenth day of the year, the stone anniversary is celebrated. This may be a vestige of stone worship which existed in different parts of China.

Stone is also a symbol of strength in China. The Lord Stonehead was invoked in order to have a child as strong as stone.

Stone was invested with magical powers to fend off fear and demons, and stones were placed at street corners bearing the inscription: 'The stone dares to be responsible.' Stone lions were erected in front of administrative buildings.

On the fifth day of the fifth month, stone battles took place as a protection against epidemics and as an aid to fertility.

• Calcified human remains possess the crystallized force of *Ki*. Intense mental concentration is supposed to bring about petrification; medication concretizes the image of an imagined person who can be found engraved in stone in the body of the person meditating. A legend tells that after the incineration of the perfect Bonze (a type of monk), his heart was gathered intact from the ashes; in the heart of someone else who was given to meditation, they found a statuette of the goddess whom this Bonze was worshipping.

According to a very old tradition, disobedience of a ritual, or an intense emotion, or the vision of a supernatural act can provoke petrification – this tradition surfaces in the story of how Lot's wife was turned into a pillar of salt.

• Alchemical ideograms show three stages in the Great Work through symbols that were adopted in Freemasonry – the equivalent of the three types of stone. In the Masonic lodge these are the immovable jewels that serve as a mirror to divine nature:[108] these jewels are the tracing board, and the rough and perfect ashlars.

– Tartar, matter from which the philosophers could extract their magistery, is represented in the rough ashlar that apprentice masons must improve, for it is a symbol of 'the imperfections of the mind and heart that the Mason must apply himself to correct',[109] and of the young soul, the candidate's undisciplined mind still plunged in the shadows of ignorance.

– The hexadron, cubic stone, or perfect ashlar, the masterpiece that each apprentice must achieve, symbolizes the balanced individual, in full possession of himself, well-adapted to the 'exigencies of the spirit',[18] an 'emblem of the soul aspiring to reach the source'.[109]

– The square surmounted by a cross or 'pyramidal cubic stone' in French Freemasonry corresponds to the philosopher's stone (perfectly purified salt which coagulates mercury and stabilizes it in active sulphur). This symbolizes the stage of the Perfect Sage, 'intellectual and spiritual perfection that the Companion must be forced to attain within himself.'[109]

• Stone monuments symbolize the human sexual organs through their shape:

– *the phallus* columns and standing stones are symbols of the creative male energy of Nature. In Arcadia Hermes–Mercury was worshipped in the form of a stone phallus erected on a pedestal;[19]

– *the uterus* grottoes, wells, hollow stones, pierced stones endowed with the power of regeneration through the intermediary of the female cosmic principle.

• An ambivalent aspect of symbolism can be seen among the American Indians who considered stone to be a symbol of destruction because their weapons were made of stone. On the other hand, Indian tradition established a link between the west wind, the bearer of thunder and rain, and rock, a personification of a cosmic aspect of God 'for the rock gathers into itself the same complementary aspects as the storm: a terrible aspect through its destructive hardness

. . . and an aspect of grace because it gives birth to springs, which, like rain, water and land.'[13]

• In the Bible and in Egypt, the soft or chiselled stone signified wrongdoing and impiety and was attributed with an infernal genie, foundation of all falsehood. (This sign always accompanies the hieroglyph of Seith-Typhon, principle of evil and wrongdoing.)[9]

The Symbolism of Precious Stones

Precious stones are symbols of perfection and the transformation of darkness to light and perfection. In the Bible they signify truth and on Egyptian monuments they have been called the 'hard stones of truth'.[9]

In the Apocalypse they are used to describe the new Jerusalem:

> And the city was pure gold . . . And the foundations of the wall of the city were garnished with all manner of precious stones. The first foundation was jasper; the second, sapphire; the third, a chalcedony; the fourth, an emerald; the fifth, sardonyx; the sixth, sardius; the seventh, chrysolyte; the eighth, beryl; the ninth, a topaz; the tenth, a chrysoprasus; the eleventh, a jacinth; the twelfth, an amythyst. And the twelve gates were twelve pearls.

Christian lapidaries were inspired by this description, and this rich symbolism of stones has traditionally been used in liturgical ornamentation and decoration.

• Just as the Egyptian supreme judge wore the goddess Ma'at engraved on a sapphire hung round his neck, the Jewish high priest wore on the outside of his breastplate twelve precious stones to symbolize the twelve tribes of Israel:
emerald – Reuben

topaz – Simeon
cornelian – Levi
beryl – Judah
lapis lazuli – Dan
carbuncle or garnet – Naphtali
amethyst – Gad
agate – Asher
jacinth – Issachar
jasper – Zebulon
onyx – Joseph
chrysolite – Benjamin

• In one of the English sovereign's crowns there are twelve symbolic stones. They symbolize virtues the sovereign (topaz) must exercise: justice (emerald), the sovereign's moral superiority (sardonyx), wisdom and prudence (chrysolite), courage (chalcedony), temperance and sobriety (jacinth), the plenteousness he or she must assure the people (jasper), knowledge of godly matters (chrysopale), detachment and purity (beryl), royal duties to which the sovereign must adhere (amethyst), regal humility, charity and sincerity (onyx).

On the fourth finger of his or her left hand, the sovereign must also wear 'a wedding ring that symbolizes his or her marriage to England.' This is a large flat ruby in a circle of gold on which is engraved a St George's Cross.

• The King of Siam (Thailand) wore a chain of nine stones which possessed a magical power. The stones were: diamond, ruby, emerald, topaz, onyx, sapphire, moonstone, jacinth and cat's eye.[19]

• In astrology the law of correspondences establishes links between precious stones, planets and signs of the zodiac.

• Since gems are incorruptible and are dug out of the 'earth that produces evil but also the remedies for all evils', they possess prodigious talismanic, curative, magical powers, recognized both in Arabic and Western tradition, giving them preventive, protective and curative roles.

– Amber is best in protecting against goitre (Pliny); it possesses absorbent and drying properties, cures croup, asthma, whooping cough, stops nose-bleeding, is an aid to virility and fertility.

– Amethyst prevents drunkenness, soothes gout, stimulates beautiful dreams and immunizes against poisons.

– Beryl belongs to the angelic hierarchy of powers, and corresponds to the eleventh hour of the day; it cures eye troubles, spasms and convulsions, protects us from perils and defeats, and reinforces intelligence.

– Chrysolite belongs to the sign of Leo in the zodiac, and to the angelic hierarchy of dominions. It strengthens the spirits.

– Coral soothes skin troubles and neurasthenia; it is an aphrodisiac, strengthens the heart, and cures gout and epilepsy.

– Cornelian gives courage in battle, calms rage, gladdens the mind, preserves us from nightmares and evil spells.

– Crystal is a receptacle for souls, brings rain, cures kidney problems.

– Diamond is the stone of chastity and the receptacle of 'an extremely dangerous power that is impossible to overcome. It kills those incapable of manipulating it or those who unknowingly dare to manipulate it.' It protects us against enemies, ghosts and insomnia, wards off fear, and brings victory. As a cut stone it is used to make liturgical ornaments.[80]

– Emerald provides confidence in life, helps us to look into the future and find lost objects, is a remedy against epilepsy, dysentery, major fevers, and loss of memory. When it is attached to the left arm, it prevents bewitchment.

– Jasper rules the sixth hour of the day, and belongs to the angelic hierarchy of thrones; it wards off epilepsy, prevents toothache, strengthens the pulse, and helps digestion.

– Onyx rules the tenth hour of the day, belongs to the angelic hierarchy of principalities, gives nightmares, brings worries and quarrels.

– Black opal brings good luck.

– Pearl, in powdered form and drunk is a marvellous antidote.

– Ruby rules the fourth hour of the day, strengthens memory, brings joy, is excellent for the heart, and vigour, and clarifies the blood.

– Sapphire belongs to the angelic hierarchy of virtues. It alleviates eye troubles, ameliorates heart problems, soothes inflammations, helps dysentery, increases courage, joy and general vitality.

– Sardonyx (a variety of chalcedony) belongs to the angelic hierarchy of seraphim and rules the first hour of the day. It wards off evil spells.

– Topaz is a holy stone, rules the second hour of the day and corresponds to the sign of Scorpio. It belongs to the angelic hierarchy of cherubim, and to Mercury.

– Turquoise rules the twenty-fourth hour of the day, preserves us from the evil eye, drownings and poison, and is a sailors' talisman.

• In dreams, a precious stone is a symbol of the Self, of our inner centre which we can reach through individuation.

STRENGTH
self-control

The eleventh major arcana of the tarot represents strength, in the guise of a woman subduing a lion by opening his mouth without any apparent effort.

This arcana symbolizes the domination of instincts, and shows us 'there is no reason to kill an animal, even within our own personality'; but it must be tamed and the energy thus released judiciously used.

Strength is ruled by the number 11, important in initiation (its components of 5 and 6 bring us back to the pentagram and to Solomon's scales of justice). It brings together in the pentacle magical strength exercised by human intelligence, and the universal soul.

Divinatory meaning: Intrepidness, domination of the instincts through reason and feeling. Natural energy, tamer of wild beasts, boastfulness, insensitivity, toughness, cruelty, crudeness and fury.[17]

STUPA
doctrinal monument

The stupa is a characteristic monument in Buddhist India; it can be a tomb, reliquary or cenotaph. It is a cosmic symbol, the synthesis of dharma (law), the supreme Word manifested through Buddha's sayings, for which it was originally the symbol. The stupa is identical to the Tibera *chorten*: it is composed of a square base, symbolizing the solid foundation of the earth, on which the four steps of knowledge give access to the globe of water, surmounted by a cone of fire. At the top of this cone is a dish of air, and above, the axis of the world, which goes beyond (the Tibetans' 'blazing droplet') and assists the cosmos's departure towards the ether (symbol of the spirit).

– The stupa sums up the stages in human life: birth and life on earth (the square); acquisition of knowledge (the steps); the trials of life (the cone); departure; entry into the world of the spirit.[3]

SULPHUR

secret fire

For alchemists, sulphur is the heat from the centre of the earth, 'an empowering heat imprisoned in the heart of every individual, and the constructive element in every organism.' For Freemasons this fire is a facet of creative light, and corresponds to the mason's spirit- or water-level, a symbol of original equality, male initiative and the sun.

• Sulphur is a male element, a symbol of the spirit, and with salt (a neutral element and symbol of wisdom and knowledge) and mercury (a female element and an attribute of Hermes) combines to form the three Hermetic principles that correspond to the spirit, the inner world, and the outer world. These principles are found in every body: in an egg, the white is mercury, the yellow, sulphur and the shell, salt.

• For Sufis, sulphur symbolizes spiritual activity, while Christian tradition associates sulphur with hell, and its colour yellow symbolizes adultery 'because when it is ignited it gives off a suffocating smoke. The rain of sulphur which consumed Sodom is the image of depraved passions which eat away at the heart of the impious and brutalize their intelligence.'

• Similarly, it is a symbol of guilt, and was once used to purge the guilty.

SUN
primordial divinity

In antiquity, numerous civilizations thought that the sun was God himself, or the visible manifestation of the Supreme Being, and made the sun a symbol of creative power.

• For theologians it was a substantiation of sacred power and the visible symbol of its intellectual existence.

• In Orphic doctrine, the sun at the centre of the universe was a guarantee of the cohesion and harmony of the planets which gravitated around it attracted by its magnetic force, while effluvia from the sun's rays provoked movement in parts of the cosmos. In the Orphic litanies it is called the chain that links everything together, the principle of attraction, the redeemer who redeems Nature's powers by animating and fertilizing them.[83]

• Sun worship was common in all civilizations which progressed from nomadic shepherds to farmers. It gave rise to Hinduism and Islam, Sabeism (star worship), and the esoterism of Zoroaster, to Sufism, Pantheism, the worship of Baal, Helios, Sab ('the Very-High'), Zeus, Apollo, Jupiter, Amun, Horus, Osiris, Harpocrates, Toum, Memon, Cronos, Shamash, Haraktes, Phoebus, Bel (meaning high, chief, king, lord, master), Ashur, Anuris, Adod, Jehovah, Mithras, Uiracocha . . .

• The sun was seen in the following ways:

– It was seen as different aspects of the god of the trinity: God the father and creator, symbolized in petrified rays (menhirs, obelisks), and in solar rays (the stick, sceptre, phallus, arrows, hand); the pastoral god protecting through the eye, the eagle and hand; and the judgmental god or boundary of the mind, through the disk, shield and hand.

– It was seen as a unique god having as symbols the sun itself, the halo, revolving figures, the tonsure, solar crosses, the disk (either winged or with rays, or again with an eye) and its derivatives, the rosace, chrysanthemum, lotus, solar star, or ball.[21]

Revolving figures representing the sun (stone carvings in the Musée de Lion)[121]

• The Egyptians worshipped it as the unique god Amon-Rê, 'the One without parallel' adored as a trinity: Kepaa in the morning, Rê at midday, and Toum in the evening.[10, 108] The Sun Creator possessed three virtues, symbolized by the three signs: of life (the ankh), strength (the sceptre of gods and kings) and duration (*djed*, the four pillars of heaven seen in perspective and the sun's rays).[19]

The setting sun was sometimes represented by an egg (because it took on that shape at the moment it touched the horizon) which passed into the underworld to reappear with its shell broken and full of vigour the following morning: 'it was called the flame born of the flame.'[108]

• In India, the rising sun is incarnated in the young, beautiful goddess Usas who 'makes darkness vanish and glitters in her clothes of light' and by the god of dawn,

Aruna. The two (passive and dynamic) aspects of this sun are represented by Surya (symbolized by a bird, a horse, a wheel or a chariot) whose luminosity dissipates the darkness, sickness and evil powers and who dispenses rain, and Savitar, the divine motor which sets Nature in motion.

• The sun is a symbol of gods and powerful characters like Vishnu, Buddha, Christ (with twelve rays representing the apostles) and numerous kings, and is also incarnated in a goddess in southern Arabia, Ilat, and in Japan by Amaterasu, a distant ancestor of the emperor, who, because of this became the Supreme Being in the Japanese cosmos. 'From this choice we can glimpse a gentler aspect of the idolized gift of light, a tender gratitude for all it enables us to see – so many traces of what once characterized the religious feelings of a great many peoples.'[66]

• For the American Indians, the sun's annual and daily trajectories are symbols of the cycle of human life: birth with dawn, descent below ground, triumphant rebirth in the east.

The sun 'is humanized to raise man's level to a divine level and is the model of true man. It symbolizes the law of eternal renewal.'[76]

• Every fifty-two years, at the moment the solar and divinatory calendars coincide, the Maya and the Aztecs thought that the sun's life could be extinguished, and to avoid the end of the world, practised outlandish rituals in the hope of appeasing the gods: the festival of the new fire involved a human sacrifice.

• Viracocha, the supreme god of the Incas, creator and animator of all things, was the spirit which manifested its power through the sun, and its incarnation on earth was the king, who was thus the son of the sun. Mummies of deceased sovereigns were taken to the market place in Cuzco and received the same religious veneration as images of the gods.

In Cuzco's sumptuous temple, the anthropomorphic image of Viracocha was placed facing east and was surrounded by an infinite number of luminous rays.[127, 126]

• For the Aztecs, the four suns were the four ages of mankind, which had preceded the fifth (in which we live). They were linked to the four elements, the cardinal points and a divinity.

The first sun, naui-Oceloti (four-Jaguar) associated with the earth, the north and the god Tezcatlipoca, symbolized the nocturnal course of the sun.

The second, *naui-Echecatl* (four-Wind), associated with the air, the west the god Quetzalcoatl, symbolized by a breathing monkey, was the setting sun.

The third, *naui-Quiahuitl* (four-Rain, or sun of the Rain of Fire), associated with fire, the south, and the god Tlaloc, yielded its place to *naui-Atl* (four-Water), corresponding to the east, to the goddess of water, Calchiutlicue, then to the fifth sun, *naui-Ollin* (four-Movement), dedicated to Tonatiuh who would be destroyed in an earthquake. The sun at its zenith was represented by Huitzilopochtil.

• The Aztecs believed that the sun had to be fed to supply it with the necessary energy for its course, and especially for its daily resurrection. And from this sprang their custom of ritual sacrifices, only human blood ('precious water') having the potential to fulfil this function of nourishment.

• In the Middle East, an identical function was fulfilled by solar walks, rituals used by Egyptians, Jews, and Phoenicians, at the time of the equinoxes and eclipses to help the sun-god during difficult periods in his annual cycle. 'Leaning on a stick, they walked continually in a circle throughout the duration of the eclipses, thus hoping to sustain the weakened sun.'

• In Japan, they would walk around Fuji-Yama, the holy mountain, at Osaka, a hundred times around the holy walls, singing their litanies.[136]

• In the sun's passage to the zenith, situated on the perpendicular of the temple, which determined the rainy season, the sun could see the whole universe. Mexicans and Maya called this moment 'the eye of the sun' and symbolized it in a double circle, in place of an eye, when they depicted Tlaloc, god of rain.[76]

• The light radiated by the sun is cosmic intelligence and symbolizes the intelligence and knowledge which every candidate seeks at initiation.

The knowledge acquired in Freemasonry after an initiatic journey (see *Labyrinth*) is identical to the sun's trajectory from east to west, defining the seasons that correspond to the stages on the perilous path followed by the candidate: birth in winter darkness, entering the menacing clouds of spring, mounting to the zenith in summer to ripen the wheat and fruit, triumphing over enemies who surround it, autumn mists, the descent before winter begins, death symbolized in the west where the sun discovers the 'secret of the renewal of existence'.[108]

The flaming star hung in the centre of the Masonic lodge is a symbol of divinity and also of the sun and its innumerable blessings.[108]

• The sun's rays transmit celestial influences to the earth. 'The sun's rays lighting up the domestic threshold symbolize communication of divine energy to the womb of the world', as it is the axis which turns the heavenly and earthly wheels.[66] Like a rainbow, they form the bridge along which God descends to man and man ascends to God.

• In India these rays are absorbed into the symbolism of the arrow and Shiva's hair, and the sun is the principle and end of every manifestation.

• In Mayan-Chortl ritual, these rays spread physical and spiritual light which, like human intelligence, illumines the world, conferring a magical power on things, which disappears with the setting sun.[76]

• The solar cycle (solstices and equinoxes) was the reason for fertility rites which still exist to this day: the celebration of the birth of the sun at the moment it begins to appear in the sky on 25 December has ben adopted by Christians, Christ being, in a spiritual sense, the new sun, the lustral branch used in purification rituals of flagellation and exorcisms during the spring equinox devoted to the resurrection and ascension of the sun god; the fires of the summer solstice (the fires of Saint John).

• The sun's heat which gives man warmth, and its light which illuminates his world are, in the Bible, the symbol of divinity which warms the heart and makes itself aware through intelligence.

• In Genesis the name of the sun symbolizes revelation and doctrine. The stationary sun is a manifestation of God's presence; the setting sun the absence of God: 'And it shall come to pass in that day, saith the Lord God, that I will cause the sun to go down at noon, and I will darken the earth in the clear day' (Amos 8: 9). 'She that hath borne seven [children] languisheth: she hath given up the ghost; her sun is gone down while it was yet day' (Jeremiah 15: 9).[9]

• The sun also has a destructive side, through its sometimes excessive heat, and the element of drought as opposed to the fertilizing element of rain. This links it to death: in every religion there is a tradition of the sun of the dead, the black sun, and of sun gods with black faces (Osiris, Hades). The Gnostics taught that the 'sun is double . . . a white sun and a black sun . . . Michael and Samuel', that it is the astronomical and cosmic symbol of two opposing lights and of two snakes symbolizing good and bad, God and Satan, an idea that they symbolized through the intertwining of the good and bad rays of the sun.

• The Bible sometimes attributes the sun with an evil meaning of devouring ardour, fury and selfishness. Job congratulated himself for not having worshipped the sun and moon: that is to say, for not having faith in his own wisdom.[9]

• The sun is the heart of the world, the centre of the system it rules, and is represented at the centre of the zodiac wheel. It plays a primordial role in the theme of the individual. Astrology defines its attributes as heat, dryness, masculinity, positiveness.

• The nineteenth major arcana of the tarot is the Sun, and it symbolizes the double action of the sun as 'giving light and heat: with twelve straight and wavy rays' (connected to the zodiac, therefore to the cycle of the year, the seasons).

The sun at midday creates life but crushes, burns and dries up if lunar water is lacking. The rain of gold pouring out from it represents spiritual riches, the riches of the heart, the philosopher's gold of the alchemists, reserved for the initiated.

This card calls to mind the conquest of the Golden Age through the wholesome soundness of the sun. It reminds us that earthly happiness is within reach of those who manage to reconcile the opposites in their nature, like the twins who are shown seated on the ground, relaxed and happy together, and 'who contribute to sorting out human chaos.'

Divinatory meaning: brotherliness, harmony, shelter, refound happiness. Honours, fame. Idealism that is incompatible which reality. Irritability, susceptibility.[17]

• When the tarot shows the sun included in a triangle, the first geometrical figure, it means in heraldic art that the creative principle had been revealed to man threefold.

SWALLOW
faithful friendship

There is a tradition that says that swallows receive the souls of dead kings and carry them from earth to heaven and back again in order to reveal the mysteries of Beyond to initiates.[80]

• The swallow was once dedicated to friendship, as a symbol of the short duration of its appearance, and to faithfulness, because it returns each year to its old nest. It reminds us of long journeys.[114]

• In Egypt, it was the symbol of paternal heritage because before it died, it rolled in mud and built a nest for its young. It was made sacred to the household gods (*lares*) because it attached its nest to human dwellings.[9]

• In China the swallow (*yan*) is the messenger of spring. It brings good luck and the 'grace of having children, when it makes its nest near the house.' Fertility rites are held at the time of the swallows' return.

In Chinese imagery depicting the five types of human relationships, a swallow symbolizes the relationship between an elder and younger brother.

• In the Middle Ages, a chalydony was a stony concretion formed in a swallow's stomach and was used to cure epilepsy and render invisible anyone who went around with it in his mouth.

SWASTIKA
eternal cycles

The symbol of the swastika has been debased by the Nazis but before them it had always been used as a universal symbol, and is linked to turning figures, solar symbols (pre-Christian crosses with three or four arms of equal length), which originally 'reflected the idea of brewing or churning seminal substances in matrix-receptacles, in time with the movement of the sun.'[121]

The swastika represented the movement of the vault of heaven, communicated 'to man and things, animating the one and moving the others. From this movement came life which in primitive thought was seen as divine.'[17]

The rotation of the sun: the ends of the sun's rays take the shape of feet or paws, an idea that gave rise to the swastika[121]

- In India, the swastika was a symbol of the sun, fire and light, and often linked to the solar wheel and lightning.

- As an image of movement rotating around a still centre, the swastika is a symbol of the 'action of the Principle in relation to the world',[35] and also symbolic of manifestation, of the cycle and of perpetual renewal.

• In China, the swastika (*Lei-Wen*, meaning roll of thunder) is a symbol of the infinite, formerly depicted by the four cardinal points. It was then used to designate the number of 10,000 or the number of infinity. Later it became 'the seal of Buddha's heart'.

• The swastika has played an important, magical role in the science of the pentacle, as a good-luck talisman. But it is only favourable if the branches bend towards the right; in the opposite direction they exert an evil influence and it is called a Sauvastika.

Prehistoric swastika of the North American Indians[144]

SWORD
fighting

Before being used as a practical weapon, the sword was a sacred ritualistic object. It signified bravery and power linked with war.

• It symbolizes internal conflict: Boddhisatva's flaming sword procures knowledge and freedom from desire; Vishnu's symbolizes pure knowledge and the destruction of ignorance – its scabbard is composed of darkness and blindness.

• Christian tradition and chivalry associated the sword with the idea of luminosity. It is the 'luminous tool for chivalrous tasks . . . the axis of light which pierces through opposing forces so that unity can be created anew.' Like a dagger it can 'either strike down an unworthy man, or transmit the creative spirit, and therefore endow whoever sets out in the quest for the Holy Grail with a spiritual weapon.'

Imbued with this special power that unites spirit with matter, it becomes symbolic of achievement and duty. The sword of the king of England confers knighthood, and symbolizes the vertical axis binding heaven and earth, and indicates the sovereign's need for interior rectitude that will enable him to impose lasting order.

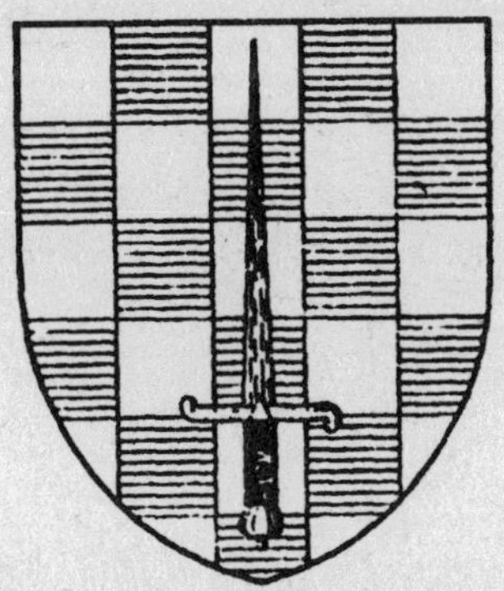

The sword, axis of light which pierces through opposing forces

The knight's sword is two-edged because with one edge it strikes infidels, and with the other thieves and murderers. Its point signifies obedience.[47]

Sword

• The heavenly sword which gathers the clouds together, or subdues fire in the grass, forms part of the treasures of the Japanese throne, along with the mirror and jewels found in the Great Dragon's tail; these are identified respectively with the virtues of *yu* (bravery), *chi* (knowledge) and *jin* (caring, charity).[77]

• Jung saw in the sword or the dagger a symbol or willpower, allied to the idea of 'penetration in a precise direction' and the desire to attain a goal.[28]

TABLE

spiritual communion

The table is associated with the idea of a gathering, of a meal, and communion (the Round Table of King Arthur's knights, the Last Supper).

T'AI-CHI, TAO

the ultimate principle

The spiral circle, one of the oldest decorative motifs known in China, where it probably had a cosmic meaning, was adopted by the Sung Neo-Confucians to express the basic concept of their philosophy in the *I Ching* (Book of Changes).

In a circle symbolizing the ultimate or absolute, yin and yang contain elements of each other and give mutual birth to each other in a perpetual circular movement. 'When the yang is at its apogee it changes into yin . . . then the yin grows and when it has reached its maximum it changes into yang. In fact yang contains an element of yin (the black spot) and yin conceals the embryo of yang (the white spot) which cements their interaction.'

This early perception of the existence of a rather

pronounced female element in the male psyche and male element in the female psyche gives rise to nuanced symbols to represent male and female. Green Dragon (small yang) and White Tiger (small yin) instead of Red Bird (yang) or Sombre Warrior (yin) are in fact less divided than old western image of heaven and earth.

• Unity, an abstract principle, is at the origin of all existence. When it is put into motion, its breath produces the male principle yang; it rests and produces the female principle yin. These two principles were vitalized by *chi*, the breath of Nature which thus gives rise to the 'five states of change' (elements) which produce the 10,000 things (an infinite number), following immutable laws (*li*), and obeying mathematical principles which rule the cosmos (*so*).[103]

This ideogram, the *Am duong*, is the Eastern expression of androgyny, the double principle of universal life, of every duality.

• Yin, the female element, proceeds from everything that is dark, negative, cold, female, existential, potential and natural: night, the darkness of primordial chaos, fertility, the west and northern regions, earth-mother, garden, peacefulness, alchemical coagulation, moon, waters, silver, pearl, the forces of contraction, condensation and retraction. Its counterpart in the body is flesh.

On the level of the individual, it is the maternal side, indulgence and wisdom, passivity, gentleness and sweetness.

• Yang, the male element, is born of virtuality, light surging from the shadows. It becomes real and is essential. Yang is everything positive: movement, summer and the sun in the east, light, day, southern regions, solar energy. the house, gold and jade. In alchemy, it is the solution, the forces of expansion, dissipation and evolution.

• On an individual level, it is the paternal side, method, justice, severity. In the body: bones.

• The alternation of yin and yang is present in all changes in the manifested world, all the cosmic, human and physical rhythms (seasons, heartbeats) that rule man's life, as well as animals' and plants' lives, and psychological life (the alternation of joy and sorrow, of relaxation and concentration).

• Its Japanese equivalent is the *tomoe*, which has a triple spiral.

T'ai-chi

• T'ai-chi, the circle of unity or monad symbolizes Tao, the unchanging unity of the cosmos and man, supreme order. Tao is a true philosophy of human responsibility and indicates the Way (that of heaven, stars and the sun in perpetual movement influencing the earth), the principle which must guide man's conduct so that it does not disturb the order and progress of the world, for it is responsible for universal harmony.[69, 86]

• 'Tao is the spirit that animates cosmic change . . . the eternal future which, like the dragon – the Taoists' symbol – rolls up on itself . . . the essential spirit of the universe . . . the eternal principle in which the whole of life participates and at the same time transcends . . . It is in the immutable principle which presides over the transformation of the world of multiplicity.'[86]

This states of inner balance is achieved through meditation and discipline in life. It is valuable for society as a whole and can be found in the *Tao te Ching* or the Book of the Way and Virtue.

TALISMAN
conjuration of fear

The talisman (*telesma*, meaning sacred object) is a little more elaborate than the amulet, and is also intended as a protection or for achieving certain powers. It exerts a magical influence by way of symbolic or analogous reasoning. It has a precise, determined goal and its manufacture follows certain laws and correspondence.

Early talismans were representations of dangerous animals such as snakes or wolves. By flattering the soul of the wild beast, it was thought that man could be protected from its attacks. There are also jewels, gems, plants and parchments covered with mysterious letters.

TAROT
spiritual journey

Tarot is a very old card game, and what remains of an ancient wisdom: 'it contains the common origins of all the myths that Jung called the collective memory.'[79]

It is used for divination and as part of a process of initiation, and has seventy-eight cards (seventy-eight being the sum of the first twelve numbers). The cards are divided into two categories.

• The first contains twenty-two cards or the major arcanas (twenty-two being the number of letters in the

Hebrew alphabet). These cards are the archetypes: the Magician, the High Priestess, the Chariot, Justice, the Hermit, the Lovers, the Wheel of Fortune, Strength, the Hanged Man, Death, Temperance, the Devil, the House of God, the Star, the Moon, the Sun, Judgement, the World, and, finally, the Mat or Fool which has no number (see under each card for its symbolic interpretation).

This series of cards expresses progress and transformation in human and cosmic development.

• The second category contains fifty-six minor arcanas divided into four series, symbolizing the elements (an ordinary pack of cards is derived from the minor arcanas).

– The coupe or cup suite corresponds to water, fertility and sensitivity, and to 'intellectual and physical female receptivity: the mother.'
Divinatory meaning: Ace – woman, house, hearth; II – amorous or friendly intimacy; III – total love; IV – family; V – jealousy; VI – friends, VII – a happy event; VIII – celebration; IX – joy; X town; Valet – a lover; Cavalier – a passionate lover; Queen – a consultant or friend, daughter, mother; King – consultant, friend, sun, father.

– The épée or sword suit is associated with air and action. It is the 'sword of equivocation, the arm signifying a cross and the fertile union of the two male and female principles, fusion, and cooperation of opposites,' a symbol of the penetrative action of the Word or Son of God.
Divinatory meaning: Ace – marriage; II – a decision to be made; III – obligatory decision; IV – protection; V – betrayal, suffering or loss; VI – the unknown; VII – grief renunciation; VIII – high protection; IX – waiting; X – distant future; Valet – destiny; Cavalier – fatality; Queen – unelected; King – lawyer, doctor, comedian or judge.

– The baton or magic wand suit corresponds to fire and life; it is 'the insignia of command and virile domination, and emblem of male reproductive power: the father.'

Divinatory meaning: Ace – strength, activity, erotic love; II – struggle; III – an obstacle; IV – affairs, earth; V – unknown man; VI – anger, revolt; VII – word, exchanges; VIII – travel; IX – transport; X – foreigner; Valet – man in love; Cavalier – short event to do with love or action; Queen – independent female; King – aggressive ambitious male.

– The denier or coin suit corresponds to earth, and expresses possession, pentacle disk, synthesis of threefold into unity, trinity or tri-unity.
Divinatory meaning: Ace – money, firming up an affair; II – exchanges; III – birth, flowering; IV – inheritance, sum of money, result of an affair; V – initiative, constant thoughts of someone; VI – a small sum or an uncertain affair; VII – certainty; VIII – a situation; IX – success; X – fortune; Valet – a proposition for an affair; Cavalier – unexpected success; Queen – woman with a sense of reality; King – businessman or man with fortune, the direction of an affair.

Symbolism of the Tarot

As a projection of the collective unconscious, the tarot relies on:

– the symbolism of *space* (with a reverse meaning). A person seen full face or sitting expresses a static act (Justice); facing left, he has an active or physical role (the Emperor); facing right is translated as turning in on himself in meditation or spiritually; standing means dynamic and active.

– *body* symbolism. Head: thought. Neck: importance of feelings. Bust: feelings. Abdomen: instructiveness. The meaning of limbs (hand, foot, arm) conforms to spatial symbolism. Hair: instinctive female force. Beard: virility.

– the symbolism of *clothes*. Necklace: dependence, Belt:

domination of instincts. Hairstyles: submission to a physical or spiritual authority.

– *colour* symbolism. White: light or divine wisdom. Black: shadows. Red: fire or divine love. Yellow: revelation. Blue: life. Green: the manifestation of divine wisdom and goodness in deeds.

– the symbolism of *numbers* (see under various numbers).

Taurus
21 April–20 May

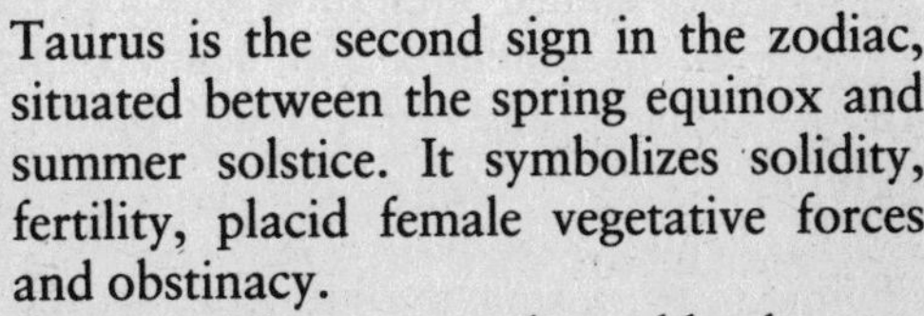

Taurus is the second sign in the zodiac, situated between the spring equinox and summer solstice. It symbolizes solidity, fertility, placid female vegetative forces and obstinacy.
Correspondences: earth, cold, dryness. Night, spring, femininity, fertility. Parts of the body: back of neck, neck. Metals: bronze, brass. Minerals: alabaster and white coral, agate. Planets: Venus has her nocturnal house here. Mars is in exile, the Moon exalts.
Characteristics: possession, attachment, desire, patience, stillness, strength, work, perseverance, tenacity, anger, beauty.
Negative characteristics: excessive need for pleasures and possessions, sensuality, obstinacy, heaviness and avarice.[14, 122]

TEA
mystery of divinity

The myth of tea is intimately linked to everyday life in Japan. Legend has it that the tea bush sprang up on the place where Bodhidharma, tired of his nine-year meditations, lowered his eyelids to the ground. His disciples used to infuse the leaves of this bush in boiling water to help them in their meditation.

• Tea is a symbol of the essence in which the Self participates in contemplative silence.

• The tea-house or 'asymmetrical house' has a low entrance, and the *cha-no-yu*, or tea company, corresponds to the Taoist idea of earthly paradise. The ceremony takes place in the tearoom or 'home of the imagination', which has no ornaments and is decorated with only an ikebana or a painting, and in silence 'which holds the secret of temporal existence' and allows each person to deepen the experience in contemplation. The host must bow in front of the ikebana and the tea urn before kneeling on the ground.

This is an occasion for Taoist masters to experience the divine and transmit the influence to the house and from there to the whole nation.[66]

The ritual surrounding this ceremony favours peace, relaxation, and frankness: a silent preparation, minute, precise gestures . . . all serve to free the spirit, detach it from everyday occurrences, make it receptive.[53]

TEMPERANCE
dynamic balance

The fourteenth major arcana of the tarot, coming between Death (of the body, the ego) and the Devil (temptation, enslavement to passions), presents us with a young girl pouring liquid from a silver urn (influence of the moon, sensitivity) into a gold urn (conscience, reason), polarities which determine a current of cosmic fluid, of fundamental energy, which uses all the opposing elements to construct, create or undo. It symbolizes the free passage of vital energies from one level of the personality to another, through the liquidation of complexes and inhabitants, and through the sublimation of unsuitable desires.

Her wings symbolize spirituality, he red dress 'inner spiritual activity', her blue cape 'serenity of the soul' and its green border 'inflow of vigour'.

Temperance tells us that life is maintained through a combination of energies, the union of opposing forces, and urges us to have equable harmonious behaviour, to be moderate. This reconciliation of opposites is the first stage of initiation, the first process in the alchemist's Great Work.
Divinatory meaning: equable temper, appeasing calm, health, disinterestedness, resignation, impassiveness. Unstable, changing nature, cold, apathy, impressionability. Laziness, passivity, lack of foresight, prodigality.[17, 79]

TEMPLE
sacred centre

Originally a temple was a section of sky, which, when auguries were used, was designated for observing the passage of birds thought to be messengers from heaven. Then it became the building where this observation was practised, a faithful reproduction of the temple of heaven or celestial space, which Etruscan diviners divided into four sections by intersecting two straight lines at right angles, with the *cardo* running from north to south, and the *decumanus* from east to west. Each section was subdivided into four, which gave sixteen parts, each of which was devoted to the sixteen separate groups of gods. It was in such a temple that they observed the birds' flight and classified the different kinds of lightning.

This divination into sections was adopted by the Romans when they constructed their temples and towns.[95]

Temple

• The Orphic temple was the symbol of the solar system, the principle of faith in ancient times. It consisted of columns (with no vaults or walls), and these symbolized the parts of the universe mastered by fire, the essence of the god who occupied the place of the sun in the centre.[83]

• The ancient Persians saw the universe as God's temple and fire as a symbol, but had neither temple nor altar. They were content with a circular enclosure where the sacred fire was lit in the middle of a stone circle. The same was true of the Celtic temple.

• Every temple (whether church, cathedral or mosque) is a sacred place of adoration or veneration and can help in productive meditation, for it is the synthesis and centre of the world, the earthly reflection of the divine world, the link between high (heaven) and low (earth), the earthly home of God, whose radiance it gloriously spreads as a symbol of his presence. Anyone entering a temple abandons the profane world. 'Anyone who, with a clear conscience, accomplishes the ritual of circumambulation and who visits the temple, point by point, following the prescribed rules, follows the course of the mechanism of the world. When he reaches the holy of holies, he is transfigured for, having attained the mystic centre of the sacred building, he becomes identified with primordial unity.'[12]

• The temple's structure echoes the spatial directions and therefore fulfils the same function as the Buddhist mandala, as an image of the cosmos (whose layout serves as a model for Indian and Buddhist temple construction). In India, as in China and Japan, the temple building conforms to the universe in order to assure meteorological order as well as order in the state.[98]

• But while the entrance porch to a temple, church or cathedral is accessible to everyone, the uninitiated remain in the peristyle (the church nave), where they prepare for a second birth bestowed upon them in baptism. They can then ascend the steps leading to the portal, symbols of ascension, of mounting towards God.

• The cathedral was orientated 'towards the place in the sky where the sun rose on the feast day of the old god, which has been replaced and perpetuated by the Christian saint.'

• The roof of the building was the cloak of heaven, protecting the earth from too great an intensity of the sun's rays. The roof tiles were knights of the grand master fighting demons. The rafters were a forest, supporting the inner life supplied by the Word. The towers symbolized prelates and preachers who pronounced on what is as yet unrevealed. Sometimes the towers expressed the sun or the murky reflected light of the moon.

The belltower repelled the devil and attracted angels, and the bells within it restored the cathedral's vibrant soul, its sonorous expression, the echo of chanting rising to the roof. The spires, descendants of obelisks, attracted the magnetic fluxes of subtle energy which maintained the unison of the church with the celestial harmonies. The cock perched aloft fended off nocturnal demons with his early morning crows and symbolized the risen Christ who reigns in glory.

The gargoyles, which originated in Egypt, had a dual symbolism: they dissipated the shadows, warded off cosmic disturbances and also symbolized the vices and hostile forces forbidding man entry into the sanctuary.

Inside, the nave was the incarnation of reason in its medieval sense, that is, as a collection of laws that constituted what is sacred. Its floor is faith and knowledge and corresponded in man to humility and a desire for knowledge. It contains the labyrinth, a complicated figure representing heavenly Jerusalem (it had to be cross on hands and knees to reach the heart of the holy city). Its black and white mosaic reminds one of the duality of the world and invites the initiate to reconcile opposites.

The transept symbolized Christ's arms: the left arm, receptiveness to all that is divine, the right arm, implementation. The crux of the transept was where the small and great mysteries met, where revelation took place. The keystone, the hollow crown in the centre, was the celestial eye through which God gazed down and man gazed up towards God. It was like the crown of acacia used in ancient initiation rites and signifying the candidate's final acceptance.

The windows symbolized transparency, and directed filtered and purified light from the outer world into the human heart. Their rosaces showed man how light was generated within the mysterious rose, and explained the double outer and inner movement, following the eternal movement of the cosmos.

The vault, which integrated circle and square and created the dynamic of the sphere, was like the vault of heaven and curved in on itself like the heavens containing the planets. The flying buttresses symbolized 'hope which raises man's spirit towards the divine by giving him strong foundations. They expressed the temporal on which the spiritual relies in order to reach its full potential.[80]

The pillars and columns symbolized simple virtues; the diagonal ribs symbolized the mystery of the Trinity. The large archway at the entrance to the choir or triumphal arch, replaced by the rood screen, reflected the triumph of man over his enemies within and gave him access to the most secret part of the temple.

The choir, formerly reserved for dancers when they performed the mysteries, was the beginning and end of the cathedral, the holy of holies, 'the perfect image of the sphere, a geometric figure in which divine acts are revealed in their glory.' And the ambulatory along which the worshipper moved around the centre was the symbol of the eternal journey.

The main altar is the heart of the grand master; it is

reached by three steps symbolizing the initiate's three successive births.[80]

The stones in the wall (that marked the limit of the sacred area) symbolized the members of the Christian community and the Holy Scriptures that teach the right way. Every one of them incarnates a virtue: charity, humility, patience and purity.[80]

• The Temple of Jerusalem was a condensed replica of the universe, and had three parts which corresponded to the three regions of the cosmos. The courtyard symbolized the infernal regions; the sacred house corresponded to the earth, and the Holy of Holies to heaven.

The twelve months of the year were represented by twelve loaves of bread (the Bread of the Presence) on the table; the decanates (division of the seven planets into tens) by the seventy branches of the candelabra.

TEN
marriage

As a composite number, 10 combines the meanings of 2 (sharing, reason) and 5 (Eros, natural forces). It therefore represents rational, legalized love (Eros), that is to say, marriage.[135] In the same spirit, it also symbolizes the first couple: 1 = man; 0 = the egg fertilized by 1.

• It is also the number of totality (there are ten numbers), of the universe, of the sephira in the Cabbalah. Then are ten fingers, ten divine names, ten scholastic predicates (substance, quality, quantity, position, place, time, relation, humour, action, passion).

• It is the number symbolizing the circumference + its centre, the tetractys (the Pythagorean symbol of ten dots, arranged in four rows (1 + 2 + 3 + 4) within an equilateral triangle). It is the perfect number since it represents 'all the principles of divinity evolved and brought together in a new unity'.[22] It is the symbol of creation in which a 'natural balance preexists between the whole and its parts . . . the root of creation and its eternal flow . . . the key to all things . . . the nature of equal and unequal.'[29]

• Ten was the end of a cycle (10 in the decimal system) and beginning of another. For the Maya, 10 was the number of life and death.

THIRTEEN
beginning of a new cycle

In antiquity, even before Christianity, 12 was a perfect, complete number, so 13 indicated the beginning of a new cycle, a new life; from this it became a symbol of death.[32] To death was added the idea of renewal (the end of one cycle and the beginning of another).

• It was probably in memory of the Last Supper (with thirteen people at table – the twelve apostles and Christ) that the number 13 took on its sinister meaning. The same idea can be found in the symbolism of the thirteenth major arcana of the tarot: this is Death (ineluctable fatality, unavoidable check, cessation in order to begin again in a completely different way),[17] which is the Cabbalist's thirteenth Way of Wisdom and corresponds to sleep, the chrysalis and night.[81]

• For the Aztecs, 13 was a cosmic number associated with the world of daylight and heaven. They thought there were thirteen levels to the sky. The first, the one nearest earth, contained the clouds, the moon and planets. The second was the home of the gods and the night sky, the sky of the Milky Way and stars. The sun circulated in the corridor of the third sky. In the fourth were the birds and the goddesses of the sun, and in the fifth shooting stars, comets, and fire snakes; the sixth sky or green sky was home of the winds. The seventh or blue sky was home of the sun god and god of war; in the eighth obsidian knives clashed; the ninth was the white sky of the morning star; the tenth or yellow sky was the home of the sun gods; the eleventh or red sky that of the god of fire; from the two uppermost levels, reserved for the original couple, which had a milk-tree, came children, and it was there that they returned if they were still-born.[73]

• Thirteen was also a unit of time in the ritual calendar based on a cycle of fifty-two years (13 × 4) or small cycle, marking the concordance with the lunar period and serving to fix dates: a series of thirteen days associated with the twenty signs of the zodiac formed 260 combinations or binomials by which dates were designated (5-snake, 13-flower, etc.). Four was used as the multiplier because there were four chief gods of the cardinal points.

The great cycle of 104 years (13 × 8) was a period related purely to astronomy.[34]

• Thirteen is frequently encountered in Gallic romances: thirteen precious things, thirteen marvels of Brittany, thirteen royal jewels, etc. which matched the thirteen consonants of the Breton alphabet.[107]

THORN
virginity

The thorn is one of the most ancient symbols in the world: thorny plants were an emblem of primitive mankind, of prehistory and the beginnings of society, preceding the discovery of agriculture, the golden age.

• As a symbol of virgin soil, the thorn became symbolic of

virgin womanhood: the orange blossom in the bride's coronet is a thorny plant, and the Egyptians used a crown of thorns to symbolize an ascetic betrothal. This is not to be confused with Christ's crown of thorns, a symbol of eternal life in Nature, to which was added the inscription INRI – *Igne Natura Renovatur Integra* or *Ignem Natura Regenerando Integrat*, to which the ancient sages attached one of the greatest secrets of Nature, that of universal regeneration.[3]

Christians adopted it as Christ's monogram (*Iesus Nazarus rex Iudaerum* = Jesus of Nazareth, King of the Jews).

This crown of thorns also symbolized a natural crown of white hair.[3]

• The symbolism of the thorn has also passed down to the broom and acacia shrubs.

THREE
receptacle of totality

Three is the first uneven number (1 was considered both even and uneven, male and female). It is an active number, a symbol of heaven, the spirit, 'a perfect number and the sensitive image of divinity' which has been variously symbolized as three interlocking circles, three candles, three crosses, three suns, three colours (white – Father; blue – Son; red – Holy Spirit), or by the trefoil.

• This Trinity of Father, Son and Holy Ghost, or the triple god Mithras, symbolizes the triple divine energy pouring out its benefits threefold over the world. It appeared to Ezekiel in the combined shape of an 'eagle, bull and lion, symbols of the ethereal spirit and destructive and creative powers which were united in the true God.'[83]

The same principle is present in all the divine triads: the

Hindu *trimurti* (Brahma the creator, Vishnu the conserver, and Shiva the destroyer), the Egyptian Memphite triad (Ptah, Sekhmet, Nefertum), the Osiris triad (Osiris, Isis, Horus), the Theban triad (Amon, Nut, Khonsu), and the Persian triad (Ormuz the wise genie, Vahu Mano the good thought, and Asha Vahista, perfect justice).

• In China, 3 (*san*) is the number of finishing. A host of ternary cycles are derived from the trinity of heaven, earth and moon. There are three god-stars of happiness, long life and rank, and the Taoist triad (heaven, man, earth). The 'three friends' are bamboo, pine and plum tree, symbols of long life. The three taboos (not to be eaten) are wild duck, a symbol of conjugal love; dog, a symbol of fidelity to his master; and black eel, a symbol of fidelity and devotion to the sovereign. The three yang correspond to the three months of spring, where yang becomes stronger and stronger and is symbolized by a sheep.[7]

• According to the *Book of Rituals* (*Li-ji*), man, as the intermediary between heaven and earth, corresponds to the number 3.

• In Tibetan Tantric Buddhism, they recognize:

– three meanings to the term Buddha: the Enlightened One (he preached the sacred doctrine); 'the spiritual principle which is the foundation of Buddhism'; and the manifestation of human appearance 'but impregnated with splendour and gifted with "thirty-two superhuman signs" mentioned in the canon';

– the triple jewel or three precious islands incarnated by the Guru: the Buddha (principle of enlightenment represented by the line of gurus ascending to Shakyamuni); the dharma (sacred doctrine and principle of enlightenment existing in the heart of the adept); the Sangha (the sacred community and principle of enlightenment, the active quest for freedom and the ultimate reality of the myriad forms of life);

Tiratna, the triple jewel[90]

– the three fires of evil (or poisons, or three daughters of desire or death), symbolized in the green cockerel (lust, pride, vanity); the tawny snake (hatred, anger, betrayal); the wild black pig (ignorance, gluttony, idleness);

– three characteristics of human existence: the transitory nature of things; suffering (*duhkha*); the absence of one's own self.[132]

• In yoga there is a ternary hierarchy that corresponds to the three stages of development.

– instinctive life, instinctive man, elementary needs, confusion of the ego and personal desires;

– emotional life, judgements based on the concepts of sympathy and antipathy, subordination of intellectual life to emotional life, confusion of the ego and the heart;

– mental life, domination of reason and use of intelligence, confusion of the ego and thought.[5]

• For the Maya, 3 was the sacred number of woman; the hearth near which she stood often had three stones placed in a triangle.[60]

• The Aztecs believed in three regions of death: there was

a heavenly paradise for women who had died in childbirth; a lower compartment of the sky which was the domain of the gods of rain or Tlalocan, where edible plants grew in profusion; and Mictlan, the kingdom of the dead, the lower section of the underworld, governed by the god and goddess of death.[60]

• The Greeks had three dwelling-places (heaven, earth and hell); three Graces (Aglaia, Euphrosyne, Thalia); three judges of the underworld (Minos, Rhadamanthys, Eaque); three Furies (Alecto, Megaera, Tesiphone); three Fates (Clotho, Lachesis, Atropos); three Gorgons (Medusa, Euryale, Stheno); and the dog Cerberus had three heads.

• The third sephira of the Cabbalistic tree of life, Binah, symbolizes intelligence, and life-giving spirit.[73]

• Three is also an archetypal number in the Christian world: there were three wise men symbolizing the three roles of the King of the World (king, prophet and priest); Jesus prayed for three days in Gethsemane; the cock crowed three times; there were three people crucified on Cavalry; Jesus died at 3 o'clock, at the age of thirty-three, and rose again on the third day.

• Multiplying a sum or a quality by three places it in a divine category: 'Holy, holy, holy, Lord God of Hosts', 'Thrice blessed is His holy name'; Hermes Trismegistus (thrice great).

• The cathedral builders had three initiatory degrees: apprentice, companion and master mason, or, in England, entered apprentice, fellow craft, master mason.

• For the ancient Egyptians, 3 was the number of the cosmos, which contained three elements: heaven, earth and Duat, the zone surrounding the world, between the world and the celestial spirits.[80]

• Life is articulated on past, present and future in relation to the notions of space: left–west, centre, right–east.

• The principal symbols of the ternary are: the trident, the trefoil, the triangle, turning figures, like the three revolving rabbits in ancient Egypt, symbols of the conscious awakening in the movement of life.[80]

• In dreams, 3, produced from 2, is the number of the future. It indicates a solution and a new life. 'When three appears . . . energy flows, life takes on a direction.'[24]

THYRSUS
fire

The thyrsus is a staff that has at its tip an ornament like a pine cone, sometimes wreathed with ivy or vine stems. It is an attribute of Dionysos and the Bacchantes, and a symbol of fire.[83]

TIGER
destruction

In ancient symbolism, a tiger stands for the destructive power of the god it is accompanying. Harnessed to the god's chariot, it symbolizes 'the destruction preceding regeneration and development.'

• In China it is the king of animals, linked to autumn, the season of storms and devastating winds. It is the symbol of robustness, courage, heroism, but also destruction and fierceness.

The white tiger (*po-hon*), corresponding to the west, autumn, Venus, cold, metal and the small yin, symbolizes woman. When associated with the green dragon (man) in magical and alchemical literature, it stands for sexual relations between man and woman and their respective power.[75] It also symbolizes the earth, matter, as opposed to the action of spiritual forces.

• The tiger is also associated with the symbolism of the moon (because it can see in the dark) and the chthonian world (the world of the ancient Greek gods of the underworld), and to regions in the west associated with death.

The chthonian tiger is a symbol of riches, and guardian of treasures.[86] Its effigy on the doors of houses protected the householder from demons. And when a tiger was shown with bamboo it symbolized a hero.

• It is the third sign in the Chinese zodiac and corresponds to the east, winter, and wood. It symbolizes passion, power and audacity. The Year of the Tiger is explosive, difficult for diplomacy, and marked by flashes of lightning. It favours war, misunderstandings and disasters. But it is a propitious period for important changes and for the development of innovative ideas.

• Among the Aztecs the tiger symbolized the sun of the earth, the star travelling through the night in order to join forces with dawn.[48]

• In dreams the tiger is a symbol of the dawning of consciousness and represents a collection of hidden instinctive impulses, therefore dangerous ones, ready to flood the unconscious, 'home of tendencies that become completely autonomous and are always ready to attack us unexpectedly and tear us to pieces.'[24]

TIME
eternity

Time has always been an essential, crucial factor for man, but also an anguishing enigma. It is impossible to preserve, though man has attempted to measure it and record it in a permanent way, first of all through megalithic circles, which were probable forerunners of the calendar, through which a jealously guarded past was, as it were, fastened down, petrified: the menhirs at Stonehenge give precise markings for the position of the sun and moon; 'the gaps between the stones provide a system of counting the years, one gap for each year.'[131]

In Orphic doctrine, time is a personification of eternity, the eternal father, the unknown being who fills infinity and eternity. But the ancient Egyptian followers of Ammon and Platonists made a distinction between time and immutable, indivisible eternity.

• Time is measured in years, months, days, hours, etc. and is distinguished by a past, present and future.

The present is 'a moment suspended between the two voids of past and future' and is symbolized by the central face of the 'three-headed dragon', raised above the other two, and signifying the point in time between yesterday and tomorrow. In fact, in primitive languages, there is no ideogram to represent the present, 'which is passed over in favour of the two factors that merge into it: the past and the future which are shown as a pair of opposites meeting on the line of the solstices.'

• So cults have fixed time down by establishing two constants in the sun's cycle: the two solstices, when the sun is at its highest point in the sky at noon on 24 June (the summer solstice), and the birth of the year's new sun on the night of 24 or 25 December at midnight (the winter solstice).

To symbolize this they chose dragons' wings to express the volatility of the moment, their long tails curled over on themselves in a circle to symbolize 'the eternal duration of time.' This is the meaning of the ouroboros (see entry). Man passes, time remains.

• In ancient times it was thought that time was a spiritual reality that was part of the spiritual life animating the whole universe, the stars and earth. Time was thought to be a collection of living entities (what the Gnostics called eons) which passed through earth and the cosmos like Chinese shadow puppets.

• This notion is also found in Islamic esotericism: 'Time is one of the bases of the world . . . the foundation of serial succession, and esoteric practice forbids us to condemn the age, for "the age is God".'

• This idea can also be found in Hindu religion: 'The Bhagavad [Lord] is the beginning, middle and end of mankind . . . in the form of Time, he carries the world along' or again, 'I am Vishnu, Infinite Time.' This concept of living time is the foundation of cycles worldwide, and of cyclic astrology 'which in antiquity was something much more profound than the periods of the stars' revolutions.'[4]

For Hindus, time and eternity are two aspects of a unique principle, and coincide in Brahman (in Hindu thought, Brahman is the abstract, impersonal Absolute), whose sacrifice is cosmological repetition. The sacrificial altar is conceived as a 'creation of the world'. The water in which the earth-symbol of clay has been mixed to build the altar is primeval water. Air is symbolized in the side walls. The aim of the sacrifice itself is the reconstitution of the primordial unity that preceded creation, the regeneration of time.[97] (See *One*.)

It is this time that is transcended through the sacred drunkenness procured through *soma* (see entry): ecstasy, ritual orgy.

The Hindus divide time into four ages that refer to the periods of Jaina, symbolized in a wheel with twelve spokes (epochs) divided into two groups of six: the descending series begins with the Age of Paradise, the era of supergiants whose size progressively diminished through the following epochs, which generated sorrow, vice and all the faults that afflict mankind. The ascendant series will appear with the rains of the Great Inundation that will last for seven days; man will slowly make his way towards a normal size and happiness.[66]

• This was the focal point of religion and a great preoccupation of the Maya, who tried to 'fix' it with monuments, stelae (upright stone slabs), pyramids and temples built to celebrate important periods of time.

• The year, month, week, day and hour form the symbolic architecture of time.

– The **year**, a segment of time, expresses sacred and profane time. 'It is none other than God curled up in a circle, touching all epochs and all countries . . . there is no day or night without him.'

It is symbolized in the Roman god Janus who has two faces and is endowed with double knowledge of the past and future. He is the gatekeeper of heaven who opens and closes the years (and who, for the Romans, became the god of doors, arrivals and departures); it is also symbolized in the wheel of the zodiac, marked with crucial reference points.

In the year's circle the supreme moment is the summer solstice, the moment when the triumphant sun reaches the apogee of its course and reorientates to begin its downward curving trajectory which brings together past, present and future. The Greeks symbolized this culminating point of the sun's curved trajectory in hunchbacks, ancestors of the wicked fairy Carabossa and Pulchinello.

The winter solstice is associated with birth and the expression: 'to be born, to live and die'.[121]

– The **week** is a smaller segment of time 'linked to the system of the planets'.

– The **day** is a symbol of life and eternity. 'We emerge from a deathlike sleep, reach the apogee of our wakefulness at noon, and final peace in the evening.'[80] And the division of the daily cycle into three or four parts (sunrise, noon, afternoon and night, invisible sun) reminds us of the stages in the process of initiation. The third grade in all the initiatic systems corresponds to sunset and the death of the old personality.

• The eternal flow of time is symbolized in the cup or chalice overflowing at the summer solstice, in great rivers, in turning figures, the wheel, the rosace, and the circle of the zodiac.

TOBACCO
link with the spirits

The American Indians used tobacco primarily for religious purposes. It had a part in puberty rites, funerals, ceremonies preceding warring expeditions, New Year festivals. The shamans used it to establish contact with the spirits to drive away sickness in a patient.

Tobacco was sometimes swallowed or cooked in a potion with datura, but more often mixed with other plants and smoked in a peace-pipe to conclude a pact, or to make the rains come, or to seal a friendship.

• In the Sioux peace pipe ritual, tobacco was used as a symbol of man and, on a macrocosmic level, of the universe; it was the mediator between man and divinity. The pipe was the axis joining man to supernatural powers;

its hollow stem the bond, the means of communication through which contacts were established.

• The fire which consumed the tobacco leaves represented God; the smoke released marked the spiritual presence of man faced with the supernatural presence of God. As it rose, the sacred smoke bore the Sioux's message away, and expressed its sincerity. With it he absorbed the scent of grace, breathed out to infinity, divine space being incarnated in the sacred pipe's fire. The Indian would offer a puff of it in the six cardinal directions (north, south, east, west, nadir and zenith) and pass the pipe around among the participants in the direction of the sun's course.

TORTOISE
vital force and long life

In Chinese symbolism the tortoise (*koei*) is an image of the universe: its shell is square underneath (like the Chinese idea of the world and round above (like the sky). It symbolized the irruption of the created world.[86]

• It was venerated as a symbol of long life because it lives for a long time; it was linked to the idea of immortality and seen as an embodiment of vital forces. It was held sacred and used in pottery decoration.

To wish someone 'many happy returns' on their birthday, you gave him a card featuring the words 'Loe-ling' ('the great age of the tortoise').

• In Japan and northern and central China the tortoise has still kept its sacred significance (in Amoy, in the first week of the New Year, they make offerings to heaven of cakes with a picture of a tortoise on them. But the tortoise can have a pejorative meaning and in popular parlance can symbolize cowardice: 'like a tortoise who draws his head back in, that is to say withdraws in on himself for fear of confronting a situation head on.'[75]

• In myths it had the role of a civilizing hero and symbolized unchanging solidity; it established the stability of the world by holding it up with its strong feet and presented the picture of the yellow river (*Lo-chu*) to Yu the Great. Its shell was used for divination.

• For the Maya, the turtle was a symbol of the earthly moon goddess,[76] a symbol of animal's fraternity with man. In the imagery of the *Mayan Book of the Dead*, it expressed a hope of long life beyond rebirth.[88]

– In Hindu tradition, the tortoise retracting into its shell symbolized spiritual concentration, a return to the primal state.[1]

TOWN
celestial city

In antiquity, the topography of the earth was a reflection of the topography of heaven. A map of the world made in 2750 BC was drawn in concentric circles, analogous to planetary circles, surrounded by an outer zone identical to the belt of fixed stars, situated beyond the planetary heavens.[4]

For the town or building to last, the 'world had to be built' around this new centre of the universe, that is, the plan of towns and buildings had to reproduce the layout described in the cosmological myths (the vault of heaven resting on four quarters-caryatids of the earth, itself upheld by pillars). This explains the importance attached by tradition to the solution of squaring the circle, which gave the key to transposing heavenly forms into earthly ones.[66]

• The layout of ancient towns is therefore rectangular or

square (both symbols of stability), and provides two main roads from north to south and east to west (in Rome, these were the Cardo and the Decumanus) intersecting at right angles, because of their link to heaven and the stars.

Foundations were laid on a day chosen by the auspices and 'the surrounding wall was marked by a ploughed furrow'; since agriculture was generally the guiding influence in the creation of a new town.[98]

This conception of the arrangement of the world, which echoes the mandala, and this ritual are universal. The most striking example is Peking, orientated to the four cardinal points, framed by four temples: of heaven, earth, agriculture and the ancestors of the imperial dynasty, symbolizing the outer cosmic elements and the four celestial palaces. In the centre, the Imperial Palace is the image of the fifth element and the replica of the Central Palace of Chinese cosmology, with the throne-room representing the North Pole from which 'the Pole Star looks towards the south.'[4]

In India, the four castes correspond to the four orientations. Jewish cities distributed their twelve territorial tribes into four groups of three tribes. Earthly Babylon was both a symbol of the heavenly city and a giant map of the sky. It was an enormous quadrilateral surrounded by a wall, punctuated by 360 square towers (the degrees of the zodiac). Egyptian Thebes was called 'the orb of the whole earth.' Its corner stones were 'placed on four pillars. They were with the winds and they upheld the firmament of the Hidden One.'[80]

This ritual, which relied on a concept of the cosmos, is still practised today in certain traditional societies: the ritual validation of the choice of site, the erection of a square or circular enclosure with four gates corresponding to the cardinal points.

- The town is a symbol of the mother, of protective and enveloping maternal power, according to Jung. 'From time immemorial it is a symbol of perfect wholeness: of eternal existence, such is heavenly Jerusalem which incarnates the fullness of the heavens, a durable state beyond the reach of time.'[28]

TRAIN

life in motion

Train symbolism is related to social life, and a train journey to development, destiny, fatalism.

The type of locomotive (power) tells us about the quota of available, usable energy.

A missed train reminds us of occasions when the dreamer has allowed things to slip by or important things in life that he has neglected because 'he arrived late'.

A derailment is an expression of neurotic behaviour, or a complex which is blocking psychic development. A train crash reveals inner conflict. The train which threatens to crash into the dreamer incarnates the profound anguish associated with a feeling of being crushed by physical or social life or by the importance of the contents of the unconscious.

When you travel first class with a second-class ticket, you have found a higher place in life than your capacities can cope with. From whence the anguish of being unmasked, which is translated into a fear of failure. Or perhaps you are living above your means. The opposite situation denies the existence of any feeling of inferiority.

The ticket collector represents inner justice which reestablishes equilibrium.

The characteristics of fellow travellers tell us about elements of our personality or attitudes we adopt.

Luggage represents aptitudes, capabilities, plans or the persona, the external aspect of our personality, our way of life. Bulky packages are useless burdens that we drag around with us: obligations we create for ourselves, unconscious fixations, excessive anxieties or feelings. Their disturbing absence reflects the anxiety that is caused by uncertainty about the choice of means that will lead to a project's success. Dreams of losing luggage always translate a deep feeling of powerlessness and inadequacy.

Leaving the station is a symbol of the beginning of a stage of development, of a physical or spiritual enterprise. Arrival at a station signifies that unconsciously we have reached the end of a stage with our luggage (newly acquired experience).[24, 25]

TREE
uprightness

Pliny said the earliest temples were trees. In ancient times, sacred trees, whole forests even, were attributes of the gods: Jupiter's oak, Venus' lime tree, Apollo's laurel, Minerva's olive tree, Bacchus's vine, etc. Oak and the mistletoe which grows on it were venerated by the Gauls.

People went into the forest to make offerings to the gods. Even today statues of saints are placed in trees, and votive offerings placed in front of them testify to the persistence of these traditions.

• Myths of giant trees abound; such trees served as paths of communication between heaven and earth (in the same way as a ladder or rainbow) and were used to reach the gods. There was the Chinese sun-tree used by sovereigns to climb up and down; the Scandinavian *Yggdrasil* ash tree with its branches in heaven and its roots in the underworld; *Heimdallr* (heavenly button), the cosmic ash tree mentioned in the Icelandic *Edda*; the tree of life Gilgamesh sought in the middle of the ocean; the oak over which Zeus stretched continents and seas; and the golden apple tree guarded by Iduna in Scandinavia mythology.

• The tree of knowledge in the Garden of Eden is a symbol of the immortality man lost because he lost his sense of eternity and primordial unity. It symbolizes 'the active ego's field of awareness that has learned to adapt to contingencies. Like the mythical giant tree its length and breadth is travelled by mankind, climbing up and down the natural ladder made by its branches, or some other ladder made especially for man': man has to undergo an initiation in order to find paradise and his lost unity once more.

• This universal tree of life bearing twelve fruit (twelve being the number of divisions in a year, the number of new Jerusalem's foundations in the Book of Revelations, the number of golden apples in the garden of the Hesperides) symbolizes a spiritual centre. The origin of this may go back to the apple tree on Mount Meru in the Hindu creation myth. This was a tree that satisfied every desire. It was also known as the tree of periods, the axis of the world, and it grew in the centre of the garden of paradise on Mount Meru. It was surrounded by four other gardens, each having a miraculous apple tree, all emanations of the central, cosmic, tree. This tree formed a link between heaven and earth and was used by spiritual influences that came down to mankind via its trunk.

• In the Jewish Cabbalah, the tree of life is identified with the sephirotic tree of life (the ten sephiroth are emanations through which the infinite is in touch with the finite). This tree forms a link between heaven and earth, extending through the three worlds of emanations, creations and formations, and ending in the world of forms, below which lies the underworld of hell and the tree of death. It thus depicts the whole cycle from life to death.

• The Chinese tree at the end of the world almost exactly replicates the sephirotic tree; its trunk is a hundred leagues high; on its branches hang ten suns which extend into ten hells.[4]

This is reminiscent of the Christmas tree, a descendant of the cosmic tree that lights up at midnight in midwinter (some attribute its origin to the old custom of decorating the inside of a house with pine branches to ensure they will see the end of the year).

• Note that the interpretation of the pine's symbolism is close to the evergreen's. It denotes vitality, prosperity, things that last, as opposed to things that are condemned to die or change (the seasons, living entities . . .). It is for this reason that cypresses are usually found in cemeteries, because they remind us of the life of the soul after death.

As a prickly tree it symbolizes virgin Nature, the burning bush that holds the entire universe within its branches: the candles we decorate it with are replicas of constellations impregnated by the ether, the reflections of stars on the cosmic tree; gold and silver balls symbolize sun and moon, and coloured balls the planets and their influx.[3]

• In the Vedic Upanishads, an inverted tree symbolized creation, and God. 'May its rays shine upon us', the Rig-Veda says. It is a widespread decorative theme in the East, and the tree of life can be seen in many Indian and Islamic silk paintings, and on carpets.

• Up until the seventeenth century, the May tree in full leaf and tied with ribbons played the role of messenger, when young villagers planted it on 1st May outside the doors of people they wished to honour, or under the windows of young girls. It did not specifically refer to a hawthorn. Lilac was used as a homage to their beauty, holly reproached them for bad behaviour, and the elder for laziness.

• During the French Revolution, the oak (in deference to Gallic tradition) and the poplar (because of its Latin name 'populus') were chosen as symbols of the people, and of liberty, hope and continuity. These trees were treated as public monuments, and were protected by law. Peasants burn landowner's deeds at their foot; important acts were signed and the civic oath sworn in their shade.

• Trees were also symbols of fraternity, and as such were planted on the French frontier of the canton of Geneva as testimony of the good relations between the two countries.

• The tree was seen as a gushing spring of life, and with its thick foliage and profusion of fruit, a symbol of fertility. Its trunk, rising towards heaven, evokes strength and power and is a phallic symbol. Its roots plunging into the ground where the dead lie buried symbolize the physical transitoriness of life.

• With its spreading branches, the tree is also a symbol of man.

• In dreams the tree is an intermediary between heaven and earth, and represents possibilities of development and progression. It invites us 'to stand up, find the axis of our life, plant our roots in the ground, and touch the heavens with our highest endeavours.'[80] See also *Cross, Forest.*

TRIANGLE
the cosmos's motherly breast

The triangle is the earliest known geometric figure.

In Egypt it symbolized a triad made up of man's spiritual will, intuitive love, and superior intelligence, that is, man's individuality or soul.[108]

• In Hermetic ideography, a triangle with its point at the top represented fire (mounting flame), and corresponded to ideas of ascension and spirituality, dry, heat, summer and red, iron, the sign of the lion, March and St Mark the Evangelist.

With a horizontal line through it, the triangle became a

symbol of passivity, air, and moderate fire. It corresponded to heat and wet, autumn, blue, tin, Jupiter, an eagle, scorpion and St John the Baptist.

Upside down, the triangle symbolized a cup waiting to receive water, and corresponded to femaleness, passivity, the creative wisdom of the governing idea, wet and cold, winter, green, copper, Venus, angel and St Matthew the Gospel writer.

With the horizontal line through an inverted triangle it symbolized earth, and stagnant, viscous water. It corresponded to cold and dry, spring, black, lead, Saturn, the ox and St Luke.

• The Aztecs used the triangle pointing up attached to one pointing down to represent the cycle of time.

• The Hermetic sign for sulphur was a triangle combined with a cross. Upside down, it signified 'accomplishment of the Great Work', that is, the transmutation of base metal into gold.[7]

An *equilateral triangle* is a symbol of perfection in Jewish tradition, and has come to represent the Christian Trinity of God the Father, God the Son and God the Holy Ghost.

• In Freemasonry, a triangle symbolizes the threefold cosmos. Written on its sides are light, darkness, and (on the base) time.

• The *sublime triangle* (with an angle of 36 degrees at the top and two angles of 72 degrees at the base) forms the point of a pentagon: multiplied by 10, it forms the 360 degrees of a circumference. Added together ten triangles form a decagon.

• The *luminous delta* is an isosceles triangle (with an angle of 108 degrees at the top and two angles of 36 degrees at the base). At its centre is the divine eye (the sun, the visible distributor of light and life, logos, the creative principle, or the sacred tetragram IEVE, the name of God that the high priest of the Jews pronounced once a year.

Its three sides are translated into the formula: 'Think well, say well, act well' or liberty, equality, fraternity. The three points signify past, present and future, and the whole triangle signifies eternity.

The three angles mean wisdom, strength and beauty. They are divine attributes and represent the three kingdoms of Nature, the three phases of human life, birth, life and death.[109]

• The Egyptians' *sacred triangle* had a vertical side measuring 3 lengths (a symbol of the male element), a base measuring 4 lengths (symbol of the female element) and a hypotenuse of 5 lengths (symbol of what is born from us). This gave a perfect right angle which symbolized the nature of the universe whole. According to Plutarch, in this triangle 'the number 3 is superior to others and perfect; 4 is the raised square on the side of the double even number; as for number 5, this belongs on one side to the father, on the other to the mother, being composed of the triad and dyad.'

• Arab architects built their cupolas using these two joined triangles to trace an ellipse.

• In dreams, a triangle symbolizes the cosmos's motherly breast.[75]

TRIGRAM

secrets of the universe

Trigams or *pa kua* take their name from a series of eight figures made up of complete or broken lines, linear representations of yin and yang. The activity of these two elements, these symbolic figures, which are set out in the *I*

Ching or Book of Changes, depicts everything that happens in the universe and expresses the movements of things and their transformations. 'The circular representation of yin and yang [see *T'ai-chi*] shows the duality of Nature; in other words the unity of man and the diversity of the world of manifestations.'

Each trigram represents a fundamental element of passive (yin) or active (yang) nature.

Khien, creative energy has as its symbols: sky, father south, summer, dark red, circle, dragon, gold precious stone. Yang.

Khwan, earth, square, north, winter, mother passivity, receptivity, black, trunk. Yin.

Chen, alarm, thunder, north-east, reed, dark yellow decision, shaking. Yang.

Sun, wind, wood, white, indecision, south-west, end of summer. Yang.

Tui, bog, south-east, beginning of summer, pleasure. Yin.

Li, fire, sun, lightning, beauty, east, springtime, red. Yang.

Khan, abyss, water, darkness, west, autumn, trap. Yin.

☶ **Kan**, arrest, mountain, north-west, beginning of winter, ascension. Yang.

These trigrams are placed in an octagon of which the circumference symbolizes time and its contents space. The diagram must be read from top to bottom and anticlockwise.

When combined, they form sixty-four hexagrams which together show the interaction of the negative yin and positive yang forces in the universe, and the transformations produced.[86, 63]

TURQUOISE
rebirth

Turquoise was an attribute of Persephone (or the Roman Proserpine) and sometimes of Juno. It was a symbol of renewal of the earth, and a sailor's talisman.

In Egypt it ruled the twenty-fourth hour of the day. In geomantic-astrological tradition, it exerted a favourable influence on sinusitis, rhinitis, head colds, and chills on the kidneys.[114]

• Turquoise is associated with Huitzilopochtli, the Aztec god of war, and with fire and the sun.

TWELVE
order

Twelve is a synthesis of the duodecimal system and the circular system; it regulates space and time and symbolizes order and good.

• According to the Persians, all good came from the regular movement of the twelve signs of the zodiac, the creation of Ahura-Mazda (the Persian god of light), while irregular movements of the seven planets provoked evil.

• In Jewish and ancient Eastern civilizations, 12 corresponded to fullness, completion, and integrality of a thing. Ancient peoples adapted their local history to this cosmic number: twelve royal ancestors, twelve wives of the king, twelve Malagasy sovereigns. The twelve ethnic groups of the Winnebago Indians (Wisconsin), representing the union of heaven and earth, realized perfect harmony with the sky. Twelve emperors (corresponding to the signs of the zodiac) reigned in Peru.[4]

• In addition to the signs of the zodiac, there were twelve great gods in ancient mythology, twelve disciples of Christ, twelve French peers, twelve knights of the Holy Grail, twelve months in the year, twelve angels in the Bible, twelve tribes and twelve patriarchs, twelve hours of the day.[30] The Christian tree of life bore twelve fruit.

• The Chinese also had a duodecimal system: twelve imperial insignia, twelve government posts created by the mythical Emperor Shun. In medicine there are twelve viscera; music has twelve notes.

TWO
duality

Two symbolizes polarity, opposition, division of unity into male/female (yin/yang). It is also a symbol of sexuality.[30]

• It represents the divine, twofold power of creation and destruction (personified in the god Shiva).

• But primarily it symbolizes ambivalence, duality, personified in the hermaphrodite with its mixture of male and female characteristics, having both breasts and penis, or in a creature like the snail which has both male and female reproductive organs.

- In dreams it is a dynamic moving number. Paneth sees it as the number that symbolizes dissociation, sharing, decomposition, and the ferment of separation.[135]

UMBRELLA/PARASOL

power, protection

If a parasol is a symbol of the sun, an umbrella is a symbol of shade, a turning in on oneself, a need for protection, fear of reality, a lack of dignity and independence.

• It was once a badge of royalty reserved for princes and kings, and in Asia it was a symbol of sovereign power linked to heavenly power; the canopy represented heaven, the umbrella's handle the cosmic axis, with which the sovereign was identified. Similarly the Buddhist's *atapatra* is a symbol of spiritual royalty.

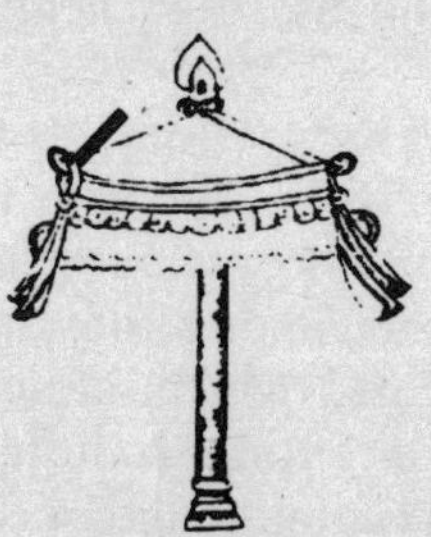

In India, a parasol is a badge of sovereignty[90]

• The golden umbrella, the *Chattah*, is one of eight

Buddhist symbols, and is the emblem of power and dignity (it is held over the heads of dignitaries)[7]. There are many tiers to these ancient umbrellas, the replica of a pagoda roof.

• In Laos, a parasol is a link between heaven and man, and at funerals it is placed on the top of a column to help the soul escape to heaven.

• In India it is Vishnu's emblem and Tantric Buddhists liken the *chakras* situated along the vertebral column to parasols.

• Like the parasol, the Moslem *baldaquin* is a link with paradise.

UNCONSCIOUS
secret life

Jung distinguishes three parts of the psyche: the conscious, the preconscious and the unconscious, corresponding to decreasing levels of consciousness.

Consciousness allows us to face the exigencies of daily life intelligently, and use our energy and will constructively.

'When something escapes our consciousness, this thing does not cease to exist . . . We have merely lost sight of it . . . A part of our unconscious consists therefore of a multitude of thoughts, impressions, images that have been temporarily obliterated which, although they are lost to our conscious mind, continue to influence it.'[42]

The unconscious contains all that is repressed and which constantly tries to flow back into our conscious. C. G. Jung went further and more precisely: he saw that the personal unconscious 'contains a mass of forgotten memories, painful, repressed experiences and ideas, and items which are not yet ready for the conscious; the unconscious retains all the contents or all the psychic processes which are not conscious, that is to say, whose connection with the ego are not perceptible.'

Below this stratum is the collective unconscious, a reservoir of ancestral experience and race memories which can never be brought into the conscious mind, but which are revealed in dreams through archetypal images connected with myths, legends, etc.

UNICORN
purity

This fabled beast with a horse's head is linked to the symbolism of the horn, which signifies divine strength and power. In Exodus it is said that when Moses descended from the mountain, he had horns, which signified that he 'was elevated to a position of command and power.' This explains why in antiquity portraits of kings were decorated with horns.

• The horn is a phallic symbol evoking the idea of fertility and spiritual fertility, and also has associations with the sun's rays, enlightenments and intuition, the intellect, the divine light entering the mind of man.

• In the Middle Ages, Christian tradition maintained that the unicorn could be captured only by a virgin, and so it became a symbol of purity and religion. Its horn, which had the power to detect and neutralize poisons, was, for instance, part of the church's treasures in the Abbey of Saint Denis.

• In ancient China, the unicorn along with the dragon, phoenix and tortoise was a fabled beast which brought good luck and symbolized 'the happiness of having children; above all sons,' and 'kindness, for it is careful never to trample on a living creature, not even the grass that grows.'[7]

• The unicorn is also the idea or dream, the inaccessible that is always present in man's heart.

URANUS
discoveries

The planet Uranus was not discovered until 1781. Its influence is interpreted as brusque changes, upsets, revolts, revolutions, preludes to major advances on a world scale.

At a social level, it is responsible for great inventions in the area of microwaves, electronics, information technology and communications.

On an individual level, it reveals how independent of spirit a person is and confers intuition. Its harmonious effects are felt towards the age of thirty and again at fifty-eight, coinciding with the trigons (sets of three signs of the zodiac – either airy, earthy, fiery or watery), periods when the individual, who has acquired self-confidence and autonomy, is able to enjoy his independence.

Its dissonant effects are felt at the time of squaring the circle towards twenty-one and sixty-four, coinciding with a period of aggression and revolt. Opposition is revealed at forty, when values are questioned.[112]

VAMPIRE

divine spirit

For the Maya, the vampire bat had a procreative role. It was the personification of the agrarian god, and symbolized the process of germination, and, by analogy, death followed by regeneration through the sun's rays. It is depicted falling from the sky accompanied by torrential rain, to symbolize the fall of divine substance to the earth, at the time of the sun's journey to its zenith, a time that produces rain which germinates the maize.[76]

VASE

receptacle for the spirit

A vase is an indispensable element as a receptacle for the divine spirit in Hindu ceremonies, during which the *avahana* or descent of the divine essence from the celestial plane to the recipient takes place. The essence will be projected onto a statue or object. This small, circumscribed sacred space becomes the universe, in the centre of which the adept is identified with the supreme forces, the power of which he gathers to himself.[2]

• In China, the same ideogram (*ping*) designates both vase and bottle.

• In antiquity, the 'vase of treasures' filled with five nourishing fruits (different kinds of cereal) was used in a fertility ritual during the wedding ceremony. Hot-water bottles were called warming women and the penis a bottle of oil.

• In the iconography, a vase with branches of pine and plum with a narcissus signified: 'Life for ever green, love, happiness and peace.'

VENUS
seduction

In antiquity, the goddess Venus was the personification of Nature and the passive principle of creation. She appeared under different personae (Ceres, Juno, Diana, Isis). It was also thought that 'she caused the production and growth of the seeds of every living thing in water . . . she was Nature, the mother of things, or the female creator.'

As Isis she symbolized 'the fertile matter on which creative and destructive organisms worked.' Water was her earthly essence, the moon her heavenly essence 'which drew up the vapours from the sea through her power of attraction.'[83]

• She was a symbol of femininity and seduction, and for alchemists she was the goddess who dispensed voluptuousness which 'draws the soul into the body with the promise of a langorous, sensual self-existence . . . teaches man to love life for itself and taste its charms while avoiding anything unpleasant.'

• In astrology, the influence of the planet Venus is all femininity, gentleness, sensuality, harmony, the inner meaning of balance revealed in charm, living warmth and intimacy. She confers an agile mind, subtlety of faculties and reflexes, dexterity and mental finesse, *savoir-faire*, sensitivity, imagination, the capacity to understand, all of which generate a remarkable efficiency and a certain prestige. In practical terms, however, this does not exclude a certain naïvety that ensues from a freshness of mind.[111, 100]

• In Mexico, this planet is linked to the idea of death and rebirth. The Aztecs created a year lasting 584 solar days, based on the synodic revolution of Venus (*Citlalpol*), the great star (eight solar years were the equivalent of five Venusian ones). The concordance was made every 104 years (an Aztec century).

Quetzalcoatl, transformed into Venus after his death, was resuscitated from the dead eight days afterwards (the period of the darkening of the planet in its lower conjunction), like Venus, the morning star.

According to astronomers' calculations on the length of Venus's cyclic revolutions and on the correspondence with other cycles of the Mayan solar and divinatory calendars, the planet reappears at this time every 104 years.[98]

VINE, WINE
divine drunkenness

The vine was a sacred wine-producing plant, a drink of the gods, and in ancient tradition it was identified with the tree of life in paradise (which in the iconography is often shown as a vine).

The vine and wine are inseparable from the myth of Dionysos, dispenser of life, and god of wine whose superhuman existence became absorbed into the drink that made his worshippers divinely drunk, and proved to them the real presence of a god.

The cult of Dionysos had connections with phallic worship and consisted of outdoor revelries, ceremonies of purification which took place at the beginning of January (the winter solstice) to make fertility more potent, assist fermentation of the wine and protect it from the pernicious influence of evil spirits.

• Wine is a symbol of the revelation that results from the delirium produced by the divine presence, and the vine symbolizes immortality. The rites which prepare the initiate for immortality were originally intended to renew the fertility of the soil. Immortality, because the god of the grape, Dionysos, who was hacked to pieces so that his blood became wine which the Bacchantes and Maenads drank, could experience resurrection.[134]

• The myth of Dionysos, who suffered the passion and experienced resurrection, has echoes in the story of Christ who declared: 'I am the vine', thus attaching himself to a whole tradition in which the gods are incarnated through wine. The sap is the light of the spirit, the grape of the Eucharist and wine are similar to the blood of Christ.

VIRGIN
purity

Virgin births can be found in every mythology and every religion. Buddha's mother received him direct from heaven in the form of a milk-white elephant; the Aztec goddess whose dress was woven with snakes, Coatlicue, was visited by the plumed serpent; nymphets and goddesses were fertilized by a hazelnut or a puff of wind . . .

The virgin of myth is a symbol of the passive female principle of Nature in winter, the counterpart of Hermes enclosed in his sheath, personifying the positive virile principle in Nature.

Virgins who die, sleep, or 'descend into the underworld' illustrate agricultural myths and symbolize the burying of virgin seed which had not been used to make bread, or young shoots emerging from the ear of corn at the time of sowing. Pluto abducting Proserpine, Hades abducting Persephone, Hecate plunging into Acheron all symbolize the grain disappearing into the winter soil.[121]

• The sun of truth was conceived in the bosom of black Isis who, under the guise of the black virgin, still makes her presence felt at the founding of cathedrals, like the one at Chartres. She can be seen again in Marseilles (the church of Saint-Victor), at Rocamadour, Boulogne sur Mer, at Fourvières, in Barcelona and in Poland.

This black virgin, who was honoured by the Celts, is identified with the black rock. In fact, the black and white rocks which are objects of Muslim veneration were replaced by Asali, a male idol, and Mayel (Mary), a female idol.[121]

• We can recognize Isis holding the infant-god Horus in the Christian Virgin, a symbol of purity and maternal love, holding the infant Jesus on her knees, 'an affirmation of the Virgin as the throne of wisdom. The name "Isis" in Egyptian probably signified "throne", a tradition preserved for the Christian Virgin.'

• In the Middle Ages, the Virgin was defined by masons as 'heaven and the throne of God, heaven which raises the sun of truth . . . clouds containing light' and identified with the symbolism of the Egyptian goddess Nut, a relative of Isis to whom was consecrated the sycamore or 'Pharaoh's fig tree' which sheltered the Virgin Mary when she fled into Egypt with Joseph and the Christ child. 'And so the Christian Virgin, in the shade of the Egyptian tree, became an integral part of the axis of the world, the symbolic axis procured through Pharaonic tradition.'[80]

• In the tarot the Virgin is symbolized in the Empress in the third arcana, queen of heaven, virginal mother of all things connected with Venus–Uranus and Babylonian Ishtar, who flies above the sub-lunar world.

Virgo
22 August–22 September

Virgo is the sixth sign in the zodiac, ruled by Mercury, and symbolizes secrets, moderation, discernment and analysis. Virgo is a sign of physical wisdom, intelligence turned inwards in the quest for principles which allow for synthesis.
Planet in exile: Neptune. Falling: Jupiter.
Correspondence: cold, drought, earth, night, femininity, vitality, sterility. Metal: mercury. Minerals: flint, jasper. In the body: intestines, abdomen, duodenum, small intestine, solar plexus.
Main qualities: critical and practical sense, moderation, logic, precision, order and method.
Negative characteristics: exaggerated critical sense, aridity, excess of method, tendency to get bogged down in detail, lack of assimilation, of discrimination, poor memory, scruples, pedantry, uncontrolled nervousness.[145, 122]

VULTURE
old age

In Mexico, the royal vulture (*cozcaquanhtli*) was a symbol of old age and long life.

• The vulture, one of the twenty signs in the divinatory calendar, is associated with the south. It communicated to natives of its sign qualities of wisdom, prudence, calm, thoughtfulness and discretion, a talent for teaching, but also a taste for gossip.[125]

• For the Maya it was a symbol of death, and also a god of abundance, and the regeneration of vital forces. It was associated with watery signs, and ruled the storms that brought about a renewal of plant life.

Egyptian amulet depicting a vulture[124]

• In Egypt, it designated maternal love because it was said to feed its young with its own blood, and it represented the sky because its nest was inaccessible. It was also seen as a symbol of knowledge of the future, because its flight was interpreted by the auguries as meaning conquest in battle.[9] From this came its use by Greeks and Romans as a divinatory bird.

WAR

inner conflict

The fights which the gods indulged in in myths represent the confrontation between the unconscious and the conscious, the fight between the ego and the shadow, according to Jung.

• War in dreams expresses an inner sense of difficulty and conflict, resulting from the battle of opposing vital forces. It can also reveal a difference of opinion with someone close. Often it is a question of a truth that the dreamer refuses to admit, or a situation whose gravity he or she has minimized.

WATER

origins, the unconscious

Water is the source and symbol of life. Water worship can be found in every mythology.

• In early times, the Sumerians taught that heaven and earth emerged from the primal waters, and then gave birth to the other gods.[45]

• In Egyptian cosmology, in Genesis and in Jewish and

Hindu belief, water is 'the essence of passive or female power'; moisture is the most fertile of the elements, the basis of creation.

• In Chinese philosophy, the original female force (yin), water (*shui*), united with fire (yang) to give birth to the five elements (earth, wood, metal, fire and water) which in turn engendered the ten thousand things (totality). In the system of correspondence, it is related to cold, the north, kidneys, the number 6, the colour black, the moon, the trigram *kh'an*, a symbol of difficulty and danger.[6]

• Water was a symbol of purity in ancient Egypt, 'and symbolized the birth of the pure in heart or the initiated.'[9]

It has remained the commonest means of regeneration and of physical and spiritual purification:

– holy water, a symbol of the primal waters which protect us from demons and help us renew ourselves each time we enter a holy place.

– baptismal water for Christians, which is poured over a child's head, purifies and admits the child into the Christian faith. Once associated with initiation rites, baptism was formerly a royal, initiatory ritual, indicating admission into a community of initiates. The Essenes performed this ritual many times in the course of their lives – and on a cosmic level, for the baptismal fonts had twelve sides, like the zodiac, or stood on 'twelve bulls, evoking simultaneously the sea of bronze in the Temple of Jerusalem and the cosmos in its all-powerfulness.'[80]

– the druids' lustral water, enemy of evil spells.

– sacred Gregorian water, used to re-sanctify, therefore regenerate profaned churches.

– water for ritual ablutions, used by Moslems or for ablutions of holy statues in India and the Far East.

Ritual bathing in cold water is highly valued in Japan,

where it forms part of the *misogi* (purification exercises). It is practised in total nudity and in a very precise order: the mouth, face, sexual parts, chest and stomach, legs and feet, shoulders and arms, back, chest and stomach again, and finally the entire body.

These symbolic baths remind Shinto followers that in order to please God it is not enough to rid oneself of bodily dirt, but bad habits must be restrained, a straight, moral path must be adhered to.[77] Water fulfils a dual role: purifying and moralizing.

It is water's renovatory property that modern man makes use of when he visits thermal baths or steps pleasurably into his own.

• Water is a blessing for people who life in drought-ridden countries: the fertilizing properties of rivers and streams are thought to have had a divine origin. The Koran says that water falling from heaven is blessed.

• From being a gift to mankind from God, water becomes a symbol of wisdom and spiritual life. In heraldry, 'water symbolizes the primal cosmic sea, that is to say, the "reservoir" of possibilities whose depths God plumbs to create his worlds. Limpid waters symbolize harmony of feelings, nobility and sensitivity.'[47]

• In India, water is the symbol of superior consciousness, 'of the supreme universal conscious existence . . . in its form and movements, the conscious being.' The Vedas speak of 'two seas, the waters above and the waters below', corresponding to the dark subconscious and the super-ego.[44]

The rivers of the hidden superior world produce *soma*, the drink of the gods, ambrosia which is 'the sweetness in the seven waters', the indispensable element of Vedic sacrifice, the sap of life. Related to blood, the vital liquid, and Dionysian wine, *soma* symbolizes the rise of the libido, vitality, the link with the unconscious, often guarded by monsters because this vital force comes from animal instincts that must be mastered before knowing true pleasure.

• 'Water symbolizes goodness, that is to say, desire purified into its most sublime form; water symbolizes the purification of personality' (Paul Diel).

'Water falling from heaven in the form of rain and cloud represents sublime fertilization. Human life, its desires and feelings are symbolized in the river crossing the land and rushing into the sea. The sea represents that mysterious immensity towards which our life is leading and from which it emerged. The sea is thus a symbol of birth.'[36]

The waters under the sea symbolize the subconscious, frozen water, ice, cold, stagnation at its most intense level, the lack of warmth of soul, psychic stagnation, the dead soul.[36]

Another interpretation has been given by G. Bachelard: he sees stagnant water as silent, dark, sluggish, unfathomable, a practical aid to death. Sluggish waters are a symbol of 'total sleep from which there is no desire to waken, a sleep from which we are protected by living human love. From it we learn the lesson of motionless, profound death, death that lives with us, near us, within us.'[46]

• In dreams, water is the symbol of the unconscious. Baths reveal a desire for regeneration, a need to forget the past. 'A calm or moving source of life . . . but contained within limits, a bath is a good sign in a dream.' But floods warn of the danger presented by feelings that have become too overwhelming.

WEAPON
aggression

Associated with the idea of war, a weapon is an ambivalent symbol, implying struggles against enemies or domination. The pleasure felt in handling firearms or other types of weapon can reveal sublimation of aggressive tendencies.

• Weapons which appear in dreams reveal the existence of internal conflicts, connected with sexuality, if they involve revolvers, swords or daggers.

WEEK
segment of time

The division of time into weeks goes back to earliest antiquity, and observation of the seventh day was practised not only by Jews, but also by the Phoenicians and in several Eastern countries. The seven days were already symbolized in myth by the seven sons of the sun, of which 'the seventh was devoted to birth.'

• In China on the seventh day, known as the great day, the emperor would order the doors of houses to be shut and on that day trading was forbidden. Among the Arabs, it was sacred to Venus–Uranus, a long time before the advent of Mohammed.

• The days of the week correspond to a planet: Sunday – Sun; Monday – Moon; Tuesday – Mars; Wednesday – Mercury; Thursday – Jupiter; Friday – Venus; Saturday – Saturn.

WELL
life, truth

A well is a medium of communication between air, water and earth, and in every tradition it is a sacred place. In the Bible, providential encounters, pacts, unions and alliances all take place near a well.

• For Jews and those people who live in desert regions, it is the source of life.

• In the *I Ching* a well (*tsing*) symbolizes the union of the inner self with the secret riches of the unconscious, learning from the past, the roots of human life, the central place, the bringing to light of whatever is hidden.[63]

• In erotic writing, it means the vagina.

WHEEL
vital movement

The symbolism of the wheel is similar to that of the circle, with the addition of the idea of movement, which is linked to the sun god's revolutions around the earth (as it was once believed).

• The wheel was a symbol of the sun because its spokes were reminiscent of the rays of the sun which seemed animated by a circular movement. And so images of the wheel can be found on ancient monuments in Egypt, Chaldaea, India, Mexico, Palestine, Peru, and on monuments belonging to the Gauls, as well as in Scandinavia, and in temples devoted to Vishnu, mounted on a pyramid, in monasteries where Buddha is worshipped as the 'king of wheels' or the 'precious wheels' or the 'precious wheel of religion', in caves at Adjanta and at Ellora in relief on Buddha's lotus-throne.

• To produce fires for both practical and sacred use at sun and fertility festivals two pieces of wood were rubbed together by rapidly turning a wheel. The symbolism of this act was added to. On the Isle of Mull, the wheel was turned from east to west, that is, in the direction of the sun's course. In Swabia, heavenly fire was obtained by setting fire to a cartwheel decorated with straw and fixed to the top of a twelve-foot pole.

The Gauls' sun wheel

The Gauls' sun wheel transformed into a Christian emblem[12]

• From this came the tradition of the flaming wheel of the summer solstice. On 24 June, the even of the solstice, a large wheel wrapped in straw was set in motion from the top of a hill and became a circle of fire, symbolizing the moving sun.

In some countries, including Scotland, this act of worship and faith was moved to 25 December, becoming the ceremony of the *clavie* or Christmas sun wheel in which a barrel of flaming tar was taken through the streets of the town and then rolled down a hill. This became part of the celebrations on gala night. The same happened in Sweden. In Nordic languages the name for Christmas, *Iul* is also the name of the sun wheel. It means revolution, or wheel, and December is called *Iul-Manat*, the month of the return.

This cult of the sun wheel, 'the beautiful, shining wheel', as it is called in the Icelandic legends of the Edda, lives on. The Christmas period in England is called yuletide and there is a yule log. In Lincolnshire, they still call the fork they put in the fire on Christmas Day the *Gule-block* (Iul's fork) which must stay there for the entire eight days. In old Breton almanacs, Christmas Day was marked by a huge wheel, and traditional ceremonies at the beginning of the century still harked back to the cult of the sun wheel.

• Inside their temples the Greeks used to turn a luminous wheel, a perfect symbol of the sun god, as a sign of worship, a custom borrowed from the Egyptians. The Saxon sun god also carried a wheel of fire.

• The sun's revolution is also symbolized in revolving figures: originally these were solar crosses (swastikas), usually with four arms, each ending in a foot or paw all facing the same direction, symbolized by animals or arms coming out from around an axis, a theme which in ancient Egypt expressed the omnipresence of the trinity in the movement of the worlds[47] and was evidence of a syntonic concern with the cosmos.

The swastika-symbol of the sun's rotation[121]

• Rondos, whirling dances, circumambulation, processions, relay races with torches, roundabouts, all originate from the same quest: the hope of obtaining the sun's benefaction. It is still perpetuated in the rogations (three solemn processions to ask God to fend off contagious diseases from man and animals, and to bless work in the fields).

• The four-spoked wheel symbolizes expansion into the four directions of space, the quaternary rhythm of the moon and the seasons.

• The six-spoked solar wheel, a horizontal projection of the cross with six branches, was worn by the Gauls as an amulet, and later became Christ's monogram, its spokes transformed into the letters I and X or into P.

It is also the Buddhist Wheel of Existence whose spoke represent *loka* or worlds: worlds of the gods, of man, of Titans, of hells, of ghosts, and of animals.[4]

• With eight spokes, it becomes the Celtic wheel, symbolizing the eight directions of space and regeneration and renewal. It is identified with the lotus flower and the octagon in Chinese *Pa-kua* (trigrams).

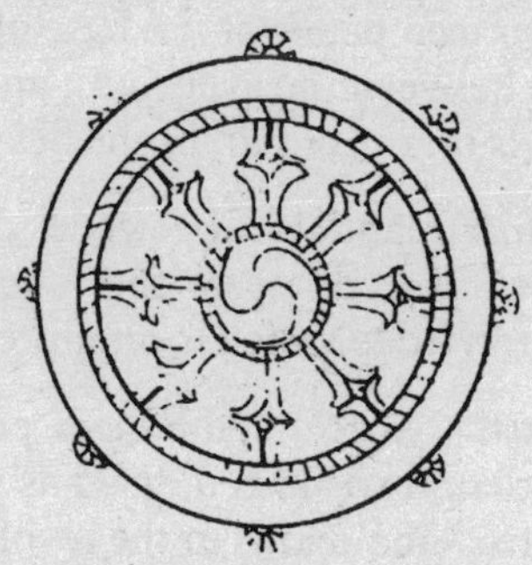

The Dharmachakra *or wheel of law*[121]

• The *Dharmachakra* or wheel of law is in perpetual motion, and is a kind of cosmic and spiritual zodiac, a synthesis of Buddha's teachings, the principal symbol of Buddhist schools.

Wheel

From the wheel of law come space and divisions of time. Its rays symbolize the eightfold path of noble truths, that consist of right understanding, right aspiration or purpose, right speech, right bodily action, right means of livelihood, right endeavour, right mindfulness and right concentration. The Noble Eightfold Path is often associated with the *vishudda chakra*, situated in the throat, that has sixteen petals (2 × 8), and is the gate to great freedom.

The centre of the wheel, the hub, symbolizes the enlightened point of consciousness from which our psychic faculties emanate.[112]

• Tantric Hindus call the vital centres situated along the vertebral column *chakras* because they have the appearance of a wheel. There is the *muladhara* with four petals situated in the testicles; *svadhistana* with six petals above these glands; *manipura* with ten petals in the navel; *anahata* with twelve petals in the region of the heart; *vishudda* with sixteen petals at the base of the throat; *ajna* with two petals between the eyebrows; and *sahasrara* with a thousand petals on the crown of the head.[96, 102]

• In the Buddhist mandala, the wheel derived from the syllable *bhrum*, placed over the square, symbolizes transcendent knowledge which is omnipresent.[12]

• In heraldic art, a wheel symbolizes perpetual motion, 'that ancient Oriental wisdom defined as whatever is most stable in existence,' analogous to the revolving castle in the Holy Grail stories, the unmoving centre of the world that is in perpetual motion. It invites the knight to seek out the location of this castle, this spiritual centre, 'without ever believing that he can one day obtain the definitive truth.'

• The five-spoked wheel symbolizes the harmony that must exist between the heavenly and material worlds.[47]

• The sun wheel was, in early agriculture, a symbol of

fortune, as it related to the success of the harvest. From this came the idea of the wheel of fortune which was spun at fairgrounds, a debased copy of the sun wheel, symbolizing material sovereignty, power and fame, pictures of which were made popular by Italian miniaturists. It symbolizes the vanity of human values, and features a woman (fortune) attached to an endlessly turning wheel (emblem of worldly fame), impelled by perpetual movement. Her head, alternatively raised and lowered, symbolizes people who rise to power and riches only to be cast down into misery and poverty.[121]

• But the degeneration of the symbol goes even further and becomes confused with cruelty. The sun wheel became an instrument of torture. Libyans would tie a dwarf or beggar on to a wheel on top of a post and whizz it round; the Romans would put a Jew in a barrel which they would then roll down from the top of the Capitol. Jews had to wear a picture of a wheel on their clothes in the Middle Ages.

• In dreams, a wheel is a symbol of the Self, denoting that the dreamer has reached a new stage in psychic development, a new state. If the dreamer is at the hub of the wheel, it shows he has resolved his contradictions and is freed from the domination of the ego and selfishness. He has been reborn with a new identity and is now aware of the whole significance of the universe.

• The Wheel of Fortune, the tenth major arcana of the tarot, reminds us of the samsara, the Oriental wheel of fate. It is also an image of duality: a wheel with two concentric rims, an image of the double, procreative whirlwind of individual life; two small boats in contrasting colours side by side are reminiscent of the caduceus (held by Hermanubis) and symbols of the vital positive and negative currents of yin and yang. The two figures attached to the wheel represent the constellation of Sirius, summer heat, life and joy; and Capricorn, the fish-goat, winter, selfishness and the passions.

Dominating all this, the impassive sphinx symbolizes the principle of immobility and balance, which guarantees the stability of individual forms, and counsels us to avoid excesses, and, like the wise man, 'keep away from the current that carries the crowds along . . . and await the call or sign that will give the order for action.'

Divinatory meaning: lack of seriousness, carelessness, speculation, Bohemian character. Unstable situation, changes of mind. Adventures, gains and losses. Inventive aptitudes, drive. Opportunities, initiative, fortuitous success.[17]

WILD BOAR
brutal strength

In the myth of Adonis, the wild boar, which is sacred to Diana, incarnates the Mesopotamian god of plant life and corn, symbol of the fertile sun and ferocious winter: at the winter solstice the wild boar disembowelled the god who had descended into the underworld (the disappearance of the sun below the horizon).

• The wild boar became a symbol of destruction, and in Christian tradition, of the devil because of its piggishness and impetuosity.

• In Japan, the wild pig (*cinoshishi*) is a symbol of courage, in memory of the 300 pigs which saved the imperial throne from the usurper Do-kyo.[77] Wild boar defended the entrances to temples sacred to Wake-no-kiyomaro.

• In China the wild boar is a symbol of debauchery and violence and appears at the centre of the Buddhist Wheel of

Existence as a symbol of ignorance, idleness and gluttony.

The wild boar (*zhu*) is the twelfth sign of the zodiac and corresponds to the north, autumn and water. It symbolizes sensuality, abundance and satisfaction. The Years of the Wild Boar are excellent for business and industry, favourable to friendly settlements of court actions, social and charitable activities, but also to excesses of every kind.[118]

WILLOW
forbidden pleasures

In China, a willow (*liu*) is a symbol of spring and is often associated with eroticism. The expression 'the willow's feelings and flowers' wishes' express sexual desire; 'sleeping among the flowers and resting under willows' signifies going to a brothel.

• It is a symbol of immortality and similar to acacia in Freemasonry; but the male weeping willow which bears no fruit is a symbol of purity.

• The weeping willow is associated with sadness and death.[1]

WIND
messenger of the gods

The Mexicans recognized four winds which corresponded to the cardinal points: the good wind from the east, earthly paradise; the furious wind from the direction of hell in the north; the west wind; and the south wind as furious as the north wind.

• The winds sometimes had an intrinsic beneficial power,

but more often an evil one: the bad north winds were responsible for sickness.

The Chortis practised a curious ritual to fend off their influence: they trapped the winds which had been taken over by infernal spirits with the help of a 'capital lasso of the wind', so that they would be unable to harm the maize plantations. These rituals have their equivalent in the popular dance of the tumbo bull, a fantasy animal that they try to capture and tie up with a lasso.[76]

• In ancient China, the god of wind was Feng-Po, the heaven's mouth and tongue, who was the source of cosmic breath. In the *I Ching* it corresponded to the wood element in the *sun* trigram and to the north-west.

• The eight winds (*feng*) were used in divination, following the compass-card method based on the direction of the wind, in relation to the five musical notes and denominations of cycles. The wind from the south announced drought; from the south-west a small drought; from the west, military disturbances; from the north-west an abundance of beans; from the north, an average year; from the north-east, a very good year; from the east, a great flood; from the south-east, a great epidemic.

The *Kong* wind (doh), whose noise was like an ox bellowing, announced a lucky year; the *Chang* wind (ray), that sounded like galloping horses, announced war. The *Tche* wind (soh), like a flock of birds, announced drought. The *Yu* wind (lah), like the beating of a drum, announced floods. And the *Kio* wind (me), that sounded like a thousand men, presaged a bad year.[65]

• Wind resulted from the combined activity of the breath of Nature and the breath of the earth (on wood, it caused rain; on fire, heat; on metal, fine weather; on water, cold).

When associated with water, it designated *feng-shui* (the science of wind and water) or the 'art of provoking the harmony of the mean,' linked to alternating and complementary rhythms common to all things, to interaction and to combinations of yin and yang, contrasting manifestations of universal life.

Originally, *feng-shui* was restricted to forecasting rain and fine weather for farmers, but later it extended its prognostications to human enterprises, according to what day it was and whether the orientations were good or bad.

This system involved geomancy, astrology and alchemical medicine, based on the effects of the course of the sun and moon across the twenty-eight constellations, the correspondence of the five elements with the five parts of the human body, the five viscera, the five colours and the direction houses and tombs faced.

The *feng-shui* studied in turn the vital breath of Nature (*Hi*), the normal order resulting from its regular activity (*Li*), its material effects (*Ki*), the mathematical rules involved in making the calculations (*Su*), and the way in which they were applied to the forms of man and colours (*Ying*).

Whoever ignored these laws 'upset the living breath that impregnates every stone, tree, and flower; he risks going against the forces of earth and the heavens and causing his own loss.'[133]

• In Hindu mythology, the wind is Vayu, breath, associated with Prâna and the vital energy it inspires, the master of the intermediary world between heaven and earth which rules the vital levels that link physical and mental being.

Vayu and Indra, lords of thought, free the energies and powers enclosed in the subconscious.[44]

• In Christian tradition, wind is synonymous with breath; the spirit, and the flow of spiritual power from heaven.

• The Sioux saw the wind as a heavenly agent, and made analogies between the four cosmic winds and the four cosmological periods.

• The Aztecs dedicated circular temples to the god of the night wind, Checatl, because the wind detested corners.

Their zodiacal sign of the wind stands for witchcraft and black magic. Natives of this sign are indecisive, inconstant, capricious and lack perseverance and courage.[125]

• The ancient Greeks thought winds were active gods living in the caves of the Eolian islands, governed by Eolus, Aquilen and Boreus (north winds), Zephyr (evening and west wind), Eurus (morning and east wind) and Auster (south wind).[1]

• In dreams, a wind means mental disturbance, vanity, inconstancy, instability and violence.

WINGS

freedom, alleviation, attainment of spirituality

In early Greek theology, God was attributed with wings as an emblem of his gentleness, and of incubation. 'Through his gentleness he entered into the world, and through incubation he caused the egg to hatch from chaos.'

• Wings are symbols of spirituality in every tradition, of winning through only after a difficult, perilous initiatory education. Allegorical tales, stories of the Christian mystics or Sufis and shamans all illustrate this, as do the wings of the Taoist immortals of ancient China, who, by eating a special diet, acquired the ability to ride the clouds, and reach the islands of paradise, home of the gods.

• Wings also denote the ability to understand, knowledge and, in the Bible – as in Christian tradition – spirituality, the spirit (angels are depicted with wings), elevation to the sublime, transcendence of the human condition.

This explains why certain symbolic figures have wings: the snake (an image of spiritual perversion) becomes, with wings a symbol of spiritualization, of divinity. The hero who kills ferocious monsters also has wings.

• Wings are, naturally, associated with the symbolism of air, the most subtle element of all, and with the bird who inhabits it.

• In dreams, wings symbolize the release of creative forces.

WOLF

cruelty

The wolf is seen as a voracious monster, and is one of the mystic symbols in ancient sun worship. Its name in Greek signifies 'light' and it was worshipped in the same way as Apollo, dispenser of light. It is a maternal symbol associated with the idea of fruitfulness: a female wolf fed Romulus and Remus.

• In its negative aspect, and in Celtic mythology the wolf represented Lok, the great destroyer.[83]

• It is this dangerous aspect that is highlighted in folk tales and legend where the wolf personifies ferocity and blind, uncontrolled forces, appearing as a hypocritical tempter, the male seducer, full of greed, and devoid of scruples, as in Little Red Riding Hood.

This archetypal image of the undisciplined libido is typical of legendary monsters, and represents oral greed, and the selfish, antisocial, violent, and virtually destructive tendencies that stem from this.[67]

• Like the snake and the bear, the wolf also symbolizes the shadow (of Jungian psychology): the dark, unconscious aspect of a personality whose emergence can be dangerous because of the energies it awakens which threaten to swamp the conscious.[16]

WOOD
supernatural knowledge

In China wood is the third of the five elements (earth, metal, wood, fire, water), and corresponds to the east, spring, the colour green, love, the Chen trigram – the vibration of thunder – the awakening of yang (masculine energy) and the beginning of its upward movement. It symbolizes suppleness, for it is in the nature of wood to be bent and straightened.[8]

- In India, it symbolizes raw material, universal matter.
- In Catholic liturgy, wood is synonymous with the Cross.

THE WORLD
unity of the created world

The twenty-first arcana of the tarot shows a young woman dancing with two sticks in her hand (to capture aerial and terrestrial energies), surrounded by a crown of leaves (the rhythms of Nature). In the four corners are the Evangelists – Mark (lion), Luke (ox), John (eagle) and Matthew (angel) – symbols of the elements that form matter.

This arcana depicts the unity and interdependence of all the elements of creation, the dance of atomic particles of which movement is made, the life of the universe. It invites us to stay awake, 'awake to the world, to oneself, to others.'[79]

Divinatory meaning: passivity, impulsiveness. Pawn of occult forces. Inability to recognize wrong and show remorse.[17]

WRITING
divine gestures

Writing was once a sacred activity, the reserve of priests, a symbol of a spoken language; the shape of its letters were intended to transmit the idea 'of the world as a book containing messages from God.'

• Inscribing the letters was a magical activity, repeating the initial feature of the demiurge. The 'science of letters', wrote René Guinon, meant a knowledge of everything, and calligraphy, which reproduced the cosmological process, was a preliminary ritual in a scribe's initiation.

• In the same way, hieroglyphics were thought to possess a life of their own, and to have such potent powers of evocation, that in order to limit their effect and avoid any harm they might do, people broke them up by leaving gaps in the strokes or splitting them up. This rescued them to a few fragmentary indications (a detail: an arm, head), and prevented them from provoking delirium, collective trances, anger, contortions, wild enthusiasm, or frenetic movements of pleasure or fear.[136]

• The magical and sacred character of letters (like pictures) was employed in the making of pentacles, as well as their correspondence with the planets, elements and signs of the zodiac:
A – Saturn; B – Aries; C – Taurus; D – Gemini; E – Jupiter; F – Cancer; G – Leo; H – spirit; I – Mars; J – Mercury; K – the triplicity of Earth; L – Virgo; M – Libra; N – Scorpio;

O – Sun; P – Sagittarius; Q – triplicity of water; R – Capricorn; S – Aquarius; T – Pisces; U – Venus; V – Moon; X – air; Z – fire.[4]

The science of pentacle-making also employed spectacled or circled letters (letters with circles as finials) similar to cuneiform writing, and known as heavenly writing or Malachim's writing; the Greek *epsilon* (a reversed 3) signified silver, and the moon; Z, a symbol of life, corresponded to the number 7 which, crossed and with a circle, became Jupiter's sign.

Spectacled letters: Hebrew and Ethiopian letters[136]

• The Hebrew alphabet forms the basis of the sephirotic tree of life in the Cabbalah.

• The Irish Celts had a tree alphabet of eighteen letters, which the druids used for divination, each letter drawing its name from a tree for which it was the initial. Five vowels and thirteen consonants formed a calendar of arboreal seasonal magic:

B – Beth – silver birch. The month of the silver birch was from 24 December to 21 January

L – Luis – service tree. Month of the service tree: 22 January–17 February

N – Nion – ash tree: Month of the ash: 18 February–17 March

F – Fearn – elm. Month of the elm: 18 March–14 April

S – Saile – willow. Month of the willow: 15 April–12 May
H – Hath – hawthorn. Month of the hawthorn: 13 May–9 June
D – Duir – oak. Month of the oak: 10 June–7 July
T – Tinne – holly. Month of the holly: 8 July–4 August
C – Coll – hazel. Month of the hazel: 5 August–1 September
M – Muin – vine. Month of the vine: 2 September–29 September
G – Gort – ivy. Month of the ivy: 30 September–27 October
P – Peith – lime. Month of the lime: 28 October–24 November
R – Ruis – elder. Month of the elder: 25 November–23 December
The vowels:
A – Ailm – spruce
O – Onn – gorse
U – Ura – heather
E – Eadha – poplar
I – Idhu – yew.[107]

• Writing is an essentially symbolic activity, where 'the immense reserve of primordial images' that has accumulated through the long history of mankind finds an ideal place for display. The collective unconscious, in fact, still guides our pens as it does our actions.[136]

The symbolic interpretations of writing is based:
1 on two essential symbolic shapes: the stick, represented in the vertical stroke, and the sphere, in the oval;
2 on the symbolism of the four spatial directions reflected in graphic zones: upstrokes high on the page and the height of the letters in relation to height; downstrokes to depth.

Whether the writing slopes backwards or forwards reveals the writer's basic attitude – if towards the right, then the writer is extravert, if to the left, introvert.

The body of the letters, the middle part of the writing,

reveals the importance of emotional life to the ego. The marked development of one or more zones is indicative of a preponderant interest in the values they represent.[137]

YANTRA
linear mandala

The Hindu *yantras* are linear diagrams used as aids to meditation instead of the mandala, although they are very similar.

While the line replaces the mandala's pictures of the gods, the principle is the same: 'it is only a matter of a quintessential reduction of an identical idea.'

An example of the *yantra* is the *Srí* wheel, that is to say, the *shakti* or divine force, the motor power of the universe, through which God manifests himself in things. It is composed of four intersecting isosceles triangles of different sizes, with points upwards, and five triangles pointing downwards. In the centre rests an invisible point, the *bindu* (the condensed universe, the meeting point of creative forces, the massive conscious which is aware of all the worlds and beings which will be manifested), the mother seed, around which male forces (Shiva, the upright triangles) and female forces (Shakti, the inverted triangles) are balanced in equilibrium.

Drawn on the first circle surrounding these figures are eight petals, symbolizing the lotus of creation; on the second circle, a lotus with sixteen petals, then a third circle (*trimekhala*) contained in a square, open to the four cardinal points, symbolic of the earth.

The whole is intended to illustrate the reflections of primal power in its basic aspects.

The five triangles pointing downwards symbolize the quintuple aspects of power, and their peaks symbolize the tendency towards realization.

The four triangles pointing upwards symbolize Shiva, and their peaks symbolize the tendency to return.

• The images of the Buddhist mandala are sometimes replaced by Sanskrit letters placed in the angles. Each of them, written with a special nasal ending is (as each petal, each angle, each figure) identified with a specific energy that man has, and with a goddess (*yogini*) residing in a part of the body.

Each divinity or power man has possesses its *yantra* and its formula of invocation, the mantra, which is, it is said, the *yantra*'s soul.

• As in the mandala, the meditator starts from the outside, from external physical powers of the body and moves towards the inside, to the internal, supersensitive powers.

• At initiation ceremonies, a vase filled with perfumed water is placed in the centre of the *yantra* to receive the divinity.[1, 38, 96]

YIN–YANG

see *T'ai-chi*

YUGA
cosmic cycle

The *yuga* or age is a unit of measurement in the Hindu cosmic cycle. A complete cycle (*mahayuga*) lasts 12,000 years and ends with *pralaya* or dissolution. It is composed of four *yugas* of unequal length.

– *Kriti-yuga*, lasting 4,800 years, is the perfect 'accomplished age', that is to say, the Golden Age (the equivalent of the paradisal period in other traditions), a time of justice, wealth and happiness, during which dharma (law) was respected.

– *Trela-yuga*, lasting 3,600 years, or the 'triad' is characterized by work, suffering and death; the dharma is only three-quarters respected.

– *Dwapara-yuga*, lasting 2,400 years, is ruled by vice and ill-fortune, and the shortening of human life. Only half the dharma is left.

– *Kali-yuga*, lasting 1,200 years (the present-day period) is 'the bad age' of discord, intellectual decline and lax morals. Only a quarter of dharma remains.

Each *yuga* is preceded by a dawn and followed by a dusk, linking the ages together.[92]

ZERO

dead point

The concept of zero was discovered by the Maya more than a thousand years before the Europeans. It was depicted as a closed shell, like the foetus in the womb, and symbolized the disintegration of the maize seed which precedes the appearance of the seedling. It signified cyclic regeneration and represented 'the passage from one life to another . . . the dead point', from which sprang the ascending numbers 'like the beginning of the development of all natural life.'[76]

• With the contour of a sphere, the symbolism of zero is similar to that of the cup, vase or coffer in fairy stories, in which a prince or a hero is enclosed, an image of the philosopher's vase used in Hermetic initiation. It then becomes a symbol of the womb, an image of fertile woman.[136]

ZIGGURAT
cosmic mountain

Sumerian ziggurats were massive towers made up of seven superimposed platforms, which became progressively smaller, and were of different colours; the whole was surmounted by a sanctuary in which to welcome divinity, and which linked heaven to earth.

The best known of these 'hills of heaven' or 'mountains of God' were those of Babylon: the *Etemenanki* or 'house of the seven directions of heaven and earth', situated beyond the sacred way, and the *E-eur-imin-an-ki* situated to the south-west of the town.

The ziggurat was both an observatory and a protective talisman. It was an artificial mountain, built according to a plan, each part of which had a symbolic meaning. It was an image of the cosmos orientated towards the cardinal points, its floors symbolizing the seven planetary heavens and dedicated to the gods of those planets.

The first floor, painted black, was sacred to Saturn; the second, orange in colour, to Jupiter; the third, coloured red, to Mars; the fourth, gold, to the Sun; the fifth, yellow, to Venus; the sixth, blue, to Mercury; and the seventh, silver, to the Moon.

The storeys of this beneficent tower and the chapel were reached by a spiral staircase (spiritual development), the steps of which were about 80 cm high.

'Halfway up there was a room with seats where people who had undertaken to climb to the top sat and rested. In the upper tower was a great sanctuary and in this sanctuary a great, richly decorated bed, near which was a table made of gold. Every morning at sunrise, the Hymn of Fire was recited, facing the rising sun at the top of the tower.'[190]

• The hill of heaven is part of the symbolism of the ladder with its initiatory rungs. The pilgrim's or priest's ascent is the equivalent of an ecstatic journey to the centre of the world. When he reaches the upper terrace and enters the sacred space 'he breaks through a level, transcends profane space and enters into a region of purity.'[92]

• The Chinese replica of the ziggurat is T'ien Tan the 'altar of heaven' or 'round eminence' situated to the south of Peking. Four staircases placed at the cardinal points give access to three round terraces one on top of the other, of different sizes, decorated with balustrades. The second door has tablets dedicated to the sun, moon and Great Bear, to the five planets, the twenty-eight lunar houses (*Sieu*) and to the stars.

The altar on the upper terrace symbolizes the zodiac of the heavenly sphere. At the time of the winter solstice, the emperor and his dignitaries went with great ceremony to T'ien Tan to worship heaven.[4]

ZODIAC

Before the zodiac became a way of predicting the future, it was used to measure the cycle of a year. (Ancient scholars had noticed that the sky was at the same point every 365.2422 days.)

The zodiac is a circle symbolizing an imaginary belt of the celestial sphere, made up of twelve constellations, each covering 30 degrees of the sun's course, which helps to determine the positions of sun, moon and planets.

The original zodiac was probably laid out by using the visible, fixed stars, which explains why we have two zodiacs: the astrological zodiac based on groups of fixed stars, which advances by a day every seventy-two years, and the movable zodiac. This is worked out from four points where the sun changes direction: the two celestial tropics (Cancer and Capricorn) marking the furthest points the sun reaches in relation to the equator (the solstices) where it seems to stop and change direction from north to south or from south to north; the two other points correspond to the equinoxes, points where the apparent movement of the sun crosses the celestial equator in March towards the north and in September towards the south.[110]

• The zodiac is a replica of the universe. In the zodiacal circle can be traced the story of Christ whose birth coincides with the winter solstice, and, by extension, a history of the world.

The zodiacal circle has become a part of everyday life. The Round Table of medieval legend, and the twenty-first arcana of the tarot, the World, are linked to its symbolism. Nor has it disappeared from our lives in the twentieth century: the arena of a bullfight is nothing other than a symbol of the zodiacal circuit, as are horse races (symbolizing the planets) in an oval circle (the universe in the image of a temple), which once upon a time symbolized the course of the planets which regulated human existence and determined the seasons. But we have only looked at the profane meaning of these rites; in antiquity they had a sacred or symbolic meaning too.

• Spacewise, the zodiacal circle used to be positioned beyond the fixed stars, and appeared as the shell of the cosmic egg (this is why the symbolism of the egg is closely linked to the zodiac); it was the sphere where universal life and its possibilities were born. Timewise, the zodiac was linked to the symbolism of the circle, a figure without beginning or end, representing eternal cycles evolving in time.

• Each sign of the zodiac has its attributes, its own characteristics, and corresponds to its own forms and psychological types, and to a stage in psychic development.

– early impulses, impetuosity, new plant life and its potential, with **Aries**;

– taking possession of earthly goods, with **Taurus**;

– principle of comprehension with **Gemini**;

– physical and psychic gestation, sensitivity, stimulating creative forces, with **Cancer**;

– autonomy, individual self-control, individuality, with **Leo**;

– awareness of useful acquisitions, assimilation of useful data, with **Virgo**;

– knowledge of balance in relationships, with **Libra**;

– black art, disintegration and rebirth, with **Scorpio**;

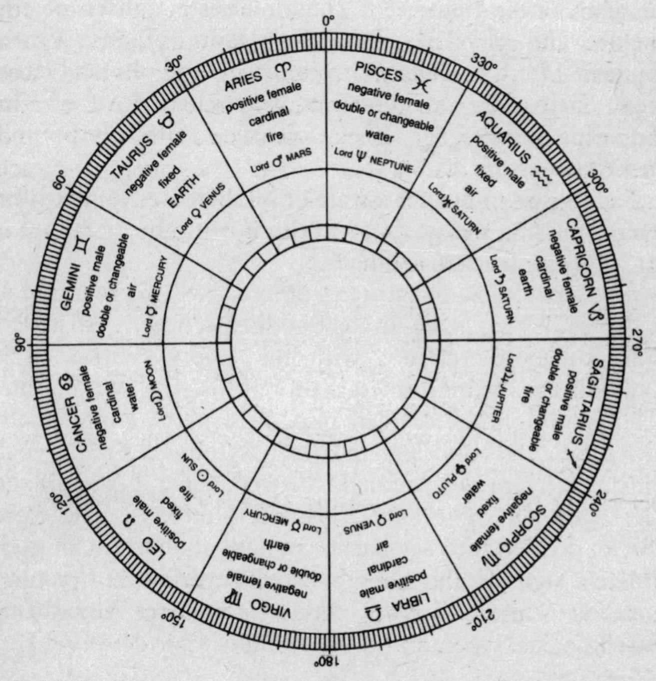

The zodiac

– wisdom, philosophy, religion, with **Sagittarius**;

– solar will, the realization of ambitions for whoever reaches the zenith of life, with **Capricorn**;

– knowledge of patrimony common to all, but exceeding personal interests, with **Aquarius**;

– awareness of origins, of life, prevarication between contradictory currents, with **Pisces**.[14]

• Buddhists see the zodiac as a road that must be followed and believe that the twelve signs symbolize the chain of causes determining rebirth and links with karma.

Aries is a symbol of ignorance and error, which makes us mistake the transitory for the permanent; Taurus is the sign of aggregates; Gemini of consciousness; Cancer of the mental and physical; Leo, the sensory organs; Virgo, contact; Libra, feelings; Scorpio, desire and physical cravings; Sagittarius, covetousness; Capricorn, love of life; Aquarius, renaissance; Pisces, old age, death, disappointment, depression and despair.

Each sign symbolizes a state of mind in ascending order, finally leading the adept to freedom from the astral yoke, to 'a rupture with the zodiac'.

These twelve zodiacal states of mind, which are found in most traditions, make up the Buddhist Wheel of Existence: four concentric circles, with the empty central circle symbolizing the motionless centre of the whirlwind of life. The second circle, divided into three parts, contains the three daughters of desire and death, symbolized in the cock (lust, vanity, pride), the snake (hatred, anger, betrayal) and the wild pig (ignorance, laziness, gluttony). The third circle, divided into six parts, contains the worlds of gods (*lokas*), men, Titans, hells, and twelve *nidanas* or picture-symbols. The wheel is encircled by a monster symbolizing fate.[4]

• The Chinese zodiac also has eight divisions connected with the trigrams:

– *Li* from the spring equinox to halfway through the zodiac sign of Taurus, corresponds to the Heavenly Western Palace, yang, the active period of the white tiger, and symbolizes the individual's natural tendencies.

– *Tui* (stagnant water) from halfway through the sign of Taurus to the summer solstice, yin, passive period of the black tortoise, corresponds to the Northern Palace and physical pleasures.

– *Khien* (sky, father) from the summer solstice to halfway through the sign of Leo, yang, active period of the black tortoise, linked to the Northern Palace and advancement in life.

– *Sun* (wind) from halfway through the sign of Leo to the autumn equinox, yin, passive period of the green dragon to the Eastern Palace and fertility.

– *Khan* (rain) from the autumn equinox to the middle of Scorpio, yang, the active period of the green dragon, to the Eastern Palace and to difficulties coming from outside.

– *Kan* (mountain) from halfway through Scorpio to the winter solstice, yin, the passive period of the red bird, to the Southern Palace and rest.

– *Khwan* (earth, mother) from the winter solstice to halfway through Aquarius, yang, the active period of the red bird, to the Southern Palace, to darkness and submission to fate.

– *Chen* (thunder), from halfway through Aquarius to the spring equinox, yin, the passive period of the white tiger, to the Western Palace, to a return to life.

Bibliography

1 *Dictionnaire des Symboles*, J. Chevalier-Gheerbrant, Laffont-Bouquins, 1982.
2 *Les Religions de l'Océanie*, J. Guiart, P.U.F., 1962.
3 *The Third Eye*, T. Lobsang Rampa, Ballantine, New York, 1983.
4 *L'Esotérisme de l'Astrologie*, A. Volguine, Dangles.
5 *Le Sphinx*, P. Weil, Epi, 1972.
6 *Le Manuel des superstitions chinoises*, P. H. Doré, 1970.
7 *The Dictionary of Chinese Symbols*, W. Eberhard, Routledge, 1988.
8 *Chinese Thought*, M. Granet, Ayer, 1975.
9 *Les symboles des Egyptiens*, F. Portal, Guy Trédaniel.
10 *The Egyptian Book of the Dead*, G. Massey, Society of Metaphysicians, 1986.
11 *Théorie & Pratique du Mandala*, G. Tucci, Fayard, 1974.
12 *Terre Wakan*, S. Bramly, Laffont, 1974.
13 *Les Rites secrets des Indiens Sioux*, Héhaka sapa, Payot.
14 *Comment comprendre voitre horoscope*, G. Holley, éd. du Rocher.
15 *Book of Signs*, R. Koch, Dover Publications, New York.
16 *Man and his Symbols*, C. Jung (ed.), Penguin, 1990.
17 *Le Tarot des Imagiers du Moyen Age*, O. Wirth, Tchou, 1978.
18 *Le Symbolisme hermétique*, O. Wirth, Dervy-Livres, 1969.
19 *Amulettes, Talismans, Pantacles*, J. Marquès-Rivière, Payot, 1950.
20 *Les Figures de Tabernacle*, Mouv. Missionnaire Laïque, 1937.
21 *Traité d'histoire des religions*, M. Eliade, Payot, 1975.

22 *Le Mystère cosmique*, A. Ferriére, Cahiers Astrologiques, 1948.
23 *L'Arche de Noé*, G. Romey, Laffont, 1977.
24 *Les Rêves et leur interprétation*, E. Aeppli, Payot, 1986.
25 *Ce que disent les rêves*, A. Teillard, Stock + Plus, 1944.
26 *Mythologie grecque et romaine*, Larousse.
27 *Les Bestiaires du Moyen Age*, Stock + Plus, 1980.
28 *Modern Man in Search of a Soul*, C. Jung, Ark, 1961.
29 *Les Présocratiques*, J. Brun, Q.S.J., P.U.F., 1968.
30 *Signes, Symboles & Mythes*, L. Benoist, Q.S.J., P.U.F., 1975.
31 *Le Coq*, A. de Grémilly, Flammarion (Symboles), 1958.
32 *Des Couleurs symboliques*, F. Portal, Guy Trédaniel.
33 *Le Test Marabout des Couleurs*, N. Julien, 1984.
34 *Les Signes sacrés*, R. Guardini, Spes, Paris, 1938.
35 *Le Symbolisme de la Croix*, R. Guénon, Vega, 1957.
36 *Le Symbolisme dans la Mythologie grecque*, Paul Diel, Payot.
37 *Peinture islamique et indienne*, Recontre (Lausanne), 1967.
38 *L'Inde secrète et sa magie*, J. Marquès-Rivière, Œuvres Françaises.
39 *Le Surnaturel et la Nature dans la Mentalité Primitive*, L. Lévy-Bruhl, P.U.F., 1963.
40 *The Origins of the Zodiac*, R. Gleadow, Stock, 1968.
41 *Traité pratique d'Astrologie judiciaire*, G. Muchery, éd. du Chariot.
42 *Psychology of the Unconscious*, C. Jung, Routledge, 1992.
43 *Guide des Pierres précieuses*, W. Schumann, Delachaux-Niestlé.
44 *Interprétation psychologique du Veda selon Shri Aurobindo*, J. Herbert, Dervy-Livres.
45 *L'Histoire commence à Sumer*, S. Noah Kramer, Arthaud, 1975.
46 *Water and Dreams*, G. Bachelard, Dallas Institute, Dallas.
47 *De Sable et d'Or*, C. Jacq, éd. des Trois Mondes, 1976.
48 *Teotihuacan*, Métropole de l'Amérique, L. Séjourné, Maspero, 1969.
49 *Mexican and Central American Mythology*, I. Nicholson, Newnes Books, 1983.
50 *Les religions de l'Inde*, J. Gonda, Payot, 1979.

51 *Dictionnaire de la Psychanalyse*, Larousse.
52 *Développement de la Libido*, K. Abraham, Payot, 1966.
53 *Les Japonais*, J. C. Courdy, Belfond, 1979.
54 *Aspects du Mythe*, M. Eliade, Idées Gallimard, 1963.
55 *Le Test de l'Arbre*, C. Koch, E. Vitte, 1969.
56 *Initiation, rites, sociétés secrètes*, M. Eliade, Idées Gallimard 1959.
57 *L'Inde du Bouddha*, Calmann-Lévy, 1968.
58 *Zarathushtra et la tradition mazdéenne*, J. Varenne, Maître spirituels, Seuil, 1966.
59 *La Nostalgie des Origines*, M. Eliade, Idées/Gallimard, 1971.
60 *Grandeur et décadence de la Civilisation Maya*, Thomson Payot.
61 *Blasons des villes d'Europe*, J. Louda, Gründ, 1972.
62 *Histoire des Fleurs*, L. Guyot, Q.S.J., P.U.F., 1972.
63 *Le Yi-king*, Hadès, éd. Niclaus, 1980.
64 *Lao-Tseu*, M. Kaltenmark, Seuil (Maîtres spirituels), 1965.
65 *Divination, Magie & Politique*, Ngo Van Xuyet, P.U.F., 1976.
66 *Le Héros aux Mille Visages*, J. Campbell, Laffont, 1978.
67 *Psychanalyse des contes de fées*, B. Bettelheim, Laffont, 1976.
68 *A Dictionary of Symbols*, T. Chetwynd, Thorsons, 1994.
69 *Les Symboles de la Chine*, F. Wion, Courrier du Livre, 1970.
70 *Méthode pratique de devination chinoise*, Yüan-Kuang, Guy Trédaniel, 1977.
71 *Le Yi-chou*, Kim-Tawn, Guy Trédaniel.
72 *La clef des grands mystères*, Eliphas Lévi, Marabout, 1974.
73 *L'origine des religions*, M. H. Gobert, Baudouin.
74 *Psychological Types*, C. Jung, Routledge, 1971.
75 *La vie sexuelle dans la Chine ancienne*, R. Van Gulik, Gallimard, 1971.
76 *Le Popol-vuh*, R. Girard, Payot, 1972.
77 *Aux Sources du Japon*, J. Herbert, Albin Michel, 1964.
78 *La Grande Initiation*, J. L. B. Léonard, PIC, 1970.
79 *L'Esprit des Jeux*, (coll) Seghers, 1980.
80 *Le Message des Constructeurs des Cathédrales*, C. Jacq, éd du Rocher, 1980.

81 *Les 33 Voies de la sagresse*, Th. Terestchenko, Cahiers Astronomiques, Nice, 1947.
82 *The Aztecs of Mexico*, G. C. Vaillant, Penguin, 1944.
83 *The Cult of the Priapus*, R. P. Knight, E. Losfeld, 1786.
84 *The Baghavad Gita*, Swami Prabhavanda, NAL-Dutton, 1989.
85 *Le Voie des Lettres*, J. Canteins, Albin Michel, 1981.
86 *Tao Philosophy*, J. C. Cooper, Dangles, 1972.
87 *The Buddha and Buddhism*, M. Percheron, Overlook Press, US, 1984.
88 *Le Livre des Morts Maya*, P. Arnold, Laffont, 1978.
89 *Soleil & Lune*, A. Barbault.
90 *Om Mani Padme Hum: The Sound of Silence – The Diamond in the Lotus*, Rebel Publishing, Germany, 1989.
91 *L'Astrologie lunaire*, A. Volguine, Dervy-Livres, 1972.
92 *Images and Symbols, Studies in Religious Symbolism*, M. Eliade, Princeton University Press, US, 1991.
93 *La Vie quotidienne des Aztèques*, J. Soustelle, Hachette, 1955.
94 *15 Tests pour découvrir votre vraie Personnalité*, N. Julien, Flash Marabout, 1983.
95 *Les Dieux de la Gaule*, P. M. Duval, Payot, 1976.
96 *Le Secret de la Reconnaissance du Cœur*, Ksemaraja, G. Trédaniel, 1987.
97 *The Myth of the Eternal Return*, M. Eliade, Penguin, 1989.
98 *La Pensée de l'Asie & l'Astrobiologie*, R. Berthelot, Payot, 1938.
99 *Le Langage des Fleurs*, M. L. Sondaz, Solar, 1974.
100 *Influence des Planètes*, J. Gerson-Lacroix, Cahiers Astrologiques, 1947.
101 *Les Silencieux Messages du Corps*, C. Bonnafont, Buchet/Chastel.
102 *The Art of Tantra*, P. Rawson, Thames and Hudson, 1978.
103 *Book of Chinese Beliefs*, F. Bloomfield, Ballantine, New York, 1989.
104 *Dictionary for Dreamers*, T. Chetwynd, Aquarian Press, 1993.

105 *The Psychology of Motivation*, P. Diel, Hunter House, 1991.
106 *Le Caractère révélé par le corps et les gestes*, R. Demazière, Famot, 1980.
107 *White Goddess: A Historical Grammar of Poetical Myth*, R. Graves, Faber, 1961.
108 *Le Côté occulte de la Franc-Maçonnerie*, C. W. Webster, Slatkine, Genève-Paris, 1981.
109 *La Symbolique maçonnique*, J. Boucher, Dervy-Livres, 1948.
110 *Naissance de l'Homme*, R. Clarke, Seuil, 1980.
111 *L'Apocalypse*, J. Forest, Musée d'Art Moderne de la ville de Paris, 1961.
112 *Prévoir par l'Astrologie*, H. Hirsig, Delachaux & Niestlé.
113 *La Cosmogonie des Rose Croix*, M. Heindel, La Maison Rosicrucienne.
114 *Dictionnaire pratique des Sciences occultes*, M. Verneuil, Les Documents d'Art Monaco, 1950.
115 *Histoire de l'Art*, C. Terrasse, H. Laurens, 1938.
116 *La Symbolique des Nombres*, R. Berteaux, Edimaf, 1984.
117 *Diagnostic & Conduite des Tempéraments*, P. Carton, Le François, 1972.
118 *Le Grand Livre des Horoscopes chinois*, T. Lau, Le Jour, 1982.
119 *Comment interpréter vos Rêves*, F. Kennett, éd. Princesse, Paris, 1976.
120 *Les Songes et leur interprétation*, S. Sauneron, Seuil, 1959.
121 *Le Cercle, un Symbole*, M. Loeffler-Delachaux, Mont-Blanc.
122 *Initiation à l'Astrologie*, Hades, Bussière, 1984.
123 *De la Psychanalyse à l'Astrologie*, A. Barbault, Seuil, 1961.
124 *Who's Who in Egyptian Mythology*, A. Mercatante, Clarkson, N. Potter, New York, 1978.
125 *Astrologie Aztèque*, C. MontGs, Laffont, 1984.
126 *La Civilisation indienne*, P. Radin, Payot, 1953.
127 *La Civilisation de l'Empire inca*, R. Karsten, Payot, 1952.
128 *Les Aztèques*, M. Simoni-Abat, Seuil, 1976.

129 *Poisons sacrés, ivresses divines*, P. de Félice, Albin Michel, 1936.
130 *Calendrier, histoire de monde*, P. Vidal, éd. Traditionnelles, 1978.
131 *Les Horloges cosmiques*, M. Gauquelin, Denoel, 1970.
132 *Le Bouddhisme tantrique de Tibet*, J. Blofeld, Seuil, 1976, Famot, 1975.
133 *La Maison de la Réussite*, F. Bonhoure, éd. Encre, 1983.
134 *La civilisation chinoise*, M. Granet, Famot (Lausanne), 1975.
135 *La Symbolique des nombres dans l'inconscient*, L. Paneth.
136 *La Préhistoire de la Graphologie*, M. Loeffler-Delachaux, Payot, 1966.
137 *Ecriture & Personnalité*, N. Julien, Marabout Service.
138 *Les Masques*, G. Buraud, Seuil, 1948.
139 *Les Agni devant la mort*, J. P. Eschlimann, Karthala, 1985.
140 *L'Epopée celtique en Bretagne*, J. Markale, Payot, 1971.
141 *Introduction au Bouddhisme tibétan*, Dervy-Livres, 1971.
142 *Primitive Art*, F. Boas, Dover Publications, New York.
143 *Rites et Mystères au Proche-Orient*, J. Q. N. Callebaut, Hayez, Bruxelles, 1979.
144 *Designs on Prehistoric Pottery*, F. Fewkes, Dover Publications, New York.